NEW CRITICAL NOSTALGIA

Sara Guyer and Brian McGrath, series editors

Lit Z embraces models of criticism uncontained by
conventional notions of history, periodicity, and culture,
and committed to the work of reading. Books in the series
may seem untimely, anachronistic, or out of touch with
contemporary trends because they have arrived too early or too
late. Lit Z creates a space for books that exceed and challenge
the tendencies of our field and in doing so reflect on the
concerns of literary studies here and abroad.

At least since Friedrich Schlegel, thinking that affirms
literature's own untimeliness has been named romanticism.
Recalling this history, Lit Z exemplifies the survival of
romanticism as a mode of contemporary criticism, as well
as forms of contemporary criticism that demonstrate the
unfulfilled possibilities of romanticism. Whether or not they
focus on the romantic period, books in this series epitomize
romanticism as a way of thinking that compels another relation
to the present. Lit Z is the first book series to take seriously this
capacious sense of romanticism.

In 1977, Paul de Man and Geoffrey Hartman, two scholars
of romanticism, team-taught a course called Literature Z that
aimed to make an intervention into the fundamentals of literary
study. Hartman and de Man invited students to read a series of
increasingly difficult texts and through attention to language
and rhetoric compelled them to encounter "the bewildering
variety of ways such texts could be read." The series'
conceptual resonances with that class register the importance
of recollection, reinvention, and reading to contemporary
criticism. Its books explore the creative potential of reading's
untimeliness and history's enigmatic force.

NEW CRITICAL NOSTALGIA

Romantic Lyric and the Crisis of Academic Life

Christopher Rovee

Fordham University Press

New York   2024

Fordham University Press has no responsibility for the persistence or accuracy of URLs for external or third-party Internet websites referred to in this publication and does not guarantee that any content on such websites is, or will remain, accurate or appropriate.

Fordham University Press also publishes its books in a variety of electronic formats. Some content that appears in print may not be available in electronic books.

Visit us online at www.fordhampress.com.

Library of Congress Cataloging-in-Publication Data available online at https://catalog .loc.gov.

Printed in the United States of America

26 25 24   5 4 3 2 1

First edition

for Giovanna
and in memory of Remo Ceserani

Contents

When we go out into the fields of learning
We go by a rough route
Marked by colossal statues, Frankenstein's
Monsters, AMPAC and the 704,
AARDVARK, and deoxyribonucleic acid.
They guard the way.
Headless they nod, wink eyeless,
Thoughtless compute, not heartless,
For they figure us, they figure
Our next turning.
They are reading the book to be written.
As we start out
At first daylight into the fields, they are saying,
Starting out.
                          —Josephine Miles, "Fields of Learning"

Introduction:
Our Elegiac Professionalism

A vague sense of loss has long permeated the study of literature.[1] Whether explicitly named as a "longing for the lost unities of bygone forms" or merely implied in a wistful terminology that, to cite a typical example, recalls the late 1950s as "the heroic age of Spenser studies," this nostalgic strain suffuses our disciplinary vocabulary.[2] It's not necessarily a *new* nostalgia—two wellsprings of modern literary study, philology and New Criticism, were underwritten by it after all—but it's an *intensifying* nostalgia, this widespread belief "that something has gone missing" from our work, that "the discipline, as currently configured, is missing something that it once had."[3] The last two decades have seen calls for assorted disciplinary "returns"—to philology, to aesthetics, to the common reader, to the archive, to the classroom, to the text—and the range of practices associated with the twenty-first century's "method wars" often attest to a similar desire to reclaim something that's slipped beyond our shared professional grasp.[4]

This is the elegiac sense conveyed in my book's title, by which I don't mean a nostalgia *for the New Criticism* (though in some cases it manifests that way) but rather a nostalgia for something indeterminate which the New Criticism is regularly identified with, namely the fleeting cohesiveness and relevance that our histories tend to associate with the postwar era of the 1940s and '50s. Nor do I mean "nostalgia" only in a regressive sense. The term may be shorthand for a false consciousness that basks in dreams of yesteryear ("Nostalgia tells it like it wasn't," in David Lowenthal's much-quoted phrase), but it can also register protest against an unjust present and signal forward-looking engagement with the past. Nostalgia also evokes desires that are endemic to literary study and inextricable from the experiences of dislocation and compulsive mobility that define life in the modern university.[5] All of these aspects feature in Edward Said's mournful (yet deeply political) 1982 observation that "there has been a historical erosion in the role of letters since the New Criticism"—where Said employs "New Criticism" less to denote a methodology than a lost Eden, in which literature was both the spiritual center of academic life and capable of "*interference*" in "the everyday world."[6] The image that he summons may be pastoral—the sun casting its light through autumn leaves into the window of a book-lined seminar room, among students in earnest discussion around a heavy wood table—but it is potent. It is the image of a time when literary criticism, the humanities, and the university all seemed on a surer footing vis-à-vis society at large; when it could be taken for granted that the study of books played a role in public life.

The story of this "golden age of robust confidence and prestige" is widely familiar.[7] After World War II, we're told, the humanities took on the responsibility of developing the nation's leaders, cultivating the values that the United States had defended in the war and stabilizing what the Harvard "Redbook" Committee in 1945 called "a centrifugal culture in extreme need of unifying forces." In the face of a perennially modern fear "of losing touch with the human past and therefore with each other," the literature classroom assumed a central place in the national imaginary, uniting a new generation around shared texts and a common cultural heritage.[8] "College English" became a near-mythic space of socialization, where adolescent students grew up under the tutelage of a progressive and energized professoriate, honing their close-reading skills within an intimate classroom community whose members attended, all at once, to the same thing. The shared study of books, in this idyllic image, compensated for the disunity seemingly incarnated in the period's modernized large universities with their newly disparate student bodies. For a tantalizingly brief space of time, while the American university benefited from a massive infusion of state and federal funds for scientific research, its liberal core remained essentially intact, the government's largesse benefiting what would still be, for a few years longer, a humanities-centered institution.[9] This fleeting happenstance made possible an argument which no generation of American academics has been able to make since: that the humanities, as crystallized in the practices of literary study, bore a recognized social value. Our New Critical nostalgia looks longingly toward this transient period when it was possible to articulate and believe in such a claim—a period that is metonymically associated, in the historical imagination, with the close-reading practices of the American New Criticism.

I don't wish to hypostatize this optimistic view of mid-century literary study. Whether things were this way or not, whether there really is something particular that's gone missing and is the source of our nostalgia, this is a story that's taken hold. There are plenty of contemporary anecdotes to support it, and there is just as much contemporary worry, expressed under titles like "Can the Study of Literature Be Revived?," to counter it.[10] There is also, we know too well, a popular and conservative fixation on this story of literary study's bygone eminence, fed by a facile media caricature that points to politicization and over-specialization as the reasons for our falling-off. A little more than a decade ago, a characteristic requiem in *The American Scholar,* titled "The Decline of the English Department," lamented the replacement of "books themselves" by "a scattered array of secondary considerations (identity studies, abstruse theory, sexuality, film and popular culture)."[11] But this fantasy of a simpler, apolitical, and pre-specialized time is of course amnesiac. The 1950s classroom was not some Rousseauvian idyll where students "naturally" gravitated toward imagery and away from politics, and even at the height of New Critical sway, there was no clear consensus about the disciplinary object of literary study; formalist close reading existed and thrived in a vital dialectic with varieties of criticism, historicism, and reception study. As for the supposed salad days of postwar relevance, literary study (and humanistic study in general) has never *not* struggled for academic and cultural legitimacy. The nineteenth-century Swiss historian Jacob Burckhardt identified crisis as the humanities' permanent condition, noting the struggle of sixteenth-century "poet-scholars" to explain their social purposes.[12] Even if we accept the hypothesis of a postwar boom, it is easy to lose sight of how fragile and fleeting such a moment would have been.

The most obvious sign of interest in an older period's practices of literary study is the curiosity that has lately been swirling around close reading. No disciplinary concept has made quite so strong a return in recent years, whether in varieties of the new aestheticism, or in the Common Core curriculum, or in the frequency with which critics have weighed the merits of close reading against alternatives ranging from surface reading to distant reading to hyper-reading.[13] "Reflecting on how we read has become a metacritical genre unto itself," writes Elaine Auyoung, and a glance at JSTOR shows that the phrase "close reading" soars in our critical literature after 1995—an admittedly imprecise measure, but one that at least marks a distinct phase in the history of criticism, with close reading more and more at the center of the discipline's collective thought.[14] It is not surprising that interest in a reading practice which approached poems as self-sufficient objects would have revived at the very moment when academia was being forced into economic self-sufficiency (the early 1990s representing, as Mary Poovey notes, a key moment for the public divestment from higher education).[15] Since then, there have been repeated attempts to turn up the forgotten origins of this "sacred icon of literary studies."[16] Close reading's inception has been found in London extension schools and in Skinnerian behaviorism, in British aestheticism and in Southern agrarianism; it's been sourced to Nashville (home to the Fugitive poets), Baton Rouge (birthplace of *Understanding Poetry*), Cambridge (practical criticism), New Haven (Yale-School formalism), Chicago (neo-Aristotelianism), Paris (*explication de texte*), St. Petersburg (OPOYAZ). It's sprung up in so many places that the pursuit has a kind of Whac-A-Mole quality about it—tracked down to one place only to pop up in another.[17]

This resurgent interest in the origins of close reading is not a sign that close reading has gone missing in itself. It obviously has not. Rather, it is a sign of close reading's imaginary relation to something that *has* gone missing: a confidence—underwritten by political culture and enabled by asynchronous funding streams, and thus possible only in the fleeting and contradictory circumstances of the postwar academy—that what happens in college literature classrooms and in the pages of academic periodicals is valued by the culture at large.

Dispensing with the myth of a single point of origination for close reading and the professionalism it instantiates, *New Critical Nostalgia* instead pursues a period of cultivation, establishment, and dissemination between the 1930s and the 1960s. I put gentle and corrective pressure on the received view of these decades by historicizing the institutional changes and critical exchanges out of which our current practices and predicaments grew. I refract all of this through the prism of the romantic lyric's reception, an integral but much-caricatured feature of the disciplinary past. More often talked about than read, New Critical treatments of romanticism have mainly been known by their reputation for hostility. But they are more than this; they are quirky and unpredictable, with a compelling strangeness that derives from the spectacle of America's most ambivalently nostalgic critics taking on Britain's most explicitly nostalgic body of literature. In these frequently cathectic engagements with the romantic lyric, the question of nostalgia is overdetermined in ways that would prove consequential for the later development of criticism.

By turning the narrative of romantic studies toward this earlier period of reaction, and away from the presumptive core of romanticism's disciplinary history—the rehabilitative phase of the 1950s and '60s and the deconstructive apotheosis of the 1970s—*New Critical Nostalgia* enables a different perception of the relationship between the field of romantic lyric and the discipline of literary studies. For one thing, it reveals the dislocation of romanticism from its curricular perch in the mid-twentieth century, which is typically seen as a causal feature in the rise of the modern field, as more a rhetorical feature of our professional self-understanding than a fact of disciplinary history. To say so is not to downplay the very real antagonism expressed toward romanticism at the time (an antagonism that the following chapters will amply document), but rather to interrogate its causes and effects. The period's vaunted anti-romanticism is traditionally chalked up to a basic clash of worldviews, as was summarized even by the MLA's research guide to romantic studies, published at the end of New Critical hegemony in the early 1970s:

> The trouble with the Romantics was [seen by New Critics as] their ability to detect intimations of immortality or to create myths which enabled them to wander in gladness. The New Critics spoke for a generation which was world-weary, materialistic, and skeptical; which regarded the human situation as a hopelessly perplexing existence in a barren, wasted land; and which despised any literature that envisages it otherwise. Hence they asserted that Romantic literature as a whole (including Shakespeare) is too emotional, too soft (not "dry, hard, and classical"), too hopeful that the good in man's nature may overcome the evil, too desirous of simplifying human experience into intelligible design, too credulous in sensing a harmony in the apparent discords of the universe, and, above all, too certain that Imagination, cooperating with Reason, can reveal such truths through the beautiful.[18]

Irreconcilable differences of sensibility probably do inform some anti-romantic writing of the early twentieth century, though another way of understanding the phenomenon has been to identify an originary moment or epochal turn within the institutional adolescence of the discipline. The historical scholar Carl Woodring, for instance, recalled anti-romanticism as taking root at the 1947 MLA Convention in Detroit, where "New Critics spoke in the large section meetings, and the teaching of English was transformed as if by fiat." According to Woodring, this episode turned intellectual aversion into institutional contagion, with the assault on romanticism "spread[ing] from T. E. Hulme and the new humanists to the classroom, through textbooks prepared by the new critics or by eager disciples."[19] The claim is compelling—that American New Critics transformed New Humanist antagonism into a field-wide phenomenon rooted in teaching practices—and as I discuss in Chapter 2, some of the readings in Cleanth Brooks and Robert Penn Warren's popular classroom textbook of the time, *Understanding Poetry*, did indeed codify anti-romantic sentiment. But the notion that fields are "transformed by fiat" is an example of the exaggeration that too often mars an anecdotal history, preventing clear understanding of the complex development of the discipline in its relation to one of its core subjects.

While the rhetoric of disparagement invites such exaggeration, another way to read that rhetoric is as a symptom of countervailing investments. The English poet-critic Hulme's lurid and foundational assault on romanticism as "spilt religion," defined by its "sloppiness," its "moaning or whining," and its drug-like addictiveness, may have laid the groundwork for later denigration of romanticism by ethical and aesthetic critics, but it also established a bombastic tone that was sometimes more theatrical than critical.[20] For all their avowed and vigorous anti-romanticism, critics like Brooks, John Crowe Ransom, and W. K. Wimsatt cared intensely about romanticism, and to closely attend to their writing about it is to encounter an affective involvement that runs far deeper than our histories of literary criticism typically acknowledge. They produced influential readings of romantic poems, took intellectual inspiration from romantic literary theory, and shared with the leading romantic writers both an interest in the language of everyday life and a powerful anti-industrial and anti-capitalist bent. Even as New Critics argued for the decentraliza- tion of romanticism in the curriculum, they framed the literary field as, in some sense, a response to romantic ideas. In keeping with a historical pattern wherein romanticism was consistently seen, in James Chandler's words, "as the prestige field of methodological advancement," the romantic lyric rode shotgun with the New Criticism as the modern discipline developed its initial vital sense of itself.[21]

At the same time, American New Critics habitually tamped down their involvement with romanticism, both willfully and defensively. As students, many had been dazzled by the romantics, suggesting that the achievement of critical maturity demanded the surmounting of early literary passions. T. S. Eliot, a key influence on New Critics, described the "invasion of [his] adolescent self" by Shelley, which he called "a kind of daemonic posses- sion."[22] Soon after, Brooks experienced his own boyish enthrallment by the romantics, which he claims to have conquered by the end of college: "In my own senior year, I at last began to grow up."[23] Austin Warren, arguably the most moderate and representative of the New Critics, described a similar process of adolescent fascination and recuperation. A "youthful Shelley and Keats man," Warren remembered being whipped into "confusion" by his undergraduate romanticism class at Harvard with Irving Babbitt. Having an- ticipated appreciative lectures on poets he considered as "spirits like myself," Warren instead "experienced conversion"—a word used by many others of his generation to describe their intellectual maturation away from the romantics. "I burned what once I had adored," he later reminisced; "Once so proud of my effervescent 'enthusiasm,' I grew so ashamed of the thing and name that to this day I cannot write the word without encasing it in prophylactic quotes." Warren's metaphor of "prophylactic quotes" suggests the severity of the threat posed to his scholarly identity by a "sheer romanti- cism" that he learned to repress.[24] For critics in like remission, an exaggerated anti-romanticism seems almost to operate as a defense against backsliding. To detach from romanticism's perceived immaturity and from their own remembered "enthusiasm" for it, it appears, is to establish and preserve an objectivity of judgment, keeping those identifications that Eliot associated with the "intense period before maturity" at a safe distance from the mature critical self.[25]

This pattern—youthful enthrallment giving way to critical maturity, and grown-up critics on guard against their "burning memories" of romantic poetry—shaped mid-century attitudes toward the romantic lyric. Repeatedly, by ethical and aesthetic critics alike, romanticism was defined as a psychopathological condition.[26] When Eliot says that "the only cure for Romanticism is to analyze it," or when Ransom states that "a romantic period testifies to a large-scale failure of adaptation," they are framing it in terms of the regressive and dangerous desires traditionally associated with a pathological nostalgia.[27] "The poetry I am disparaging is a heart's-desire poetry," Ransom explained, which "denies the real world by idealizing it: the act of a sick mind."[28] In this analogy, romanticism is unfitness, a form of arrested development or state of enervation in which the hardness and critical capacity required for modern life and privileged in the modern university are lacking. "[T]he awful result of romanticism is that, accustomed to this strange light, you can never live without it," writes Hulme; "Its effect on you is that of a drug."[29]

Paradoxically, however, the agrarian sensibility that gave rise to a major branch of the New Criticism was nothing if not nostalgic and romantic. As Gerald Graff puts it, a "condition of becoming institutionalized" in the modern American university was that the New Criticism had to "sever its ties with the social and cultural criticism" of its "first generation" practitioners—had, in other words, to guard against becoming defined by their virulent longing for an idealized past.[30] Such, perhaps, is one explanation for the American New Critics' Janus-faced attitude toward romanticism— sometimes admiring and sympathetic, sometimes dismissive and hostile. The strategic dislocation of romanticism from its place atop the mainstream canon might be seen as self-protective, a way to defend against an identification of literary study as undisciplined, merely nostalgic, while simultaneously avoiding the opposite extreme of a hard-scientific model of study.

The Romantic Crisis Narrative

The intense repudiation of romanticism by the New Critics may be a conventional plot-point of disciplinary history, but romantic scholars have played their own meaningful role in generating and reproducing the narrative. Harold Bloom in a 1990 *New York* magazine feature called the New Criticism "a neo-Christian, neo-Catholic attempt to destroy Romanticism," and while this may have been comic hyperbole, it fit a longstanding pattern of romanticists fretting what they perceived as an existential threat to the field.[31] In the immediate postwar years the worry centered on Shelley, target of the most extravagant critiques. Richard Fogle wrote in agitation that the "reputations of all the English Romantic poets" had been "vigorously attacked," with the New Critics "succeed[ing] in damaging Shelley seriously in the minds even of intelligent readers."[32] Frederick Pottle, Bloom's usually even-keeled supervisor at Yale, similarly waxed alarmist: "within fifty years practically everybody will be saying about Shelley what the New Critics are saying now. The disesteem of Shelley is going to become general, and it may continue for a century or more."[33]

Theatrical distress is characteristic of a field whose structural signature is crisis.[34] Romanticism, as an intellectual and thematic rubric rather than a historical one—"the period metaphor that both stabilizes and disrupts the very concept of period metaphors"—is uniquely vulnerable to the efficiency-driven business model of the modern university.[35] Though historically central to the conceptualization of literature as a field, with a foot in two separate centuries it is assimilable on either side, with the result that jobs in romantic studies are now typically absorbed in the more economical categories of a "long eighteenth" or "long nineteenth" century.[36] But there are important differences between English's (and by extension romanticism's) "market retreat," an intricate economic event of the late twentieth century that has only worsened since then, and the storied decline of romanticism in the wartime and postwar era, which was largely an invented crisis.[37] Romantic studies was not, to be clear, a field in decline at mid-century. It did, however, come to figure decline around that time—and soon enough, in keeping with the pattern familiar to any reader of *The Prelude*, to figure recovery as well.

Romanticism's founding myth of crisis-and-resurgence is almost too obvious to mention, being so dear to the field's self-understanding, but it is worth pausing over this myth in conjunction with the broader emergence of literary study. "Rehabilitation," "rebirth," and "revival" are the familiar medical tropes: Aidan Day claims M. H. Abrams as "arguably the most important single voice in the post–Second World War critical rehabilitation of Romanticism"; Thomas McFarland invokes an "astonishing rebirth of romantic attitudes" and dates "the new flowing of romantic currents" to "the early 1950s"; James Chandler points to Abrams, Bloom, and Frye as primary vectors in "the American revival of Romanticism after the debilitating critiques of humanist ideologues like Irving Babbitt and new critics like T. S. Eliot."[38] Abrams's subsequent formulation of the "Greater Romantic Lyric," a seminal account of the lyric pattern of crisis and recovery, resonates with the perceived trajectory of the field as a whole.[39] A narrative of recovery, though, presumes prior debilitation: that the field of romanticism had suffered a diminishment of legitimacy, had been weakened, impaired, enfeebled. This is the story we tell, and it was the story told at the time.

Yet to be embattled is not to be debilitated, and if questions of legitimacy dogged romanticists, this was partly in consequence of the field's undeniable centrality in the debates taking place at the time. In all my archival research, I have yet to come across a single expression of concern, however fleeting or facetious, about the academic job market for romanticism at mid-century. A series of scholarly reminiscences published in *Studies in Romanticism* in 1981 under the title "How It Was," on the contrary, paints a picture of relative (if paradoxical) health—at least for the white, male scholars surveyed for the issue. The great Keatsian Jack Stillinger recalls abundant positions available for romanticists, despite Wordsworth being "very little taught," Shelley "mentioned only to be ridiculed," and Blake "practically unheard-of." By the time he began traveling for on-campus interviews, "the offers were piling up" for his Harvard grad school colleagues, all of whom would, "before the end of the year, get good jobs." Herbert Lindenberger, author of *On Wordsworth's Prelude* in 1963, recalls his graduation year of 1954 as "a bad job market," though it was not bad enough to prevent his becoming "decently ensconced at the University of California's brand-new campus at Riverside." The Coleridgean Thomas McFarland, meanwhile, shares in the same issue a self-aggrandizing and self-mythologizing recollection: blowing up interviews and opportunities right and left, resigning from his first job "in a romantic frenzy," announcing in an interview for his next job that he didn't "believe in teaching hard," refusing yet another position for reasons so trivial he can't even remember them, and finally resigning the next position he got "in another romantic paroxysm, this time taking half the department with me."[40] It is no stretch to say that young female scholars of the time could never have survived professionally had they played so lightly with "frenzy" or with "paroxysms." A tale such as McFarland's underscores the special privilege informing these earlier iterations of the academic job search, which barely merits the term "market."

It might even be said that romanticism in the middle of the twentieth century thrived as never before, assuming an integral role in contemporary skirmishes over the future of literary study. Crisis may have been (and may still be) the field's byword, but this is part-and-parcel of what Eric Lindstrom remarks as its "centrality to twentieth-century methodological change."[41] Whether this centrality will define romanticism's position in post-liberal, mid-twenty-first-century academia remains an open question. Orrin Wang writes that "romanticism has always been structured by its own legitimation crisis," meaning that its "discursive operations" can "provide a tropological resource for understanding literature's present predicament during the global reorganization of knowledge in and beyond the humanities."[42] This would partially explain the correlate relation that often seems to subsist between "the state of the field" and "the state of the discipline"—for Romanticism's fortunes do tend to ebb and flow with those of literary study as a whole.[43] That relation could also be explained by Poovey's recognition that modern American literary criticism is predominantly organized around the romantic conception of "the organic whole."[44] (In 1948, Brooks tied up his tour de force reading of "A Slumber Did My Spirit Seal" by calling organicism "the best hope that we have for reviving the study of poetry and of the humanities generally").[45] Or it could have something to do with the romantic consolidation of high culture as a reaction to the marketplace for reading, an early paradigm for the academic privileging of "elite," "difficult," "literary" writing.

I don't wish to overstate this correlation (which in any case is probably not causal), yet I find the overlap between the much-vaunted revival of romanticism in the 1950s and the so-called golden age of "College English" intriguing. Jacques Barzun, who helped design Columbia's Great Books program, advertised romanticism as the intellectual muse of American democratic liberalism, and in *Romanticism and the Modern Ego* (1943) he grandiosely hailed America as "the land of Romanticism par excellence"—a claim repeated in a *Time* magazine cover story in 1956.[46] Hyperbole aside, the postwar health of romanticism reflects the postwar health of the American university. And analogously, as Jon Klancher argues, when the postwar's optimism about institutions finally faded into disillusion, romanticism again proved central, this time negatively, as the face of the post-1968 "'legitimation crisis' of liberalism, textual representation, and historical narrative."[47] In its prestigious role as "the paradigmatic field in Anglo-American criticism," romanticism became the discipline's central ground of loss—the field with the most intimate relation to the vanished liberal consensus of the postwar period, and the field whose mid-century crisis and recovery stands as a central if distant object of present-day nostalgia.[48]

I wish here to step back and explain my use of "crisis," which is informed by Reinhart Koselleck, who recalls the word's Greek origin as a verb meaning "to 'separate' (part, divorce), to 'choose,' to 'judge,' to 'decide'; as a means of 'measuring oneself,' to 'quarrel,' or to 'fight.'" In surveying a multitude of variations on the term, Koselleck ties this flexible metaphorics of judgment to the "expression of a new sense of time" in modern life, "the fundamental mode of interpreting historical time"—a usage that accelerates, he argues, during the years that we associate with British romantic thought ("around 1770" or "since the last third of the eighteenth century").[49] Koselleck recovers the important etymological relation between crisis and criticism:

> "Crisis" also meant "decision" in the sense of reaching a verdict or judgment, what today is meant by criticism (*Kritik*). Thus in classical Greek the subsequent separation into two domains of meaning—that of a "subjective critique" and an "objective crisis"—were still covered by the same term. Both spheres were conceptually fused.[50]

For literary study, as several have pointed out, the mid-twentieth century is both an age of criticism and an age of crisis. René Wellek made this point in "The Crisis of Comparative Literature" (1959), writing that the field of literary study "has been torn by conflicts of methods" since the Great War. With different aims, Paul de Man observed an affinity between "the notion of crisis and that of criticism," famously writing that "all true criticism occurs in the mode of crisis."[51] The particular crisis *New Critical Nostalgia* describes, however, is neither a "mode" intrinsic to the act of criticism nor a "mood" of urgency or imminent doom (the feeling, as de Man puts it, that the "edifice threatens to collapse"—which also describes the crisis-discourse of job hires or tenure lines). It refers rather to the juncture of various techniques for reading, a sundry assortment of criticisms ranging well beyond the typical opposition between critics and scholars. This is crisis as the essence of a profession's daily practice, crisis as the air that a discipline breathes: the disputational foundation of a professional community that believes in the significance of its internal debates.

Keeping in mind this distinctive sense of crisis, I approach the methodological experiments and disputes of this period in terms of the decision-making essential to defining modern practices. Jonathan Kramnick and Anahid Nersessian have recently pointed to "the diversity of approaches" within literary studies as "the mark of a discipline in good enough shape to adapt its distinctive idiom to changing and specific contexts"—an expression of "the discipline's good standing, not its crisis."[52] One can certainly question, with Ellen Rooney, the seductive appearance of methodological exchange's affability, but the point here is that, much as in recent decades, practitioners of English at mid-century strenuously contested their work as readers and as teachers, and not always affably.[53] One symptom of this contest is the genre of popular "How to Read" books: How to Read *Poetry*, How to Read *Fiction*, How to Read *Literature*, How to Read *Better*. It's a genre with two readily identifiable moments, the first located roughly between 1910 and 1940, the second between 1995 and the present day. A slightly upscale version of the

Idiot's Guide or *For Dummies* series, books in the "How to Read" genre depart from the more delicately named *Understanding Poetry* in that their explicitly didactic titles imply, without equivocation, a crisis of technique seen as applicable to a wider public. The kind of book I am talking about does not include books about how to read a certain subject—e.g., *How to Read Sartre*, or *How to Read Beauvoir*, books that emphasize content rather than method. Instead, it focuses polemically on proper practices, the "right way" to read.[54] Mortimer Adler's *How to Read a Book* (1940), an offshoot of his work with Columbia's General Education program, is a classic instance of the genre, and two years later, I. A. Richards's *How to Read a Page* would downsize Adler's populist Gen Ed mode. Terry Eagleton's latter-day version, *How to Read a Poem* (2007), starts from our by-now-familiar premise of loss: "Like thatching or clog dancing, literary criticism seems to be something of a dying art."[55]

The rise of the "How to Read" book in the first two quarters of the twentieth century reflects a discipline at odds over its main terms. The "profession of college English teaching shares the general predicament of a world in which all values are tossing about in confusion," wrote R. W. Short in 1944.[56] In a time of global economic crisis and war, the challenges facing society inevitably found expression in the college classroom. The ideological fracturing between communists and conservatives, and the radical pedagogical innovations of the New Critics, generated yet more uncertainty about values, with scarcity intensifying the disputes and leading to a rhetoric of crisis in its direst sense. In a "period of hardship, with departments pared to the bone, with advanced courses curtailed or laid away on ice, with research facilities impaired," English professors needed desperately to articulate the practical value of what they did.[57]

The establishment of *College English* in 1939 is a monument to this critical moment, and after Pearl Harbor the journal was filled with essays such as "English in Wartime" and "The Study of Literature During the War," which staked a claim to moral purposiveness by foregrounding literature's impact on the growing minds of students. The maturation process had historically been part of the American university's purview, but previous generations' hand-wringing about maturity referred mainly to students' behavior: whether they could be trusted to elect their own courses, for instance, or whether they would go to class without an attendance policy.[58] In the 1940s, the unmistakable danger of the world at large, combined with greater access to college for middle-class and non-Christian students, provoked a wave of Arnoldian concern for students' intellectual and moral development. "Not much hope remains for the adolescents of our time if they are not trained to think courageously and for themselves," declared H. A. White, Graduate Chair of English at Nebraska, in a forum on the question of the humanities during wartime; "We shall need much clearer thinking along the way to world security."[59]

The English classroom thus became a sort of proxy battleground. What was taught there could lift spirits on the home front, could assist students in understanding what was being fought for and against, could even prepare them for the problems of peacetime that were to come. Curricula were seen as patriotic or unpatriotic, purposive or irresponsible, mature or childish. In a piece dealing with "the problem of undergraduate reading in a time of war," William Riley Parker (namesake of *PMLA*'s esteemed essay prize) offers this strange but representative example:

> Whether we like it or not, in a time of war we teachers of English become, automatically, guardians of civilian morale. We cannot escape this grave respon- sibility; we ignore it at our peril and to our shame. But I am suggesting here that if we merely continue to teach those books which satisfied the mind in days of peace, and do not show their value and relevance for minds absorbed by war, we are not only shirking our duty as citizens but also shirking our great opportunity as teachers. If we muff this opportunity, we deserve the worst that can befall us, for we shall prove ourselves incompetent as well as unpatriotic.[60]

It was the professor's "duty," both to students and to a profession struggling to claim a sense of public purpose, to connect the classroom to the world outside of it. Still, the dominant strain of this discourse focused less on the choices that professors made than on the growing minds of students. "The military has taken over the liberal-arts college," announced the *Saturday Eve- ning Post* in 1943, describing an emergency situation in which the typical undergraduate urgently required "as much mathematics, physics, navigation, engineering drawing as he can possibly absorb before he is called to active duty."[61] Competing for a share of this disciplinary currency, humanities advo- cates fashioned English, History, and other so-called soft fields as part of the nation's arsenal, by making students' growth from adolescents into mature adults a matter of wartime and postwar strength.[62]

To be sure, the sense of crisis brought on by global war only exacerbated a preexisting condition. In 1941, a Yale Victorianist-turned-dean named William DeVane wrote that it was in "about 1930" when neighboring fields began to usurp the study of literature:

> I judge that the English major was the most important major in our colleges, as well as often the most populous, until about 1930. Since that date we have had to give ground—partly to the economists who fancied they had the answer to the ills of the world, partly to the historians who could assert with some cause the greater significance of their field, partly to the social scientists who are

constantly expecting to hatch chickens from the doorknobs they sit upon and who keep up a steady premonitory cackle.[63]

After the war, Marvin Herrick bemoaned the "overwhelming aggression" of "engineers, chemists, physicists, biologists, and the champions of the 'social sciences,'" adding a sharp warning about the perils of a professional nostalgia. A Renaissance scholar at Illinois, Herrick urged his discipline to leave off its hankering for an idealized past, lest English follow "the downward path" of Classics half a century before—the inevitable consequence, he predicted, if "the teachers of English do not stop yearning for vanished glory...and try to build something that our students want, or think they want, as much as they now seem to want chemistry and physics and 'personnel management.'"[64]

We conventionally assume that the profession's successful response to this crisis was some monolithic consensus around close reading. In fact, though, it was a *practice* of crisis—a culture of disputation and experimentation around varieties of reading—that marked the tenuous and temporary health of literary studies in what we fondly look back on as our institutional golden age. Jane Gallop is not necessarily wrong in identifying close reading as "the very thing that made us a discipline, that transformed us from cultured gentlemen into a profession," but what falls out of her succinct formulation is the diversity of other ways reading was practiced at the time: philological slow reading, impressionistic criticism, critically relativist historical analysis, archetypal criticism, ethical criticism, statistical description, and so forth.[65] In 1928, nearly a decade before Ransom championed criticism as the proper business of literature professors in his essay "Criticism, Inc.," a romanticist at Goucher College named Elizabeth Nitchie produced a meticulous and non-exclusive survey of professional critical practices in which she anatomized a variety of approaches, ranging from author-centered and responsive criticism to ethical and philosophical criticism.[66] And beyond criticism, there were strong claims made for sundry other methods and practices: for data analytics, for literary history, even for a version of literary Darwinism. Edith Rickert's 1927 book, *New Methods for the Study of Literarture*, laid out an array of dazzlingly inventive visualizations and statistical tables for the description of literary history. Edwin Greenlaw in 1931 defended the legitimacy of literary history as "a learning, having its own method, its own right to exist among the learnings." And Elisabeth Schneider published a strenuous psychobiological account of literary pleasure, *Aesthetic Motive*, just as aesthetic criticism was taking off in 1939.[67] As exemplified by the establishment of the breakaway English Institute in 1939, crisis was less a condition to be overcome than a state of quickening dispute that helped to consolidate "English" as a profession.

Critical (and Uncritical) Nostalgias

The past few years have seen a striking upsurge of interest in the histories and techniques of literary criticism. Deidre Lynch's *Loving Literature: A Cultural History* (2014), Rita Felski's *The Limits of Critique* (2015), Marc Redfield's *Theory at Yale: The Strange Case of Deconstruction in America* (2015), Joseph North's *Literary Criticism: A Concise Political History* (2017), Rachel Sagner Buurma and Laura Heffernan's *The Teaching Archive: A New History for Literary Study* (2021), among many others, all attest to this blossoming interest. The turn of the discipline back onto itself, through essential questions about how to read and even what it means to read, can be seen as a sort of return to first principles in a time of uncertainty. As a pursuit of what's supposedly gone missing in our professional rationales, it represents a nostalgia not merely symptomatic of present angst but rooted in our history, dating at least as far back as the 1930s.

To look back at the critical nostalgists of the 1930s, a decade when "critical reading" was advanced as "the holy grail of literary studies," is to consider the possibility that nostalgia is simply cooked into the discipline, operating pervasively before, during, and after any specific loss as its fundamental ground.[68] The proverbial longing for "books themselves" took shape at that time as the echo of another longing. Here is Ransom in *I'll Take My Stand*:

> Nostalgia is a kind of growing pain, psychically speaking. It occurs to our sorrow when we have decided that it is time for us, marching to some magnificent destiny, to abandon an old home, an old provincial setting, or an old way of living to which we had become habituated. It is the complaint of human nature in its vegetative aspect, when it is plucked up by the roots from the place of its origin and transplanted in foreign soil, or even left dangling in the air. And it must be nothing else but nostalgia, the instinctive objection to being transplanted, that chiefly prevents the deracination of human communities and their complete geographical dispersion as the casualties of an insatiable wanderlust.[69]

The historical backwardness here is clear enough: in the American South of the 1920s and '30s, the idealization of "human nature" as torn from its home and "even left dangling in the air" speaks to an enormity of historical projection and displacement on Ransom's part, which will be pursued at greater length in the chapters that follow.[70] But when he plaintively adds, "Will there be no more looking backward but only looking forward?," Ransom seems less nostalgic for the Old South than for nostalgia itself, as a mode of thinking antithetical to the critical discipline that he would soon call his professional home. Just a few years later, in his much-cited case for the professionalization of criticism, he would adopt a radically different tone, albeit with tongue in cheek. Literature professors, he urges in "Criticism, Inc.," ought to form a professional community around a "more scientific, or precise and systematic" method for reading. Sounding anything but nostalgic, he appears to press for a modernization of the discipline along masculine, businesslike lines: "I should think the whole enterprise might be seriously taken in hand by professionals. Perhaps I use a distasteful figure, but I have the idea that what we need is Criticism, Inc., or Criticism, Ltd."[71]

Ransom's prior nostalgia does not just vanish when he advocates for a new professionalism. Although he tells Allen Tate that to gain "a professional level of distinction" a critic must make "no reference to local setting whatever," Ransom's endeared "local setting" persists metaphorically into his professional practice, as what he and his fellow critics (perhaps echoing Heidegger) refer to as "the poem itself," or "the work itself," or "the text itself."[72] Agrarian nostalgia provides a template for understanding the literary object—what it is, where it begins, what its boundaries and exclusions are. A locally oriented cultural politics dovetails with a locally oriented approach to poems, which also happened to be, at the time, a revolutionary way of understanding poems as aesthetic events in their own right. The objective in both cases was to preserve a particular unfallen region, whether geographical or textual, from external forces, be these the encroaching industries of the Northeast or the encroaching disciplines of the modern university, such as sociology, history, psychology, ethics, politics.[73]

In part because of these historical resonances, close reading has been particularly vulnerable to the charge of a regressive nostalgia that "exiles us from the present."[74] The very first sentence of Susan Wolfson's 1997 *Formal Charges* anticipates the suspicion: "Why care about poetic form and its intricacies, other than in nostalgia for a bygone era of criticism?"[75] At a time when reading for form was commonly dismissed as collaborating with an older critical politics, Wolfson pre-empts the accusation, casting her work against type as an interventionist and counter-nostalgic commitment of attention. She also exposes the expectation that close readers will disproportionately elicit the charge of nostalgia. But nostalgia can propel even the most self-consciously progressive criticism. The anti-nostalgic polemic of Joseph North's *Literary Criticism*, for example, is dense with nostalgia of its own. North repeatedly invokes "nostalgia" as his term of critical analysis: condemning the main streams of disciplinary criticism for embracing "a nostalgia for idealist aesthetics," targeting the "new aestheticism" in particular as "a nostalgic attempt to reinstate an idealist model of the aesthetic as the philosophical foundation for the discipline," and arguing that it "simply rebounded into a nostalgia for older modes."[76] Yet, longing for a different object, North laments that literary studies "is failing" in all its "genuine attempts to move forward onto new ground" because of the "lack of something that it once had"—this "missing something" being what he regards as disciplinary criticism's true origin in the non-idealist project of I. A. Richards.[77] The paradox that defines North's argument, as Alastair Bonnett puts it, is that "nostalgia is integral to radicalism" while "radicalism has been offered as a narrative of anti-nostalgia."[78] North longs for a forsaken, left-liberal project of criticism, and in this he has much in common with a romantic strain of radical politics, one shared by the Agrarians whose idealism he condemns: "it is precisely the nostalgia for what has been lost," as Michael Löwy and Robert Sayre write, "that is at the centre of the Romantic anti-capitalist tradition."[79]

Caught in this paradox, a vividly apparent but unacknowledged nostalgia cedes a potentially critical function. This move is in keeping with nostalgia's history as a diagnosis, for from the time Johannes Hofer coined "nostalgia" as a medical term describing a patho-physiological response to dislocation, it has signaled malady of one kind or another.[80] In the Napoleonic era, national armies had to account and plan for nostalgia, which Erasmus Darwin defined as an "unconquerable desire of returning to one's native country" and classed among "diseases of volition."[81] In the late nineteenth and early twentieth century, nostalgia was linked to criminal behavior (a penchant for arson was seen as one of its signature manifestations).[82] As late as the 1940s—concomitant with literary criticism's emergence as a "precise and systematic" way to stamp out affective and historical modes of reading—the U.S. military was screening recruits on the belief that the "greatest single factor in waging successful warfare . . . is the preventing or overcoming of nostalgia" ("no place for weakling emotions" among "fighting men").[83] This long history of pathologization, Nauman Naqvi argues, has reinforced the dismissive modern view of nostalgia as a sign of "incompleteness and impoverishment," transforming it into a practically self-justifying accusation with the "air and verve of diagnostic certainty."[84] Merely to "name" nostalgia, as Nicholas Dames puts it, "is to already have found, and denounced in advance, the characteristics that all nostalgias supposedly possess."[85]

More productive (if less polemical) than wielding nostalgia as a bludgeon is to consider the circumstances that have made it so pervasive. Nostalgia is practically hardwired into the idea of the university as a place of complex negotiation between past and present, where tradition meets experience in the form, often, of polemical collisions between generations. (The coining of the term "nostalgia" is itself such an event in the university's early-modern history.)[86] Nostalgia is also integral to literary studies, whose work originates with the pursuit of reading's reference, the lost object of figuration—meaning that all critics, whether idealist or materialist, interventionist or apolitical, must reckon with it eventually. Instead of employing nostalgia as an evaluative term synonymous with "the amelioration or cancellation of the past," therefore, I use it here to describe certain postures within the practice and history of criticism and to examine the undeniably intense attachments to this history that characterize much literary criticism today.[87] In this, I build on the work of those who have in recent years sought more nuanced ways of understanding nostalgia's critical potential. Svetlana Boym, for instance, has described a skeptical and "reflective" nostalgia (opposed to what she calls a conservative "restorative" type), which fixes the past as elsewhere and "does not pretend to rebuild the mythical place called home."[88] Peter Fritzsche elaborates this idea of a nostalgia that grants the past its historical otherness:

> There is no nostalgia without the sense of irreversibility, which denies the wholeness of the past to the present. If this were not so, nostalgia would not mourn the exhaustion of tradition or lovingly attend the bits and pieces that are scattered about, but rather protest widespread ignorance of tradition's validity, which is the duty of the reactionary. In other words, nostalgia constitutes what it cannot possess, and defines itself by the inability to approach its subject, a paradox that is the essence of nostalgia's melancholy. This displacement is lost on those critics who simply deride yesterday's questionable merits. Nostalgia is therefore premised on a fundamental break with the past. It maintains a necessarily troubled relationship to the past which is regarded as *past* and it is quite foreign to the ordinary reactionary, who inhabits wholly, without the nostalgic's dread, a verifiable universe in which today corresponds with yesterday.[89]

Taking a similarly reflective tack, *New Critical Nostalgia* acknowledges and explores our cathected and ambiguous attachments to the early professional era—attachments made all the more intense by the sense of fantasy and loss they involve. Taking the critical cosmos of the mid-twentieth century as my subject, I seek not to reify an imagined past or to rejuvenate one that is no more, nor to excavate "a verifiable universe in which today corresponds with yesterday," but rather to make another world of professional crisis available to us, that it might helpfully frame our own of today.

I gathered many of "the bits and pieces" attesting to that separate world of crisis in the most alluringly nostalgic of institutional spaces, the archive, home to documents and artifacts that tempt with the promise of a fully habitable past.[90] Lisa Jardine is forthright about the affect involved: "it is generally an archival document, handled and deciphered for the first time, that gives me the particular thrill of connecting with the distant past."[91] The recurring thrill of this literal encounter has been mine too: reading mimeographed mid-term examinations or deciphering the hand-scrawled notes for classroom lectures delivered more than eighty years ago, I've had to guard against the temptation to believe myself privy to what actually went on in those bygone pedagogical performances. Connecting with a "true" past is not really possible. In part this is because archives are never the past's neutral vessels. They are the outcome of work put in by collectors, librarians, and scholars, all of whom must negotiate institutional constraints, public imperatives, and financial pressures, not to mention their own engrained (and perfectly understandable) biases. The contents of an archive are the result of fraught processes of selection and exclusion: "what gets into an archive," Lorraine Daston writes, is never "accidental: just because the costs of curating and preserving its contents are so high, absorbing fortunes and lifetimes, selectivity is paramount and access is jealously guarded."[92] Josephine Miles, the longtime Berkeley professor who is the subject of my fifth chapter, had to cajole the Bancroft Library's directors to take her papers (the basis of that chapter). And this was distinctly a partial collection, as my colleague Brad Pasanek discovered when he visited Miles's former house in North Berkeley and found therein the repository rejected by the Bancroft: bookshelves bent with the weight of old marginalia-filled books, and a small closet stacked with cartons of yet more papers. This unarchived archive is a register for all the documents and artifacts never kept in publicly accessible space, a symptom of what even the most sumptuous resources do not record. If the university archive seems to house what Daston calls "the literal fact" of the distant past, it is also a construction, assembled by devotions of all kinds, and on principles of selection that themselves need to be recognized and read.[93]

One determinant is financial. It takes money and paid staff to assemble materials, process them, curate them, and make them available, whether for primary or online encounters. No surprise, then, that the personal archives of our discipline's well-known figures tend to be at elite institutions, even when they've taught elsewhere. Cleanth Brooks left his papers to Yale, not LSU; John Crowe Ransom left his to Vanderbilt, not Kenyon. Austin Warren's papers are not housed at Boston University (his first teaching job), nor at Iowa (his second), nor at Michigan (his third and last), but at the John Carter Library of Brown University, whose faculty he never joined. No surprise, too, that the archival record is thinner when it comes to faculty papers and curricular matters at public universities, and particularly at historically Black public colleges and universities, where the word "underfunded" does not begin to do justice to the situation. While elite institutions are able to preserve the papers even of their more obscure faculty members, with digital databases making access to those papers easier than ever, scholars typically have to make formal inquiries at less well-supported places, where after decades of inadequate funding, overworked archivists face the most formidably disorganized base of materials.[94]

The archival situation of materials from literary criticism's past is inseparable from larger worries about the discipline's future. *New Critical Nostalgia* tracks these worries back to the mid-twentieth century, when the idea of the American university underwent a massive renovation with far-reaching social consequences. It traces a set of cathectic encounters between mid-century readers and romantic poets that put romanticism at the center of the modern discipline's growth: Keats's Odes are set in dialogue with Cleanth Brooks's nostalgic classroom practices, Shelley's lyrics read as fetishes of New Critical hostility, Wordsworth's pastorals framed by Josephine Miles's innovative arithmetical readings and by John Crowe Ransom's ruminative Agrarianism. Attention to these critical engagements creates, among other things, a geography of the mid-century discipline, a sense of the academic locales where this seminal phase in American literary studies was staged, from land-grant schools in the Deep South, to elite Ivies in the Northeast, to the emergent public "multiversity" out West. As professional mobility developed into a key characteristic of modern academic life, a complicated sense of regional inflection (whether in Southern New Criticism of the 1930s or in the West Coast "lit-labs" of the early 2000s) became legible as a feature of the field's methodological disputes and as a key node of our endemic critical nostalgia.

My first chapter, "Ransom's Melancholy," focuses on the Southern New Critic John Crowe Ransom, treating his complicated sense of the relation between place and discipline. It reconsiders Ransom's symbolically fraught move from Vanderbilt University to Kenyon College in 1937, which is often seen as a pivot between his cultural and literary phases and as symbolic for the commencement of the discipline's professional era. I here explore Ransom's challenging nostalgia in relation to his professional mobility, as it manifests in his later writing about poetics and William Wordsworth. Reading Ransom-reading-Wordsworth, we encounter the queasy feelings that come with the kinds of professional dislocation and reorientation that are only too familiar today.

My next three chapters turn in different ways to the relationship between mid-century literary criticism and classroom teaching. Chapter 2, "Shelley's Immaturity," explores the New Critics' extraordinary hostility toward Percy Shelley's poetry. Academically central and yet beloved outside of the academy as well, Shelley had long been a prime object both of professional scrutiny and of pre-professional affection. This chapter argues that the New Critics' overdetermined aggression against him was part of an effort to distinguish these modes—to define disciplinary reading's difference from non-disciplinary reading. After looking at some of the early, "adolescent" responses to Shelley on the part of mature professionals like T. S. Eliot and Frederick Pottle, the chapter turns to a primal scene of interpretation: the notorious critique of Shelley's "The Indian Serenade" in Cleanth Brooks and Robert Penn Warren's anthology *Understanding Poetry* (1938), where questions of maturity and development (the poet's, his readers', and the discipline's as a whole) come together.

If *Understanding Poetry* turns the classroom into a site of discipline, with Shelley served up as a textbook example upon which students could sharpen their critical teeth, in Chapter 3, "Brooks and the Collegiate Public, Reading Keats Together," the classroom is a friendlier (if somewhat inscrutable) place. Here I approach New Critical pedagogy as a subtle negotiation of authority between professional critics and new readers of poetry. Shuttling between Brooks's renowned teaching and his modeling of pedagogy through criticism, I read his landmark study of John Keats's "Ode on a Grecian Urn" as a dramatic text, which represents close reading as a nostalgic and communal practice. Infused with social and moral purpose, and idealistically figuring the reading of poetry as an exercise in social inclusion, the Brooksian scene of instruction—whether taking place in print or in a university classroom—self-consciously draws a poem near to its readers and draws those readers near to one another.

My fourth chapter, "The Case of Byron," takes a different approach to the relation between mid-century criticism and the mid-century classroom. The case of Byron overturns the usual understanding of literary study in the 1940s and '50s as an age of New Critical consensus, for despite neglect by formalist critics, Byron continued to be enthusiastically taught in American universities as well as consistently treated in some of the field's leading historically oriented periodicals. I pursue the complexity of this disciplinary moment via Byron's paradoxical reception: first by examining the political and historical criticism on Byron that thrived in these decades of his formalist neglect, and then through a pair of archival case studies—one on Byron's odd exclusion from the criticism of M. H. Abrams, and the other on Byron's surprising role in the teaching of William Kurtz Wimsatt. In both cases, Byron provokes unexpected fits of critical nostalgia.

My last chapter, "The Emergence of Josephine Miles," examines the work of a twentieth-century poet, scholar, and critic who has recently attracted notice as a forerunner of twenty-first-century interests in digital humanities, disability studies, and postcritique. Miles emerges here as a counter-nostalgist who signposts the resemblance implicit throughout these chapters, between our own crisis period and a similar disciplinary crisis three-quarters of a century ago. Using archival study of her voluminous handwritten visualizations and poetic word counts, this chapter treats Miles as a central figure of the mid-century discipline, who speaks to our present moment precisely because she was so integral to her own. She committed herself to principles of continuity that she idiosyncratically read into the work of William Wordsworth, principles which ran counter to the main streams of her discipline in multiple ways. Eschewing the notion of a poem's organic wholeness, embracing an evolutionary view of periods as the historical flows of literary change, and dedicated to the notion of interdisciplinarity, Miles pushed against the methods and values being consolidated at the outset of higher education's liberal period. Her story brings into view these tensions over how to read, a crisis once again centered on the romantic lyric.

An epilogue, "The Fields of Learning," juxtaposes the subjects of my first and last chapters: Ransom and Miles, exponents of opposing views on the large public university whose divergent pastorals of academic life augur a post-1968 era. Ransom's nostalgic protest against the huge technological "plant" of the modern university, together with Miles's counter-nostalgic embrace of the multiversity as a forward-facing "city of intellect," previews a complex era of increased student agency and decreased faculty governance—an era paradoxically catalyzed (in an irony that I reflect on in closing) by the New Criticism's insular engagements with the lyric.

---+---

Throughout these chapters, I am careful to avoid describing the history of our discipline as a sequence of discrete movements and counter-movements, each ceding logically or reactively to the next like presidential administrations ("philology gave way to literary history, which gave way to New Criticism, which gave way to poststructuralism . . .").[95] A minority formation can appear hegemonic thirty years on. The eclectic and pragmatic criticism that grew up in the 1950s, mixing attention to context and imagery, was testament to a flourishing (but harder to summarize) *Realkritik* that resists our neat methodological classifications. This dynamic sense of methodological experimentation and mutual influence provides the crucial backdrop to *New Critical Nostalgia*, which examines some seemingly familiar nodes of our critical history, not to rehearse well-worn encounters between the New Critical and the romantic but to make sense of them within the complex story of a disciplinary past whose outlines we too often take for granted.

1. Ransom's Melancholy (Reading Wordsworth in Gambier, Ohio)

> Within the same poem, we can pass from one world to another.
> The first world is the hustling one we have to live in, and we
> want it to be as handsome as possible. The second world is the
> one we think we remember to have come from, and we will
> not let it go.
>
> —John Crowe Ransom, "Humanism at Chicago"

Among John Crowe Ransom's papers in the Vanderbilt University archives sit the remnants of an unfinished poetry anthology: projected tables of contents, hand-scribbled page allocations, entire transcribed poems.[1] These scraps reveal the special status Ransom accorded to William Wordsworth, no fewer than ten of whose lyrics—more than by any other writer—turn up in each of the anthology's fragmentary variants. The selections are unorthodox, reflecting a quirky and non-canonical taste: "On the Extinction of the Venetian Republic," but no Intimations Ode; "The Pet-Lamb," but no Tintern Abbey. Indeed only one poem by Wordsworth appears in every variant, and it is the least-known of his Lucy poems:

> I travell'd among unknown Men,
> In Lands beyond the Sea;
> Nor England! did I know till then
> What love I bore to thee.

> 'Tis past, that melancholy dream!
> Nor will I quit thy shore
> A second time; for still I seem
> To love thee more and more.

> Among thy mountains did I feel
> The joy of my desire;
> And She I cherish'd turn'd her wheel
> Beside an English fire.

Thy mornings shew'd—thy nights conceal'd,
The bowers where Lucy play'd;
And thine is, too, the last green field
That Lucy's eyes survey'd![2]

Tense, ambiguous, seemingly remote from history and politics, the Lucy poems were ideal set-pieces for New Critical close reading, with Cleanth Brooks famously devoting three virtuoso pages to the eight lines of "A slumber did my spirit seal" in his classic essay on ironic poetry. "I travelled among unknown men," however, never quite made the critical cut, and for Ransom, its value seems to reside in the qualities that made this so: transparent longing, an iconic nostalgia for a lost world of both nation and region, conveyed with an earnestness that was out of keeping with a post-1945 canon in which ironic detachment reigned supreme.

Ransom had been shaped by his own experience of "travelling among unknown men"—early, as an American studying in Oxford in the 1910s, and late, as a native Tennessean who left Vanderbilt for tiny Kenyon College. A mood of dislocation pervades all his writings. Even before leaving Nashville, he produced work infused with nostalgia, not only in the usual sense of the Agrarian's wistful yearning for an irretrievable past but in the term's original reference to painful feelings of spatial displacement: *nostos algos*, homesickness. Whether treating the literal human migrations associated with industrial capitalism, or the existential migration away from the already "fugitive first moment" of primary experience, or the migration of "foreign [metaphorical] matter" into the language of modern poetry, Ransom's thinking, both early and late, is structured by nostalgia.[3]

His affection for Wordsworth's "I travelled among unknown men" fits neatly into a related story commonly told about the emergence of American New Criticism: that it required migration both literal and ideological. Cutting a path from small southern cities like Nashville and Baton Rouge up to college towns in Gambier, Ohio, and New Haven, Connecticut (so this story goes), Southern Agrarians carried a methodology born from regional, cultural, and political commitments and transplanted it, as a deliberately apolitical reading practice, at the center of the discipline. "In the early 1930s," Stephen Schryer narrates, they were "political Agrarians chiefly interested in protecting the South from industrialism; by the 1940s, they were formalist aesthetes interested in disseminating the apolitical practice of close reading throughout the academy."[4] This migratory paradigm makes for a compelling myth of the professionalization of literary study, yet it is overdetermined in ways that have obscured the complexities of this transitional period. A closer look at Ransom's part in the story illuminates the sometimes-messy ways that his Agrarian and professional phases ran together, even as he sought to distance himself from both.

Ransom is an apposite figure through whom to interrogate the queasy feelings that come with the kinds of professional dislocation and reorientation that we are only too familiar with today. He emerges in this chapter as something like a Wordsworthian halted traveler, paused amidst the fields of criticism and brooding on his participation in a profession undergoing rapid change—embodiment of the self-conscious mournfulness that shadows disciplinary progress. This is a Ransom less defined by regional attachments than by mobility and distance, less the champion of systematic "close criticism" than the epitome of a circumspect historicism. I read him here with an appreciation of the ambivalence that his later critical output luxuriates in: a capacity to historicize his involvement in a swiftly transforming profession; a hyperconsciousness about the ascendancy of the modern university; a piercing awareness of living and working in time. Ransom's melancholy, an elegiac professionalism that would quietly become paradigmatic for an entire discipline, permeates his late thinking about Wordsworth especially, which is imbued by a keenly resigned recognition that modern liberal societies are rootless in ways that both intensify feelings of loneliness and enable exhilarating change. Revisiting Wordsworth in 1950, Ransom mourns the losses endemic to literary study from the front-end of the historical plot that binds him to us, as readers approaching the end of that same story.

Criticism Goes North

There is something hyperbolic about the way Ransom came to be identified almost single-handedly with the professionalization and practice of American literary study. "No man," wrote Hugh Kenner in the 1970s,

> has had more effect on the way the subtle operations of language are apprehended in this country in this century. There is probably not a freshman in the United States today whose experience of the English survey—three classroom hours a week plus three more hours of preparing his assignments plus whatever time for term papers his conscience impels or his roommate permits—is not in large part traceable to concerns of Ransom's.[5]

This exaggerated stature is rooted in the year 1937, when Ransom left his longtime post at Vanderbilt to join Kenyon College as Professor of Poetry. Rarely has a professor's move from one university to another been so freighted with symbolic significance. Nothing less than the institutional emergence of the New Criticism and the modernization of the discipline have been metaphorically compressed into that 500-mile drive from suburban Nashville to rural Ohio. As Gerald Graff puts it: "If there was a single career whose personal trajectory perfectly coincided with the institutional fortunes of criticism, it was that of John Crowe Ransom."[6]

Ransom's move to Kenyon has been described in various ways—as a "new corporate accommodation," as a "transformation of Agrarianism's politics into . . . political quietism or conservatism," as a "calculated and strategic" way of accruing "institutional power"—but whatever the narrative, the grammar is mobility and the affect is loss.[7] Ransom, circa 1937, epitomizes a modern academic phenomenon: the moveable professor, able to negotiate the best deal for himself in an open competition among universities eager to add his prestige to their rosters, yet simultaneously entangled by a nostalgic relation to previous professional locales and relations. Only a half-decade earlier, he fretted about contemporary American life that there would "be no more looking backward but only forward"; now, he disciplined himself forward, trading in his stature as the South's premier intellectual for a thousand-dollar raise and the reins of the *Kenyon Review* (notwithstanding the locator, a periodical of national consequence). On the mere news of his imminent departure, letters poured into local editorial pages and onto the desks of Vanderbilt administrators. It was such a resonant event that *Time* magazine dispatched a reporter to Nashville to look into it.[8]

Kenyon was by no means a paradigm of the behemoth modern university, and Ransom's arrival at the tiny liberal arts college hardly changed a thing about the way "Criticism, Inc." did business. It did, however, feed various narratives about the rise of modern literary study, one of these being the so-called academic hegira from the South, which saw some of the New Criticism's protagonists move to prestigious posts north of the Mason-Dixon line.[9] Southernist scholars of the later twentieth century liked to emphasize that story, attributing the coherence of the discipline to "the changing geography of the New Criticism, as its leaders moved from Nashville to Baton Rouge to Gambier, Ohio, and finally to New Haven, Conn."[10] This account, written by Thomas Daniel Young, marks Ransom's move to Gambier as preliminary, bypasses Robert Penn Warren's 1942 move to the University of Minnesota, and treats Brooks's move to Yale in 1947 as a triumphant finalé ("finally") marking New Criticism's decisive entrance on the national stage. Ransom's, however, was the archetype. Before considering how intellectual migration was naturalized as disciplinary progress, I want to pause over the details of his move and reflect on its incorporation into regional mythology.

By the late 1930s, Ransom was almost completely identified with the

South. He wrote about Southern style, Southern regionalism, Southern history, Southern economics, and Southern aesthetics, all while holding an influential professorship at one of the South's wealthiest universities. Soon after he announced his intention to depart, regional publications began churning out worried features and editorials. "Ransom is logical to the South," the *Chattanooga Times* declared; "For all of his forty-nine years . . . he has lived in the South; he has given his brilliant mind to the consideration of the problems of the South; and he possesses a Southern citizenship that is both intuitively and insistently traditional."[11] At the height of the commotion, in June 1937, a banquet in Ransom's honor attracted a crowd of admirers and a flood of telegrams, including one from Wallace Stevens. Even a Northern insurance salesman could appreciate the magnitude of the move: "Sorry to see you making a myth of such a very real person as John Crowe Ransom who is contributing as much to life in the South as any of its politicians and more than all its preachers and story tellers."[12]

Ransom's departure was quickly incorporated within a regional tradition of lost causes.[13] Ransom's "going to Ohio will leave the South so much the poorer," wrote the literary scholar Samuel Holt Monk (then teaching at Memphis's Southwestern College), and Lawrence Lee, a minor Southern poet and editor of *Virginia Quarterly Review* from 1938 to 1942, described the event in existential terms: "In intersectional exchange it has long been our tragedy to give up the best of our human material and to receive, in exchange, the worst. In permitting the loss of Mr. Ransom we show by what violent gullying and washing away we are willing to see our contemporary civilization made sterile."[14] That the South's leading humanist could be poached by a tiny Midwestern college with an endowment one-tenth the size of Vanderbilt's was seen as a special humiliation. For his part, Ransom would not collaborate in the genre of "tragedy," the "violent gullying and washing away" of the South's "best . . . human material." He was, to the contrary, worn out by the genre. As he confessed to his former student Allen Tate in 1936, "*patriotism* has nearly eaten me up, and I've got to get out of it."[15] He was also well-aware that his decision might be perceived as a betrayal. "Some of my friends may regard me as a renegade to run away from my region," he said at his farewell banquet, and more than a decade later a few of those friends still felt the wound.[16] "Things have been rather soft and easy for him at Kenyon," wrote his Vanderbilt colleague and fellow Agrarian Donald Davidson in 1950; "In effect, when he went there, he left the field of battle to sit in an Episcopalian, quasi-Oxfordian parlor, where, over the teacups, he could refine his aesthetic refinements, pretend that he had never heard of a Southern Agrarian, and study the beauties of the Middle Ohio landscape."[17]

Satire, not tragedy: Davidson imagines Ransom's new situation as a fantasy of professional maturity, amounting to little more than effete pretension and Anglophilic indulgence.[18]

What actually motivated Ransom was material more than mythic. He had financial obligations to meet; he craved additional time to write; he was impatient for a change of institutional setting. When Kenyon's President-Designate Gordon Keith Chalmers went to Nashville to make his pitch in person, Ransom's closest friends read the cards.[19] Outside offers had come fairly regularly throughout the 1930s, but Kenyon's brandished a nearly twenty-percent raise in salary, rent-free campus lodging, and a lighter teaching load. Most appealing of all was the editorship of the *Kenyon Review*, a new vehicle for professional relationship that replaced local attachments with national ones. To top it off, Gambier was pastoral, nearly idyllic. "I live in a well-to-do residential neighborhood of a mid-sized city," Ransom wrote in 1932 of his unremarkable, semi-urban situation in Nashville. Of Gambier: "It's rural, there are no politics." Agrarianism is "a fine doctrine that does not have much to do with Ohio," he put it, with no little relief.[20] Kenyon was also far removed from the modern-progressive higher-education complex. Half a century older than Vanderbilt, it boasted a curriculum rooted in classical education and a small, all-male enrollment. In 1934, its freshman class of 110 was the largest on record. The senior class when Ransom arrived was a mere 57, also a record, and half the number of students he would have taught in any given semester at Vanderbilt.[21]

If Ransom was the South's latest cause, his own critical cause—New Criticism—kept its Southern growth. Brooks and Warren were still there in 1938, lecturers at Louisiana State University when they published *Understanding Poetry* and prepared their follow-up, *Understanding Fiction* (1943). Brooks and Robert Heilman, another colleague, put out *Understanding Drama* in 1945. It was only in 1947 that Brooks left for Yale, precipitating what Mark McGurl has called the "moment of crisis for regionalism." Reaction in the South was imprinted with a rehearsed dismay; an editorial in the *Chattanooga Times* was plaintively headlined "Why?"[22] Brooks took pains to answer with a long letter to the editor, blaming the South's assimilative institutional culture. Each of the departing Agrarians "genuinely wished to remain," he said, but university administrators proved so "indifferent or hostile" to the culture of ideas that it seems they "actually preferred to see him go." To Brooks, this was "a timid and cowed provincialism," emblematic of the Southern university's "anxiety" to "imitate what it takes to be the national norm":

> The typical Southern college or university is highly sensitive to the figure
> that it cuts in the public eye. It is embarrassed at the thought that it might

appear "cloistered," unworldly, visionary. It prefers, on principle, bowl games to poets, techniques to the humanities, "practical" subjects to "impractical" ones. In general it likes to be thought of as a bustling technological plant, the able and tireless assistant to business and industry. The Agrarian—the very name sounded bad—with his talk about tradition, his independent criticism of aspects of our contemporary society, and his unabashed concern for values, looked fatally like a crank.

The northward migration of Agrarian intellectuals, paradoxically, was a migration toward the very institutional culture (the university "as a bustling technological plant") that had provoked this desire of imitation. Brooks, repelled both by modern institutional culture and by the aspirational Southern assimilationists, rejects the charge of "looking forward" by preserving his regional affiliations intact: "It might almost be argued that the Southern Agrarians have proved themselves too Southern for the South."[23]

So intellectual migration it was, though this was rapidly naturalized as disciplinary progress. Narratives of the late 1940s almost completely disregard Southern Agrarianism, treating the rise of formalism as a merely institutional fact.[24] A full-page advertisement for *Understanding Poetry* in *The Saturday Review of Literature* indicates that erasing Southern ties was good business. Headed by a vignette of a gun-wielding owl positioned behind piles of books, the ad's copy touts a "conservative revolution" in literary study, led by the "rebellions" of "young instructors" against an "old guard . . . whose tastes had been formed at the end of the century." The Southerners' revolution, though, was depicted as the Northeast's pride:

> The obvious need for a new approach to the teaching of English poetry in American colleges was the spark that set [the revolution] off, and by 1940 it was well underway. At a great Eastern university, where the same Freshman course—the usual Carlyle and Ruskin, Browning and Tennyson—had been taught since the middle nineties, a group of young instructors organized a rebellion. . . . In 1940 the Brooks and Warren revolution was not complete; but the victory won by the young professors at the Eastern university was the beginning.[25]

This mythologizing ad, in which "rebellion" is a secondary stage in a diffusive professional process, is just slippery enough to imply that *Understanding Poetry* itself originated at this "great Eastern university." The textbook's Agrarian provenance gets replaced here by an offshoot "victory." Perhaps this is meant to summon the nebulous aura of Eastern prestige, or even to connect it with Yale, where Brooks was soon to move. The book's title page names Brooks and Warren's institutional affiliation, but this was as Southern as it got. Henry

Holt and Company had its sights set on national sales—and as the university became ever more "incorporated," the dividing line between discipline and market was getting harder to discern.

This particular elision of the Southern university reflects a general pattern. The change in the higher-educational environment after World War II led to a number of disciplinary self-assessments starting in the late 1940s, one striking aspect of which is the repeated erasure of regional context.[26] Stanley Hyman's *The Armed Vision* (1947) seemed its only chronicler, discerning a distinctive "Southern school" of criticism whose "leader" and "outstanding theoretician" is Ransom, scion of "a more or less concrete political program of Southern regionalism and agrarianism."[27] At the same time, Hyman carefully disentangles the Southern thinkers' criticism from political sources, emphasizing the influence of non-Southerners like Richard Blackmur (Princeton) and I. A. Richards (Cambridge and Harvard) and noting the substantial institutional foundation: "it has had a base to work from, in two or three Southern universities, as well as what amount to 'colonies' in Northern universities," and "it has always had one or two excellent literary organs."[28] Hyman's contemporary account was doubly deviant, both acknowledging the role of Southern regionalism and refusing the typical dichotomy, one that even Agrarians liked to tout, between the rural and parochial South and the institutional and cosmopolitan North.

What we have, then, are competing early accounts of the development of literary study: a Southern story of intellectual flight and regional exploitation in which the South's loss is turned to the modern university's gain, and a professional narrative in which the spread of formalism belongs to the internal and systemic evolution of a discipline. In the former, what matters is the pathos of loss, the mythologizing perception of the South's cultural impoverishment by forces originating elsewhere. This is the story told by what Paul Bové calls the "Professional Southernist"—nostalgic historians of the New Criticism such as Thomas W. Cutrer and T. D. Young, who recover the Agrarians as heroic and prophetic anticapitalists while occluding the problem of race.[29] In the latter, we find a romance of professionalism, in which ideas are shared, techniques are disseminated, and fields evolve. It's not that close reading simply grows (like a stalk of cotton), but that the social and political elements that informed it are not seen as meaningful in that growth.[30]

If Southernist scholarship tends to invest in the regional dichotomy of South-versus-North, institutionalists tend to invest in a story of heroic severance from the backward South. Graff's exemplary claim that the New Criticism's success was predicated on cutting ties with its regionalist roots, however, is not so much inaccurate as it is too simply polarizing, assuming a neat dichotomy between the institutional and the sociocultural.[31] Neither of these narratives adequately explains the shift that took place in literary study between the 1930s and the 1950s, a shift for which Ransom's decisive move to Ohio has come to seem symbolic. A third story might account for the impact of regional cultural politics without mythologizing or reifying those cultural politics—without rationalizing the northward migration of Southern intellectuals as intelligent strategy, or mourning it as a noble defeat, or bemoaning it as ignoble surrender; but also without essentializing the North as a progressive haven from the illiberal South (another assumption borrowed from Agrarian ideology). Subtle and ambitious explorations of the interplay between institutionalism and regionalism by Stephen Schryer and Alexander MacLeod have begun to re-map this critical narrative.[32] Yet we continue to lack an account that asks what "the flows of nostalgia and anti-nostalgia" that characterize this early moment in the discipline's history have to tell us.[33] It is only by attending to the centrality of loss in the old formations as it becomes formalized in new regions of reading that we gain a deeper appreciation for the residual nostalgia of the forward-looking discipline.

Poetry, Unincorporated

Ransom's "Criticism, Inc." (1937) was an early capital of these new regions of reading. The history of the discipline is studded with nuggets from the essay's first two pages alone:

> . . . it is from the professors of literature, in this country the professors of English for the most part, that I should hope eventually for the erection of intelligent standards of criticism. It is their business.

> Criticism must become more scientific, or precise and systematic, and this means that it must be developed by the collective and sustained effort of learned persons—which means that its proper seat is in the universities.

> Rather than occasional criticism by amateurs, I should think the whole enterprise might be seriously taken in hand by professionals. Perhaps I use a distasteful figure, but I have the idea that what we need is Criticism, Inc., or Criticism, Ltd.[34]

In rethinking the institutional past, we need to move beyond these sirenic early paragraphs of the essay that they've practically come to stand in for. To glance at "Criticism, Inc." is to grasp its investment in the growth industry of close reading, seen as the practical mechanism for the Wall Streeting of literary study. But to trace the essay's migratory impulse through to its very end is to encounter its elegiac quality, a newly critical nostalgia, which shadows the modern discipline in its formative era.

The affective drive of "Criticism, Inc." is at odds with Ransom's near-Swiftian satirical distance—a paradox that explains in part how he is able so presciently and single-handedly to write the history of the critical turn that he participates in. "Criticism, Inc." is usually read in earnest, without an ear for its author's comic sensibility, yet Ransom's satirical edge reflects his abiding ambivalence about this history. The essay's very title plays this business jargon as a ruse, while sentences like those above are practically written to be quoted (indeed the history of literary study can hardly be written without them). But criticism is about investments—in practices of reading, styles of teaching, and in the end, a theory of poetics—and so "Criticism, Inc." drifts from its initial, cagey insistence on the incorporation of criticism.[35] It is no small irony that the essay is so strongly identified in the disciplinary imaginary with its boldly progressive claims, for to read to the essay's end is to encounter the nostalgic longing that characterizes this transitional phase in Ransom's career, conveyed through respect for the local and concrete, indictments of teachers whose "salesmanship" imposes upon students in the manner of Northern imperialism, and critique of academic norms that mirror the practical and purposive ideology of American culture.[36]

The declarative confidence of the essay's opening sentences, in fact, is belied by their uncertainty. When Ransom says that "what we need is Criticism, Inc., or Criticism, Ltd.," he leavens his claim with doubt: "Perhaps I use a distasteful figure." But he does mean to suggest a corporate venture ("The idea of course is not a private one of my own"), then nods to "Professor Ronald S. Crane, of the University of Chicago" as "probably" the source for his thesis: "It is possible that he will have made some important academic history." However, it is Ransom, not Crane, who makes this history—which is not the tragic Southern plot but what he enigmatically refers to as "comic history."[37]

The comic plot frames Ransom's frequently cited distillation of the New Critical revolution, that "students of the future must be permitted to study literature, and not merely about literature." What comes next is not as much cited, being harder to parse: students "have not always been amiable about" being denied this permission, and "the whole affair presents much comic history."[38] There is no elucidating footnote here, no account of this unamiability, yet the mere mention of "comic history" colors the rest of the epigrammatic and occasionally exaggerated "Criticism, Inc." The voice of this essay steadfastly keeps a distance—sometimes naïve, sometimes satirical, sometimes indifferent. "(My information is not at all exact.)," Ransom playfully inserts.[39]

Theatrical from the start, a tonally adventurous performance of double-meaning, "Criticism, Inc." is performative in another sense as well, for it champions a disciplinary turn while seeming to make that turn happen. Ransom "makes history," enrolling various figures in the record of the time. Two hapless roles in this comic history are assigned to professors mocked for "read[ing] well aloud": Charles Townsend Copeland, professor at Harvard and part-time theater critic known for his poetry readings in the 1930s (and praised for his instructional style in Helen Keller's autobiography); and a less renowned Ethan Allen Cross, English professor at Greeley Teachers' College (later the University of Northern Colorado).[40] "Mr. Austin Warren," little-known in 1937, gets a slightly more sparing role: he "is evidently devoted to the academic development of the critical project" but, like other skeptics, "sees no reason why criticism should set up its own house."[41] The cast of characters also includes Crane, leading figure of Chicago's neo-Aristotelian school; Irving Babbitt, head of the New Humanist school; and T. S. Eliot, hero of an "aesthetic" approach embraced by New Critics. Wielding terms like "intoxicating" to describe ethical criticism, and "dull" and "perfunctory" to describe traditional historicism, Ransom evokes a deadening binary as his comic plot: "dryasdust" learnedness over and against "new and seductive [critical] excitements."[42]

However, the central dispute staged in "Criticism, Inc." is less that between scholars and critics than among different kinds of critic: moral, neo-Aristotelian, aesthetic or literary, and appreciative. Ransom's wiliness in laying out these critical categories becomes visible when he invokes the name "romantic"—famously damned by Babbitt for lacking a mature moral sensibility. Ransom finds it "perfectly legitimate" for Babbitt "to attack romantic literature . . . on the ground that it deals with emotions rather than principles, or the ground that its author discloses himself as flabby, intemperate, escapist, unphilosophical, or simply adolescent," reflecting an entire "romantic period" that has failed in mature response to the demands of "the social and political environment."[43] Such a critique, Ransom concludes, "is probably valid" for the moralist, but to its side is an equally forceful *aesthetic* objection, articulated in terms transparently imported from Eliot's "Tradition and the Individual Talent":

> the literary critic also has something to say about romanticism, and it might come to something like this: that romantic literature is imperfect in objectivity, or "aesthetic distance," and that out of this imperfection comes its weakness of structure; that the romantic poet does not quite realize the aesthetic attitude, and is not the pure artist. Or it might come to something else.[44]

Lest we assume this to be Ransom's view, note how deftly he ventriloquizes the figure of "the literary critic," presented here as a floating persona. The closing, sly escape from the constrictive taxonomy—"Or it might come to something else"—is his comic position, ironically detached from any single view.

Later in the essay, Ransom will elaborate this dissociative stance, posing the question that "the superior critic" concerns himself with: "why poetry, through its devices, is at such pains to dissociate itself from prose at all."[45] These were the pains taken by Wordsworth and Coleridge (Wordsworth with some equivocation on the necessity of meter, Coleridge on all the devices) and "dissociation" moreover has T. S. Eliot's fingerprints all over it (the problem with poetry after the seventeenth century is famously a "dissociation of sensibility" that separated thought from feeling). "Dissociation," the most prominent feature of Ransom's rhetorical stance, also proves the key problem of the poetics he lays out here—a poetics that transvalues terms like distance and logic, irrelevance and foreignness, and that is propelled by claims of attachment that define its fundamental nostalgia.

Ransom wants a criticism of poetry and prose as conceptual categories rather than as genres. Richards's *Practical Criticism* (1929) is his forerunner, setting a poem's "prose sense, its plain, overt meaning, as a set of ordinary, intelligible, English sentences, quite apart from any further poetic significance." Readers "travesty" a poem when they "fail to understand" even this "prose sense," according to Richards, but for Ransom, the relation between the prose and poetic senses that are active in any poem is more tense and charged with feeling.[46] The "two terms" that describe the content of any given poem, he argues, are "the prose core to which [the good critic] can violently reduce the total object, and the differentia, residue, or tissue, which keeps the object poetical or entire."[47] The "prose core," capable of paraphrase, represents logic, function, communication. It moves toward a reader and toward an end. It embodies an entire way of being—prose as the medium of "practical interests [that] will reduce their living object to a mere utility," and of "sciences [that] will disintegrate it for their convenience into their respective abstracts."[48] We recognize in the deadening effects of Ransom's "prose" a version of Viktor Shklovsky's "automatization," with the human agent reduced by habit into a voluntarily functional unit, and an anticipation of Adorno's "the lie of being truth": "our own minds," he writes, "have acquired such a prose habit that those parts which are not active in prose are thoroughly suppressed, and can hardly break through and exercise themselves."[49]

Poetry, on the other hand, is strange and alienating, illogical and perverse, residual and insubstantial. Years before Brooks would employ "the residuum" to describe what survives after a poem has been "referred to a cultural matrix," Ransom mobilizes it for his own poetics.[50] He uses "residue" three times in a row to describe poetry's character: he refers to the "residue, or tissue, which keeps the object poetical or entire"; to the poem's "way of exhibiting [its] residuary quality" as the key to its "character"; and to the poet's "way of involving [the poem] firmly in the residuary tissue." The poetic residuum is what's left behind after the prose core has been "scienc[ed] and devour[ed]," subjected to the various heresies of criticism (paraphrase, moralism, personal feelings, appreciation, biographical reading, and so forth).[51] Crane and the Chicago-School neo-Aristotelians, invested in paraphrase, took issue with such fetishizing of poetic content, but Ransom's nostalgic poetics needs to be distinguished from the New Critical mode that would become increasingly dominant in the 1940s.

While other New Critics talk about the organic body, for example, Ransom, the homesick intellectual, talks in terms of houses, monuments, habitations: the architecture of poetry. "A poem is a *logical structure* with a *local texture*," he writes in "The Concrete Universal I." Its structure is like the house's integral scaffolding, its joists and stanchions, foundation and walls, all of which can be mapped on a blueprint and reduced to a set of engineering problems solvable through calculation. It is abstract, moveable. The texture, by contrast, is the paint or wallpaper, the color and design. It is not essential—"It is logically unrelated to structure"—yet this is what finally distinguishes one poem (or house) from another.[52] Texture, in other words, *resides*. It lives in a place, not as a logical abstraction but as local detail. Its affinity is with the native environment, not the built one. A critic who "has nothing to say about [a poem's] texture" therefore "has nothing to say about it specifically as a poem, but is treating it only insofar as it is prose."[53]

Ransom's interest in poetry as "residue" or in its "residuary quality" deepens the emotional charge associated with architecture through the idea of residing, staying-on. "Residual" is also a legal term referring to what's left of an estate after its debts have been paid: the residuum is technically what does not matter (and so doesn't get devoured) in the socio-legal sphere of exchange. The residuum of texture never goes on the market, for it belongs neither to the house proper nor to the extended sphere of exchange in which the contents of a house participate. The residuum instead belongs to what Ransom calls "a tissue of irrelevance," a tissue that, as he elsewhere elaborates, "imports and carries along a great deal of irrelevant or foreign matter which is clearly not structural but even obstructive."[54] Imported, irrelevant, foreign, non-structural, obstructive: this woven tissue of irrelevance is the very stuff of poetry. It encloses a poem's "prose core," simultaneously part of and apart from the logical structure. As Catherine Gallagher sees it:

> Ransom tells us that the poet must encase the internal enemy, the "prose core" or paraphrasable meaning of the poem, in "a tissue of irrelevance," which violates prose logic. Just as the prose core of the original object begins to "emerge" from the language-shattered edifice of particularity, it must be precariously arrested by a poetic tissue of "superfluity" and irrelevance. The poet thus uses a language of connotation, peculiarly indirect and metaphorical, to repair the damage done by his language of denotation. Thus detained in "a tissue of irrelevance from which it does not really emerge," the immobilized prose core is not transformed into crystal, as in Pater, but is locked, permanently twitching, in a state of tension with the poem's own linguistic superfluity.[55]

Gallagher measures the internally divided nature of poetry for Ransom, its aesthetic echo of the internal divisions that condition his ambivalent rhetoric. She reads this poetics in terms of violation, arrest, detention, and immobilization, adapting the unified logic we associate with the New Criticism (the rhetoric of the organic whole) by making the poem into a self-policing system.

I would lay more stress on the pathos of Ransom's figures—the gentle longing conveyed by his "differentia, residue, or tissue," his nostalgic investment in survival—as well as on a violation of "close prose logic" that does not, I think, so easily resolve into a "permanently twitching" state of New Critical tension. Tissue and texture are both, etymologically speaking, text: the Old French *tissu* and the Middle English *texture* derive alike from the Latin verb *texere*, and they serve Ransom as object-lessons in residual survival and elegiac attachment. He describes the poetic act as a "desperate" effort to hold onto "something" that is vanishing, what he calls an "agony." The poem, he proposes, is "nothing short of a desperate ontological or metaphysical manoeuvre" on the part of a poet who "perpetuates in his poem an order of existence which in actual life is constantly crumbling beneath his touch." Robert Frost would call it a momentary stay against confusion, but Ransom ups the stakes. Practicality, history, information, paraphrase, instrumentalism, industry, all are aligned with "devouring" prose reductions, against which the poet works to safeguard a whole "order of existence." In this, his desire is essentially conservative: "Something is continually being killed by prose which the poet wants to preserve."[56]

This preservational urge is couched as deviance, a positively valued "lapse" from "the prose norm of language, and from close prose logic."[57] In "The Affective Fallacy," Wimsatt and Beardsley will work a similar transvaluation, interpreting Ransom's "tissue of irrelevance" as metaphor: "an obstruction to practical knowledge (like a torn coat sleeve to the act of dressing)," which "operates by being abnormal or inept, the wrong way of saying something."[58] Derived from the Greek for "transfer" or "carry over," metaphor is also a figure of foreignness or importation, and in characterizing it, Wimsatt and Beardsley use a vocabulary ("abnormal," "inept," and "wrong") that echoes Ransom's account of the poetic residuum as a form of deviance.

Ransom, however, spatializes rather than moralizes, making poetry's resistance to the "prose norm" into a dynamic of closeness and distance, enclosure and escape. He later would exaggerate this spatial dynamic by describing poetry as closed-off—the lodge of secret, undisclosable, and even unknowable forms of desire—with criticism an abettor of escape and explanation. In "The Bases of Criticism" (1944), Ransom revives the incorporative rhetoric of "Criticism, Inc." by revaluing what is most incommunicable about poetry: "in welcoming the strange foreign content that crowds in [to poetry], we are finding our real satisfaction in a sub rosa sort of activity." The secrecy and silence of the sub rosa may seem out of place in a discussion of poetics, but it suggests how utterly unknowable and transgressive of prose logic Ransom considers the formal essence of a poem to be. That essence speaks to a "motive for wanting poetry" that "may be obscure even to ourselves," a desire to "lapse" from the constraints of "prose habit" and thus to recede from expression, to move downward and inward, toward the silence of the poem's linguistic residuum. Prose, in this argument, is a code of straightness and regularity, linearity and automaticity, its essence being to guard against surprise. Its nature is tamed; "close prose logic" is a closed and enclosing logic. The "actual life" of poetry is the "alienating" force of its "strange" and "foreign content."[59]

To say this another way, Ransom conceptualizes the relation between poetry and prose as a movement across space, defined by confinement and vagrancy, proximity and distance. Poetry's technical devices are for Ransom a means of "*escaping* from prose," of getting distance from its argumentative logics.[60] He would later summon the term "distal" to describe this relation—*distal* being a variant of *distant* that is used in medicine or anatomy to indicate parts of the body "farthest from the center" (the thumb in relation to the wrist, for instance, or the hand to the shoulder).[61] This was no turn to organicist metaphor, for Ransom instead employs "distal" to indicate remoteness from an origin (the opposite of "proximal"), and it defines the relation between "differentia, residue, tissue" and the poem's "prose core." He even turns it into a noun, placing it opposite "syntax" in the lyric ecosystem: "It is only by determining the syntax of the [poem's] argument" (what is communicable as direct statement) "that we can throw into relief the distal of the poem" (what cannot be paraphrased).[62] This "distal of the poem" can only be sensed in "relief," belatedly. The distal may be "as proper to the poem as the syntax is proper to the argument, being the character of a discourse which is poetical," yet readers' view of it is recessive and flickering. To "figure [the poem's] actual distal" is to "take leave with their glance lingering not upon the paraphrase of a poem but upon a poem."[63] Readers gain the poem itself only while taking leave, in a figurative backward look during the motion of departure. Poetry is a mode of alienation, and the techniques that distinguish it are what make possible this double-movement of close attention and recession. Poetry's "metric; its inversions, solecisms, lapses from the prose norm of language, and from close prose logic; its tropes; its fictions, or inventions," are the means "by which a poem secures 'aesthetic distance' and removes itself from history."[64]

Ransom's "removal from history," paradoxically, aims to preserve historical content. This refusal of history's prose logic I'll call the nostalgia of close reading; I find Frederic Jameson's comments on "historicity" closely analogous. Jameson describes historicity as a "perception of the present as history, an understanding of "the here and now ... as a kind of thing—not merely a 'present' but a present that can be dated and called the eighties or the fifties."[65] This same sense of "the present as history," untamed by prose habit and full of residual matter, illuminates Ransom's attraction to the enclosed and distant vantage afforded by the railcar or automobile, which we see in several of his Agrarian-era essays. It also inflects the analogously dissociative perspective of his later writings about poetics. If history's "prose logic" is what one experiences on a train moving steadily forward, poetry evokes a multidimensional awareness of one's historicity, that disorienting double-consciousness of living in one world while feeling the tug of "the one we think we remember to have come from."[66]

Entering the 1940s, this complex nostalgia could well describe the institutional situation of criticism along with Ransom's relation to the professional age that he'd helped usher in. As if in recoil, he grew more skeptical of the "business-like" manner. Close criticism had become unsettlingly prose-like in nature, "perfunctory and academic," a way to simplify complex texts for students in an age of mass education and a touchstone for career advancement.[67] On the threshold of the "academic revolution" that would uproot collegiate life from its local communities and re-align it with disciplinary ones, Ransom's nostalgia found a special focus in a poet who was neither

Southern nor American: Wordsworth, an agrarian and a regionalist, and the English tradition's preeminent poet of place.[68] Wordsworth gives Ransom a way to articulate the migrancy of his own professional life, while expressing a new readerly ideal invested in affective connection and attachment. One of the constitutive "exclusions" in Ransom's definition of criticism had been, anticipating Wimsatt and Beardsley, "personal registrations": "The first law to be prescribed to criticism, if we may assume such authority, is that it shall be objective, shall cite the nature of the object rather than its effects upon the subject."[69] A dozen years after this, Ransom would court these very effects in writing about Wordsworth, reflecting his own distanced historical sense of the mid-century world he helped to make: his nostalgia for the present.

Reading Ransom-reading-Wordsworth

"William Wordsworth: Notes Toward an Understanding of Poetry" (1950) is a peculiar piece of criticism, lightly regarded in its time and little known today. There's no mystery to its obscurity. The essay is full of contradictory insights, alternatively effusive and chiding, and is oddly personal throughout. Ransom's interest in Wordsworth involves a strong emotional response to the poetry and an even stronger identification with the poet. In this and in other ways, Ransom doesn't abide by the received orthodoxies of critical history; he qualifies the iconic title of *Understanding Poetry* with the provisional "notes toward." For a reader expecting a tightly formed, New Critical take on romantic poetry, this meandering essay will surprise and disappoint.

And yet there is something representative about the essay's origins. Ransom wrote these "Notes" mostly in Bloomington, where he spent the academic year 1949–50 as Indiana University's first annual Visiting Professor of Criticism, a position that symbolized the mobility increasingly being built into the modern academic profession. The essay thus took root in a freshly energized intellectual atmosphere characterized by the growing prestige of literary research (as the mere fact of his visitorship attests). A blossoming PhD program and the migration of "English" into neighboring disciplines, such as Comparative Literature, Linguistics, Folklore, and Drama, were the most obvious signs at Indiana of the discipline's strength, as it moved past its previous role as "a service department of the University" and into a fully enfranchised research program.[70]

This material efflorescence lagged somewhat behind the "conservative revolution" with which Ransom is so intimately connected. By 1950, the American New Criticism had put down roots, and in "William Wordsworth" Ransom pulls back from his immersion in the discipline's "here and now" to assume a historical vantage, grasping the recent past "as a kind of thing" that he can comprehend and date. Deliberating the two consciousnesses of his own past—the Agrarian nostalgic who longed for a past that never was, and the New Critical professionalist who projected a "business-like" future for literature—Ransom in 1950 comes (back) to Wordsworth as a partner in elegy and a fulcrum for his burgeoning historical sense.

The essay is an exercise in revisiting, pervaded by retrospection, as if Ransom were taking the measure not merely of Wordsworth but of his own intellectual journey. The promise and the disappointments of a disciplinary narrative in which he had participated weigh on his reading of Wordsworth, which is filtered by his personal history:

> many of us for the first time, when we were young, discovered in the poetry of Wordsworth what poetry was; but turned from him as we became experienced in other poetry of greater virtuosity; and through some need felt in our maturity have finally come back to him with admiration for the purity of his style.[71]

This mature gravitation toward Wordsworth is given with just enough vagueness ("through some need felt in our maturity") to prompt wonder at its intensity. Ransom had previously associated Wordsworth with a "confessional" strain that he deemed "unfortunate for the prosperity of the art." In *The New Criticism* he filled five pages with unimpeded quotation of William Empson on the "muddled" thinking of "Tintern Abbey," one of the longest quotations in all of modern criticism, which Ransom punctuates with a curt assent: "I think this comment is lucid and just."[72] Now having "come back" to Wordsworth, Ransom stakes a personal claim in grandiose literary-historical terms: "Our poet was one of the giants," the essay begins; "he reversed the direction of English poetry in a bad time, and revitalized it."[73] Ransom may have felt he'd done the same for criticism, with some regret.

Neither his mature "need" nor his "admiration" for Wordsworth's "purity of . . . style" were main lines of reception in twentieth-century criticism. In the best-known account of Wordsworthian reception, M. H. Abrams describes the "two roads" by which critics traditionally approach Wordsworth. One, blazed by Matthew Arnold, reveres Wordsworth as a "simple, affirmative poet of elementary feelings, essential humanity, and vital joy"; the other, that of A. C. Bradley, finds him a "complex poet of strangeness, paradox, equivocality, and dark sublimities."[74] To Ransom, however, Wordsworth is both: affirmative humanist and theologically inclined poet of consciousness. The merging of these two roads in Ransom reflect his appreciation of Wordsworth as simultaneously poet of migrancy and poet of rootedness. This contradiction defines his sense of the "elementary" Wordsworth: a localist who attaches himself to the "little tract of land" he himself could call home, and an exile battered by experience, whose "long journey home" is, as Abrams argues, both literal and spiritual.[75] Ransom frankly admires Wordsworth's devotion to a fully realized sense of place within a world of transients and vagrants in which he is always potentially one of them, but he feels as well (especially perhaps in the aftermath of his Agrarian renunciations) the irresistible pull of the dark possibility this contains: that home is no guarantee.[76]

The divergence of these two roads to Wordsworth represents a potent juncture in Ransom's thinking not only about the poet but about the history of literary criticism that he had quite consciously helped to create. To read Ransom-reading-Wordsworth is to discover, in one of the protagonists of the discipline's history, an abiding ambivalence as it entered its triumphal decade. The 1950s, heart of the postwar era and great age of the public university, are when the ideals of "Criticism, Inc." blossom as a vehicle for the social mission of liberal higher education, but for Ransom they represent a watershed, a moment of literal crisis that demands he look back upon the history he'd participated in.

But why was Wordsworth his proxy? Wordsworth was never really a stable subject in New Criticism. Brooks begins *The Well Wrought Urn* (1947) by reading "the language of paradox" in two compact sonnets, "It is a Beauteous Evening" and "Composed upon Westminster Bridge," and even his most polemical turn against romanticism, *Modern Poetry and the Tradition* (1939), opens with extended discussion of Wordsworth's conception of fancy and imagination.[77] At the same time, Wordsworth's "unprecedented" capacity to "talk so much about himself" (his description of *The Prelude*) was at odds with the ideal of impersonality set forth by Eliot.[78] He may have been the visible face of a romantic revolution that served as a model for the New Critics' own, but he was also too propositional for them, too spontaneous, too emotional, and not sufficiently ironic. His poetry of "the frontal attack" was especially dubious; Brooks worried that students would read the Intimations Ode as the voice of "a very fuzzy sentimentalist," and he had his work cut out in recovering its multiple paradoxes.[79]

Ransom's own formal interest lay in the push and pull of Wordsworth's style, specifically what he calls its "prose-poetry diction" or "prose-poetry language."[80] The appeal of "prose-poetry" marks a turn in Ransom's poetics: where he previously chastised "prose core" paraphrasing, he now appreciates Wordsworth's "poetry" of "prose, when it is well-written."[81] It is precisely this equivalence that wins over the mature Ransom, who describes Wordsworth's poetry as operating almost entirely in the realm of the tenor, with "little recourse to extraneous vehicles"—hinting at its value as a poetry that stays in place, resisting the transports of metaphor.[82] This "prose-poetry diction" is beyond use or exploitation. It "registers factually a human passion for a concrete object," defined as "that plenum of the natural world which is so much denser than our appetites need it to be, and denser than our intellects can grasp."[83] A poetic manifestation of Wordsworthian innocence, the prose-poetry style is an analog to the knowledge that the joy of innocence has passed. There can be no mystical renovation of fallen reality into Edenic vision; this is a poetics of (lower-case) agrarianism, or naturalism.

At the center of this new poetics are four devices, whose names Ransom coins: Spreaders, Rufflers, Importers, and Meters. Strikingly playful, these terms figure visible movement—how words *spread* meaning, or *ruffle* it, or *import* it.[84] There is a comic quality in this technical terminology, which functions as a kind of parody of formal poetics. But the devices do real critical work. We know about "Meters," the expectation of stressed and unstressed syllables in one patterning or another. "Spreaders," Ransom proposes, are the signature feature of Wordsworth's prose-poetry style, consisting of "Singular Terms . . . words and phrases," which "explore the vivid concreteness in the objects and events, even while seeming to prosecute a discourse in logical terms which would refer only to their use." Spreaders in Wordsworth are resistant to metaphor; they operate, as Ransom puts it, "entirely within the tenor."[85]

Two other terms that Ransom lists but doesn't find as prominent in Wordsworth are "Dystactical Terms, or Rufflers; where a logical confusion is deliberately cultivated," and "Metaphorical Terms, or Importers; where vehicle is introduced."[86] While many readers of Wordsworth long for more rufflers and metaphors, Ransom admires the "plain style" that "sticks to its tenor," arguing furthermore that such a style "is not so plain absolutely as comparatively. . . . there may be a great range of sensibility carrying it on and establishing vivid and abundant content. The stylist can achieve his distinction here as well as anywhere else."[87] Ransom subverts the notion of "innovation" by redefining it as plainness, reinforcing the point through his homemade terminology. This is evidently not a technical discourse that would ever catch on in English Departments, and Ransom knew it. He was refusing the codified "scientific" language of criticism, adopting a terminology that, for all its playful directness, was no less systematic or precise.

His coinages owe a debt to I. A. Richards, who described how "the compression of poetic language . . . tends to obstruct the discursive intelligence that works by spreading ideas out and separating their parts."[88] In Richards's account, students who were asked to paraphrase a poem typically fell to "shuffling synonyms" around, substituting poetic words with similar words but without really understanding the poem's content or "literal sense."[89]

Alternatively, the word lists of Basic English, which Richards came to champion, "spread" a too-concise poem into an easier, flattened paraphrase.[90] This emphasis on "spreading" rather than on "shuffling" informs Ransom's technical vocabulary, as he defines the "plain" or "prose-poetry diction" by its tendency to spread poetry out into a decompressed idiom with "a tendency to flatness."[91] A "plain style" reliant on "spreaders" effectively locates the work of paraphrase inside of the poem. Especially because paraphrases can require long sentences and awkward phrasing, Wordsworth's "virtuous" style is its affordance—through the use of spreaders—of a compact and concise line so close to what Richards calls "its plain, overt meaning," so *concrete* (to use a term favored by Ransom), that it effectively pre-empts the need for prose paraphrase.[92] It's a poetry with its own prose paraphrase built-in, previously installed. "Spreaders" keep Wordsworth's poetry near to its "literal sense"; generic as his label might sound, Ransom is being precise when he writes of Wordsworth's "prose-poetry style," because this style literally involutes the prose sense within the poetry. Such compactness defines it as the "good" kind of prose ("when prose is well-written").

This prose-poetry style comes to the fore of the essay on Wordsworth as a formal means of resisting the migratory nature of modern life as well as of modern poetry. Wordsworthian lyric, Ransom argues, stays put, technically speaking, refusing the dynamic transformations generated by metaphysical conceit. Gone is the nostalgic vision associated with Agrarian cultural politics, and gone is the spiritualism embedded in metaphor. In an early essay, "The South: Old or New?," Ransom described the insidious ways that modern travel steals away our time under the pretense of saving it:

> [V]ehicular transportation is a peculiarly modern symbol. Rapid transit between points is properly the means of saving time to spend at the points. But the moderns have devoted such ingenuity to the problem as greatly to multiply the points accessible, and now are transporting themselves about within this multiple system with less time to spend at any one point than ever before.... [I]ndustrialism no sooner reduces the period of a given labor than it more than makes it up by inventing a number of new objectives to work at, and we are further off from freedom and leisure than we were at the beginning.[93]

Ransom wrote this in 1928, when he was at his most "Agrarian." He craved rootedness, and he viewed mobility as an illusion of freedom that overvalues the acceleration of life and material desires. Much later, this aversion to mobility would come to describe an entire poetics: Wordsworth, by sticking to the tenor, refuses the migratory vehicle; his poems remain rooted in place, and this is their "plain style."

Despite his connection with a close reading practice that "does not stray far from the literary text," Ransom travels a fast road through Wordsworth's individual poems.[94] Starting with the critique in the 1800 Preface to *Lyrical Ballads* of Thomas Gray's too-artful diction, he moves in short order through "Home at Grasmere," "Ruth," and "Michael," almost perversely avoiding direct claims about any of them. His manner is vagrant and associative, with strategic juxtapositions generating insights and doing the arguing for him.

First, Wordsworth's critique of Gray's "Sonnet" on the death of Mr. Richard West—a critique that is not about Gray's mourning or Gray's alienation from the comforts of nature, but about artificial eighteenth-century diction. Yet Ransom's focus is on what Wordsworth obscures: this is a poem of profound, life-altering, inconsolable grief, which is also the ground of Ransom's investment in Wordsworth. He sets out in a teacherly mode, quoting Gray's sonnet in full and then offering a workmanlike, paragraph-long paraphrase, covering everything from the poem's rhyme structure to its central drama, in which nature endeavors unsuccessfully to "cheer" the speaker with its various "small joys." Ransom appreciates Gray's delicate artistry: "This is about as graceful in design as the elegiac mode can well afford to be."[95] Elegy, rather than joy, is seen as the tenor of Gray's lament. Ransom next (in a vein that might surprise readers expecting the usual New Critical prohibitions) mentions the "flesh and blood" biographical backgrounds of the poem, veering into affective response: "it is touching, in some degree, that the natural objects seem to solicit the mourner to partake of their joy, and in saying joy the poet is in the heart of Wordsworth's own vocabulary."[96] Ransom too stays in Wordsworth's vocabulary, merging his critical voice with the poet's, in a kind of free indirect style that conflates their assessments of the sonnet: "the objects are too pretty, they are too petty, and the fact is that they are too meanly regarded altogether." These are Wordsworth's claims about the poem, conveyed as Ransom's own. Both poet-critics find Gray's account of nature inadequate.

For comparison, Ransom turns to "Home at Grasmere," with its patent joy in nature's beauty, recalling how Wordsworth produced "a passage about the surpassing beauty of the region in which he declares solemnly: 'On Nature's invitation do I come.'"[97] "Home at Grasmere" is mythic-nostalgic in this way, and merely thinking about the poem may have stoked in Ransom memories of his return to Vanderbilt in 1914, after three years in Oxford and a fourth year teaching in Connecticut. He doesn't say so, but this seems behind a fantasy that what really bothered Wordsworth about Gray's sonnet was not its dictional prettiness but its failure to find solace in "nature's succor." "Home at Grasmere" is the antithesis.

But Ransom does not dwell here, nor even return to his treatment of Gray.

Instead he plows forward both associatively and recursively. What reads like a passing speculation—"We will imagine that he [Wordsworth] did not like the idea of Gray's having his speaker decline the solicitations of the natural objects, poor though they might be"—gives way to another poem about solicitations, the story of "Ruth" (the very name meaning sorrow).[98] Wooed by "a youth from Georgia's shores" who sells her on America's natural beauties, Ruth falls for him, only to find herself abandoned far from her English home. Even so, what strikes Ransom is the girl's natural piety, her refusal to blame Nature for having been the source of her deception. Ransom quotes the poem's relevant passage:

> The engines of her pain, the tools
> That shaped her sorrow, rocks and pools,
> And airs that gently stir
> The vernal leaves—she loved them still;
> Nor ever taxed them with the ill
> Which had been done to her.[99]

Wordsworth's vocabulary reinforces Ransom's own: Ruth succeeds where Gray had failed. Just because nature has been misused does not mean that it should be disregarded (or "meanly regarded"). Ransom, again, does not tell us any of this; he seems constitutionally unable to clinch an argument about any one poem, choosing instead an associative method in which resonant turns echo and reinforce earlier points. He merely implies his claims, arguing vagrantly through a set of cascading implications—a critical habit that prompts a reader to do the work of revisiting what has been said previously. The brief turn to "Home at Grasmere" explains Ransom's previous remark on Gray's "mean regard" for Nature, and the turn to "Ruth" offers a belated gloss on his earlier remark on Gray's failure to see through the instrumentalization of Nature.

And then another resonant transition: "It was likewise with Michael himself."[100] In this last associative turn, Ransom connects Gray's lack of natural piety with the unfinished sheepfold that Michael hoped to complete with his son Luke upon his return. Luke did not return, and the sheepfold—like Wordsworth's "prose-poetry diction" itself—"registers factually a human passion for a concrete object."[101] The (once again tacit) claim is that Wordsworth's natural piety enables him to find value in even this object of sorrow. In Gray, sterile poetic conventions yield a Nature inadequate to the speaker's needs: "A different object do these eyes require." For Wordsworth, there is no "different object" to "require," for that object is still Nature. Only the vehicle is wrong, and the unfinished or missing natural object (though it is partly man-made, and mostly *un*-made) retains its influence over the person open to its solicitations. Like Ruth, Michael does not "tax" either "the rocks," or "the wind," or "his sheep," or "the land, his small inheritance," for the loss of the son who left in order to save those things. He may "mourn to him that cannot hear," but Michael returns again and again to that resonant spot of ground, accepting nature's barren invitation.

"Our appetitive business with a concretion," Ransom writes, "is to find some use to abstract from it, and then to abandon it."[102] The "youth from Georgia's shore" nurses his appetites by turning nature's "rocks and pools" into (rhyming) rhetorical "tools," only to abandon Ruth; and Gray, in the face of poetry's florid and unsatisfying vehicles, similarly abandons nature's small joys. But Ruth and Michael neither abandon nor feel themselves abandoned by Nature—and neither does Wordsworth himself: "In choosing to deal directly with the natural concretions, and with the feelings which engage with it, Wordsworth was willing to throw away most of the tropology with which poetry was commonly identified." Ransom here adds a personal declaration, which defines his appreciation for Wordsworth as a result of his maturation, while conveying that more was at stake in his reading of Wordsworth than a description of a style: "For some two years I have felt deeply grateful to Wordsworth for giving his authority to this special kind of language."[103]

Ransom's gratitude to Wordsworth is the response that he wishes (via Wordsworth) that Gray had felt toward Nature. To take such an acknowledgment literally is to date Ransom's gratefulness for Wordsworth to about 1947—after the war's end, and well after Ransom's public renunciation of Agrarianism. We need not unpack the psychology behind the exact timing of Ransom's return to Wordsworth—what he sought in "this special kind of language" that Wordsworth made possible for poetry, or why his "felt . . . need" for the Wordsworthian "purity of style" peaked at this particular moment. It is sufficient, for now, to remark that Ransom's turn to Wordsworth was late in his own trajectory, and that he dates it to a time when his own previous call for "close criticism" as a "more scientific, or precise and systematic" professional practice was finally coming to fruition.

This makes his highly personal and contingent account of Wordsworth's plain diction all the more striking. Ransom writes:

> The test poem for me is Michael. No part of it is less plain or more plain than the lines I have quoted. I have wavered between resistance and participation till at last it has (at this writing) won me. It has a kind of virtuosity of its own, which consists in its relentless understatement (by poetical standards) of the occasion, where other poets are virtuosos by overstatement, over-writing, aiming perhaps to overwhelm us with their "fine excess."[104]

This is not about close reading as we imagine the New Critics to have practiced it. The emphasis is on the present of reading. Ransom describes himself as having "wavered" on "Michael," like a young person fearful of commitment, but the poem finally wins him "at this writing." Not at this *reading*: it is as if he has written himself into admiration.

Ransom's judgment belongs to a particular moment, which is the present moment of composition. He is a quirky and emotional reader—less close reader operating by absolute critical standards than close responder or ruminator, concerned with ethical and existential questions as these are unpredictably sparked in him by the poetry. Ironically, considering his seminal role in close reading's history, Ransom's highly cathected approach to Wordsworth is prone to fits of sloppiness or casualness. It is a non-professional affection.[105] His take on *The Prelude*, occupying the final pages of the essay, devolves into a projection of anti-romantic prejudices not predicted by the essay's first two-thirds. He argues that later Wordsworth adds "a heavy overlay of religious experience" to his blank verse, imposes a "more or less uniform religious doctrine" on his boyhood experience, and displaces innocent perception with "the matured configurations" of the adult mind. Wordsworth's Catholic inheritor, Hopkins, did not "compel every spontaneous experience to disclose its dogmatic bearings," Ransom claims, yet in reading Wordsworth we encounter "something . . . which we feel like resisting, or more probably feel like reading very carelessly or even skipping in order not to resist."[106] Ransom generally prefers short lyrics to long ones, explaining that they are "not burdened with all [the] significance" imposed by a looser and more propositional poetry, and he thus declines a careful accounting of the epic *Prelude*, despite the fact that he identifies it as "the greatest locus of the plain style."[107]

The desire to read Wordsworth "very carelessly" comes from Ransom's sense of a mismatch between what he wants to find in the poetry and what he feels is there but won't read closely enough to confirm. His chosen critical form correlates to this practice of "reading . . . carelessly." Writing in "notes, because my impressions are speculative and imperfect, and . . . do not aspire anyway to be demonstrative," Ransom refuses professionally formed, self-contained explications of individual poems, a critical form that was becoming normative. Such discrete readings included Trilling's and Brooks's recent treatments of the Intimations Ode, a back-and-forth that Ransom short-circuits through his speculative, impressionistic, and non-demonstrative mode of surveying Wordsworth's oeuvre. For Ransom, the Intimations Ode is less significant as a poem in its own right than as a way to frame Wordsworth's poetic maturation, which Ransom understands as having taken place before the final stanzas were composed in 1804. It is in the gap between the first seven and last four stanzas of the poem that Ransom's interest migrates to another, briefer Wordsworthian lyric: "My Heart Leaps Up," composed in that gap and excerpted for use as the Ode's epigraph beginning in 1815.

By privileging "My Heart Leaps Up" over the longer and more prestigious lyric to which it eventually was attached, Ransom makes his declared "admiration" for Wordsworth a matter of personal development and maturation. Wordsworth, Ransom says, helps his readers to "obtain the sense of community with the infinite concretion of the invironing world, [so that] we may cease to feel like small aliens." Such a poetry, Ransom concludes, is "of even greater moment to us today than in the time of Wordsworth, in the degree of our increased alienation from nature and, I think, our increased anxiety."[108] This "anxiety" is often associated with the sense of modernity as a mode of historical experience given over to change and renewal—a temporal discontinuity from which redundancy and return might provide an outlet. Ransom's meditation on Wordsworth culminates with a reading in which he seems to identify a nostalgic solution to temporal discontinuity, though it might just be "homesickness by other means."[109] He quotes "My Heart Leaps Up" in its entirety—

> My heart leaps up when I behold
>   A rainbow in the sky:
> So was it when my life began;
> So is it now I am a man;
> So be it when I shall grow old,
>   Or let me die!
> The Child is father of the Man;
> And I could wish my days to be
> Bound each to each by natural piety.[110]

—and then praises the poem for its assertion of a continuity between the unselfconscious joy of childhood perception, and the conditional hope that, in maturity, one can still experience such joy:

> For me this perfect little poem seems to say by indirection that the important thing in the child's experience was the spontaneous joy of seeing the rainbow; and the full sense of God which belongs to the man with his laborious dogma may not really have been there. The joy was enough, and it is enough now if the man has never lost the gift for joy.

Ransom's commentary then takes a sudden turn, invoking Virgil in reference to Wordsworth's phrase "natural piety":

> To know what piety is we have to have read Virgil and seen how Aeneas was pious because he honored his father Anchises, and bore him upon his own back from burning Troy. That was a piety symbolic of how each day a man must take up the life of yesterday, so that no human gift or possession will be allowed to fail.[111]

The turn to Virgil comes seemingly from nowhere, though of course this isn't the case. When introducing the poem, Ransom points out that its "last lines" were "placed by the poet under the title of the *Ode* as a text," but in the poem's initial 1807 publication, a line from Virgil had actually served as its epigraph.[112] That textual history of displacement supports the deeply personal sense of history as failure that Ransom's "piety" calls to mind. While piety here is about honoring the past, it's also, importantly, about *reading*: to properly understand this poem's clinching statement, we have to have read not only Virgil, but also Wordsworth in his earlier versions, with an understanding of the way that displacement defines a text's (and our own) existence in time. To know something (even if only a poem's epigraph), we need to know what it has displaced; we need to know what is gone. Piety, in this way, is moreover about *leaving*: Ransom brings an obligation to history, processed through his history of reading, together with the necessity of moving forward. This is a sense of piety as fidelity to the past, which includes an acceptance of the past *as past*.

So this was Ransom's burning Troy. The exhortation to "take up the life of yesterday" may seem regressive, but this sense is countered by the complicated piety entailed in Ransom's effort to bear the past forward, to salvage what he can from the conflagration. Summoning through Wordsworth the idea of lived consistency, "days bound each to each," Ransom projects himself back across a tremendous fracture, encompassing a catastrophic global war, an emergent liberal hegemony, not to mention (at a personal level) a new politics, a new job, and new attachments. His changed circumstances (staid resident of Gambier, professor at Kenyon, editor of the field's bedrock periodical, leading member of the progressive disciplinary community at large) held enormous symbolic value for the discipline as a whole, and the backward glance, far from valuing past over future (or regional identifications over disciplinary ones), acknowledges the facts of dislocation and of generational displacement and finds value in the capacity to see the present clearly. "To know what piety is, we have to have read Virgil" is, with Ransom's characteristic wiliness, another way of saying that to bear the past forward "each day" is to take up a historical perspective, to discern the present as history and as shaped by a radically distinct past.

Coda

It may seem odd for Ransom to have identified Wordsworth, the Lake District regionalist, as a fellow Agrarian, effectively importing him to the American South. For Ransom, though, "Southern" was as much a style and sensibility as a fact of geographical locale. As he says in his 1935 essay "Modern with a Southern Accent":

> some writers must impress us as having Southern quality, or something like it, who are not physically of the South.... [I]t is not the specifically Southern localism that matters but the fact of localism at all; that is, the reference of everything in the story to the genius loci, or spirit of the local background. A concrete formalism is, then, the Southern sort of thing.

"Southern," Ransom claims, is "a descriptive classification," "a proper name like Romantic or Gothic."[113] This notion of "Southern quality" as a transportable style allows him to conceive of Wordsworth as, at his best, a poet of the American South.[114] Wordsworth's "concrete formalism," embedded in his "prose-poetry diction" or "plain style," is seen as attending to and preserving the concreteness of local nature, be it of Georgian shores or Cumbrian hills. Natural piety, or faith to nature, paradoxically makes Wordsworth available to regionalists everywhere.

Transportable style also defines Ransom's own vexed Southernness. When he left Nashville in the late 1930s, his friends insisted that there was no other Southerner quite like him. The notion that Ransom could remain "Southern" even after moving to Ohio seemed to depend on a fantasy of his future return. But such a return did not seem greatly to attract him; there would be no "long journey home," and the essay on Wordsworth appears to have coincided with a realization that his own route would not, as in the self-conscious design of *The Prelude*, "round back to its point of departure."[115] Shortly after publishing the piece, Ransom replied to Davidson about a potential reunion: "It's a touching thing to go back to the place where one started and see the old friends again. It seems incredible how little contacts I have these days with the Vanderbilt community."[116] The move north had taken him far from his friends and far from the political broil of the 1930s. Decades later, as his career wound to a close, he told a feature writer for the *Columbus Citizen-Journal* of his appreciation for the serene academic life he had discovered in Gambier: "It's lovely and cool up here on this hill, much nicer than anything below," he explained; "It's rural, there are no politics."[117]

One hears in this a fleeting Wordsworthianism—"For rest of body perfect was the spot.... [H]ere / Must be his home, this valley be his world"—

though the inversion of valley and hill reminds us that Ransom's journey was in a certain sense the opposite of Wordsworth's in "Home at Grasmere," one-way and not redemptive. "In the forms which [our] salvation takes," he wrote when renouncing Agrarianism in 1945, "we do go back into our original innocence, but vicariously or symbolically, not really. We cannot actually go back, and if we try it the old estate becomes insupportable."[118] Hence his mature psychic "need" for the Wordsworthian "purity of style," a need born from a realization of difference. Wordsworth's consolations could not be Ransom's own. The achieved unity of the bard striding atop sublime Helvellyn is an ironic distortion of the distal relation between Ransom, alone upon his cool little hill, and the raging social and historical tumult of "anything below" (this was 1968, after all).[119] Remote from the prose logic of political turmoil and campus uprisings, this is a Ransom removed from history in a way that faintly echoes his departure from Nashville three decades before.

Ransom never tired of wanderer figures, be they ironic or heroic. There were all those philosophical regionalists and traveling eclectics in his writings of the 1930s, comically presented; there was Aeneas bearing Anchises from the conflagration of Troy; there was Wordsworth "come to live at last at Grasmere to pursue his dedicated career"; and there was also Otto von Bismarck, creator of the German *Kaiserreich*, whose statue on the bank of "the golden Rhine" was "a firm instance of those uncompromising human spirits who travel far from their origins and make their mark."[120] Writing this in 1945, in a response to Theodor Adorno (another émigré who traveled far to make his mark), Ransom seemingly resigned himself to the fact that there would be no hero's return to Nashville, that he indeed had no desire for such a return. The philosophical regionalist of the 1930s had transformed into a kind of permanent nostalgic, member of an international academic community, living at a cool distance from the college that employed him and at a larger remove from the world that formed him. Encountered from the depths of our present higher-ed era, a period defined by humanities downsizing, student poverty, and casualized labor, Ransom's anesthetic distance from "anything below" can ring with callousness, practically arctic in its frigidity. This late-career melancholy is not our millennial despair.[121] And yet, once we recognize the alienating layers of self-protection that Ransom has learned to put on amid the turmoil of 1968, we might revisit a melancholy with the capacity to speak to us, however obliquely, from a world we think we remember to have come from.

2. Shelley's Immaturity

Most of the people who have read and enjoyed Shelley over the last 150 years never went near a university.
—Paul Foot, *Red Shelley*

The anti-romanticism of the American New Critics was more complex and ambivalent than is usually recognized, but about Shelley's poetry there seemed to be a consolidated line. Cleanth Brooks called it "slovenly" and "embarrassing." John Crowe Ransom judged it neither "bold . . . nor quick and terse; no guts," and wrote a couplet rhyming *Shelley* with *pale yellow jelly*. To Allen Tate it was "incoherent," emasculated. "Shelley's balls warn't anything to write home about," Tate quipped to John Peale Bishop, who volleyed back:

> The question, lords and ladies, is
> With what did Percy Shelley piss?
> Was light dissolved in star showers thrown
> When Percy Shelley had a bone?
>
> . . .
>
> We ask and ask, till silence palls,
> Did Percy Bysshe have any balls?[1]

This "Percy Shelley" was, as Carlos Baker summarized in 1948, "a falsetto screamer, a sentimental Narcissus, a dream-ridden escapist, an immoral free-love cultist with a highly inflammable nature, and . . . the weakling author of the lyric called 'The Indian Serenade.'"[2] More later about this lodestone of a poem; for now it's enough to note Baker's précis of the case against Shelley: childlike, irresponsible, and incapable of properly controlling or directing his sexual appetites; a boy poet, appealing to boyish (or girlish) readers.

There was nothing particularly new about this; such claims had been a commonplace of Shelley's reception from the very start. Yet here in a nut-shell are the normative criteria according to which a conspicuously selected portion of Shelley's work (the "angelist" canon, not the radical one) became the target of over-the-top New Critical aggression: good poems as manly and tough-minded, bad ones as naïve, sentimental, and undisciplined.[3] The consistent implication, rooted in biography and seeping into explication, is that Shelley the poet, like Shelley the man, was immature. Though many of the charges against him are self-canceling (womanizer or queer? oversexed or impotent?), and though they contradict his own insistence that "The Poet & the Man are two different natures," taken together they constitute an enveloping mesh of insinuation about his poetry and about his life, boiling down to one basic suspicion: *Shelley was just a boy*.[4]

The conjoined vocabulary of critical appraisal and psychosexual de-velopment was hardly unique to Shelley. The Spasmodics, Tennyson, early Wordsworth, all suffered abuse in similar terms, with Keats perhaps the best-known example of a poet derided as childish, immature, not a man for men to read.[5] But twentieth-century readers would reconstrue Keats as a complex and mature poet—including Brooks, who amended his own initial impa-tience with Keats's chaotic impressionism.[6] Shelley, though, never passed the test of New Critical maturity. In *Modern Poetry and the Tradition* (1939) Brooks defines the "characteristic fault" of Shelley's poetry as its exclusion of "all but the primary impulses—that it cannot bear an ironical contemplation." The best poetry, Brooks writes, "has come to terms with itself and is invulnerable to irony"; it accounts for "complexities and apparent contradictions" in a "mature" manner; it is "founded on the facts of experience." Shelleyan lyric lacks such toughness: potent but out-of-control (as he was); insufficiently formed (as he was); given to "embarrassing declarations" (as he was).[7] In the New Critical judgment, "I fall upon the thorns of life! I bleed!," the *cri de coeur* of "Ode to the West Wind," is the exemplary Shelleyan fault, begging "the question as to whether the statement grows properly out of a context; whether it is ironical—or merely callow, glib, and sentimental."[8] A malformed growth, the line is not just outrageously improper (the poet as existential Christian martyr), but puerile, even deviant.

There is something evidently, but not admittedly, overdetermined about such extreme judgments—more severe than what was leveled at Wordsworth's extravagances, or even at Keats's boyish sensuality. What was it about Shelley that was so unsettling that it seemed to require this aggressive sexual den-igration?[9] Our critical histories tend to elide the question, taking Shelley's radical politics and emotive lyricism to be explanation enough. And certainly those are factors, though the depth of hostility suggests more. This chapter pursues the question, first distinguishing between New Critical vitriol and the longer history of attacks on Shelley's immaturity, then looking intensively at the most damaging offensive: the massively influential disciplining of Shelley's "The Indian Serenade" in Brooks and Robert Penn Warren's popular textbook, *Understanding Poetry* (1938).

The Shelley who comes into focus in this chapter was more than just "too radical," "too atheist," or "too dreamy" for self-consciously modern critics. He was also, in a sense, too much adored—the "most beloved of all the poets in the English hierarchy of genius," a 1933 textbook raved; his "readers" are his "lovers."[10] Such intense attachment ran counter to the critical detachment that was emerging as a sign of professional seriousness, making Shelley's lyrics into a hyper-cathected focus for the difference between disciplinary and non-disciplinary reading. The derision of Shelley may have the look of a defensive formation, a reaction against a still forceful tug, but it was ultimately about redefining the work of literary study around a certain kind of resistant reading, performed slowly and consciously: a mature criticism. In this way, Shelley's twentieth-century disparagement belongs to the story of what Deidre Shauna Lynch calls "literary studies' love-hate relationship with love."[11] Entrenched within the academy and adored outside of it, Shelley was (and remains) the object of professional scrutiny and of pre-professional affection; of "mature" examination and of "pre-mature" appreciation. He disturbs the cool detachment practiced and prized among the disciplines. And particularly when the masculine erudition of philology and literary history was morphing into a more ambiguously positioned "criticism," Shelleyan lyric focused a prevalent concern that the study of literature would appear soft, impressionistic, overly subjective, gossipy, effeminate, neither disciplinary nor disciplined. Shelley was said in the *Sewanee Review* to appeal mainly to "a boy of sixteen or seventeen," but in the university, reading had to be an adult undertaking—less affect, more intellection.[12] Attacks on Shelley (the man as well as the unmanly poetry) were determined on this line of difference.[13]

Boy Shelley

The compulsive focus on Shelley's psychosexual development began in his own lifetime. Admirers celebrated his childlike imagination; critics condemned his undisciplined youthfulness. After his death, hoping to dispel his scandalous reputation (a "monster" of atheism and treason), Mary Shelley, a 42-year-old widow, established the romance of perpetual youth in her landmark edition of 1839:

It is seldom that the young know what youth is, till they have got beyond its period; and time was not given him to attain this knowledge. It must be remembered that there is the stamp of such inexperience on all he wrote. . . . The calm of middle life did not add the seal of the virtues which adorn maturity to those generated by the vehement spirit of youth.

This Shelley, an idealized "spirit from another sphere, too delicately organized for the rough treatment man uses towards man," is a figure of myth that fed the romance of youth and also fed its caricature.[14] The poet Francis Thompson felt the romance. To read Shelley, he said, is to "see the winsome face of the child": "The universe is his box of toys. He dabbles his fingers in the dayfall. He is gold-dusty with tumbling amidst the stars."[15] The Shelleys' friend Edward Trelawney reminisced about his friend "gliding in, blushing like a girl, a tall thin stripling": "Was it possible this mild-looking, beardless boy, could be the veritable monster at war with all the world?"[16] If the child is father to the man, the "beardless boy" grows into that sexually ambivalent "veritable monster" of conservative renown—the "shrieky" or "womanish" image produced by hostile critics like Charles Kingsley.[17] Whether or not one liked Shelley, by the turn of the twentieth century there was no getting around the perception that he had died before having reached maturity, and this became, for better or for worse, the essential fact of Shelleyan style.

The correlation of Shelleyan adolescence and Shelleyan style, active even in the poet's lifetime, was worked out by John Stuart Mill, who set Shelley's rapidly shifting metaphoric frames (a common target of criticism) in a biographical framework by suggesting that Shelley missed the chance to grow into a stronger style. "He had scarcely yet acquired the consecutiveness of thought necessary for a long poem," and even "his more ambitious compositions too often resemble the scattered fragments of a mirror; colours brilliant as life, single images without end, but no picture."[18] Good for a fleeting image, Mill's Shelley never developed the potent "consecutiveness" needed for sustained work, never grew out of an impetuous adolescence, stayed locked in a narcissistic world of mirrors and "single images" that never coalesced into a durably stable "picture." Mill attributes this impotency or lack of "consecutiveness" to a physiological "susceptibility of [Shelley's] nervous system," resulting in a poetry that "starts into life, summons from the fairy-land of his inexhaustible fancy some three or four bold images, then vanishes, and straight he is off on the wings of some casual association into quite another sphere."[19]

Mill's Shelley would subsequently become the poet of "eager, breathless hurry" (F. R. Leavis), whose "untrammelled, reckless speed" makes us feel "that we have somehow left our bodies behind" (C. S. Lewis).[20] Leavis found the "casual association" of this poetry even a tad licentious and genetically infectious. Forgetting "the status of the metaphor or simile that introduced them," the images "assume an autonomy or right to propagate" on their own, resulting in "confused generations and perspectives."[21] Mill had said as much in reading Shelleyan style as the pathology of perpetual adolescence, and as Leavis's later iteration makes clear, this diagnosis would be echoed throughout the century and into the next.[22] The physio-ethical lapse extended to Shelley's politics. To Paul Elmer More, Shelley lacked the "toughness of fibre" needed to resist "the insidious poison of the age," and More's fellow New Humanist, Irving Babbitt, saw a chameleon-like instability as the hallmark of Shelley's immaturity: "The man who makes self-expression and not self-control his primary endeavor becomes subject to every influence." Many others make the same points, assembling a chorus that amounts to a consensus. As Frederick Pottle summarizes: "It is not necessary to name the significant modern writers who are anti-Shelleyan; one had better save time and say that they all are."[23]

How could this Shelley be reconciled with university curricula for a new generation, a *wartime* generation, in which more than ever the goal of higher education was to foster students' maturity?[24] Esther Raushenbush, an English professor (and future president) at Sarah Lawrence, argued in 1942 that a humanities education was essential to helping both male and female students "grow out of their adolescence and become mature human beings."[25] Elizabeth Geen, a Wordsworth scholar and dean at Goucher College, urged that colleges "take into account" the average freshman's "essential immaturity and inexperience" in planning a curriculum that would account for how "the ripening processes of time and education work on the mind and character."[26] In his Presidential Address to the National Council of Teachers in 1948, Thomas Clark Pollock emphasized "civilized maturity" as college's "central goal"—the dangerous, alternative outcome being a postwar "generation of childish adults":

> We must guard against the tendency to confuse mere physical survival or permanent adolescence with civilized maturity. We must use all the forces of education to help the individual boys and girls and young men and women in America realize their full potential maturity—which is the only true goal and purpose of democracy. . . . I believe we are in less danger of trying to rush our students too abruptly toward maturity than we are of permitting them to remain too long in childish stages of growth or in permanent adolescence.[27]

For Pollock, an ethical critic at New York University, the reading of literature on its own would expose students to "a range and depth of experience" and thus help "boys and girls become men and women."[28] Aesthetic critics, however, viewed "English for Maturity" as not merely a matter of exposing young people to literary experience but of training them to read literature critically. Learning to tell a good poem from a bad poem was a part of growing up.

This was the context in which the American New Critics made a mature poetry, and more importantly a mature critical attitude, the focus of their classroom teaching. As an aesthetic term, *maturity* belonged to a constellation that included *richness, complexity, subtlety, sophistication,* and *coherence*. Ransom defined it as a capacity to see any "system of belief" (especially one's own) as "provisional," valid within a specific "context."[29] Wellek held that the "maturity of a work of art is its inclusiveness, its awareness of complexity, and that the correspondence to reality is registered in the work itself": "An incoherent, immature, 'unreal' poem is a bad poem aesthetically."[30] Brooks keyed maturity to a poetics of irony, praising the "maturity of attitude" involved in "both-and" thinking; Tate contrasted "naive propaganda" to a "mature literature" precisely on the basis of this allowance for complexity; and Wimsatt imagined "a visual diagram of the metaphysics of poetry" in which "complexity," "unity," and "maturity" served as headers.[31] (That these are all, in effect, paraphrases of the Keatsian aesthetic of "negative capability" may help to explain why Keats was ascendant at the very moment when Shelley was derided as immature.) In a complex modern world, to read a mature poetry, and to read it maturely, was to grapple with difficulty. "The kind of poetry which interests us," wrote Ransom, making clear the gender-specific inference, "is not the act of a child or of that eternal youth which is in some women, but the act of an adult mind."[32] The mid-century literature classroom was the scene of a critical coming-of-age, a training ground for maturity. And Shelley, embodying the very qualities that students were to grow beyond, was dismissed from the field.[33]

Affairs of Adolescence

In their "Sophomore Poetry Manual" for Louisiana State University students, an early dry run for *Understanding Poetry*, Brooks and Warren supplied their own italics to argue that "*the more closely one considers*" Shelley's poetry, the "*weaker*" it appears. And of "The Cloud" specifically: "we find that this poem seems better the more *carelessly and superficially we read it*."[34] None of this overwrought italicizing means that Shelley was not being read, or even adored. This was precisely the problem. Here is the staid, sober T. S. Eliot describing an affection for Shelley—somewhat like bullying in the schoolyard or the pangs of first love—as a milestone in a boy's psychosexual development:

> an enthusiasm for Shelley seems to me also to be an affair of adolescence: for most of us, Shelley has marked an intense period before maturity, but for how many does Shelley remain the companion of age?[35]

One does not grow old with Shelley's poetry but rather grows out of it. It's a passing phase. Eliot's nearly visceral condemnation—Shelley's ideas are "repellant," Shelley himself "humourless, pedantic, self-centered, almost a blackguard"—suggests feelings that exceed mere dislike.[36]

Eliot elsewhere recalls having "imitated Shelley" himself, "not so much from a desire to write as he did, as from an invasion of the adolescent self by Shelley."[37] Even if this was a convention of the young writer's development (see Robert Browning's rapture in *Pauline*), the sheer force of this "invasion" is something to behold.[38] Shelley takes "daemonic possession" of the adolescent self, in what Eliot says is "certainly a crisis," a secret "relation" touched by guilt, pleasure, and even danger:

> when a young writer is seized with his first passion of this sort he may be changed, metamorphosed almost, within a few weeks even, from a bundle of second-hand sentiments into a person. The imperative intimacy arouses for the first time a real, an unshakeable confidence. That you possess this secret knowledge, this intimacy, with the dead man, that after few or many years or centuries you should have appeared, with this indubitable claim to distinction; who can penetrate at once the thick and dusty circumlocutions about his reputation, can call yourself alone his friend: it is something more than *encouragement* to you. It is a cause of development, like personal relations in life. Like personal intimacies in life, it may and probably will pass, but it will be ineffaceable.[39]

Eliot describes an erotics of secret reading defined by an intimacy that "you" (the young writer, meaning the young Eliot himself) alone possess. It is a fantasy of exclusivity: the young man alone can "penetrate" the author's "circumlocutions," he alone is his "friend." This penetration helps to defend the young poet against other penetrations, insofar as it provides security "against forced admiration, from attending to writers simply because they are great."[40] To love a dead author is to know when one does not love. Eliot understands this "secret knowledge" of "the dead" practically as destiny; there is no other reader but himself. It is an indulgence bordering even on addiction.

And yet, for all the embarrassed secrecy of this ineffaceable romance,

Eliot was not, in fact, alone. In 1920, as a man of 32, he wrote in *The Sacred Wood* that "the only cure for Romanticism is to analyze it," but the "uncertain disease" that was Shelley—the pressure/pleasure of whose poetry seemed again and again to disorient and displace the subjecthood of his boy readers—was not to be gotten over.[41] It was a conditioned response: a century after Browning, falling hard for Shelley was practically cliché. Even Brooks, steadiest of critics, was disappointed when he went to college, inflamed with romanticism, only to find that the poets at Vanderbilt "didn't look in the least like the pictures of Byron and Shelley."[42] Another comrade in this intimacy is Frederick Pottle, ten years Eliot's junior, who would rehearse his romance over and over again, year after year, in his Yale romanticism classes. Declaring himself as having outgrown it, Pottle told his students that loving Shelley "is, in fact, the normal experience of men with a natural passion for poetry."[43]

Considering his quiet pragmatism and self-effacing personality, I was surprised to discover, in Pottle's archived teaching notes, that he introduced his undergraduate lectures on Shelley by telling his own quite intimate story of adolescent crisis. He felt strongly that crisis was an integral part of Shelley's reputation—and so, beginning in 1934, he regularly shared a poignant remembrance of "that state, so delicious and so painful, that I was in seventeen years ago," when as a senior chemistry major at Colby College he had a feverish, fervid first encounter with Shelley's poetry. Pottle's adolescent "enthusiasm for Shelley" was psychic ravishment, a visceral sensation of the power of poetry "to absorb and dominate your entire being," and he used the personal narrative to warn his students about the invasive power of what they were about to read.[44]

The strong emotions that permeate Pottle's telling are scripted into his lecture notes (with the lecture itself repeated year after year), yet there evidently is something in Shelley that discomposes him anew each time, even in his professional role. After a leery overview of recent responses to Shelley, Pottle self-deprecatingly interrupts himself: "Do I *defend* too much?" Elsewhere he apologizes for being insufficiently critical: "My own limitations. Emotional involvement." Kevis Goodman has observed the uneasy fit between "nostalgic desires, born of loss" and an empirical mode of "criticism" invested in the aesthetic tradition's cherished "principles of detachment, impartiality, and consensus," and "Emotional Involvement" such as Pottle's was a key issue for New Critics, dismissed as "The Affective Fallacy" by William Wimsatt and Monroe Beardsley in a 1946 essay.[45] It's not that they denied affect; they just excluded it as a criterion (for better or for worse) for critical judgment. Immediately debating Brooks in the same year, 1946, on this subject, Pottle argued that affect could not be so summarily dismissed; it is one of the "limitations" of personal investment that Pottle would acknowledge and pluralize, and it belongs to a work's historical meaning:

> The historical critic believes that all original criticism is subjective: the description of the impact of the work on his own historically limited sensibility. He does not for that reason conclude that there is no permanent value in his critical judgments. The fact that his measurement is relative does not make it any less a valid measurement: he must merely measure carefully and report his frame of reference. His frame of reference is his own sensibility, which to a very great extent is that of his age, or at least of his generation. . . . *He grants the general, though relative, validity of all honest critical judgments.* He knows that as he has his own areas of great sensitivity, he has also critical blind spots and critical deafnesses.[46]

One of Pottle's purposes in sharing with students the lingering effects of his infatuation with Shelley was to fold into his pedagogy a methodological debate about judgment. Pottle cites his "own limitations" in order to acknowledge that "he has also critical blind spots and critical deafnesses." He would further develop this position after reading Brooks's *The Well Wrought Urn,* and Brooks found it forceful enough to warrant a response in the second edition.

But more straightforwardly, Pottle's story of discovering Shelley is a tale about the power of poetry, and I return—as he did—to the confession that is his first lecture on Shelley. Without explanation, he begins it by reciting Robert Frost's "The Road Not Taken" (which he tellingly mis-titles "The Road Less Travelled"). It's hard to think of a less Shelleyan opening. Pottle means for the story of his Shelleyan romance to serve as a cautionary tale, but as with most cautions, the transgression has to be stated. Frost's poem, it soon becomes clear, is not about Shelley, but about Pottle, still "telling this with a sigh / Somewhere ages and ages hence":

> On an evening in early spring of the year 1917 a young man sat at a desk in a frowzy room of an old dormitory in a small coeducational New England college. He was in his twentieth year but looked younger, slender, bespectacled, large of head and thin of neck. He affected the slovenliness of dress then fashionable among men; his corduroy trousers were full of holes where he had spilled chemicals on them, and his fingers were stained yellow with picric acid. If you had asked him what he was, he would have replied with perfect seriousness that he was a chemist. The books on his desk include no text-books of literature, no volumes of poetry or *belles-lettres*; they appear to deal mainly with science: a big red book on quantitative analysis, a thick green book on Organic

Chemistry, a thinner text-book of Biology. The book which our student holds in his hands is not, however, a book of science; it is an anthology of English poetry which he has borrowed from his roommate. On the desk before him are some sheets of paper on which he has been drafting an oration on International Peace. (I may remind you that the First World War has been going on for two years and a half, but America has not entered the struggle.) If you looked over his shoulder, you would see that the sentences of his speech are composed in that mingled style of flatulence and innocent radicalism characteristic of such attempts; the general tone is deeply pessimistic, and in the last paragraph, he has been leading up to a statement that the awful struggle in Europe proves to any intelligent being that there is no God in the universe.

So begins "Confessions of an English Opium-Eater," Pottle-style (but for *Opium* substitute *Shelley*, and for *Eater* substitute *Reader*). Or to advance a century: in this Portrait of the Professor as a Young Man, we can already discern some of the conditions for Pottle's budding love of Shelley: youthful idealism, "innocent radicalism," nascent atheism. But the comic calm of this portrait does not quite prepare us for the storm that is to come.

As young Pottle opens his roommate's anthology in search of a line for his oration, he alights on a brief Shelley lyric:

... his eye is caught by a tiny poem at the bottom of the page, a poem titled *A Dirge*. His eyes wander idly through it.... He sucks in his breath with an involuntary gasp of surprise and pleasure. He pushes the pages of his speech to one corner of the desk, lays the book down, and begins to devour the pages. His whole figure grows tense, his eyes blaze, he runs his fingers rapidly through his rough hair. The steam departs from the radiator with much gurgling and knocking, and the damp coldness of early spring invades the room. His hands and feet grow cold, he shivers and gasps, but he beats his feet impatiently and reads on and on. The bells in the railroad yard cease their clamor; the jovial noises of the dormitory die away; it is very late, but he is oblivious to everything. At length he finishes the last line in the section headed "Percy Bysshe Shelley," sucks in his breath again sharply with much chattering of teeth, jumps to his feet and walks rapidly about the room slapping himself in a trance of excitement. He will never finish his speech on International Peace, he will never feel the same towards his big books on chemistry.

The effect—call it invasion—is visceral (chattering teeth, cold extremities). Shelley provokes in the young man a sense of dislocation, and a nervous need for counterpressure, for assurance of his body's physical boundaries. He moves "his fingers through his rough hair," "beats his feet impatiently," "walks rapidly about the room slapping himself." He gives up the speech, not because Shelley leads to delinquency but because he is (like Eliot) "certainly in a crisis." The young man loses himself in Shelley, absorbing Shelley's phrases (from "Ode to the West Wind") and Shelley's life as his vow:

> if you ask him what he is, he will say that he is a pardlike spirit beautiful and
> swift, that he is tameless and swift and proud, that he does not know whether
> he wishes to lie down like a tired child and weep away this life of care, or
> whether he yearns to throw himself into the harsh and grating strife of tyrants
> and of foes.

This is no mere burlesque but an entire romantic style, a feverous overflow so intense that the third-person displacement seems a necessary defense against a total reabsorption, in the present-tense rehearsal:

> he is alive as he never was before; every nerve and fibre of him alive with
> tingling sensibility, and in his brain the stream of consciousness rushes along
> swift and turbulent and rejoicing, like a springtime brook which has broken the
> bonds of winter.

Vital, unmanacled, bursting into springtime: young Pottle has *become* Shelley. We are in the midst less of a reminiscence than of a religious confession, about an errant conversion experience from Chemistry to Shelley.

Pottle will subsequently pass through an entire Shelleyan phase, throwing himself into Shelley's fashion, his practices, his dreams, his agons with university authorities (Figure 1):

> The next day he will rush to the library to get Shelley's complete poems. He
> will open the collar of his shirt and let his hair grow even longer; he will get
> a copybook, write a motto from Shelley on the first page, and begin to fill it
> with verses. He will have moments of hallucination when he thinks he actually
> *is* Shelley. He will insult the President of the College and get expelled from
> the President's class in Philosophy. He will write a Commencement Oration
> entitled "Ashes and Sparks" which the President will refuse to allow him to
> deliver.

But then, as if he were living out the plot of a romantic crisis lyric, Pottle sets himself to relinquish Shelleyan flight for Wordsworthian sobriety. This is the story he tells: the real world calls; he goes to Europe and enters the theater of war; later returns home to a humdrum life of marriage and career. But the evolution doesn't entirely evolve. Unlike Eliot, Pottle keeps Shelley as "a companion of age":

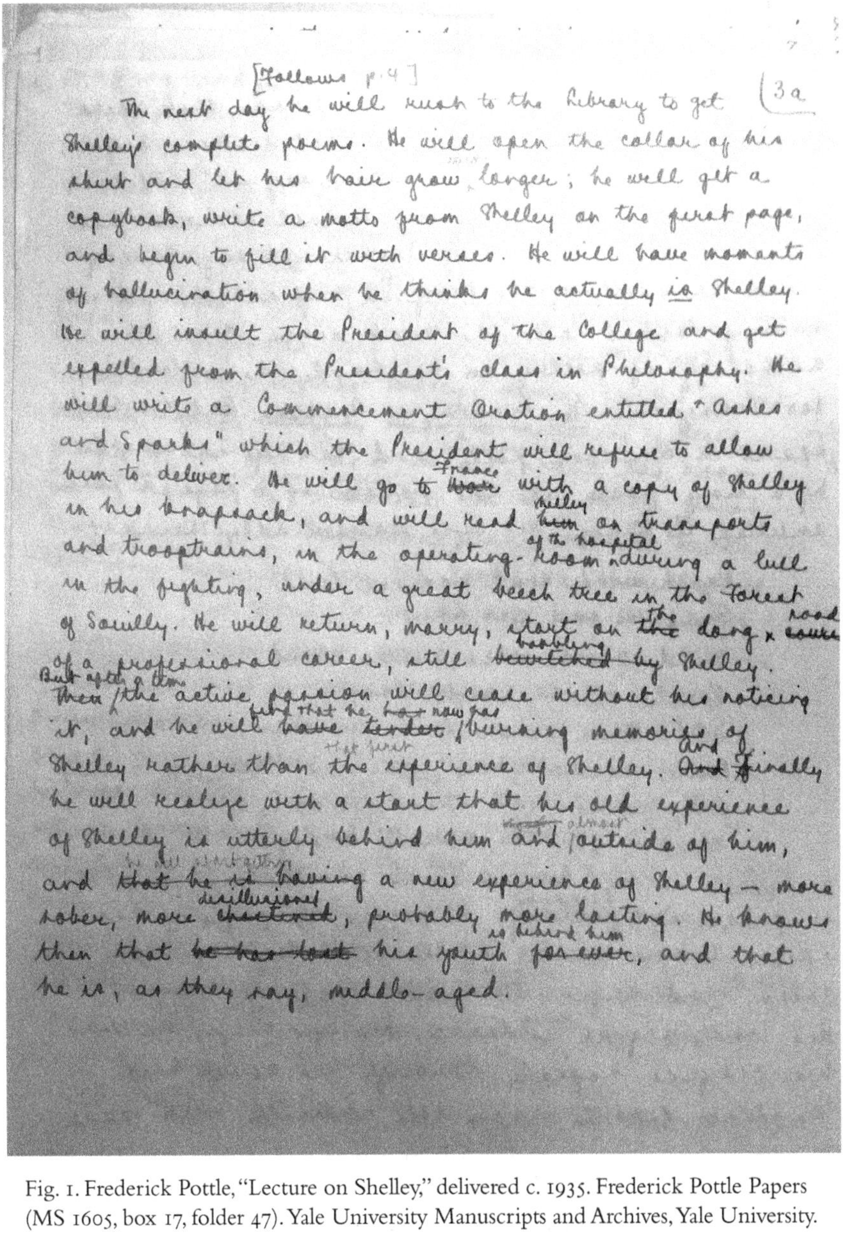

[Follows p. 4]

The next day he will rush to the Library to get [3a] Shelley's complete poems. He will open the collar of his shirt and let his hair grow longer; he will get a copybook, write a motto from Shelley on the first page, and begin to fill it with verses. He will have moments of hallucination when he thinks he actually _is_ Shelley. He will insult the President of the College and get expelled from the President's class in Philosophy. He will write a Commencement Oration entitled "Ashes and Sparks" which the President will refuse to allow him to deliver. He will go to France with a copy of Shelley in his knapsack, and will read Shelley on transports and trooptrains, in the operating-room of the hospital during a lull in the fighting, under a great beech tree in the Forest of Souilly. He will return, marry, start on the long road of a professional career, still bewitched by Shelley. Then the active passion will cease without his noticing it, and he will have burning memories of the first Shelley rather than the experience of Shelley. And finally he will realize with a start that his old experience of Shelley is utterly behind him and almost outside of him, and that he is having a new experience of Shelley — more sober, more disillusioned, probably more lasting. He knows then that his youth is behind him forever, and that he is, as they say, middle-aged.

Fig. 1. Frederick Pottle, "Lecture on Shelley," delivered c. 1935. Frederick Pottle Papers (MS 1605, box 17, folder 47). Yale University Manuscripts and Archives, Yale University.

He will go to France with a copy of Shelley in his knapsack, and will read Shelley on transports and troop-trains, in the operating-room of the hospital during a lull in the fighting, under a great beech tree in the Forest of Sauilly. He will return, marry, start on the long road of a professional career, still [warbling?] Shelley. But after a time the active passion will cease without his noticing it, and he will find that he now has burning memories of Shelley rather than that first experience of Shelley. And finally he will realize with a start that his old experience of Shelley is utterly behind him and almost outside of him, and he will start getting a new experience of Shelley—more sober, more disillusioned, probably more lasting. He knows then that his youth is behind him, and that he is, as they say, middle-aged.

There's no renouncing Shelley, yet this companion is not the same poet of fiery adolescence. "Shelley" has become a secondary experience, the terminus of the overpowering primary experience, now the subject of annual rehearsal.

Patricia Meyer Spacks's description of youth and middle age is instructive: "The young flaunt their beauty, energy, and freedom; the middle-aged assert their experience, wisdom, and parental dominance. The young press forward, the old press them back."[47] Although Pottle certainly feels the change from "energy" and "freedom" to "experience" and "wisdom," he tries to convey it without "parental dominance" or constraining authority. Far from it: for all the caution, he seems to be inviting the *Sunetoi*, the elect, into this experience of painful delight. Like the speaker at the end of a romantic lyric, having recovered from his flight into "burning memories," Pottle addresses his audience with his feet on the earth, though there is a note of Ancient Mariner in the tale as well. And while he claims the crisis of the past as his own, he warns that his young audience's is yet to come:

I should not have run the risk of presenting so much autobiography (for of course I have been talking about myself) if I did not think that it was the only honest way for a man of [thirty-six][48] to begin a series of lectures on Shelley to a group of men little more than half his age. For Shelley is not like the other poets in this course, the reading of whom is an experience on a level with other poetic experiences. Shelley will leave some of you quite cold. Some of you will actively dislike him. But for a few of you the reading of these poems will be an experience unique in its power to absorb and dominate your entire being. Some of you at this moment are in that state, so delicious and so painful, that I was in seventeen years ago, and it is to you primarily that these opening remarks are addressed. You will perhaps resent the coldness of my approach, the harshness of my critical judgements, my strictures on the private life of your idol. I wish you to know that I too once roamed in Arcadia. Once roamed, for I roam there no longer. My youthful feelings about Shelley are to me now like a lovely enchanted country girt with a wall, and I have shut myself out. I could no more enter that country again than I could write an oratory on International Peace, and I shall not insult you by trying to impersonate myself at the age of nineteen. I must talk about Shelley as I see him now.

Et in Arcadia Ego, Pottle says, though he hardly seems to have shut himself out of this hortus conclusus.

Here is Pottle's notion of historical "shifts of sensibility" reduced to (or concentrated in) the scale of the individual life. Just as people in the eighteenth century judged poetry by different values from those of the twentieth century, so too the professor in his late thirties (and forties, and fifties) experiences Shelley differently from the way he did in his youth, and differently from how his students will. It is hard to know what those students made of "so much autobiography" from their staid and serious literature professor. One rather imagines a group of nineteen-year-old boys tuning out the wistfulness of an older man recalling his "delicious" and "painful" coming-of-age, yet surely he left students curious, and maybe a little nervous, about a set of readings "unique in its power to absorb and dominate [their] entire being." Pottle's affair with Shelley would "mature" into a fall away from Shelley, a departure from "Arcadia" into sober adult life. But it isn't only this. The crisis is still there, and it needs discipline: "I have shut myself out."

Pottle reflects on these matters in *The Idiom of Poetry*, resisting the idea that reading Shelley at an impressionable age can lead a young man astray, or that it "might be dangerous to faith and even to morals." His own story is one of providential survival, rendered as a born-again salvational narrative:

> I have to testify that my own reading of Shelley (which occurred in my twentieth year), though it possessed me with the strength of a conversion and led me into ridiculous postures of identification with my idol, served, unless I am greatly mistaken, as the first stage in a conversion to orthodox Christianity. Shelley's poems seemed to me to burst the flimsy barriers of my previous narrow world, and to leave me whirling in giddy rapture amidst great new masses of almost intolerably vivid mental stuff which finally settled into that very configuration which Shelley most detested.[49]

The possession remains, only it has been reinvested. Reading Shelley was Pottle's first experience of religious passion; for atheist Shelley, substitute orthodox Christianity. Yet here is a part of the story that Pottle skips over in his undergraduate lectures: the adult struggle to achieve a "precarious equilibrium." Somewhat paradoxically, he suggests that it is the secondary, adult experience of Shelley, and not the adolescent "first experience," that is most perilous to the self. The real risk of Shelley was to grown-up men, who had matured past their youthful raptures, and in whom "burning memories" are ever poised for crisis: "Serious-minded men who have fought their way to a stage of precarious equilibrium find nothing more painful than a too-powerful recalling of their own youth."[50] Faced with the pain of remembrance, the "equilibrium" of mature adulthood seems "precarious" indeed, and this, he adds, is why "serious-minded critics, from Matthew Arnold down to Mr. Eliot, have shown so little temperance and detachment in writing of Shelley; he is a poet whom you must either adore or attack."[51]

Adore or attack: as we have seen, the most common response was to "attack," but how much was this a defense against the alternative? Pottle was unique in continuing to "adore," maturing not by purging Shelley but by developing a professional critical defense against his "power to absorb and dominate." Later in this chapter we will see how he channels that intensity into a critical defense of Shelley against New Critical attacks—the most notorious of which I turn to now.

Undemolishing "The Indian Serenade"

In their groundbreaking pedagogical textbook *Understanding Poetry*, Brooks and Warren claim to refuse the dyad of adore-attack. Their stated aspiration is to cultivate in readers a care for stable, unified forms, and an invulnerability to sentimentality and romantic excess. The book is a guide to disciplining literary affections and identifications, through critical readings that would not be hospitable to "invasions" by poets like Shelley. Rival anthologies in the 1930s, such as Louise Dudley's *The Study of Literature* (1928) and H. F. Lowry and Willard Thorp's *Oxford Anthology of English Poetry* (1935), promoted "the great classics," "the best of English literature."[52] They represented and reproduced a canon, as the Norton Anthology, debuting on New Year's Day, 1962, would do more famously. *Understanding Poetry* instead encouraged students to assess such canonical claims. Teaching evaluative criticism, Brooks and Warren liberated students from what Eliot scorned as the "forced admiration" of writers "simply because they are great."[53]

One of their signature techniques was a remorseless dissection of "bad and uneven poems," such as Adelaide Procter's "The Pilgrims," Joyce Kilmer's "Trees," and notoriously, Shelley's "The Indian Serenade."[54] The "destruction of weak and ineffective poems," one reviewer said, was their "most radical departure from standard procedures"; it was what "attracted so much attention" to the anthology.[55] It was also a risk. The targeting of negative examples led to a caricature of the editors as impossible to satisfy: "Professors Brooks and Warren seem to have become critics partly through hatred of bad poetry."[56] Hatred had nothing to do with it, though, as criticism in *Understanding Poetry* is framed as neutral appraisal (Brooks even considered calling the book *Reading Poems*).[57] The teacher's manual makes a point of cautioning against condescending to students who "like" a particular bad poem, recommending respect for such affection while keeping the focus on appraisal, without regard for a poem's reputation or a poet's prestige.[58]

The lightning-rod was Shelley, hailed as "the supreme lyrical voice in England" in the early twentieth century, "a warbler" who entered the 1930s perched atop the literary hierarchy alongside of Shakespeare and Chaucer.[59] Brooks and Warren's prefatory "Letter to the Teacher" casts doubt on his stature. Citing another textbook's praise of his "freshness and spontaneity" and "beautiful figures of speech," they ask,

> But in what, for example, does a beautiful composition consist? . . . When a student has been given no concrete exposition of the "adaptation of form and movement . . . to the word and the idea" of a poem, and has received no inkling of what the "idea" of a particular poem is, what is such a statement expected to mean to him?[60]

The problem is the praise, minus explanation: "*That* is poetry," M. H. Abrams recalls a professor at Harvard declaring after a resounding recitation of "My Last Duchess."[61] Brooks and Warren want students to understand *why* it is poetry.

They put nine poems by Shelley in the 1938 first edition of *Understanding Poetry*, appending study questions to most of these. The questions are loaded: for "When the Lamp Is Shattered," whether the images follow "any consistent principle," and for "To Night," whether the poet has "successfully avoided sentimentality"—not questions at all really, just coercions. Noting the "jigging rhythm" of the short lyric "Death," they dispense with a question altogether: "The poem is an unsuccessful poem because the parts do not work together."[62] And at the very center of the book's first edition there is "The Indian Serenade," one of the editors' "bad and uneven poems," chosen as an object of critical demonstration and as an example of poetic immaturity.

It is this extended treatment of the Serenade that interests me. If this poem is hardly on the radar for students (or critics) today, Brooks and Warren are the reason why. Their eight succinct paragraphs about the poem arguably comprise the most influential piece of romantic criticism produced in the first half of the twentieth century. It certainly is the most castigatory. The "great aim or end of liberal education," Robert Scholes writes, consists in "teaching students to be critics, to resist the very texts from which they derive textual pleasure."[63] Brooks and Warren, aspiring toward this "great aim," short-circuit the pursuit in the lesson on "The Indian Serenade." They begin by asking whether "the statements made by the lover" in the poem are "convincing to the reader," and after forensic analysis, they issue an unwavering verdict: the statements "are unconvincing, and the poem, for the mature reader, is a sentimental one." The speaker, they say, has "lost control over himself"; his exaggerated feelings strike readers only with "amusement or disgust"; the whole poem is a "violation of our sense of reality."[64]

A generation of college students came away from this lesson with methodical instructions for how to assess a poem, but more indelibly, with an image of Percy Shelley as "a flighty hysterical sentimentalist." This was a turning point in Shelley's decline from esteem. In class after class between the late 1930s and the late 1950s, his disrepute spread among students who were coming into their own as readers, and among professors who had been taught to believe that he was the preeminent lyric poet in English. Hugh Kenner, who wrote his doctoral dissertation under Brooks, would later include "The Indian Serenade" in his own edited anthology, *The Art of Poetry*, under a headnote calling attention to "the difference between an emotion presented for examination and one in which the reader is invited to wallow."[65] Decades later, the Renaissance poetry scholar H. R. Swardson recalled the "New Critical revolution" as having taken place "in a classroom during my sophomore year," when "Sentimentality" was deployed "with great zest to disapprove certain works like 'Indian Serenade.' "[66] Even die-hard Shelleyans, unwilling to base their defense of the poet on damaged goods, strategically divested. Richard Fogle, the poet's most outspoken defender against the New Critics, offloaded the Serenade as "slight and quite frankly of no great consequence." An evidently distressed Pottle called the effort to "demolish" it an unfair fight, "like training a sixteen-inch gun on a cat-boat."[67]

You could say that Brooks and Warren's storied takedown—rarely read today—is one of modern literary study's primal scenes. Before turning to their categorical treatment, though, I want to begin with my own brief reading of Shelley's poem, not to reify it but simply to show, preemptively, some possible ways of approaching it. You'll note my tentativeness: throughout this book, I treat close reading as a subject of dispute, the operations of which are as much unspoken and habitual as scripted and systematized. I moreover channel my own predilection for reading poetry closely into closely reading others' close readings. It was strange for me to realize, having completed the manuscript of a book about reading poetry, that these next few pages contain my only real reading of a poem. In starting out, it seems only right to point this out, and to acknowledge that such a reading was the desired outcome of the textbook under consideration. Now, the poem:

I arise from dreams of thee
In the first sweet sleep of night,
When the winds are breathing low,
And the stars are shining bright:
I arise from dreams of thee,
And a spirit in my feet
Hath led me—who knows how?
To thy chamber window, Sweet!

The wandering airs they faint
On the dark, the silent stream—
And the Champak odours fail
Like sweet thoughts in a dream;
The nightingale's complaint,
It dies upon her heart;—
As I must on thine,
O! belovèd as thou art!

Oh lift me from the grass!
I die! I faint! I fail!
Let thy love in kisses rain
On my lips and eyelids pale.
My cheek is cold and white, alas!
My heart beats loud and fast;—
Oh! press it to thine own again,
Where it will break at last.[68]

The essential fact about "The Indian Serenade" is its complicated, even sensational, textual history. Its appearance on the printed page is nothing if not vexed. The first publication, in 1822, was in the inaugural issue of Leigh Hunt's *The Liberal: Verse and Prose from the South*, where it appeared as "Song, written for an Indian Air." Mary Shelley included it, with slight changes, in *Posthumous Poems* as "Lines to an Indian Air," and it held this title until the late 1870s, when the scholar and editor Buxton Forman, responding to a contemporaneous manuscript discovery, gave it the name it goes by in *Understanding Poetry*. This is, as the Norton Critical editors note, a significant genre-tag, not a first-person lyric (Shelley's voice) but a "dramatic lyric."[69] Shelley's fair-copy, not discovered until 1962, goes yet further, indicating not even a male singer but "The Indian Girl's Song." True to the musical terms in all its titles, the poem has been set to song more than 150 times, second-most among all Shelley's works.[70] In the early twentieth century, it was even known among Yale undergraduates as "the air sung at the fence," its lyrics having been set to music by a former student and turned into a slightly vulgar tradition.[71]

The poem's dramatic situation is clear enough, and significant. The poem is sung, in the dead of night, from the grass below the beloved's bedchamber. Its dramatic character is the fact of the singer's performance, standing outside of the listener's chamber window. The poem is cannily aware of its various relations to embodiment, from its concentrated attention on the body of its singer-speaker, to its status as a verbal construct, to its material existence in various bodies of print. But while the title indicates that one or both of the lovers is Indian, other than this we know next to nothing about the circumstances of its address.[72] Even the gender of the poem's lovers is unspecified: the singer is usually assumed to be male, but Virginia Woolf in *The Waves* intuited the poem as a feminine utterance, or at least as gender-nonspecific, by having her character Rhoda reference it while preparing to drown herself. Woolf's allusion shows, at least, that there is nothing in the poem to indicate that its singer is a male. With the discovery in the 1960s of a manuscript bearing the title "The Indian girls song" [*sic*], some readers have even reassessed it as the expression of a female singer preparing for *suttee*.[73]

All of which is to say that there's a lot of uncertainty here. The speaker's indeterminacy reflects the lyric's generally indeterminate atmosphere. Its opening line introduces a dream-world, with a patently fictive explanation ("who knows how?") of the singer's arrival at the beloved's window. The initial anapestic foot ("I arise") mimics the act of rising that it describes, as in Yeats's "Lake Isle of Innisfree," and it recurs in each of the first six trimeter lines. The crucial rhythmic break occurs with line seven's declaration of uncertainty (and playfully, just after the self-referencing phrase, "a spirit in my feet"): "Hath led me" does away with the initial anapest, replacing it with a simple iamb, before the second foot is interrupted by a caesura—setting off, as if with a wink, the rhetorical question. Line eight, recovering the anapestic opening, shifts from "sweet sleep" to the physical reality of the beloved, now referred to as "Sweet."

This conventional, explanatory frame gives way to a middle stanza notable for its Orientalist atmospherics. These lines are characterized by incompletion, their images giving verbal form to the interrupted sexual dream: "The wandering airs . . . faint," "the Champak odours fail," the nightingale's song "dies," all of which suggests the reason for the lover's physical arrival here: to "die" upon the lover's heart. As the poem moves toward closure, however, physical communion proves elusive. These wanings of the natural world—fainting airs, failing odors, dying songs—get folded into a single paroxysm of desire, as the lover outside the beloved's window falls down in the grass. The declarations of intense affection advertise their own artifice; they are (just like the act of serenading a lover by moonlight) over the top, merely conventional—the words, that is, of a serenade, a performance of courtship. The capacity to sing, to rhyme, even presumably to play accompaniment on a guitar, all show a self-control at odds with the poem's words. The maligned effusion "I die! I faint! I fail!" is not without irony, even comedy, given the impossibility of what it narrates. The death is a contrivance, the distortion of sequence in the line (fainting and failing ought to precede dying) indicating as much. The poem ends with the lover wishing to die, yet very much alive.[74]

Negative attention to the Serenade concentrates on this abject line, but the main wish expressed in the stanza—"Let thy love in kisses rain / On my lips and eyelids pale"—is a fantasy of ideal figuration, a request for feeling ("love") to be translated via language (word-like "kisses") into a natural phenomenon ("rain"). Desire here is less sexual than textual. The process described (love-kisses-rain) reflects and culminates in a language that suggests printing: "O *press* [my heart] to thine own again / Where it will break at last." To "press" the heart (to print out a rhythmically beating "love") is to "break" the heart, to fail sentiment by breaking the spell of lyric. For all its maligned sentiment, this is a poem that understands its own material existence. It calls attention to its drawn-out life as poetry, from its source in a singing body to its impression on a printed page and ultimately to its public circulation.

"The Indian Serenade," in short, embeds an anxious account of its own materiality—only fitting, given its textual history. Shelley wrote the poem multiple times, on multiple occasions, even for multiple female recipients. One story has it that he composed the poem for a young woman in Florence named Sophia Stacey after hearing her sing in a drawing-room. He subsequently copied the poem several times, occasionally pretending to dash it off fresh on the spot.[75] He may have presented one such draft to Jane Williams and another to Mary Shelley, and he used the poem again in 1822 in a friendly competition with Byron (who composed his own "Stanzas to a Hindoo Air"). There are, though, only two existing manuscripts, both dating to 1821–1822. The first of these is the one headed "The Indian girls song." Bequeathed by Mary Shelley to her son Percy, it was in the 1850s given to the activist and writer Bessie Rayner Parkes, in whose family it remained for over a century until going to auction in 1962. The Sotheby's catalog for that sale referred to the poem as "I arise from dreams of thee"—the first time this copy was made public.

The other manuscript, titled "The Indian Serenade," has a wilder history.

It was recovered in September of 1822 from the wreck of the *Don Juan*. Many of the memorandum books, letters, and private papers salvaged from the boat were, Captain Daniel Roberts wrote to Trelawney, "so glued together by the slimy mud that the leaves could not be separated."[76] Roberts doesn't mention the Serenade, which sat in obscurity until late 1857, when Robert Browning quite by surprise found the manuscript in Italy, in the possession of a Mrs. McClelland: "Is it not strange that I should have transcribed for the first time, last night, the *Indian Serenade* . . . ?," he exclaimed to Leigh Hunt; "That I should have been reserved to tell the present possessor of them—to whom they were given by Captain Roberts—*what* the poem *was, and that it had been published!*"[77] What Browning referred to as "that divine little poem" had been reduced by the salt-water to an "all but illegible" curiosity, yet enough of it remained to reveal its title.

The fascination of the manuscript is partly due to its physical intimacy with Shelley's death. The American financier and collector J. P. Morgan (the Pierpont Morgan Library how holds this manuscript) is said to have gloated that it "was found in [Shelley's] pocket when they recovered his body after the drowning."[78] Yet the lines that were "all but illegible" were not in Shelley's hand but in his wife's, the various ink-runs and paper-creases suggesting that it was discovered folded up, "perhaps secreted within a small book or a pocket diary," along with a second folio that contained the libretto of a duet between star-crossed lovers in the Mozart opera *La Clemenza di Tito*.[79] Perhaps Mary Shelley put these twinned songs together; the transcribed duet, "Ah Perdona!," ends with the lovers singing in unison about their love for one another—a poignant contrast to Shelley's agonized first-person plea. The two lyrics, literally folded into one another in a shared physical form, might even be seen as a sort of double poem, each requiring the other for its completion (like the duet's lovers).[80]

I relate this fascinating textual history as a context for this song in order to suggest how a formal reading of the Serenade might have proceeded had evaluative criticism extended its view beyond the perceptible boundaries of the printed text. We can understand this difference between critical and philological modes as giving a logic to *Understanding Poetry*, a textbook in rebellion against the strictures imposed upon graduate students of Brooks and Warren's generation.[81] The philologist was charged with understanding *how a text was made* (which is different from the question of "how poems come about," the title of a chapter added to the 1950 second edition of *Understanding Poetry*).[82] It was a variant of biographical criticism, focused not on the life of the author but the life of the text. By subjecting individual fragments and even single words to their "art of reading slowly," philologists pinpointed when, where, and in what sequence a text came into being. "The philologist's original and still core job," writes James Turner, "was to (re)produce a text as faithful as possible in words and meaning to a putative, lost original." This laborious "art of reading slowly" was actually, Turner reminds us, "the first meaning of 'criticism.'"[83]

Understanding Poetry argued for a new meaning of criticism. The promotional materials from Henry Holt advertise it as "the manifesto for a quiet and scholarly revolution."[84] So does the table of contents, organized by formal categories rather than by chronology, with lesson topics such as "Imagery," "Tone and Attitude," and "Metrics." This drastically new logic announced a turn from philology, which examined a poem's imbrication in history (its provenance and various versions and sources), to criticism, which undertook the aesthetic analysis of "the work itself" ("the poem itself," "the text itself") to emphasize the integral unity of the object at hand.

This struck some as problematically ahistorical. In 1939 the literary historian David Daiches, then an assistant professor at Chicago, protested that there was no such thing as a "poem itself" outside of history. Later a colleague of Abrams and teacher of Bloom (and later yet, a co-editor of the Norton Anthology), Daiches wrote that anything going by the label "the work itself" was necessarily "unreal," since the bibliographic and historical dimensions of a text make it nearly impossible to locate: "What is this artistic whole about which we are asking questions?"[85] In a 1941 essay with the Arnoldian title "The Function of Criticism," Allen Tate gave this cutting reply:

> Mr. Daiches nicely balances the claims of formalist and historian. The formalist is the critic who doesn't work up, but remains where he started, with the work of art—"with the work itself," as Mr. Daiches calls it, "an end which, though attainable, is yet unreal." Its unreality presumably consists in the critic's failure to be aware of the work's relevance to history. There may have been critics like Mr. Daiches' formalist monster, but I have never seen one.[86]

For Tate, it is not "the work itself" that is "unreal," but history itself. His hyperbole distracts from Daiches's basic point, though, which is not that critics have yet to recognize literature's involvement with history ("formalist monsters" indeed), but the other way around: that history (including compositional history and provenance) is so embedded in literature that one can never quite pin down what a work "in itself" would be. Before the twentieth century, it would not even have been possible to volley such phrases as "the poem itself" (a Kantian concept) or "the text itself" (a materialist one). Elevating the intensive study of verbal structure, New Criticism in effect erased textual history. Jerome McGann saw this as one of its "signal failures," and called for a method that could "distinguish clearly between a concept of the *poem* and a concept of the *text*." But it's not that the editors of *Understanding Poetry* were naïve. This supposed failure was precisely their point: to deliberately sever reading from the "study of biographical and historical material" and the old value-system of "didactic interpretation."[87]

Understanding Poetry was an intervention at a time when the meaning and practice of philology was broadening significantly. The philologists of ancient Alexandria undertook the systematic comparison of Homeric manuscripts to come up with "standard editions" of the *Iliad* and *Odyssey*; Renaissance humanist philologists salvaged biblical manuscripts and used historical and linguistic analysis to unmask forgeries. While a sizeable segment of the field continued to do lexicographical work on ancient manuscripts, modern philologists working in English departments dealt for the most part with already established texts. They had also been literary study's prime embodiments of disciplinary professionalism (vide the founding of the major periodicals: *Journal of English and Germanic Philology* in 1897, *Modern Philology* in 1903, and *Philological Quarterly* in 1922). Of the three main branches of literary study before 1900 (textual editing, literary history, and evaluative criticism), it was textual editing, the most direct inheritor of old philology, that held prime professional prestige. The groundbreaking nineteenth-century editions of John Donne by James Russell Lowell and Charles Eliot Norton, with their exhaustive attention to variants and dedication to accuracy, exemplified the "highly skilled, professional qualities" of the textual philologist.[88] This was the professional culture that drove Ransom, Brooks, and their sympathizers to rebel, to make the work of "understanding poetry" accessible and even exciting to (nonprofessional) students.

This meant, heuristically and pragmatically, distilling "the poem itself," scrubbing off the complicating materiality of textual history. Philology operated on the assumption "that interpretation could only proceed on the basis of reliable texts"; criticism "minimized the place of editorial projects" that would have muddled the process of reading.[89] But as we've seen with the Serenade, these matters are not only interesting to consider, but can be revelatory in ways that might excite students. Yes, poems are messy, physical things: discolored, deteriorating, faded; unstable and multiple; often lacking authority, sometimes unreadable—and all of this is additive. Philology is no devouring monster, nor is it the policing action that Frances Ferguson has wittily cartooned, demanding "that texts carry their identity papers on them" and auditing them "to see if they were who they said they were."[90] "The Indian Serenade" may, it is true, have been a slightly different object had Brooks and Warren considered its identity papers, for the text they print in *Understanding Poetry* is literally and even polemically undocumented, confected from a hodge-podge of precursors. Based mainly on Buxton Forman's 1876 text (the first to incorporate the fair copy found on the *Don Juan*), their text of the poem also draws words, lines, and punctuation from George Woodberry's 1907 scholarly edition of *Shelley's Poetical Works*. As printed, the poem has no editorial authority, and no historical existence. It appears in the anthology as a free-floating lyric, unmoored from its dynamic life in manuscript and from questions of provenance or bibliography. One line follows Forman, the next follows Woodberry, and so on, the variations always slight but cumulatively attesting to the unauthorized character of the text itself.

And this ahistoricity is precisely its historical significance—no such thing, after all, as "the poem itself." There is a sort of magic in the way *Understanding Poetry* conjures its objects of analysis, which belies the effort (not to mention the tedium and expense) involved in Brooks and Warren's actual work as editors.[91] Selecting and arranging poems, counting pages, securing copyrights, all of this was beyond formidable, and yet the anthology as published subordinates this massive editorial labor to the pedagogical objective of teaching students to read: "We wrote *Understanding Poetry* with the hope of bringing something of the critical attitude, even at a very simple level, into the classroom."[92] Modest-sounding as this hope was, Brooks and Warren were effecting a seismic rupture in the historicist and philological character of literary study, with consequences for decades—and not least for Shelley.

"the poem, for the mature reader, is a sentimental one"

How surprising that the seemingly slight "Indian Serenade" not only registered but epitomized this epochal rupture. I turn now to Brooks and Warren's treatment of it, a treatment so conspicuously peculiar, and so controversial in reception, that they dropped the poem from later editions. When it first appeared, Brooks and Warren's lesson was readily understood as an attack on Shelley, and not only on Shelley, but on his sentimental admirers. No mature reader could fall for a poem like this. But to read their analysis of the Serenade carefully is to see how much their agenda depends on a performance of neutrality. They start coolly, with plot synopsis: "The lover is speaking to his mistress"; "He describes the night scene"; "overcome by his passion, he half swoons away." These first three paragraphs are plain-spoken and understated, laying an objective groundwork for evidence-based analysis. Brooks and Warren note the poem's mode of communication as "a direct method," which proceeds not "by hints and implications merely" (that would be the poetry of "relentless understatement," which Ransom associates with

Wordsworth) but "directly and to the full."[93] The approach, they point out, runs the risk that readers will feel that its "statements are overstatements," instances of romantic excess, or (the charge they'll soon work themselves up to) "merely absurd exaggerations."

Paragraph four springs the main question: "Is the method chosen successful?" It must have seemed at the time a surprising possibility, that "one of the most famous lyrics in the English language" might in fact be an artistic failure.[94] To get there, Brooks and Warren point to "the character of the lover" in the poem. They explain that the lover's hyperbolic statements cannot be judged in a vacuum; one needs to know his emotional and verbal baseline. He might say that "his love is so intense that he is dying of it," but "some people die very easily—they are always dying over this or that—always thinking that they are dying." Despite the winky jab at the caricature of Shelley falling upon the thorns of life, Brooks and Warren keep their eyes on the text. Depending on what we can learn about the lover, they argue, "The statement, 'I die,' comes with very different effect": if he is "a man of few words, cautious and well balanced," then "it comes with tremendous effect"; if he is "a flighty, hysterical sentimentalist," then "it merely provokes amusement or disgust."

I am proceeding here on Brooks and Warren's neutral terms, but clearly the lover's character has, in a sense, already been determined: only "a flighty, hysterical sentimentalist" could believe himself to be "dying" of love. There is no exculpatory account of the lover's character to be found in the poem. It takes place entirely in the swooning present tense. We only see him "at the moment of romantic ecstasy," in which he has "lost control over himself," and if "he is usually poised and restrained," the poem never tells us so. We can only judge based on what is before our eyes, Brooks and Warren say, and a man claiming to be dying of love is not just sentimental but "a confirmed sentimentalist" (and the poem a symptomatic pathology). If some students object that "Shelley felt 'sincere' when he wrote the poem," or that the poet might actually "have had such an experience," they must learn to see "the problem before us here" as nothing other than a question of whether "the statements made by the lover in this poem" are "convincing to the reader." And Brooks and Warren state the answer bluntly: the lover's statements "are unconvincing, and the poem, for the mature reader, is a sentimental one."

Having rendered this judgment, Brooks and Warren turn their criticism up a notch. A reading that began in measured tones becomes, post-verdict, actively antagonistic. Like a magistrate at sentencing, they list defects: "nowhere in this poem" is there "a sharp and definite image"; Shelley "does not perceive anything sharply and compellingly"; the lover's "hairtrigger" emotions are indulged only for "their thrilling sweetness"; the poet is so self-obsessed that "the mistress herself is not described—not even by implication," though he "does describe himself and his own feelings—in detail." (Brooks and Warren have no trouble equating "lover" and "poet," or "poet" and "Shelley"; these terms run into one another throughout the analysis.) The term "critical inspection" appears three times in this peroration: "Under anything like critical inspection [the poem] is seen to be one-sided. It is this critical inspection which the poet wishes to avoid—or rather it does not occur to him to inspect his experience critically." All of this together, argue Brooks and Warren, constitutes the poem's failure.

It also constitutes the poem's danger, for notwithstanding how "bad and uneven" the Serenade is, Brooks and Warren allow that there are conditions under which it *can* be enjoyed: "If the reader can be induced to yield himself to the dreamy sweetness of the setting, and if his intellect can be lulled to sleep, he feels that the poem is fine." Leavis had said that "it takes conscious resistance" not to fall for Shelley's "immediate feeling"; that one needs in reading Shelley to "slow down and think."[95] Brooks and Warren similarly argue that the problem with Shelley is his power to disable readers' agency: poems such as this "ask us to stop thinking so that we can exclusively and uninterruptedly 'emote.'" This is the peril of "The Indian Serenade," a poem designed to lull intellect to sleep—to produce an immature reader as the epiphenomenon of the immature poet.

I want to suggest that the real characters on display here are Brooks and Warren, authoritative wielders of "critical inspection." The Serenade is a textbook case of Shelley's "invasion of the adolescent self," and Brooks and Warren's placement of the poem in *Understanding Poetry* prepares students to judge it—indeed, practically coerces a "mature" response to it. Appearing almost precisely at the mid-point of the volume, it is set as the fourteenth poem in the section titled "Tone and Attitude," an example of "the sentimental attitude." The way is prepared by several brief examples and exercises that gradually increase in complexity: Ben Jonson's "Epitaph on Salathiel Pavy" (what is the poet's attitude toward the child actor?); Burns's "Address to the Devil" (how does the opening stanza establish a tone?); Carew's "An Epitaph" (how does this tone compare to Jonson's?). Two separate poems by Robert Herrick addressed to Ben Jonson, one playful and one serious, task students to relate tonal differences to meter and other technical elements. Finally, with Thomas Hardy's "Channel Firing," the editors dispense with exercises and offer a seven-paragraph essay of their own, explaining Hardy's handling of tone and attitude so that students can test their understanding on a polished model. Then another series of poems, each followed by brief, pointed questions: Whitman (tone in relation to metrics), Browning (tone in relation to the character of the speaker), Landor (tone in relation to metrics), Dickinson (tone in relation to stanza form), Lovelace (tone in relation to paradox and metrical variations).[96] And then "The Indian Serenade." The poems that follow it are each accompanied by some version of the question that devastates the Serenade: "Is this a sentimental poem?" More than ten pages on, following Spenser's "Prothalamion," students are still being asked to make comparisons with the sentimentality of Shelley's lyric.[97]

The placement of the poem immediately after Richard Lovelace's "To Lucasta, Going to the Wars" is especially strategic, especially in a war era. Here is a speaker who is not ignobly dying for love, but ready to die honorably in battle:

Tell me not, Sweet, I am unkind,
    That from the nunnery
Of thy chaste breast and quiet mind
    To war and arms I fly.

True, a new mistress now I chase,
    The first foe in the field;
And with a stronger faith embrace
    A sword, a horse, a shield.

Yet this inconstancy is such
    As you too shall adore;
I could not love thee, Dear, so much,
    Lov'd I not Honour more.[98]

One could hardly concoct a more "grown-up" expression than this, a poem in which the highest sexual passion of a man for a woman is redirected into an eroticized but deadly conflict between men, signifying Honor. The traditional opposition of Love and War poses an unsolvable paradox. "Tell me not, Sweet, I am unkind," the speaker pleads, even while confessing the peculiar form that his "inconstancy" must take: his "new mistress" is to be "The first foe in the field." The "maturity" of Lovelace's lyric is its riddle of double devotion: "I could not love thee, Dear, so much, / Loved I not Honor more." This is what Brooks would call a "tough-minded" poem, ironic to the core.

The contrast between "To Lucasta, Going to the Wars" and "The Indian Serenade" is a microcosm of the approach taken to periodization throughout *Understanding Poetry*. Within its deliberated anti-chronological cosmos, Brooks and Warren maintain a usable concept of historical periods but foreground style, tone, and technique. Wellek would argue for romanticism as a historical concept; Brooks and Warren accept the term but treat it as consciousness. Shelley represents the Romantic, Lovelace the Metaphysical. Instead of highlighting a rupture between adjacent periods, this juxtaposition of seventeenth- and nineteenth-century poems isolates features of each. The self-controlled "To Lucasta Going to the Wars" sets off uncontrolled Shelley.

Both poems are three stanzas, both are dramatic addresses from one lover to another, both adoringly name their addressee "Sweet." But all the rest is contrast: Lovelace's lover is departing for war; Shelley's speaker is arriving from a dream. Lovelace's mistress may require his death; Shelley's lover could die in the nighttime grass. The physical weakness of Shelley's lover might be conventional lovesickness, but after Lovelace, it invites moral judgment. Exclamations proliferate at the end of "The Indian Serenade": three times in the last nine lines, an effusive "Oh" artfully signals the lover's loss of verbal control, a contrast with the deliberated intimacies at the end of "To Lucasta." The difficulty and value of Lovelace's poem resides in its complication (even obstruction) of sexual desire, with the transfer of desire to the battlefield serving as the ultimate sign of manliness. Shelley's speaker, by contrast, is ridiculed for desiring too much; he could die of his desire. And so the reader is tacitly encouraged to show the discipline of Lovelace's soldier-lover, not to "yield" to the Serenade's "dreamy sweetness." Shelley is essentially a litmus test of the reader's maturity. "It is so easy to be immature," Kant wrote, underlining the strenuous effort required for the work of critique, and Brooks and Warren's point of departure is the assumption that young readers will find it easy to like "The Indian Serenade." But a "really grown-up person," they elsewhere write, "merely feels amusement or disgust" when reading such "a gushy sentimental poem"—and "really grown-up" readers, *disciplinary* readers, were what *Understanding Poetry* was intended to produce.[99]

Frederick Pottle was one such reader—the consummate professional— and in "The Case of Shelley," his landmark of rehabilitative criticism, Pottle pointed out some shortcomings in Brooks and Warren's analysis. He did so, strategically, in their own formalist idiom.[100] "All accomplished poetry requires close reading, and Shelley's is especially difficult," the historicist Pottle wrote. "The danger the New Critics run is that of not taking Shelley seriously enough."[101] Taking Shelley seriously meant acknowledging what is, from its very title, most obvious about "The Indian Serenade"—that the speaker and the poet are distinct and discontinuous (exactly the point Brooks will be at pains to make in *The Well Wrought Urn*). This is "a dramatic poem," says Pottle, which "follows a well-known convention":

One is not to assume that the person speaking is really fainting or failing or dying or even that he thinks he is; he is a young man (an East-Indian young man, at that) singing a serenade. Faced with a witty seventeenth-century love-poem of extravagant compliment, the modern critic knows just how to handle it; faced with Romantic extravagance, he loses all lightness of touch and becomes priggish and solemn.[102]

Pottle grounds his disagreement in Brooks and Warren's own terms. He objects to the conflation of poet and lover-singer, which is related to the elision of the marked artifice of the form, a "serenade." Referring to an evening or nighttime musical performance, often as part of a courtship ritual, a serenade is associated with calmness and tranquility—the term derives from the Italian for "serene." In this light, the apparent hyperbole of line eighteen, "I die! I faint! I fail!," is a lover's discourse, a rupture of the decorum of serenity. Nothing in the poem asks us to believe that the lover is really fainting or dying, nor does the poem ask us to read the lover's feelings as Shelley's own.

Yet Brooks and Warren are intent on collapsing aesthetic distance and difference, so as to diagnose a symptomatic Shelley. Pottle sees the maneuver as symptomatic of the critics themselves: the "failure of much New Criticism with Shelley is that it assumes a wrong unifying principle—personal emotion, biography," rather than the poem itself. He hits them with their own study question for "Ode to the West Wind" as one sign of this: "do you need to consult a life of Shelley in order for the passage to gain full significance?"[103] They repeatedly slip between calling the Serenade's speaker "the poet" and "the lover," at one point going so far as to say that it's *Shelley* who "describe[s] himself and his own feelings." "Mr. Brooks has so underrated the poet that he supposes him to be talking quite literally about himself," Fogle comments, yet it seems to be less a question of underestimation than a kind of thesis.[104]

Eliot wrote that "the biographical interest which Shelley has always excited makes it difficult to read the poetry without remembering the man."[105] The same certainly goes for Brooks and Warren: they never forget the man. Take that effusion, "I die! I faint! I fail!," which they hear it as "shrieked out by a flighty, hysterical sentimentalist." But while the poem is effusive, there is no evidence of *discordance*.[106] If anything its sound is mellifluous—more sigh than shriek, which is in keeping with its formal designation as a "serenade" and explains its renown as the epitome of Shelley's musical ease. The critics' verb "shriek" appears to come from someplace other than the poem itself.

Most likely the source is biographical. Thomas Jefferson Hogg described Shelley's voice as "intolerably shrill, harsh and discordant"; Thomas Love

Peacock qualified that Shelley was shrill "chiefly when he spoke under excitement"; Trelawney recollected "Shelley's shrill laugh." This reputation seeped into the poet's early reception and became part of his popular reputation. Thomas Carlyle recoiled from the sound of Shelley's poetry, calling "the very voice of him (his style, &c.) shrill, shrieky," and Charles Kingsley called him "Tender and pitiful as a woman: and yet, when angry, shrieking, railing, hysterical as a woman." This emphasis on Shelley's voice would become a topos of modern criticism, with Leavis referring to his "high-pitched emotions" and Wellek to his "hectic, falsetto tone" (implying a quality both frantic and diseased).[107]

Why does Shelley's voice impress itself in this way on so many readers? It could be the aura of eternal adolescence, as if he died before his voice could deepen. It could be his "passion for reforming the world."[108] Or it could, as Sister Mary Eunice Mousel argues in her 1936 essay "Falsetto in Shelley," be his doctrine: Shelley's "high pitch of ethical significance," writes Mousel, "inspired him to sing" but "betrayed him also into a falsetto key."[109] All of these ways of describing Shelley's poetic voice—shrill, shrieking, high-pitched, hectic, falsetto—attribute to his poems a specific physical sound that is not connected to the poetry itself. Brooks and Warren propose the most straightforward explanation in their foreword to "Tone and Attitude," the section in which "The Indian Serenade" appears: "The *tone* of a poem indicates the poet's *attitude* toward his subject and toward his audience."[110] To use Eliot's word, the shriek marks an intemperate "invasion" of the reader's space. The poet who "has lost control over himself" would take control of his seduced readers.

The steady beat of personal inference in *Understanding Poetry* draws from a tradition of reception absorbed by Shelley's supposed immaturity. The biographical details were widely known, perhaps even inescapable, and they undergird Brooks and Warren's analysis at every turn. The editors seem to have recognized the dilemma they created by blurring the line separating poet and speaker. When planning revisions in the mid-1950s, Brooks jotted down a note for a new "Instructor's Manual" concerning Shelley's "To Ianthe," a straightforwardly personal sonnet slated to replace "The Indian Serenade" in the anthology's third edition. In it, Brooks advised the instructor to "point out that this is one of Shelley's slighter and poorer works," adding that the "issue here is the deadening effect of clichés—not the reputation of Shelley."[111] There is no obvious explanation for the editors' decision to remove "The Indian Serenade," which played such an important part in the pedagogy of *Understanding Poetry*, but this concern about invoking "the reputation of Shelley" might be a clue. Brooks and Warren had already deleted

from their second edition (1950) the instructive comparison between a statement "wrung from the lips of a man of few words" and one "shrieked out
by a flighty, hysterical sentimentalist."[112] In the next edition, the whole unit
would be gone—and with it, for all practical purposes, went "The Indian
Serenade."

Shelley Criticism Matures

In his 1940 essay "Understanding Modern Poetry," Allen Tate joined the
attacks on "The Indian Serenade," calling it the "worst ancestor" of a poetry
in which

> the poet's personal emotions became the "poetic stimulus." The poem as a
> formal object to be looked at, to be studied, to be *construed* (in more than the
> grammatical sense, but first of all in that sense), dissolved into biography and
> history, so that in the long run the poetry was only a misunderstood pretext for
> the "study" of the sexual life of the poet, of the history of his age, of anything
> else that the scholar wished to "study."[113]

As Tate's liberal use of scare quotes shows, it wasn't just "The Indian Serenade" that was the problem; it was an entire scholarly and pedagogical
tradition that looked past the poem to its biographical and historical contexts.
"Too much Shelley criticism has been biography in disguise," wrote Graham
Hough, identifying interest in Shelley's life with uncritical affection for his
poetry.[114] Ironically, this poem's signature critique—Brooks and Warren's
"audacious lambasting" of it—had the effect of turning attention to the same
biographical materials.[115]

Biography's power to absorb even those readers most committed to ideals
of impersonality and objectivity indicates the difficulty of disentangling an
affectionate attachment to literature from a critically detached stance. This
also explains in part the extraordinary scapegoating of "The Indian Serenade"
beginning in 1938, as well as its strikingly sudden disappearance from literary discourse soon after. The poem's fame, not inconsiderable before 1938,
turned largely second-hand as it became known through its disparagement.
Wired to the ascendancy of a disciplinary critical mode, the Serenade became a punchline—literally: "It is only a matter of time," observed Clarence
Kulisheck in *College English* in 1952,

> before we will be treated to still another of these elaborate *jeux* designed to
> show with the customary cocking of the eye and strained *sotto voce* asides to the
> reader that Shelley's "The Indian Serenade" is such a veritable nest of ironies,

paradoxes, and ambiguities as to make even Donne's "The Canonization" and "Valediction: Forbidding Mourning" look like vapid pieces of late Victorian impressionism. Inevitably, of course, there will be the uproarious paragraph commending Shelley in the best deadpan manner for his artful resuscitation of the *sub rosa* potentialities of the verb "to die" in its Jacobean context. That will lead to a really side-splitting job of close reading on

> The nightingale's complaint,
> It dies upon her heart,
> As I must die on thine,
> Beloved as thou art!—

demonstrating with many a just barely concealed giggle that the passage is actually a suppressed metaphor in which the poet is making a lewd assault on the lady's inviolability by picturing her as compliantly recumbent beneath him.[116]

If parodies of New Critical procedure were testament to the movement's spread, the inclusion of "The Indian Serenade" in such "*jeux*" entailed the poem's demotion. And indeed, after *Understanding Poetry*, the poem practically vanished. Shelleyans mostly abandoned it, seeing little to gain in a defense. The Norton Critical Edition of *Shelley's Poetry and Prose* printed it under an alternative, regendered title, "The Indian Girl's Song," in which form it maintained a vestigial existence in a few textbooks, but it dropped out of the Norton anthology after 1993 and never made the cut in later anthologies. References in the critical work on Shelley are all but nonexistent.[117] Once synonymous with the poet's lovely lyricism, it became extraneous as a darker, more philosophical and political Shelley emerged in the century's latter half.

This new emergence took shape during the 1940s, in the shadow of *Understanding Poetry*'s assault on "The Indian Serenade," when positive interest in Shelley's early intellectual development indicated that a combative defense was possible. A. M. D. Hughes's *The Nascent Mind of Shelley* (1942) and Kenneth Neill Cameron's *The Young Shelley* (1950) went straight to the scene of attack, adolescence itself, in order to redeem it as a stage in Shelley's mature development.[118] For Cameron, the period 1809–1813 is key. From the ages of 12 to 17, he concedes, Shelley was merely a boy—passive in sexuality, weak, and characterized by an "unmanly dependence" that shows through in the poetry of these years. "The Indian Serenade," though written later, is tellingly assigned to these years, along with an "unmistakable" homosexual attraction to Shelley's college friend Hogg. Cameron eventually returns readers to a properly developmental narrative, reminding readers that Shelley married (twice) and fathered six children on the way to becoming an intellectually mature radical. The misperception of the case, he concludes, had been due to the poet's unrepresentative existence in print: "Shelley has suffered, as perhaps no other poet has suffered, from anthologizing. The most popular anthologies reprint, year after year, lyrics . . . unrepresentative of the main streams of his thinking and writing." The complex philosophical rebel and the radical revolutionary of longer political works was included in neither "family editions" nor in institutional ones—a process of omission that Paul Foot called the "castration of Shelley," using a bibliographic term to put a fresh spin on the long-running sexual discourse (and echoing Frederick Engels in the process).[119]

The flourishing of a new Shelley (and a new Shelley criticism) after 1950 may, paradoxically enough, have been propelled by the New Criticism's virulent anti-Shelleyanism. While true, as Orrin Wang says, that "the professional 1950s romanticist" was generally "neither reading, studying, nor writing about Romanticism as a New Critic," hybrids of formalism and historicism became common, representing a blossoming of Shelley studies that was in some sense the blossoming of a literary criticism we've grown familiar with.[120] It would be insincere to dismiss the role that the New Critics played in nudging the general tide in this direction. Enduring work of the period readily wields terms like "imagery" and "artistry" without abandoning the contextual attentions of old, a trend culminating in Bloom's *Shelley's Mythmaking* (1959), a "strong" rebellion against his critical forefathers (including some in his own department).[121] If Bloom offered one path to what Pottle called "a mature and complete criticism," soon Paul de Man's "Shelley Disfigured," framing a new era of high theory, would offer yet another.[122] Such disciplinary turns were seeded in the years when a profession struggling to come to terms with itself struggled also to come to terms with one of its central poets, Shelley, whose work focused attention on the difference between lyric personality and impersonality, and between readerly attachment and critical detachment, in ways that highlighted an entire discipline's need to mature and adapt.

3. Brooks and the Collegiate Public, Reading Keats Together

> A thing of beauty is a joy forever. But it is not improved because the student has had to tie his tongue before it.
> —John Crowe Ransom, "Criticism, Inc."

It's not uncommon for readers to cite John Keats's Grecian urn as if it were the featured piece in one of criticism's most illustrious titles, Cleanth Brooks's *The Well Wrought Urn* (1947). The confusion between Keats's "bride of quietness" and Donne's "well-wrought urn" owes to the prevalence of the conceit—urn as self-contained text-object—and Brooks himself encouraged the misidentification by making "Ode on a Grecian Urn" his book's central case study. Keats's poem abets in its own way, embedding the key adjective ("O Attic shape! Fair attitude! with brede / Of marble men and maidens *overwrought* . . .") and thus framing Brooks's title as an allusion to the differential in which he was so heavily invested: between a poem's content (its overwrought expression) and its structure (its well-wrought achievement); between figured emotion (pictures on the side of an urn) and the complex form that contains such figures (the urn itself).[1]

That the Grecian urn has become so readily identified with this touchstone of twentieth-century criticism speaks to Keats's exceptional status among American New Critics. Ernest Bernbaum's tabular accounting of romantic scholarship in the 1940s shows that Keats was the most written-about of the romantics in that decade, and in 1949 J. R. MacGillivray remarked on the "almost unqualified praise" of Keats by "the 'New Criticism' of the thirties and forties" (still "new" enough to need quotation marks).[2] Frederick Pottle introduced his students to Keats by reviewing the poet's high standing among contemporary critics. Pottle's lecture notes read:

> Probably now at the highest point of critical acclaim. Some attempt to make him out the greatest of the Romantics. Essays on positive values by Leavis,

Brooks, Tate, Burke. . . . Basic reason for their approval: however far Keats
may be from the tradition of wit or the kind of imagery exemplified by the
metaphysicals and the moderns, he invariably shows a firm grasp of objective
reality in the mode of common concrete sense perception. Disciplines and
impersonalizes his personal emotions by developing them out of real objects.
"Sensuous"—cf. what the Victorian critics thought "Adolescence." More
dramatic than Shelley. Less direct statement than W.W. Humor. Awareness
of complexity. Skepticism. Doesn't run to easy solutions.[3]

Realistic, concrete, disciplined, impersonal, dramatic, undogmatic, ironic,
skeptical, and above all, as the sum of these qualities, *mature*: Keats is the un-
Shelley, his quasi-metaphysical concreteness redeeming him from the long
Cockney shadow of boyishness and effeminacy. "John Keats is not one of the
villains of modern criticism," Brooks declared in 1957; he "may well prove
to be one of [its] heroes."[4]

Notwithstanding Keats's oft-quoted statement that he'd be counted
"among the English poets" after his death, he could hardly have foreseen
becoming a hero among academics.[5] The gap between popular appeal and
critical respect was an ongoing source of ambivalence for him, with his need
to make money from poetry proving bewilderingly hard to separate from
his grander sense of vocation. "I equally dislike the favor of the public with
the love of a woman—they are both a cloying treacle to the wings of independence," he wrote his publisher John Taylor, aligning the allure of popular
approval, as well as the money that came with it, with the allure of "la
belle dame sans merci"—or more personally, the allure of Fanny Brawne,
for a young poet in need of funds to marry her while he still could.[6] Keats
played out his resistance to that allure in romances like "Isabella," whose
gross and "wormy circumstance" mocked the standard romance-reader, and
"The Eve of St. Agnes," where a sexually explicit depiction of Porphyro with
"hoodwinked" Madeline was deemed "unfit for ladies" by his friend Richard
Woodhouse and frustrated Taylor by seeming to refuse a wider readership.[7] "I
feel it in my power to become a popular writer—I feel it in my strength to
refuse the poisonous suffrage of a public."[8] Keats distinguished his ability to
produce sensational, "overwrought" content from the "strength" required
to assimilate that content to a rigorously wrought form. His skill in giving
aesthetic shape to sensuous and complex experience would come to be seen,
during the 1930s and 1940s, as the hallmark of his admired maturity.[9] This
skill defines his most acclaimed ode, which distills "unfit" sexual scenarios (a
male viewer who "haunts about" an inaccessible "bride"; a "leaf-fring'd legend" filled with images of what Brooks would term "violent love-making")

into an encounter fit for a museum, artfully destabilizing erotic potentials into the total form of an ancient Greek artifact.[10]

Keats's repudiation of "the poisonous suffrage of the public," which in the Keatsian narrative connotes his maturity, offers an alternative way of understanding his exceptional appeal to New Critics, who evince a similar mix of popularizing and gatekeeping impulses.[11] Close reading is commonly associated with the increasing accessibility of the postwar American university, the engine of an inclusive pedagogy that, in Douglas Mao's words, "seemed happily timed to address the newly broad composition of collegiate student bodies, and in this sense to participate in a further democratization of American society."[12] Mao's judicious phrasing reflects some of the contradictory assertions about readers made by the New Criticism's leading figures: John Crowe Ransom railing against what he called the "low grade" taste of "the participating millions"; Allen Tate condemning "egalitarian superstition"; Brooks pitting a mature understanding of poetry against the "desperately bad" taste of a "young lady . . . in raptures over her confessions magazine."[13] In *Cultural Capital*, John Guillory gives such assertions an institutional context, by presenting the New Criticism as an attempt to re-order the field of literary study and, with it, American culture as a whole. "The retreat of literary culture into the university," writes Guillory, "can be understood as a kind of transcendence of the cultural conditions of modernity." Approaching the fabled formalist turn as a disciplinary response to a looming sense of cultural disorder, Guillory argues that the withdrawal of poetry into the seminar room made literature "more difficult to consume outside the school": "In discovering that literature was intrinsically difficult, students also discovered at the same moment why it needed to be studied *in the university*." The blossoming of close reading as the central activity of literary study, in his thesis, corresponds to poetry's retreat from public culture into academic space, with the urn as a figure for this retreat.[14]

Brooks gives the critic of elitism plenty to work with. Even when displaying his belief in what could make poetry genuinely popular, he derides those forms of popular culture that serve as distracting alternatives. "Even people who think that they care nothing for poetry have interests which are the same as those satisfied by poetry," he and Warren tell us in *Understanding Poetry* (1938); "they listen to speeches, go to church, view television programs, read magazine stories or the gossip columns of newspapers."[15] Brooks associates these distractions with an urgent crisis of language and imagination: "Never has language taken such a pounding perhaps in our history," he says, citing "what happens to [it] as it is used day in and day out by the journalist, the advertising man, the Tin Pan Alley lyricist, the class B movie script writer, the politician, and the bureaucrat."[16] In *The Hidden God*, he points to "the pressure of the popular arts" as particularly damaging, arguing that "cheap fiction, Tin Pan Alley, the movies, the radio, and now television makes what Wordsworth faced in 1800 seem very mild indeed."[17] Brooks was every bit at ease in dismissing popular culture as he was in citing Cole Porter or Alley-Oop to do so, and this rhetorical flair is part of his power as a prose stylist.

Brooks's cultural polemics, however, divert attention from the more para-doxical aspects of a close-reading practice that would come to be understood by many as a catalyst for inclusivity.[18] In trying to understand the convoluted interplay between accessibility, authority, and exclusion in his pedagogy, its simultaneously disciplinary and welcoming aura, we do better by attending to the exacting labor that most preoccupied him: close reading itself. In what follows, I put Brooks's professional practice of published close reading in dialogue with the evolution of classroom close reading in the years we as-sociate with the democratization of literary study. The preceding chapter posed the classroom as a site of discipline, with Percy Shelley served up as a textbook example of "bad" poetry upon which students could sharpen their critical teeth. Here, stepping back from that negative example to take account of the changing academic world in which disciplinary reading was routinely practiced, we encounter the classroom as a friendlier place, if still a somewhat inscrutable one, site of subtle negotiations over authority between a profes-sional instructor and new readers of poetry. After considering in the first half some of these aspects of the New Critical classroom, I turn in this chapter's second half to the pedagogical landmark that is Brooks's reading of Keats.

"Keats' Sylvan Historian: History Without Footnotes," though it is Brooks's central methodological demonstration, remains known more by its broadest strokes than by its finer brushwork. Yet it rewards our scrutiny. The essay shows Brooks dramatizing close reading as a collective practice that, in the classroom, hedges against the alienation of modern life by nourishing an intimate community of readers who attend, all at once, to the same poem. The imaginary seminar that is this essay's dramatic setting is a reconstituted site of a long-since-discarded Agrarian nostalgia, an institutional yet intimate space in which poetry becomes genuinely popular again. The modern read-ing public may be defined by the fact that authors no longer know the people for whom they write, but Brooksian reading turns back the clock, drawing a poem near to its reader and drawing readers near to one another. More restrained than, say, the radical formalism of Theodor Adorno, which allowed art to float free of social instrumentality as part of a revolutionary program, the reading practice that Brooks articulates in his study of Keats respects the autonomy of art but is itself infused with social and moral purpose. Its imaginary scene of reading brings into being a communal formation—call it "the collegiate public"—which is not easily pinned down, politically speaking, and which idealistically figures present as well as future scenes of reading as sites of social inclusion, even while summoning some of Agrarianism's more conservative historical fantasies.

Poetry's Collegiate Public

In "The Slaughterhouse of Literature," Franco Moretti argues for the study of novels, "the most widespread literary form of the past two or three centuries," as a way to think about "the canon controversy," while needling Guillory's "very odd" interest in the genre of poetry. "The rise to prominence of metaphysical poetry was indeed a significant change within the academy," Moretti writes, "but outside the academy it was no change at all, because lyric poetry had already virtually lost its social function. . . . English professors could do with poetry whatever they wanted, *because it did not matter.*"[19] This partly explains the New Critics' cathected relationship with a poet like Shelley, whose "sometimes embarrassing declarations" stood in for the embarrassments of lyric poetry across the board.[20] But Moretti's confident dismissal of the academic canon, and of poetry in particular, is itself very odd. Eager to define social value in numerical terms, he vastly oversimplifies the relationship between what happens "within the academy" and what happens "outside the academy"—that is, between the university and the public sphere. Moretti's claim that poetry "*did not matter*" severely underestimates the complexity of the institutional dynamic at mid-century (the overreaching italics are symptomatic of this), assuming a caricatured model of the academic "ivory tower" as a place where a learned élite are fed a diet of otherwise irrelevant poems, while fetishizing an extracurricular "real world" in which "real reading" ("socially significant" novel reading) happens.

In the 1940s, as Guillory's carefully wrought distinction between "popular" and "high" modernisms makes clear, this binary was not nearly so neat.[21] Poetry, it is true, was being read less and less, with an audience increasingly concentrated in universities. An alarmist piece that appeared in *College English* in 1948 noted that "audiences rarely hear poetry outside of high-school or college classrooms": "except in textbook format, [it] has become pretty largely a publishers' philanthropy."[22] Ransom wrote that "poetry as a living art has lost its public support," though he added, more happily, that "since the Academy has . . . put young men and women to work at understanding poetry," his reception on the lecture circuit had improved: "At the colleges and universities a poet will find almost perfect audiences."[23] Looking back in the Ransom Memorial Lecture at Kenyon College in 1975, Brooks's protegé Hugh Kenner observed that "literature in America" had taken on a merely "classroom existence," while appending (like Ransom) an optimistic quali-fication: "But the American classroom is like no other. . . . [It is] the place where that which is taught chiefly exists: where a considerable part of the nation's mental life is actually conducted."[24] By all these accounts, if it is true that the mid-century college classroom became a cloister where "professors could do with poetry whatever they wanted," it was nevertheless a vibrant cloister, where the nation did its thinking, and where poetry found a fit audience.

That audience, moreover, was growing. For as the public for classic poetry in America came to be centered in the universities, those universities were becoming more representative themselves. Enrollments soared through the 1940s, with a university degree "transformed . . . from a document earned primarily by members of the American upper class" into "the ultimate emblem of belonging in the new middle-class society."[25] Media coverage popularized the idea of common Americans "storming the ivory tower."[26] Historically Black colleges and universities, too, saw massive spikes in enroll-ment, more than doubling during the course of the decade (although paltry government funding meant that campus conditions were often deplorable).[27] The postwar surge in university enrollments jumbled seemingly pat con-ceptions like "reading public" and "ivory tower," the latter concept coming to connote not so much an insulated physical existence (life in the ivory tower, cut off from the "real world") as an overly intellectual way of being (an esoteric "ivory tower mode"). This was the charge habitually directed at New Critics by humanists who fretted that their emphasis on structure and de-emphasis of values would result in an "earnest but dull" generation of "company men"—a "Brain-Washed Generation" who, in following their professors' instructions and learning how poems held together, would come to abide by a paltry "Chamber of Commerce morality."[28]

The poet Karl Shapiro, holding onto a romantic notion of the individual genius, called *Understanding Poetry* "one of the most important works of the twentieth century" but said it had "practically put a stop to genius": "It is the book that took poetry off the street and put it in the laboratory." In a similar vein, Darrel Abel (a midwestern Americanist) in 1943 labeled Brooks, Ransom, and Tate "the intellectual critics" and charged them with upending "the traditional requirement that poetry gives pleasure" by "substitut[ing] a requirement that poetry give us 'complete cognition.'"[29] Joseph E. Baker, New Humanist colleague of Wellek and Warren at Iowa, groused about a "general public" found only "in the classroom," which would not be so bad except that the New Critical classroom did not, in his view, allow for the conversations ("about human problems, about life, about ideals and eternal verities") that would matter to members of a public. This was the result of an assumption that, in Baker's words, "literature is mainly to be written, and even read, in ivory towers." The problem was not that ivory towers were unrepresentative of the broader public, but that they were "off the street," sites of intellectual gameplay, where students learned nothing more than to "handle a poem like a cross-word puzzle."[30]

Brooks, however, took a radically different tack to the so-called ivory tower. In an urn-like chiasmus, he saw the popular as literary, and the literary as popular: "it is possible to prove that certain ... poets inhabit the Ivory Tower by measuring the size of the reading public which appreciates them," he argued, "but it would be better to say that the public is in the Ivory Tower" because of the "greater scope and breadth which the poetry of the obscure poets assimilates."[31] *The public is in the Ivory Tower.* Brooks sees student-readers as encountering, through poetry, a totality of experience at odds with the concept "ivory tower." Instead of signifying an insular place cut off from the world, Brooks generalizes the ivory tower as a metaphor for a lack of experience. In his view, the poetry classroom is the site of an expanded and profound life; Shapiro's "street," by comparison with it, is the actual ivory tower.

Brooks's redefinition of the ivory tower coincided with the intensified transformation of the collegiate public after the war, when government investment contributed to a comprehensive makeover of American university classrooms. Under the $5.5 billion GI Bill, war veterans became a prominent presence on campus, by dint of sheer numbers as well as by their visible maturity. Keith Olson, a leading historian of the GI Bill, reports that more than two million veterans attended university in the half-decade following the war, one million in 1947–48 alone.[32] Seventy percent of the class of 1949 were veterans.[33] At historically Black colleges, the enrollment of veterans increased 400 percent between 1945 and 1948.[34] College attendance was no longer the exclusive preserve of wealthy young elites, which in many places it had been even as late as the 1930s. It was "established as a social norm," more diverse in terms of class, ethnicity, and religion, and with so many ex-servicemen, there were even students of various age and maturity levels.[35] Before the war, marriage had been grounds for dismissal, but one of every five veterans arrived on campus with a spouse, and many of them had babies, meaning that for the first time there were students on campus who, instead of being children, were themselves parents.[36] In this way more than others, perhaps, the GI Bill helped to unsettle the seemingly natural equivalence between college and a specific period of life, "the adolescent years." College came into its modern identity as a mechanism or social instrument potentially applicable to all age groups—"the essential technology," as Mark McGurl says, "for producing American egalitarianism through meritocratic class mobility."[37]

The new collegiate public taking shape on American campuses, in its breadth and its visibility, generated popular desire for access to the suddenly alluring world of the campus. One reflection of this is the phenomenon of educational radio, which the cultural historian Joan Rubin describes in compelling detail in *The Making of Middlebrow Culture*. This innovative genre of radio programming, which evolved out of the "Great Books" initiatives at Columbia and Chicago, was designed to bring literary culture to a wider public. With titles such as "Invitation to Learning" and "Of Men and Books," these broadcasts took the premise of the book list—the idea that simply reading a prescribed set of "classics" is in itself enriching—and turned it into a marketing opportunity (aimed not only at men), thus capitalizing on the very technology often blamed for the decline of culture in order to sell access to culture. The programs employed the conceptual frame of the modern university: John Frederick, English professor at Northwestern and host of "Of Men and Books," emphasized his status as "teacher and professor" and promised his listeners "a classroom atmosphere."[38] The more conversational "Invitation to Learning" played on Sunday afternoons, reflecting Arnold's sense of literature as a quasi-religious object. With discussions centered on national values, the pedagogy of these programs was more New Humanist than New Critical, more public auditorium than church congregation. Nevertheless in 1941, Allen Tate began serving as a regular host (with the poet Mark Van Doren) of "Invitation to Learning," drawing praise for his avoidance of jargon, his "subtle, imaginative explication" of poems, and his "uncompromising commitment to the elucidation of ideas." The *New York Times* admired his refusal to offer "short cuts to an illusion of culture," concluding of the program as a whole, "This is the real thing."[39] Real enough, indeed, for Tate to render for the listening public his academic verdicts on romantics like Wordsworth (overly "descriptive" yet still "a great poet") and Shelley ("very sentimental and romantic").[40]

Educational radio reflected the growing confusion between the academy's inside and outside as the ivory tower turned into a major cultural crossroads. This was the metaphor employed in 1957 by Clark Kerr, chancellor of the University of California and architect of the modern "multiversity":

> the university instead of being an "ivory tower," removed from the events
> and pressures of the day, is becoming one of the most important crossroads

of society—a crossroads traversed not by students and scholars alone but by representatives of every industry, every profession, every level of government. From being maintained on the periphery of society, it is being drawn into the very center of our societal processes.[41]

As more people gained access to this "crossroads," desire intensified for what it had to offer—be that its excitement and economic promise, or a fantasy of the seminar room's intimate institutional recess. Pressing the notion of intimacy, radio offered the kind of closeness that perhaps only such a technology could achieve, by bringing a quiet and conversational voice into the private space of the home. It reflected the new collegiate paradigm, in which "campus" was no longer just a secluded outpost in a small town but a bustling site of public culture.

In this way, the ideal of a leafy and private collegiate idyll ran into the contradictory reality of the modern university as an exhilarating but potentially alienating place—a "city of intellect," in Kerr's words. An "uncritical acceptance of largeness" became the essential fact of academic life, with overcrowded sections, longer teaching hours, expanded course offerings, and towering dorms. Even Kerr had to admit that such largeness came at a cost: "Some get lost in the city."[42] American New Critics were nothing if not alert to this cost—and their alertness carries over to their pedagogy, and the fabled sense of togetherness that close reading was felt to enable in the modern university classroom.

Understanding Poems Together

The idea that close reading enabled "a counter-hierarchical pedagogy" has been part of the discipline's self-narration dating back almost to the New Critical era itself. Addressing Yale's incoming graduate cohort in 1966, Frederick Pottle, then the English department's DGS, spoke of close reading's leveling effects, reassuring the new arrivals that its practice had effectively lightened the weight of authority. Graduate students were no longer "overawed by previous judgments," he said; "No doubt this has made the study of literature more exciting." And as with canonical authority, so too with professorial authority: the student now is "on a level with the instructor, or even above him. Nobody has to be a specialist or even learned." The result was "a sense of wide horizons, room for discovery, [and] encouragement of the combative sense"—this latter encouragement hinting that students had been freshly empowered to wage intellectual battle with their professors.[43] We can discern in Pottle's words a kindly (if slightly disingenuous) welcome intended to put an anxious clutch of first years at ease. *Don't be nervous about your seminar with Misters Brooks, Wimsatt, or even Bloom,* he seems to say; *nowadays the student is on a level with the instructor, or even above him.* Without ever once mentioning "New Criticism," Pottle reproduces a familiar image of the professional close reader as an approachable pedagogue, an image that had flourished with the democratization of higher education: *Nobody has to be a specialist or even learned.*

But if the New Critics' close reading techniques facilitated participation among students of varying educational backgrounds, this was not because a new academic egalitarianism was within their purview. The odd mixture of anti-industrialist populism and aristocratic sensibility that defines the original Agrarian position in part helps to explain this split seam within New Critical thought. At issue here are two competing notions of humanities education prominent in the university of the 1930s and 1940s: the *liberal-free* and the *oratorical.* The liberal-free ideal, grounded in the Enlightenment, is critical in orientation, devoted to open-ended inquiry and to the production and accumulation of knowledge, as opposed to the dissemination of information. Its concern is for students' growth; in the liberal-free university, "maturity" is about learning how to think and is achieved through "an emphasis on freedom, especially freedom from tradition and a priori strictures and standards."[44] Conversely, in the oratorical tradition, "maturity" is about learning *what* to think. Grounded in Plato and fortified by thinkers like Arnold and Newman, the oratorical approach is cultural in orientation, devoted to the passing-down and preservation of specific knowledge, "the tradition of great texts," moral values, and an existing idea of culture.[45] The mainstream of New Critical practice effectively straddled these two approaches to education. It combined a potentially disruptive emphasis on criticism (versus philology, historicism, ethics) with a countervailing dedication to high culture. In this doubled thinking, the New Criticism practically wrote its own contradictory legacy as a movement that is as much praised for its progressive and egalitarian tendencies as disparaged for its consolidation of a restrictive view of the literary.

On the one hand, then, the New Critical emphasis on *understanding* poetry reflected an insistence that the study of literature was distinct from the sciences by virtue of its emphasis on knowledge as process rather than outcome. On the other hand, the study of poetry needed to be legitimized as a professional study, and the ready way to do this was to insist on its masculine standards. To take up the first position (which is not divorced from the second): poetry was a focus for hard thinking. It could not be properly understood through the dissemination of facts, or through the paraphrasing of its content, or through the appreciation of its aesthetic pleasures; it was instead a provocation, a basis for maturation. By engaging meaningfully with literature, adolescents learning to navigate the modern world learned how to think and act like adults. As they learned to take responsibility for their independent taste-judgments, though, they did so under the tutelage of professors who espoused and maintained a definite taste-hierarchy, in which the most difficult of literary works, which challenged readers with their ambiguities, tensions, and paradoxes, were explicitly set above the contemporary forms of cultural production most alluring to young people—radio, films, magazines, as well as the supposedly "immature" and "sentimental" poetry of writers like Shelley or Joyce Kilmer. A mature literature was touted as a difficult literature, and by providing students the tools to decipher its meanings, the New Criticism could be seen as providing access to the cultural capital that it historically represented, while securing the legitimacy of humanities study more generally.

In his 1938 essay "The Teaching of Poetry," Ransom saw this complicated legacy taking shape. There he foresees a change in the nature of English instruction, with new texts brought into discussions long dominated by classic ones.[46] Close reading, according to Ransom, would create a space for active critical assessment—for liberal-free rather than oratorical teaching. He and his fellow Agrarians had viewed lecture-style teaching as "a technique of mass-production."[47] Criticism, by contrast, promised active and inclusive "public discussion":

> The official Chaucer course is probably over ninety-five percent historical and linguistic, and less than five percent aesthetic or critical. A thing of beauty is a joy forever. But it is not improved because the student has had to tie his tongue before it. It is an artistic object, with a heroic human labor behind it, and on these terms it calls for public discussion. The dialectical possibilities are limitless, and when we begin to realize them we are engaged in criticism.[48]

Ransom takes aim at what he calls a coercive system of instruction, in which the student must "tie his tongue" in the face of Great Books lists, "dryasdust" philology, and professorial caprice. In "Criticism, Inc.," he satirizes oratorical teaching as a discipline of "men who do little more than read well aloud, enforcing a private act of appreciation upon the students."[49] Ransom expresses his antipathy to the curricular order by invoking the idea of the museum. "The professors so engaged"—that is, the professors seeking to cultivate among students an unthinking reverence for the status quo—"are properly curators, and the museum of which they have the care is furnished with the cherished literary masterpieces, just as another museum might be filled with paintings."[50]

As the inclusive counterpart to lecturing's top-down traditionalism, however, the seminar's equitable "public discussion" draws on other forms of scholarly authority. Bonnie Smith has shown in *The Gender of History* that when the nineteenth-century concept and practice of the History Seminar traveled from Europe to the United States, it conferred scientific legitimacy on historical study.[51] It was egalitarian in concept, a "*Gesellschaft*, a society, a club," as Ephraim Everton put it, "presided over by a professor, but composed, not of subject students, but of members."[52] But it was also a specifically masculine space, as Smith explains: "From the beginning, the seminar member was considered a kind of participatory, universal citizen who was implicitly gendered male and whose autonomy was shored up by the excluded and dependent status of women."[53] Ransom's liberal-free ideal of the New Critical seminar similarly legitimized itself by coopting the prestige and the manliness of historiography, as it merged (through the close reading of individual poems) professional training and evidentiary pursuit.

Problems of gender and authority insistently troubled the ideal of the classroom as an egalitarian space. At Louisiana State in the 1930s, Brooks tried to foster discussion by incorporating popular culture in his teaching, both to help him connect with students and to help students connect with the world of poetry. But his sense of popular culture was deeply gendered, and his references tended to repeat the old clichés. When teaching metaphor, for instance, he used cigarette ads to show how the girl in an advertisement bears a metaphorical relationship to the taste of the cigarette—a strategy designed (as he recalls) "to pry off the museum glass" from poems, but one that in the process excluded the idea of a female aesthetic subject.[54] In the 1960s, under pressure to revise *Understanding Poetry* so as to appeal more directly to the student market, Brooks and Robert Penn Warren set Cole Porter's "You're the Top" alongside Cleopatra's lament for Mark Antony—diminishing the woman who undid Mark Antony's power and potency. "Cole Porter is no Shakespeare," Brooks clarified in his "Instructor's Manual" (addressed to teachers, not students), but the comparison between Tin Pan Alley lyricist and Renaissance poet would nonetheless helpfully "remind the student that interesting metaphor can be found outside the collected poems of a renowned author."[55] Another iconic New Critical pedagogue, Austin Warren, similarly aimed to be inclusive in his teaching. As one former student describes: "Mr. Warren liberally, prodigally, lavishes his attention upon items of fashion (the Honda), folkways (the demand of the American tourist abroad for the American menu and the American bathroom), and headlines (Madam Nhu)."[56] Yet Warren too, as discussed below, ran into the fact that by making poems more accessible, he could do little to erase his evident teacherly authority.

It was a delicate balance to strike, between appealing to students' sensibilities and preserving the centrality of the literary work. The seminary imperative required a certain give-and-take on the part of professors, a softening of some distinctions and a reinforcement of others, and this was an even more delicate matter when it came to the choreography of discussion. In general, the more elite the university, the better it worked. For example, at historically Black land-grant universities, like Southern University or Alcorn State, low faculty salaries and high teaching loads forced professors to rely on information-based lectures, whereas at private liberal arts colleges like Dillard or Fisk, close reading was relied upon as a classroom approach.[57] Yet even at elite, historically white schools in the northeastern United States, the seminar style could prove hard. Jack Stillinger, who started teaching at Harvard in the 1950s and would go on to become a premier reader and editor of Keats's poetry, recalls "posing Brooks-and-Warren-like questions" to his classes but finding dialogue almost impossible to sustain: "class 'discussion' inevitably turned into lecture" and "the students didn't seem to mind," believing that "the professor's reading was likely to be the correct one."[58]

Anyone who has facilitated a close reading with a group of students can identify with Stillinger's struggle, and it could only have been harder at a time when students were unprepared to play along. When Ransom joined the Vanderbilt faculty in 1914, the curriculum was organized entirely along historical lines: students were expected to remember "the names, titles, and facts of English literature" and "to memorize the five thousand or so lines that in the opinion of their instructor were most representative of their literary heritage." Yet Ransom "almost immediately" began teaching in the mode that Brooks and Warren would later codify in *Understanding Poetry*, and a Kenyon undergraduate in the 1950s recalled him as "very nearly incapable of giving a formal lecture": "The effect was one of complete formlessness, but, in retrospect, it all seems to have been done with a great deal of precision."[59]

The ability to straddle the line separating "formlessness" and "precision" was essential for teachers who brought collective close reading to the center of their classroom practice, and not everyone succeeded. Despite the mythology, New Critics were sometimes thought of as *bad* teachers: "The critic is, too often, not a teacher," wrote Robert Withington, a professor at Smith College, in 1950; "the 'new critics' often talk over their students' heads."[60] In part, this was the pushback of the historicist lecturer for whom facilitating critical discussion did not count as "teaching." But the praise lavished on certain New Critics might nonetheless indicate that great teaching was not common at a time when their classroom practices were so novel.

Austin Warren, who contributed one of the first-ever pedagogical essays to *PMLA*, excelled by negotiating so adeptly the conflicting demands of class discussion. Best known for co-authoring *Theory of Literature* with Wellek, Warren took special pride, and found his deepest sustenance, in teaching. His New Critical style is chameleonic rather than oppositional, predicated on empathy and an almost novelistic ability to inhabit other voices. Reluctant "to argue for a position put forward as my own," he sought instead "to exposit sympathetically the view of the author whose text was before us, or to articulate for an inarticulate student what I divined his own views to be."[61] Myron Simon, a longtime UC Irvine professor who took Warren's under-graduate American literature survey at Michigan in 1948, recalled how the teacher "promptly disturbed the mild air of the lecture room" with his care for "rebel voices," seeking "to build a community in the classroom by making the relation between teacher and student a reciprocal one."[62] Yet Warren's explicit deferral of authority was shadowed by his nagging awareness of his power: "Empathy is next to essential, but it is dangerous also."[63] He reflected that, in ceding authority to students by placing their arguments at the center of discussion, he still could call on "the seductive powers of a teacher's per-sonality and voice," and in the short tract on teaching which he sent to *PMLA* in 1955, he claims that "intellectual honesty" demands "that the teacher shall not limit himself to asking the students: 'what do *you* think?'"[64]

Brooks's own, famously agile teaching was distinguished by the ability to manage these contradictions of the New Critical style. His reputation as an exemplary choreographer of discussion preceded him when he moved from Louisiana State to Yale. A poem published in the *Yale Record* "in Com-memoration of a Brand New Addition to the Yale Faculty," subtitled "*Mistah Brooks—he here*" (in comic allusion to the servant's voice in *Heart of Darkness*), welcomed Brooks to New Haven with a touch of Northern snobbery. The poem depicts Brooks as a Southern gentleman, "carefully, intimately" per-forming his role as a close reader at the head of the classroom:

> The Yalemen come, the English majors, the hangers-on, the dreamy architects,
> Come to know the modernists, come to listen and to gaze with doubtful,
>
> Open mouth, like old men before a bawling campaign speaker,
> But he does not bawl.
>
> He suggests to them
> Carefully, intimately.
>
> And they listen
> Carefully, intimately.
>
> And they understand.[65]

What stands out here is the student-writer's portrayal of a carefully calibrated and nearly invisible professorial authority. Brooks the teacher is seen as meticulously staging this authority, producing an appearance of reciprocity that masks the fact that knowledge moves mainly in one direction: "He suggests"; "And they listen"; "And they understand." Whereas Stillinger in the 1950s (and many of us still today) struggled with the contradictory demands of the student-oriented classroom, Brooks displays an agility that would be unique in any case but is especially so in the 1940s, when "straightaway lecturing" was still the norm.[66]

Brooks no doubt felt the difference between teaching at a large land-grant institution and at an elite private university, no matter how much the GI Bill unsettled the cozy homogeneity of the seminar room after the war. His students in Louisiana would mostly have arrived at college with the expectation of learning a trade; the older pedagogical model in which pedantic professors dispensed facts about literature would not have roiled their expectations in the least. He later recalled his "innocent Louisiana sophomores" as "bright enough and certainly amiable and charming enough," but as lacking any "notion of how to read a literary text."[67] At Yale, though, students mostly hailed from New England boarding schools, and Brooks would have met there with a confident and cliquish sense of privilege that made student participation both easier to come by and more crucial to keep in check. While the diminished stress on learnedness contributed to leveling the relations between professor and student, we should not overstate the degree to which close reading superseded context in Brooks's classes. He took a pragmatically eclectic approach to teaching. Former students have remarked on his inclusive, outside-in classroom approach, through which he framed the work of close reading by always beginning with historical and biographical details external to the text. Susan Wolfson cites the Shakespearean Lawrence Danson, a former student of Brooks, as saying that in graduate seminars "the first half of the term was spent reading historical background, biography, and literary history, the second half reading the poetry. While the curriculum was not dialectical, it was also not exclusionary."[68] This feature of Brooks's teaching method is confirmed by the many typed-out lectures preserved among his papers, which regularly intersperse historical and biographical information with occasional close readings. While true, as Rachel Buurma and Laura Heffernan say, that in guiding students through poems he "works to make his classroom as self-contained as good poems should be, and guards against a referentiality that would connect his classroom to the world in nonfigural ways," he also freely brings biographical and cultural contexts to bear when they can be of assistance.[69] And rather than belabor the "unity" of individual poems, he more often attends to the images, metaphors, and diction of individual passages read in isolation, often in an appreciative mode.[70]

Still, if Brooks was more permissive of historical study in his teaching than he lets on in his criticism, to undergraduates—who could compare his approach with that of traditionally historical professors—he seemed downright revolutionary. In the 1963 *Yale Course Critique*, a student publication, a reviewer praised his "informal approach" in the classroom as a consequence of his formal approach to poems:

> Few students take notes. Aesthetic analysis in the manner of the New Critics is stressed while the historical, sociological, and psychological aspects are necessarily de-emphasized. A great deal of personal interest and initiative are necessary for the student to gain from the informal approach since Mr. Brooks emphatically does not "spoon-feed" his students with factual information about the modern poets.[71]

This student's easy reference to "the New Critics" suggests that already a certain stereotype was taking shape and influencing perceptions, though transcripts of this same class, preserved in Yale's Beinecke Library, confirm this informality. At one point, when one of the students is trying to describe his boredom at Archibald MacLeish's insistence on illustrating every one of his poetic statements, the transcriber inserts a stage-direction: "as opens eye with a thumb." This moment (the student gesturally describing his boredom) shows how easy Brooks's students felt in class; they did not always passively follow him and apparently felt comfortable engaging with him in spite of his professorial mastery:

> Mr. Brooks: Taken in its own context, measured by its own illustrations which are imbedded within it, I think it intimates pretty well an idea of poetry which makes sense and which perhaps all of you are familiar with.
> Student: I disagree with the qualification. I can't agree with that qualification at all.
> Mr. Brooks: Which qualification?
> Student: Well, the qualification that it does sort of preach and it is sort of didactic. Just the same after every statment [*sic*] he presents an image to make the point be where it starts to mean—here comes his qualification—dull. [handwritten insertion: "as opens eye with a thumb"] It starts with an abstraction and always ends with an image and somehow you can feel — — — and the only reason I think its [*sic*] a good image, that he gets away with it is that it's not a rhetorical didacticism, it's—

Mr. Brooks: No, not at all. The didacticism here if we call it that has certainly been tamed and modulated. . . .

Brooks repeatedly meets the students' confident resistance with his characteristic complaisance, here wrapping up the point with grace and moving on: "Quite right. I don't think we have any basic disagreement here."[72] For someone so conflict-prone in his published work, Brooks is remarkably conflict-averse in his teaching. As students continue to break in on his lecture with questions and comments, he seamlessly merges each of their points into his flow. Analogous to his work with poems, his impulse to unify and smooth out transforms haphazard classroom repartee into the coherent discussion of a community bonded by his almost imperceptible guidance.

Playing the Critic

"Brooks the critic emerged from Brooks the pedagogue," Jewel Spears Brooker appreciatively wrote in 1995, and this view of the American New Criticism as, first and foremost, a pedagogical movement has had broad purchase in histories of criticism.[73] But with Brooks, it works the other way around as well. The critic *is* a pedagogue, whose prose models the work of teaching by bearing in mind the many others he reads closely with.[74]

A gentle teacherly authority characterizes Brooks's signature study "in the structure of poetry," his essay on Keats's "Ode on a Grecian Urn." First published in the 1944 *Sewanee Review* as "History Without Footnotes: An Account of Keats's Ode," the piece reappeared as Chapter 8 of *The Well Wrought Urn* with its title slightly modified: "Keats' Sylvan Historian: History Without Footnotes." (In both titles, Brooks playfully links the essay's lone footnote to that word.) This landmark of romantic criticism answers the criticisms of T. S. Eliot, John Middleton Murry, and H. W. Garrod, by accounting for the speech of the urn at the poem's conclusion, which Eliot had called "a serious blemish on a beautiful poem."[75] Brooks observes that "some critics have felt that the unravished bride protests too much," and he catalogs the complaints, noting that the lines have been cast as "an intrusion on the poem," and as a descent into messaging that "injures the poem" because it "does not grow out of it" organically.[76] This language of violation and injury was straight out of the New Critical playbook. Allen Tate called the last stanza "an illicit commentary" and a "radical violation," and Earl Wasserman later observed that New Critics tended to figure the crossing from one disciplinary mode or discourse into another as a sexual "transgression," with the act of "reaching outside the text for information" akin to straying beyond the marital bond between text and reader. Most "explicators are sensible men," writes Wasserman; they "wish the work of art were so self-sufficient it could not tempt them to sin."[77]

This question of formal "violation" is precisely what Brooks claims as his special interest in the ode. It is "as neat an instance as one could wish" of "the problem of belief," as I. A. Richards termed the relation between a poem's aesthetic quality and the verity of its assertions.[78] Exploring this instance, Brooks recasts the urn's speech as a problem not of content (the closing statement's "truth or falsity") but of context (whether the statement "was properly prepared for"). "The very ambiguity of the statement, 'Beauty is truth, truth beauty,' ought to warn us against insisting very much on the statement in isolation," he argues, "and to drive us back to a consideration of the context in which the statement is set."[79] The poem's most celebrated lines, in other words, should matter less than the structure in which they appear. Brooks thus pursues his account of Keats's ode as what he calls a "test"—an endeavor to see whether those lines are indeed a "blemish," or whether they are "dramatically appropriate."[80]

Brooks begins his essay by casting aside extra-poetic materials ("Keats' reading, his conversation, his letters"), leaving a reader face-to-face with the poem itself.[81] The effect is both personalizing and de-personalizing. On the one hand, the reader is enfranchised to make judgments; on the other hand, those judgments are to be based on an empirical procedure. Accordingly, Brooks relinquishes his own speaking "I," assuming a passively coercive and pedagogically strategic voice: "The poem is to be read in order to see whether the last lines of the poem are not, after all, dramatically prepared for."[82] What Brooks calls "the paradox of the speaking urn"—which he identifies with the oft-quoted conclusion of MacLeish's "Ars Poetica," "A poem should not mean / But be"—morphs into a matching paradox, that of the speaking critic.[83] Poems should avoid making direct statements, and critics should demonstrate like scientists: *the poem is to be read.*

This distancing of the reader, however, is followed by a minor crisis in the identity of that reader, whom Brooks exhorts:

> Yet there are some claims to be made upon the reader too, claims which he, for his part, will have to be prepared to honor. He must not be allowed to dismiss the early characterizations of the urn as merely so much vaguely beautiful description. He must not be too much surprised if "mere decoration" turns out to be meaningful symbolism—or if ironies develop where he has been taught to expect only sensuous pictures. Most of all, if the teasing riddle spoken

finally by the urn is not to strike him as a bewildering break in tone, he must not be too much disturbed to have the element of paradox latent in the poem emphasized, even in those parts of the poem which have none of the energetic crackle of wit with which he usually associates paradox. This is surely not too much to ask of the reader—namely to assume that Keats meant what he said and that he chose his words with care.[84]

While there's some risk in over-reading Brooks's characteristically qualified idiom, it is not at all clear just who this "reader" is—whether Brooks is describing, in the third person, *his own task* in the essay, or whether he is simply dramatizing a reading practice that he expects *his readers* to imitate. Helen Vendler writes that "lyric is a role offered to a reader"; for Brooks, *criticism* is a role offered to a reader, with detailed stage directions.[85] The refrain "He must not be," repeated three times, catalogs the conditioned responses that readers of Keats should resist. With the flatly ironic "This is surely not too much to ask," Brooks admits that to pay strict attention to the words on the page is, in fact, a lot to ask of readers accustomed to seeking out messages or history. Even beyond these echoing *must-nots*, a subtle air of coercion haunts the essay's vocabulary—readers are "forced to conclude" or "forced to accept"—suggesting that good close reading means repeatedly resisting one's scholarly training.[86] This recurrent idiom of force implies that it's not the artwork that awaits ravishment by a reader, but readers who have always already been ravished by conventional disciplinary practices.

Within "Keats' Sylvan Historian," Brooks reveals his own coercive streak as an integral part of the drama of reading. For all his probity and care to anchor statements in the evidence supplied by the poem itself, he has a penchant for drawing attention to those moments when probity fails him. In a minor instance, he misleadingly quotes stanza five's reference to the "overwrought" urn, removing some of Keats's "well-wrought" ambiguity:

> . . . the urn, like the "leaf-fring'd legend" which it tells, is covered with emblems of the fields and forests: "Overwrought / With forest branches and the trodden weed."[87]

Is it the *urn* that is *overwrought with natural emblems*, as Brooks here indicates, or the *maidens* pictured on its side who are *overwrought with emotion*, as a different reading might suggest? We can interpret it either way; the ambiguity lies in the enjambment. This movement of poetry in time, the way its meanings shift with the turn of the line, is an important feature of a poem that in Brooks's own account pits the nominal against the participial and verbal—"frozen, fixed, arrested" figures against "flesh-and-blood men and women"; a world "beyond time" against "our time-ridden minds."[88] But Brooks does not acknowledge this other way of reading "overwrought"; indeed by capitalizing the word he actively dismisses any other reading, giving the impression that the reference moves only forward. Can he have missed the ambiguity? It's not likely—and later in the essay he quotes the very same passage from the opposite side:

> ... the rich, almost breathing world which the poet has conjured up for us contracts and hardens into the decorated motifs on the urn itself: "with brede / Of marble men and maidens over-wrought."[89]

Here he gives "over-wrought"—now hyphenated, but neither capitalized nor enjambed—as a postpositive adjective, again unambiguously. In pointing this out, I don't mean to catch Brooks out in a bit of expository duplicity or inattentiveness, but simply to show how peculiar, even playful, his reading practice can be. It is possible that he's ironically dramatizing the fact that poetic evidence is never entirely stable. The figure of the "well wrought urn," often misread as a figure for radically internalist understandings of the autonomous aesthetic object, allows room for deviance. The notion of an impartial reader who dutifully extricates and explicates the truth of the text itself is of course a fiction, and much as we like to think of Brooks as a reader who is always faithful to the text itself, here is a counter-instance in which he proves mischievous, or liberal, or perhaps even just careless with the text—readers can decide which it is. For an even more striking example of this Brooksian play, I turn to what I consider the essay's strangest and most nostalgic moment: when Brooks considers the "little town" and "green altar" of stanza 4.

Brooks's Stranger

Brooks transports his readers to this town, the home from which the people painted on the side of the urn have come. It is also the home to which they "can ne'er return," being frozen forever in the image's suspended present. Small, quiet, secluded, this imaginary town bears for him "a poignance beyond anything else in the poem." It is curiously present to his mind's eye, and through his translation, to ours:

> it is small, it is quiet, its people are knit together as an organic whole, and on a "pious morn" such as this, its whole population has turned out to take part in the ritual. . . . [T]here is the suggestion that the little town is caught in a curve of the seashore, or nestled in a fold of the mountains—at any rate, is something secluded and something naturally related to its terrain.

The town's "special character of desolation and loneliness," its "strange emptiness," is for Brooks the poem's "most moving" feature, a testament to the power of literary language to conjure what is missing. And the town is nothing if not missing. It "has not been pictured on the urn at all." It is fabulous, unrealizable, forever stilled: "No one in the figured procession will ever be able to go back to the town to break the silence there." Such is the power of formed language, in this allegory of reading, that it can bring an unnamed, undated, and largely unknown mode of existence into being, for "nobody will ever discover the town except by the very same process by which Keats discovers it: namely, through the figured urn." The reader—a collective identity encompassing everyone from the questioning Keatsian spectator to any number of later students and critics—is both Cortezian discoverer ("like some watcher of the skies / When a new planet swims into his ken") and Odyssean nostalgic (sick for home at the end of each day's journey), left to dwell on this newfound "enchanted world" that is forever out of reach. The "magic of effect" in stanza four's "well-wrought" verse is its reanimation of the "communal life" that once coursed through emptied buildings. This quickening "magic," an effect of formed language, is inseparable from the town's vanished world of stable repose, its embodiment of Home, Nature, and Community, and from a nostalgic sense of its loss as a feature of our literary modernity.[90]

William Empson complained of Brooks's "anti-emotional bias," but there is clearly none of that here.[91] The description of this notional town, whose "people are knit together as an organic whole," brings to mind the fading agricultural communities of the Deep South, idealized in the Agrarian polemics of *I'll Take My Stand*. Whereas Yeats, in Rapallo, was reminded of "the little Greek town described in the *Ode on a Grecian Urn*," Brooks's nostalgia moves the other way, triggered by Keats's phantom village.[92] He once argued that *Light in August* could not survive a transplant "to the east side of Manhattan Island" because "community, in Faulkner's sense, does not exist" there.[93] But it exists here in stanza 4.

Yet something quietly troubles Brooks about this stanza, and in a curious parenthesis, he admits to being puzzled by one of its lines, the line addressed to the abandoned town: "and not a soul to tell / Why thou art desolate, can ere return." To solve his confusion he devises an anonymous stranger, a belated visitor who has stumbled into an abandoned town, to stand in as the object of the line's address. As he explains parenthetically, "(I can see no other interpretation of the line, 'and not a soul to tell / Why thou art desolate can ere return.')."[94] William Empson would solve it differently, glossing the line as an address to the procession, "none of [whom] will ever go home again, so that their town will be mysteriously desolate."[95] Neither of these exemplary close readers, Brooks nor Empson, will abide an apostrophe to a merely hypothetical, empty locale; both feel compelled to read the address as directed to *somebody*. But Brooks, unlike Empson, invents his human addressee, casually inserting the stray detail of this "stranger" into the poem: "No one in the figured procession will ever be able to go back to the town to break the silence there, *not even one to tell the stranger there why the town remains desolate*."[96] Who is "the stranger there," and where did he come from? However one reads the ode, there is no "stranger there." Practically winking at his reader, Brooks coyly adds: "If one attends closely to what Keats is doing here, he may easily come to feel that the poet is indulging himself in an ingenious fancy."[97]

Of course it is the critic "indulging himself in an ingenious fancy," by inventing a human figure to mediate the affect, the "poignance," of the town. Brooks is knowing—he recognizes how seductive this fantasy is, and that it speaks to real needs, particularly when it comes to the community of readers attending closely to Keats's poem:

> The poet, by pretending to take the town as real—so real that he can imagine the effect of its silent streets upon the stranger who chances to come into it—has suggested in the most powerful way that he can its essential reality for him—*and for us*. It is a case of the doctor's taking his own medicine: the poet is prepared to stand by the illusion of his own making.[98]

Analysis has brought Brooks so far into the poem's world, has made him so alive to its conjurings, that he and his fellow readers (now generously included in the consensual "us") encounter this enigmatic wanderer on the little town's "silent streets" as a real being—thus entering into a "mythic history" of this fictional town that is said to be "richer and more interesting than the history of actual cities." Why does Brooks insert this stranger, an "illusion of his own making"?[99] Why insist on a human recipient of the speaker's address, a human witness to the town's poignancy, a human wonderer at its incomprehensible emptiness? Might the stranger be a figure for Brooks himself, the professional critic in New Haven, gazing longingly upon the Agrarian origins that he has since abandoned on the procession toward the green institutional altars of academe?

Ruminating on this stranger's presence can help us to understand why Keats's ode suits Brooks's purpose in *The Well Wrought Urn*. The poem may represent a freestanding aesthetic artifact, but this is finally less significant than the fact that it represents a *reader*, interrogating the urn in hopes of making human sense of it.[100] By inventing this stranger, Brooks effectively duplicates the dramatic tableau of the poem as a whole. Like the questioner of the urn and like the reader of the poem, the stranger in a forsaken town wonders at a past that he cannot begin to comprehend. Moreover, that act of reading calls into existence a small community of *other readers*, who attend all at once to the same thing—to the urn, the pictures on its surface, the conjured town and the altar beyond it. By becoming one of those readers ourselves, reading Brooks reading, we join this quasi-organic community.

It is a dynamic that, for Brooks, bears a clear moral and social value. This is evident in his affection for the imaginary town as the lost site of a genuinely popular form of art. There are two ways of thinking about popular art: as an art of the people, which organically expresses the will of the community from which it emanates (this is the idealized sense of a socialist art that is so well-integrated into society that one ceases even to recognize it as art); and as an art that is popularized by modern means (this is the vitiated sense of mainstream media and consumable mass entertainment). Brooks might accept that a genuinely and organically popular form of culture is no longer possible in a modern world, but he locates in close, collective reading an antidote to the enervating and commercial versions of popular culture. By turning Keats's imaginary town into a version of the Southern agricultural idyll, he also reminds us of something that's proven easy to forget in our disciplinary histories: that the Agrarian ethos, which contributed to the rise of academic close reading, lingers on in the nostalgic practices of modern literary study.

Coda

In its idealized recuperation of this communal rapport, Brooks's "agrarian anticapitalism"—Frederic Jameson's term for early New Criticism—departs from the aestheticist anticapitalism of an avant-gardist like Adorno, for whom the purposelessness of the artwork is precisely its parody of means-end capitalism.[101] As Adorno writes in his late fragmentary work, *Aesthetic Theory*, the displacement of the artwork from its native soil allows for a salutary destruction of its meaningfulness. It falls "helplessly mute before the question 'What's it for?'"; its significance is its insignificance.[102] For Adorno, it is when art is most visibly estranged from the social, paradoxically, that society most powerfully exerts itself. Brooks, on the other hand, is uncomfortable with "the strange emptiness of the little town," insisting instead on a human "stranger" to serve as recipient for the poem's apostrophe and as stand-in for the community of readers engaged with the poem. Where Adorno would argue that "only what exists for its own sake, without regard to those it is supposed to please, can fulfill its human end," Brooksian analysis valorizes that human end.[103] The "masochistic" project of "autonomous art," Sianne Ngai argues in an essay on Adorno, is "an incessant, guilt-ridden meditation on its own social impotence."[104] But Brooks denies that impotence, viewing close reading as an activity imbued with social and moral value, in its potential for returning a less alienated relationship with the products of culture and, in a sense, with the community that those products stand in for.

Nothing if not invested in that community, Brooks in 1949 went on a New Haven radio program, *Yale Interprets the News*, to talk about "the difficulty of teaching literature" in an age of cinema and mass media. "Small wonder that the student sometimes feels that Shakespeare is dry and that modern poetry is incomprehensible," he afterwards told a reporter; "remember that he is unconsciously measuring both by popular entertainment."[105] Moments like this, when Brooks registers a cultural polemic against consumer culture, are among the loudest notes in his corpus, and they speak to his deeply felt sense that something substantial was at stake in the direction of literary study and in the practice of close reading. These polemics are hardly representative, however, of a critic whose main labors were the intensive and often playful analysis of literary texts and the genial modeling of such analysis in the literature classroom. By the 1950s Brooks could jokingly refer to himself as "the monster" when introducing himself to a new group of students, aware of the distance between his radical reputation and friendly demeanor. One former student offered this memory of meeting Brooks at Yale:

> "I want to warn you, you're in the hands of the monster now." These words, delivered in the gentlest of border-state accents, were the first I ever heard Cleanth Brooks utter. The year was 1951, the setting was a Yale College classroom. I was a junior, and this was the opening session of Brooks's class in modern poetry.[106]

This habit of self-deprecation belies the image of the cultural radical spearheading a conservative revolution, while also indicating that the real revolution was taking place quietly, not in inflammatory claims about the dangers of popular culture but in the day-to-day work of a reading practice that was simultaneously public and private.

We learn more about Brooks, and more about New Critical cultural politics in general, by attending to this great bulk of his professional output. Brooks's practice as a close reader is more complex than its reputation suggests. It is sometimes downright bemusing, though to trace that bemusement can lead us quite unexpectedly to the center of his thought. By reading Brooks reading, we learn to approach some of his more extreme judgments as forays into the sensational and too-loud world of public language—necessary advertising for a reticent practice. We might at the same time ponder the paradox at the end of "Keats' Sylvan Historian," where he offers to readers (by this point a communal "we"), as the poem's ultimate assertion, a "healthy" skepticism toward the free-standing statement. He repeats the word "distrust" four times in his essay's final three sentences, culminating in a statement that might itself tease us out of thought: "Such a distrust is healthy. Keats' sylvan historian, who is not above teasing us, exhibits such a distrust, and perhaps the point of what the sylvan historian 'says' is to confirm us in our distrust."[107] Considering the strategic pedagogy on display in Brooks's essay, distrust is perhaps the essential attitude for navigating teaching's subtle coercions. The danger, it seems, is not that students might *dislike* poetry, that they might find Shakespeare "dry" or Eliot "incomprehensible," but that they might *trust* poetry, along with the way they've been taught it, rather than working up in themselves a well-wrought attitude of resistance—not just toward poetry and criticism, but toward all of the claims that culture, in its disparate forms, makes on us.

4. The Case of Byron

As we try to overcome our fear of literary history ... we begin
to suspect that that fear has been a fear of history itself.
—Roy Harvey Pearce, "Romantics, Critics, Historicists"

Unlike Keats (their golden boy) and unlike Shelley (their whipping boy),
Lord Byron almost never turns up in the writing of American New Critics—
not as the subject of a book chapter, of an article, even of a protracted close
reading. He is minimally represented in Cleanth Brooks and Robert Penn
Warren's *Understanding Poetry*, allotted just three lyrics in the first edition
of 1938 and none at all in the second edition of 1950.[1] He gets scattered
mentions in Brooks and W. K. Wimsatt's *Literary Criticism: A Short History*
and in René Wellek and Austin Warren's *Theory of Literature*, and he turns
up in a footnote to Wimsatt and Monroe Beardsley's "The Affective Fallacy,"
but nothing in any of these works approaches what we would call a "reading."[2] The New Critics' neglect of Byron is thorough and only occasionally
barbed. "Human nature being what it is," Brooks later joked, "a good many
people ... would much rather read a life of Byron than *any* of his poetry."[3]
Such was the outer limit of an intermittent critique that never really shaded
over into hostility. In a twist that would have disappointed him deeply, Byron
merely provoked the New Critics' indifference.[4]

But he did not provoke everybody's indifference. While the New Criticism is often made to stand in for mid-twentieth-century literary study more
broadly, in the case of Byron it was out of sync with the field at large. Byron's
poetry continued to be widely and enthusiastically taught in American classrooms between the 1930s and 1950s. A staple of the literature survey and
a mainstay in courses on the romantic period, he remained unmistakably
canonical, with even those who paid him little heed in their published work
finding a regular place for him in their syllabi. He was also consistently treated
in some of the field's leading periodicals, especially those with a historical-

philological or history-of-ideas slant, such as *PMLA* and *Studies in Philology*. To attend carefully to mid-century trends in publication and teaching is to see that Byron's peculiar non-significance in the writings of the New Critics is not representative of the discipline as a whole—indeed is to discover an institutional context from which his poetry never really disappeared.

Byron's curious double status presents a fascinating problem for histories of literary study in America. The contradictory treatment of his poetry adds a twist to Catherine Gallagher's argument that the American New Criticism effectively joined the research mission of literary study (located in the graduate school and centered on specialized scholarship) with its public service mission (focused on undergraduate teaching and the dissemination of culture).[5] When it came to the criticism and the teaching of Byron, these competing missions were not so readily conciliated; instead, the case of Byron asks that we revisit our received view of the field at mid-century and consider fissures within the story of romanticism's postwar rehabilitation. Certain aspects of these narratives, such as the formalist turn or the democratization of higher education, have been flattened by repetition, but through Byron, whose twentieth-century reception history is frequently rehearsed without reference to the decades around World War II, we summon a less familiar and unusually dynamic critical and curricular moment. This chapter pursues the complexity of this moment, first by examining the political and historical criticism of Byron that thrived in these decades of his formalist neglect, and then through a pair of archival case studies, exploring his odd exclusion from the criticism of M. H. Abrams and his equally odd inclusion in the New Critical classroom of William Kurtz Wimsatt. In both instances, we see Byron provoking unexpected fits of critical nostalgia—in Abrams, for the aura of an earlier generation's criticism; in Wimsatt, for the sorts of historical continuities that happen to teach well. Byron's mid-century reception offers more than just a case study in critical inattention; it also restores the ferment of this era's criticism, around a subject who at first glance seems absent from it.

The Neglect of Byron

There is no shortage of explanations for the New Critics' disregard of Byron. His poetry operates in a patently different register from the one that most interested them, on multiple fronts. He tended to write long rather than short, fast rather than slow. His ingenious rhyming seems to invite swift scansion rather than close reading, its formal energies skimming the auditory surface rather than convoluting in poetry's inner circuits. He "must be read very rapidly," W. H. Auden said, "as if the words were single frames in a movie film; stop on a word or a line and the poetry vanishes."[6] As readers are propelled forward from one clinching vowel sound to the next, Byron's verse feeds an appetite for sonic closure that it simultaneously creates.

Slow or intensive reading was, in part, a strategy for escaping from authorial personality into the impersonality of aesthetic form, a way to disenthrall oneself from the poet's voice, and here was another crucial site of disconnect between Byron and the leading edge of the American New Criticism. There is, as Peter J. Manning argues, an "endless slippage between Byron's poetry and Byron the man."[7] Byron seems to encourage what Tom Mole calls a "hermeneutic of intimacy," an assumption that his poems "could only be understood fully by referring to their author's personality, that reading them was entering a kind of relationship with the author."[8] This proximity between poetry and personality (intertwined, in Byron's case, with the world-historical moment he inhabited and embodied) troubled the New Critical belief in poetry's autonomy from history and biography. Brooks's joke that "a life of Byron" would make for better reading than the verse itself is less a judgment on the quality of that verse than another argument for the separation of poetry from biography. His surviving teaching notes on Byron show him valuing the poet almost exactly as one might expect, presenting *Childe Harold's Pilgrimage*, "sad to say, as pure 'camp,'" and emphasizing "Byron's 'inconsistencies' and 'histrionics.'"[9]

The obtrusive presence of Byron's personality fed a prevalent critique of "Byronism" among other formally inclined critics of the period.[10] Allen Tate, Austin Warren, and Kenneth Burke all expressed some version of the argument that readers' feelings about Byron, and the extent of their identification with him, must necessarily vary because such feelings have nothing objectively to do with art. Developing longstanding assumptions about the poet's "bad workmanship" (Matthew Arnold's complaint), Warren wrote in 1933 that "only the embryonic Byrons, [*sic*] will be attracted to Byron by his Byronism; while workmanship, technique, form are elements which make for relatively greater permanence."[11] The implication, a common one, is that the appeal of Byron's personality, itself associated with "the careless and negligent ease" that comes with aristocratic privilege, diverts attention from his alleged lack of technique or formal shoddiness.

Such assumptions have since been energetically rebuffed by readers who have pointed to Byron's sophisticated management of *ottava rima*, for instance, or to his genius for the couplet form.[12] But for most of the twentieth century his reputation as a craftsman suffered. As the adjectives used to condemn him moreover imply, this formal critique was closely affiliated with a moral attitude. The literary historian Frederick Pottle, in his role as tactful pedagogue, began his classes on Byron in the 1950s by explaining what he called the "unfavorable" "climate of opinion" of the preceding twenty years. "Brooks dislikes, Wimsatt dislikes—all of [the] verse, not merely *Childe Harold* and *Giaour,*" Pottle's notes read; the "distaste of the American New Critics to Byron's comic and satiric verse" doubled as "a distaste . . . for satire that is not firmly and overtly rooted in traditional morality and orthodox religion." Reflecting his practice of citing the opinions of Yale colleagues whom his students would have known, Pottle calls them "very serious men," to whom "Byron seems irresponsible, horsing around, fiddling while Rome burns."[13]

Pottle's allusion to the decadent Nero conveys his colleagues' political and moral aversion to Byron, a stance at odds with their professional commitment to reading literature apart from such concerns.[14] Yet as Pottle well knew, having engaged in a long back-and-forth with Brooks over methodology, the two positions were inextricable. Brooks's deeply felt belief that Rome was in fact burning, that traditional forms of culture were in decline, was part and parcel of his endeavor to keep the spheres of literature and culture separate. Lamenting in *The Well Wrought Urn* "the state into which literary criticism, and ultimately the Humanities in general, have fallen," Brooks protested that literature professors had ceded their unique disciplinary function to deleterious professional and cultural effect. If they "are to be merely cultural historians," he wrote, then "they must not be surprised if they are quietly relegated to a comparatively obscure corner of the history division . . . [or] treated as sociologists, though perhaps not as a very important kind of sociologist."[15] Wellek called it a "flaccid surrender to relativism and historicism," the sexual slur consistent with the ideal of the humanities classroom as a site of moral and psychosexual maturation, a virile and virtual home front where the values fought for in Europe were cultivated, maintained, and re-produced.[16] The endurance of traditional culture lay in acknowledging and embracing what made the study of literature different: "If the Humanities are to endure," Brooks concluded, "they must be themselves."[17] To promote literature's cultivating power was to perceive it aside from the changeable conditions of its production. Yet those conditions were precisely what the topical Byron, however much he fiddled, never let his readers forget.

For all Brooks's anti-historicist rhetoric, when it came to his own peda-gogy he did not simply dismiss history—or Byron. As we saw in the preceding chapter, Brooks took a pragmatically eclectic approach in the classroom, regularly bringing in historical contexts to frame literature for his students. His lecture notes on Byron's "The Prisoner of Chillon" have him telling graduate students that the poem is "rather shaky as history and does not represent the best of Byron as a poet."[18] And his end-of-semester exams—at least when it comes to romanticism—exhibit a perverse devotion to factual specificity. Students in English 150, "The Age of Wordsworth," which Brooks regularly taught at Yale beginning in the 1950s, were required to list "the chief events in the lives of Byron, Shelley, and Keats for the year 1816 *or* the year 1818"; to list the dates and the contents of individual volumes of romantic poetry; and finally to produce a one-hour essay on one of six set topics, several of which explicitly concern the poets' views—of Christianity, of Wordsworth, and of one another.[19]

It should come as no surprise when professors employ teaching methods that clash with their published critical positions, though the difference between Brooks's polemical writing and his pragmatic classroom approach is marked enough to give pause. In *The Teaching Archive*, Rachel Sagner Buurma and Laura Heffernan have illuminated the potential in exploring such dis-junctions, as well as in other forms of connection between pedagogical prac-tice and literary theory. By accounting for the everyday teaching materials that form the practical backbone of academic work, Buurma and Heffernan uncover an alternative history of literary study, one that is less subject to criticism's own self-representations and more attuned to "the many real yet under-studied, under-archived, and undervalued classrooms" in which, they argue, "our discipline's history has really been made."[20] Their thesis reverses the usual sense of the relation between teaching and theory, that literary study's core methods trickle down from its most prestigious scholarship; pedagogy, they argue, more often constitutes the practical foundation of the methods that define the discipline. But nothing is quite as we expect when it comes to the New Criticism's cathected engagement with romanticism, where there turns out to be a formidable disparity—even a total rupture— between critical methodology and pedagogical practice, as the case of Byron vividly demonstrates.

Not Donne, but Byron

The prevailing narrative of Byronic neglect is grounded in a common ten-dency, in histories of criticism, to conflate formalist interests with those of the field in general. That tendency is one feature of our New Critical nos-talgia, which distorts our perception of the rise of modern literary study at a time when we ought to be most vigilant about how disciplines "turn" during crises. There is no shortage of passing mentions of New Critical "dominance" between the 1930s and the 1960s, or of characterizations of this period as one in which romantic poetry surfaced intermittently only to be rebuked or unflatteringly compared with metaphysical poetry. This, however, is a false chronology. The American New Criticism remained a minority position in English departments well into the 1940s and only really became what we might call dominant in the 1950s. And throughout this period in which formal methodologies accrued significant professional authority, romanticism retained a strong critical and curricular presence. Not even Byron disappeared.

Overviews of Byron's reception around this time give the impression that he mattered only to British and Continental thinkers, like Bertrand Russell and Mario Praz, or to cosmopolitan poet-critics, like Auden and T. S. Eliot. This is true even of the very best treatments. In her monograph on Byron, Caroline Franklin offers an insightful account of the poet's reception between the 1930s and 1950s, as does Jane Stabler in her edited collection, but both nonetheless allow New Critical inhibitions to obscure the surge of American historicist writing about Byron in that same period.[21] Symptomatic of our overinvestment in the New Criticism, critical histories tend to assume that Byron's absence from mid-century American formalism signals his absence from that period's American academic writing in general. This was not the case. American New Critics may have disregarded Byron, but their colleagues most definitely did not.

Some numbers might help here. In the 1940s, *PMLA* printed as many articles about Byron (four) as it had in the preceding five decades combined. If we look at the production of doctoral dissertations, we similarly find that the received narrative of Byron's neglect doesn't hold. Although, as my previous chapters have shown, it is difficult to pin down disciplinary trends, the production of dissertations can be reasonably indicative, considering dissertation work's status as a sort of middle ground between the curricular and the critical. The production of dissertations at a given time indicates which literary subjects are animating advanced students during their preparatory coursework, and any dissertation additionally would require the go-ahead of a faculty committee. Thus, for example, the EBSCO dissertation database shows that John Donne's poetry experienced a discernible boom in the 1950s: there was one Donne dissertation produced in the 1930s, one produced in the 1940s, and *twelve* produced in the 1950s—numbers that would seem to match the common narrative of metaphysical ascent and romantic decline, which is so crucial to stories about the rise of the New Criticism.

Yet the numbers don't bear the story out in its entirety. As much as the New Critics helped make Donne fashionable, when it comes to the production of dissertations, his numbers are almost exactly replicated by Byron's. (Byron's numbers, meanwhile, exceed those for Wordsworth and Shelley, and are twice those for Keats.) Eleven single-author dissertations on

Byron were produced in the 1950s, when intellectual shifts occurring in the preceding decade came to fruition in emerging scholarship. This number, as with Donne's twelve, is well more than in any preceding ten-year period, and we can reasonably infer from it that advanced students were already acquiring, in the 1940s, the familiarity with Byron's verse that would soon culminate in heightened scholarly attention.

While it is important not to let statistics substitute for the history of criticism, the notable statistical congruence between Byron and Donne is a valuable supplement, indicating among other things that the stories often told about literary study in the mid-twentieth century don't transparently express curricular realities of the time. There certainly was, in those years, a vigorous emphasis on aesthetic criticism that ran counter to ethical, historical, and philological approaches. But the apparent spike of graduate student interest in Byron suggests that the dramatically "intrinsic turn" that we typically associate with these decades (to the point that it can even stand in for them in histories of the discipline) may have been gentler than is usually acknowledged.

If we put pressure on this data by asking what the upsurge of work on Byron consisted of, we discover a dynamic critical climate that was evidently in flux. The sense of rivalry between established historical and philological scholars and upstart formalists fashioning themselves as critical revolutionaries is evident on both sides of the debate. And though the rhetoric vastly oversimplifies (scholarship and criticism were hardly exclusive), it points to a discipline less in the midst of a formalist turn than on the brink of a pluralist turn—a transition not-quite-arrived, whose outcome was yet in doubt. The upstart critics, as we have seen, liked to deride historical and philological scholars as "pedants," their exacting work as "drudgery." Austin Warren recalled the phrase "Literature *as such*" as "a kind of warcry or party-shibboleth" on the critics' side. Feeling under siege, scholars could be just as harsh. At Iowa in the 1940s, a colleague denounced Wellek (hardly an ideologue) to his face as "no scholar." On another occasion, after Wellek had praised "a good historical scholar" for "some criticism" he had written on Milton, that colleague "turned red in the face" and called it "the worst insult anybody had ever given him." Yvor Winters remembered being told by his chair at Stanford "that criticism and scholarship do not mix" and "that my publications were a disgrace to the department." Ransom related the story of a graduate student interested in criticism, who was told by his department's chair that "we don't allow criticism here, because that is something which anybody can do."[22] The aggression represented in these anecdotes not only belies the common image of unquestioned New Critical hegemony but gives as well the unmistakable impression of a discipline in flux. And while this frisson might seem to reinforce the dichotomies that structure principal understandings of literary study in the 1940s (intrinsic-extrinsic, aesthetic-historical, and metaphysical-romantic), it also betokens the pluralism and methodological vibrancy that was in the discipline's near future.[23]

The fact that Byron and Donne got an equal amount of play in *PMLA* opens a window onto the situation. Between the 1930s and 1950s, *PMLA* remained an outpost for historicist, bibliographical, and philological criticism. In a letter, Brooks's colleague Robert Heilman gave a quick read of Marjorie Hope Nicolson that illuminates the annoyance this caused: "maybe I have her wrong but I thought she was straight PMLA and that if she panned the old boys it would be merely because their footnotes were getting a little shitty around the roots."[24] "Straight PMLA" meant "dry, dusty, scholarly." It also implied "Northern" and "national," as opposed to the regional, rurally based, and often Southern periodicals that heralded and spread a distinctively "literary" method. These outlets were crucial at a time when the establishment venue was widely seen as protecting the entrenched scholarly interests. "I can't show any array of Ph.D.'s and contributions to *PMLA*," the poet-critic Donald Davidson, a Vanderbilt professor and member of the original Fugitive group, confided to Tate: "My appeal to scholarly bugs is flabby."[25]

Byron's poetry was more than amenable to "scholarly bugs." The lead paragraph of T. G. Steffan's 1947 essay "Byron at Work on Canto I of *Don Juan*," published in the newly retitled *Modern Philology: A Journal Devoted to Research in Medieval and Modern Literature*, neatly encapsulates the brand of professionalism indicated by that journal's name, while underlining Byron's compatibility with its sense of disciplinary mission:

> The composition of the first canto of *Don Juan* can be approached by more than one avenue. The letters of Byron and his circle tell a straightforward story of its beginning, its progress, its expansion, and its shrinkage, attended by delays, disputes, and irritations. This is the external chronicle. The manuscript also can be made to tell its own story, although the path has to be cut through a bramble wrought by Byron's own methods, which were simple enough to him who was writing but are intelligible to us only after close analysis of the handwritten pages. Finally, a consideration of various psychological forces that controlled composition will enable us, at least conjecturally, to interpret what the letters and the manuscript show that Byron was doing. In all three parts of the study, the additions to the original draft figure prominently, for these offer the most tangible clues to the workings of Byron's mind, to the mental and emotional processes that made the canto what it is today.[26]

Instead of modern criticism or modern historiography, this is modern philology—yet still a way of understanding poetry. Steffan, a major figure in the history of Byron's editing, here applies his erudition to *Don Juan*, no ancient work, allowing the manuscript a semblance of autonomy under scholarly pressure: it "can be made to tell its own story." Instead of drawing this story out of a study of "the external chronicle," as a literary historian would, the modern philologist compels it through attention to its composition, not close reading but "close analysis of the handwritten pages." A mixture of biographical, psychological, and critical analysis assist, with the final objective being to take the reader inside "the workings of Byron's mind," to access "the mental and emotional processes that made the canto what it is today." In this single paragraph we can see the problem that Wimsatt and Beardsley set themselves against when, as discussed below, they exposed "the intentional fallacy" as part of the discipline's nostalgic symptomology, a rampant compensation for the dissociation of sensibility that had in their judgment led to romanticism—and to Byron, subject par excellence for modern philology.

At a time of deepening concern about the history of the present day, Byron's appeal was especially strong for scholars wishing to nuance the problem of his egoism and to densely historicize his political views and entanglements. As early as 1927, Tate presented Byronism as a highly individualized concept with potentially damaging moral consequences:

> Persons in 1815 were not all aroused by Byron's poetry. They were stirred, as Mr. Kenneth Burke has said, in their own capacity for Byronism. Mr. Burke and I might not have that capacity; and Byron, as far as we are concerned, would cease to exist. But if we had it, he might do us moral injury by making us sad and disillusioned, or perhaps morally unconventional.[27]

By the later 1930s, when moral injuries like sadness and disillusionment were being shaped to more invidious ends, Byron's association with hero-worship, most notably in his admiration for and identification with Napoleon, made his work a politically risky proposition. The European view of him as a larger-than-life symbol of gloomy and melancholic Satanism (i.e., the Byron of Mario Praz's 1933 *The Romantic Agony*) fed straight into the anti-fascist prejudice against Byronism. Bertrand Russell first sounded the alarm in his 1930 book *The Conquest of Happiness*, noting the "destructive and anti-social" nature of Byron's "overmastering passions."[28] The natural sequel to "Byronic Unhappiness" (Russell's chapter title) came in 1945, when Russell devoted a chapter of his *History of Western Philosophy* to the Byronic Hero as a type of "aristocratic rebel," defined by a "titanic cosmic self-assertion" with potentially catastrophic results. Byron's "aristocratic philosophy of rebellion,"

Russell argued, "has inspired a long series of revolutionary movements, from the Carbonari after the fall of Napoleon to Hitler's *coup* in 1933."[29]

Against this prominent, presentist worry about Byron, much of the contemporary work done by American Byron specialists in these years specifically set out to defend the poet's politics. In *Romanticism and the Modern Ego* (1943), the Columbia historian Jacques Barzun sought to dissociate romanticism from fascism. Eric Bentley's *A Century of Hero-Worship* similarly exalted what he called "Heroic Vitalism," transvaluing individual ambition as a crucial element in a democracy—a position with which Burke, for one, took vehement issue:

> does not Mr. Bentley end by here offering as his *solution* the very proposition that most succinctly states the essence of the *problem*? Is it not precisely the inducement to individual ambition that has led to the pushing, elbowing, and scramble characteristic of democracy, even inciting men to strive after improvement of their social status? . . . The author here ends by discovering as his solution precisely the unsettling aspect of our bourgeois society which induced our Heroic Vitalists to shape their own bourgeois careers by the reversal of bourgeois values. Sublimating the ideals of their class, they liked to imagine a careerist so great that he might abolish careerism, turning a few into leaders and calling upon all the others to rest content in their status as the led.[30]

This was the overarching tenor of the conversation about Byron circa 1940, into which scholars like David Erdman, E.D.H. Johnson, and Leslie Marchand brought a bevy of minute and comprehensively researched historical details.

Erdman, best known for his editing of William Blake and his influential historicization of that poet's social vision, sharpened his scholarly teeth on Byron in the early 1940s. During the war, while he held positions at the University of Wisconsin and at Olivet College in Michigan, he published two long pieces in *PMLA* that addressed Byron's political thought. In "Lord Byron and the Genteel Reformers," he illuminates "the practically unexplored problem of Byron's political connections and ambitions during his life in London"—a period usually defined by "gentle apathy" and "detachment from human concerns."[31] Acknowledging Byron's status as "a radical aristocrat in Regency England," Erdman situates his emerging political thought squarely among the concrete focal points of an incipient Reform movement (anti-taxation protests, constitutional rights, suffrage) while noting the irony of espousing a radical politics in genteel social circles. The "radicalism of an aristocrat," he writes, "was a self-contradiction, a fata morgana," for "the Reform aims of either lower or middle 'orders' or both, if *realized*, would undermine the basis of aristocracy."[32] By showing how Byron committed himself to the difficult and practical work of petitionary and parliamentary reform, Erdman forcefully counters the abstraction of the "aristocratic rebel" as well as the familiar assumption that Byron operated in the political realm with a merely amused detachment.[33]

Erdman's 1942 sequel, "Lord Byron as Rinaldo," appearing in the next issue of *PMLA*, continued to flesh out Byron's early involvement in Parliamentary politics. Against a common view among biographers that (like Tasso's Rinaldo) Byron operated under the romantic spell of the radical Lady Oxford when he entered Parliament in 1811, Erdman details Byron's political ambitions and describes his mortification at failing "to do great things in Parliament," thus lending a rich context to the poet's better-known "gloom" and "grumbling."[34] Later in the decade, a young Leslie Marchand, recently tenured at Rutgers, again brought a historical and biographical account of Byron's politics to the pages of *PMLA*, this time by describing correspondence related to his life in Ravenna from 1819 to 1821. In "Lord Byron and Count Alborghetti," Marchand exhaustively positions a set of unpublished letters alongside Byron's involvement in "political events of the country," which was defined by sympathy with "the secret, anti-government, free-Italy, insurrectionist society" of the *Carbonari* and, consequently, a life under surveillance by the Italian authorities. But Marchand stresses how the letters prove Byron's ultimate commitment to humanism over ideology, which shone through in the intimate friendships he formed in Ravenna as well as in his "charities and sympathies for the common people" of the city. "What a queer revolutionary Byron was!," he writes; "Individual humanity was always stepping in to blur the clear picture which partisan zealots see before them."[35]

I do not mean for these details of some prominent Byron scholarship in the 1940s to obscure the fact that Byron was conspicuously disregarded by the American New Criticism; I mean only to emphasize that disregard was not the default setting of the profession writ large. It is striking to see Byron, whose mid-century reception is often skimmed over in overviews of scholarship, transformed into a major node in the intellectual contest over critical "objectivity," a contest bound up with the question of disciplinary prestige. The future of the discipline seemed at times to hinge on this debate about whether an emphasis on verifiable historical and bibliographic facts or a theoretical understanding of the objectivity of form would carry its torch. But as we turn from the wide-angle view to a more close-up perspective, we find that these polarities were themselves less pronounced than is typically presumed.

"Byron I omit altogether"

Having taken a broad view of Byron's complicated standing in mid-century American criticism, I want in the last half of this chapter to zero in on these dynamics of inclusion and omission as expressed in a pair of archival case studies: M. H. Abrams and W. K. Wimsatt. First, Abrams.

Abrams's exclusion of Byron from *Natural Supernaturalism* is perhaps the best-known snub in all of romantic studies. Noting that his study "does not undertake to be an inclusive survey of thought and literature in the early nineteenth century," Abrams makes it plain: "Byron I omit altogether; not because I think him a lesser poet than the others but because in his greatest work he speaks with an ironic counter-voice and deliberately opens a satirical perspective on the vatic stance of his Romantic contemporaries."[36] *Natural Supernaturalism*'s redemptive thesis about the secularization of Judeo-Christian theology in romantic literature centers on the paradigm of the "journey home," as represented above all by Wordsworth's recuperative return to Grasmere. It was not designed to accommodate the skepticism and wayward drift of Byron.

The omission would not go unremarked upon. In *English Romantic Irony*, written within a decade, Anne Mellor pursues a representation of the romantic period able to account for Byron's "ironic counter-voice," and a few years later in *The Romantic Ideology*, Jerome McGann points again to Abrams's exclusion of Byron, while calling into question the project of trying to construct a historical paradigm, "the romantic period," on an often contradictory conceptual basis.[37] McGann, who like Abrams works under Lovejoy's influence, would later argue that Byron's marginalization in representations of romanticism was overdetermined as a result of Wellek's unitary conception of "romanticism," which reduced the field to an encompassing and constrictive tercet: "imagination for the view of poetry, nature for the view of the world, and symbol and myth for poetic style."[38] Seen through Wellek's integral model of a unified romanticism, McGann argues, Byron can only appear as "a problem or an irrelevance," his marginalization in the field of romantic studies between 1945 and 1980 "not an anomaly" but "a theoretical and ideological fate."[39]

Byron's omission from *Natural Supernaturalism* may have realized this "fate," but already in the early 1950s, in a meaningful echo of the poet's disregard by New Critics, Abrams was nudging Byron quietly to the side. Abrams himself was no New Critic, but he does bear an intriguing relation to that movement. Trained at Harvard in literary history, historical philology, linguistics, and the history of ideas, he defended his dissertation in 1940 and came of age professionally just as the New Criticism was becoming influential. He had some qualms about what he considered the new approach's "lack of humanity," and in one of the most lauded sections of *The Mirror and the Lamp* (1953), he detailed the romantic origins of the metaphor of the "organic" work of art while mostly ignoring the New Critics who made this their master concept—noting only the "curious twist of circumstance" by which it was so persistently used to derogate the poetry of the period which gave it birth."[40] Yet Abrams could hardly avoid the New Critics' influence, as attested by the fact that, as "one of the young bucks" in Harvard's PhD program, he pushed for "a New Critical kind of question" on the general examination for undergraduate English majors, eventually persuading "the old timers in the department" to include one.[41]

Abrams's dexterously realized perch between the historical-philological methods in which he was trained in the 1930s and the formalism that blossomed in the succeeding decade is nowhere more evident than in *The Mirror and the Lamp*. Revised for more than twelve years in an intellectual climate increasingly attuned to technique and evaluation, it is sometimes said to have achieved its tremendous influence because it approached the romantic lyric in terms amenable to both the old historicism and the New Criticism.[42] The fall and resurrection of romanticism in the 1940s and 1950s may be an exaggerated feature of our critical histories, but to point this out is not to downplay the impact of *The Mirror and the Lamp*, the book usually credited with returning romantic studies to currency after the war. It did not, however, bring *Byron* back. Byron is not even mentioned until fifty pages in, and across its entirety, only eight sentences even glancingly refer to him. Leigh Hunt, William Hazlitt, even John Keble, all receive more attention than Byron does.

The New Critics' apparent indifference to Byron might have had something to do with this. Byron hadn't been wounded as Shelley had; as we have seen, he was thriving in the literary-historical discourse of the time. There was no urgency to make his case. But Abrams's antipathy to Byron appears to run deeper than this. His class notes from the period show a disinclination even to teach Byron. While undergraduate surveys of romantic poetry, which Abrams taught starting in the late 1940s, always included a small unit on Byron, more specialized courses, such as honors seminars and graduate classes, were typically light on Byron if they touched on him at all. Syllabi for graduate seminars on "Studies in the Romantic Lyric" (1955), "Romantic Poetic Forms" (1956), and "The Romantic Period" (1963) list no Byron. Even in those pedagogical windows where one would most expect to find Byron taught, such as a course on "Longer Romantic Poems" (1964) or a unit on "The Romantic Hero: Solitary and Rebel" (1956), he is usually missing.[43] Abrams did fit Byron's shorter lyrics into a single classroom session for a romantics survey that he taught at Harvard in the summer of 1954, but his class notes show that he introduced those lyrics with a heavy dose of qualification. He summarized the commonly accepted defects—Byron's stylistic "effects [are] direct, even blatant"; he writes a poetry "of flat statement"; his craftsmanship is "often slovenly, careless, hasty" and his "metrics heavy, . . . too obtrusive"; he is "obvious" and "uninteresting"—before offering tepid justification for the day's assignment: "no one thinks of Byron as [an] exemplar, in [an] age of W[ordsworth], Shelley, Keats," yet "on the few occasions when he was at his best, [he] wrote 2 or 3 of the great love-lyrics."[44]

So the omission of Byron in *Natural Supernaturalism* was no anomaly. What was it that Abrams found so aversive? An uncharacteristic slip in *The Mirror and the Lamp* affords a hint. I refer to an odd repetition of Byron's oft-quoted statement, "Poetry is the lava of the imagination whose eruption prevents an earthquake"—a repetition that would be unremarkable but for the fact that Byron is so little discussed in the book.[45] (Fully one-quarter of the words that Abrams devotes to Byron are contained in the two appearances of this one quotation.) Not that a statement figuring lyric expression as an incinerating force born of latent madness is out of place in a thesis about romantic metaphors of expression, but its redundancy makes visible what the idea of Byron called up for Abrams. This is not romanticism on a human scale, in which a poet journeys home or addresses a dear sister or friend in lyric conversation and trusts that his voice will be heard.

I would moreover suggest, more generally, that Abrams's discomfort with a dark Byronic romanticism is connected with his sense of himself as an institutionalist. Here, for context, a brief biographical digression will help.

The son of immigrants who ran a paint-and-wallpaper store at the New Jersey shore, Abrams spoke only Yiddish until the age of five yet earned a scholarship to Harvard—experience that shaped his understanding of higher education as an engine of American meritocracy. He was deeply and personally invested in the structures he rose and worked within. This liberal faith in the positive and progressive relationship between the academy and democracy was of a piece with his work for the U.S. military during the war. Having co-taught a summer course on "The Psychology of Literature" in 1942, he was invited to join Harvard's top-secret Psycho-Acoustic Laboratory, a research outfit subcontracted to the Department of Defense to study verbal communications in battlefield environments—essentially, how language could best be transmitted amidst the noise of gunfire and military vehicles. (Abrams's traditional philological training was part of his appeal to the laboratory's director, because of the understanding of phonetics that it had given him.) Abrams's governmental status was official: he held a diploma from the "War Manpower Commission," certifying him as a "professionally qualified scientific research worker engaged in research and development important to the conduct of the war."[46] One of his first assignments was to travel to Washington, D.C., to brief an army general on details of the lab's research.

And so for a brief period in the early 1940s, this giant of modern literary study, arguably the twentieth century's most influential scholar of romanticism, crossed the well-known boundary separating the university's "two cultures."[47] Abrams is listed as a co-author on no fewer than nine different laboratory reports, each a classified, hundred-plus-page description of experimental objectives, methods, summaries, and conclusions, with many illustrations and tables.[48] Some of the practical outcomes of the research included lists of the words that could be most clearly heard in the midst of loud noise (for use as oral code), and recommendations for designing the audio systems in the Combat Information Center on the aircraft carrier USS *Independence* (Figure 2). In later interviews, Abrams would occasionally mention his work on psychoacoustics, always maintaining that it "had nothing to do with [his] critical work."[49] Still, it is hard not to think about these studies on voice and communication in relation to his belief in a communicative model of the lyric, his belief in poetry as "the product of a purposive human author addressing human recipients in an environing reality."[50]

Although Abrams almost comes around to these precise concerns in his last book, *The Fourth Dimension of the Poem*, I'm less interested in speculating about his wartime work's relation to his thinking about poetry than I am in the simple fact that, as a research scientist embedded deep in the nation's defense infrastructure, Abrams had first-hand experience of a phenomenon so often talked about in histories of the modern university and so intensively fretted over by humanists at the time: the financial windfall for defense-related research.[51] Working at the Harvard Psycho-Acoustic Lab, Abrams experienced the power (both cultural and financial) of scientific research in the American university, and this could only have reinforced his already-strong, liberal faith in the positive relationship between the academy and American democracy. His ultimate return to academia, following several years at the Psycho-Acoustic Lab, was like the culmination of a providential narrative, a Wordsworthian *nostos* that contrasted with Byron's perpetual *algia*.[52] When McCarthyites began scouring university faculties a few years later, with even the New Criticism being called out in the *American Scholar* for a perceived flirtation with anti-democratic and anti-liberal values, Abrams remained

HARVARD UNIVERSITY   *M. H. Abrams*

RESEARCH ON SOUND CONTROL

Under the auspices of the
National Defense Research Committee

S. S. Stevens
L. L. Beranek
Directors

Psycho-Acoustic Laboratory
Memorial Hall
Cambridge, Massachusetts

IC-29, No. 1

December 3, 1942

Informal communication concerning:

A VOCABULARY OF HIGHLY INTELLIGIBLE WORDS
FOR MILITARY COMMUNICATION IN NOISE

 Experience in the field has demonstrated that it is always difficult, and sometimes impossible, to communicate over radio-telephone or interphone systems in the din of modern warfare. This difficulty is due in part to the use of words which are intrinsically of low intelligibility when heard against a background of noise. Replacement of these words, whenever practicable, by speech signals of known high intelligibility will lead to substantial improvement in communication.

 At the request of various branches of the Armed Services, this laboratory has already conducted a number of experiments to determine the most intelligible words for use as standardized signal codes.* These experiments were intended to supply only small stocks of speech signals for various special purposes. It is evident that the techniques developed in these experiments could be employed on a larger scale to provide an extensive vocabulary of highly intelligible words which could be utilized in communication by all branches of the Armed Services. This project was approved by representatives of each of the Armed Services, and was undertaken at the formal request of Major A. A. McCrary of the U.S. Signal Corps.

* See the following reports from the Psycho-Acoustic Laboratory, Harvard University: The Comparative Intelligibility of Alphabetic Equivalents in the LCC, USA and NDRC Lists, August 29, 1942; The Comparative Intelligibility of Alternative Pronunciations of the Numerals "0" Through "9," September 30, 1942; Intelligibility of "Telephone Directory Names for Unit Headquarters," October 26, 1942.

Fig. 2. M. H. Abrams et al., "A Vocabulary of Highly Intelligible Words for Military Communication in Noise," Informal report by the Psycho-Acoustic Laboratory, Harvard University (first page). M. H. Abrams Papers (14-12-4080, box 17, folder 1). Kroch Library, Division of Rare and Manuscript Collections, Cornell University.

fully committed to the notion of the university as a "home for serious intellect" and as an institutional embodiment of American liberalism.[53]

 Abrams's marginalization of Byron in his main critical works reflects this abiding faith in the institution of academia; indeed, the shadow Byron cast over this faith never completely dissipates. His perceived association with the darkness of twentieth-century history made Byron a poet to be regarded with wariness by some, and with fascination by those of a more skeptical mind. The destructive and destabilizing Byronic imagination, figured by explosive lava and the potential for earthquake, represented everything that Abrams, the tactful optimist, was not.[54] Byron's archetypal lyric mode was to call into the abyss of ocean or Alpine gorge—a far cry from Abrams's belief in poetry as "the product of a purposive human author addressing human recipients in an environing reality."[55] Abrams's highly public arguments with J. Hillis Miller in the 1970s, pitting the practical critic and believing liberal against the "unrelenting destroyer—or nihilistic magician" of the deconstructive enterprise, staged opposing belief systems in a way that practically explains his omissions of Byron.[56] Abrams understood such manifestations of "theory" as a "genuinely revolutionary" turn against "the enduring Western paradigm," shifting the basis of literary production away from the world of human communication and dispersing it into signifying systems, linguistic constructs, and institutional forces—into anything but the world in which humans live and speak to one another. He mourned the disappearance of a "tacit consensus" centered on notions of "truth, rationality, and objective knowledge," a consensus summarized in the much-reproduced opening chapter to *The Mirror and the Lamp.* This loss left him, by the 1990s, unable "to recognize literary studies."[57]

Somewhat surprisingly, Abrams eventually came to associate this missing "consensus" with the American New Criticism of an earlier generation. I quote from his "Reply" to the essays collected in his honor in *High Romantic Argument* (1981):

> What I have said, then, is really an announcement of *where I take my stand*—I stand on certain primitives to be used in our explanative discourse about human talking, doing, and making. Which amounts to the confession that, despite immersion in the deconstructive elements of our time, I remain *an unreconstructed humanist.*[58]

The allusion here is to the Agrarian manifesto *I'll Take My Stand,* published in 1930, whose cultural politics were soon to morph into the literary formalism of the Southern New Criticism. John Crowe Ransom opened the volume by posing nostalgia as a deviant stance:

> It is out of fashion these days to look backward rather than forward. About the only American given to it is *some unreconstructed Southerner,* who persists in his regard for a certain terrain, a certain history, and a certain inherited way of living. He is punished as his crime deserves. He feels himself in the American scene as an anachronism, and knows he is felt by his neighbors as a reproach.[59]

Abrams shared neither a politics nor a methodology with Ransom. His first published article in 1942 was in fact a *critique* of Ransom, in which he questions whether "critics who seem to have formed their manner of reading largely on the poetry of the metaphysical school" could accurately judge "passages from Shelley, or Wordsworth."[60] Later that decade Abrams interpreted the New Critics' intense focus on a poem's verbal elements as a disregard for poetry's character "as a human product."[61] The explicit illiberalism expressed most vividly by Allen Tate assured Abrams's ideological distance.

And yet, in this later allusion to *I'll Take My Stand*, we see a consciously shared sense of embattlement, as well as a consciously shared desire to "look backward." Like Ransom in 1930, and somewhat like Byron in his own day, Abrams in 1981 poses himself as an anachronism and a reproach. He takes his stand against the decline of an older order and proclaims an almost theological commitment to its remains. The notable difference is that Abrams takes his rhetorical stand not *in a place* (Ransom's "a certain terrain") but *on disciplinary values* ("certain primitives to be used in our explanative discourse about human talking, doing, and making"). He recasts the Agrarian community as a community of scholars and critics. The contours of shared belief are no longer provided by the Arcadian region but by the incorporated profession.

There is a certain logic in the fact that Abrams's intention "to omit Byron altogether" leads, ultimately, to an identification with the lost ideals of an earlier age—a literal statement of New Critical nostalgia. The New Critics' indifference to Byron, however, was involved with a different sense of critical nostalgia, integral to their central ideas but not, as we see in turning to W. K. Wimsatt, always extending to their classrooms.

"Byron as bridge to Eliot"

In closing this chapter, I follow the road from Ithaca back to New Haven. Abrams's archive opens onto the world of higher education after the war, a golden age without much use for the volcanic Byron. The papers of W. K. Wimsatt lead instead to a classroom "Byron," who is strikingly absent from Wimsatt's published criticism.

Hugh Kenner calls classroom teaching "the most evanescent of performances, unless we count skydiving," but archived pedagogical materials allow provisional access to this otherwise fleeting work.[62] Wimsatt's unusually thorough and well-kept notes make for an especially interesting case, providing an index to his teaching of the romantic Byron and enabling an extended consideration of how poetic principles ill-fitted to Byron's poetry fared in the university classroom. They reveal the disparity between Wimsatt's critical writing and his pedagogical practice, while showcasing the struggles and unique rewards he experienced in teaching a poet whose work was seemingly so much at odds with the formalist program.

A 1939 Yale PhD who stayed on for a long and illustrious career there, Wimsatt was an eighteenth-century specialist, a Johnsonian above all, but also a generalist, prosodist, and theorist. He produced several classics of New Critical theory, including the two "Fallacy" essays co-authored with Monroe C. Beardsley—"The Intentional Fallacy" (1946) and "The Affective Fallacy" (1949)—leading his colleague Wellek to proclaim (correctly, as it's turned out) that he "would be remembered mainly as a theorist of literature."[63]

The intentional and affective fallacies refer, respectively, to "a confusion between the poem and its origins" and to "a confusion between the poem and its *results*." The intentional fallacy "begins by trying to derive the standard of criticism from the psychological causes of the poem and ends in biography and relativism"; the affective fallacy "begins by trying to derive the standard of criticism from the psychological effects of the poem and ends in impressionism and relativism." In both cases, "the poem itself, as an object of specifically critical judgment, tends to disappear."[64] Taken together, the arguments encompass a repudiation of all manner of "externalist" approaches (expressionist theory, biographical reading, Freudianism, history of ideas and historical determinism, affective criticism, psycho-physiological and cognitive studies, semantics, and more), privileging instead the study of the poem itself, "hypostatized as an object, and metaphorically as a spatial object."[65] The fallacies represent what Wimsatt and Beardsley diagnose as the pathological nostalgia of early twentieth-century academic professionalism: a confusion of "personal and poetic studies" resulting from a massive poetic-historical sundering in the seventeenth century, when "feeling and the act of valuing were theoretically detached from a certain something—an Aristotelian structure of ideas, a substantive belief about God, man, and the universe."[66]

This was another way of saying "dissociation of sensibility," Eliot's term from "The Metaphysical Poets" (1921), which Wimsatt and Brooks redescribe in *Literary Criticism: A Short History* (1957) as "a dissociation of the feeling and responding side of human consciousness from the side of knowing and rational valuing" that had led "toward the inspirations of the author of poetry, and toward the responses of his audience."[67] Wimsatt and Beardsley's "Fallacy" essays set out to treat the (romantic) effects of this dissociation by relocating value in the objective poem itself. If the goal was not exactly to recover that lost "certain something" (the modern critic had no such power: mature poetry would always hold "a certain nuclear area of the indefinable"), it might at least dispel this "prominent ... disorder of the age," embodied and exacerbated by romantic modes of valuing.[68] The compulsive return to authors' designs and to readers' responses was a symptom; a difficult modern poetry was one form of alleviation, a mature criticism was another.

Byron's personal story, his emotive power, and his world-historical stature constitute a great deal of his literary-historical prestige—meaning that he was no desirable object for Wimsatt the objectivist with his anti-nostalgic critical project. Yet Byron appealed plenty to Wimsatt the teacher. We can turn to Wimsatt's archived classroom notes for a sense of this. As archived faculty papers go, Wimsatt's are unusual, in that his teaching materials are sorted not by course title and year (as Abrams's and many others' are) but for the most part by individual authors. This was no doubt a logical and convenient system for Wimsatt in his lifetime, though it complicates the effort to situate the notes in a defined classroom context. Some items are notated or dated, or clearly belong to a certain course or kind of course, but most belong to a wider history of use in courses of varying size and focus.

Still, they are systematically organized. Each folder starts with an extensive bibliography, which is followed by newspaper and magazine clippings related to the writer. These clippings range from humorous news items that might have been shared with students—in his Blake folder, for instance, there is a *New York Times* article titled "Sociologist Predicts End of Romantic Love"— to long book reviews in venues like the *Times Literary Supplement* or the *Saturday Review*, which Wimsatt presumably used to jumpstart his thinking, or to update himself on the present state of discussion of an author.[69] Finally, there are the classroom notes themselves, handwritten on octavo-sized sheets of paper.

Some of these notes disclose aspects of Wimsatt's teaching approach that are poignantly mundane, considering his staunch methodological commitments. For example, in introducing Byron he presents all the romantics' birth- and death-dates in a timeline. He also draws a graphic representation, likely meant for the blackboard, of what he calls the "romantic circle of ideas" (Figure 3), in which the "big six" shoot off in every direction, each embodying particular "romantic" qualities ("Nature" for Wordsworth, "Emotion" for Shelley, "Individualism" and "Rebellion" for Byron).[70] Wimsatt called himself "an invincible Ramist and visualist," and his penchant for diagrammatic rather than syllogistic logic—graphs, pictures, charts—is on display throughout his teaching notes, which consistently push in his desired "direction of clarity."[71]

Wimsatt kept three folders of material on Byron, which he could draw upon for multiple courses and teaching situations. He asked students to read an uncommon diversity of Byron's poems, including the Oriental Tales,

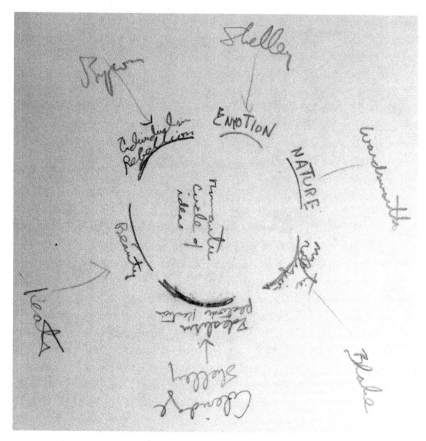

Fig. 3. "Romantic circle of ideas," in William K. Wimsatt's teaching notes on Byron. William Kurtz Wimsatt, Jr. Papers (MS 769, series 1, box 7, folder 99). Yale University Manuscripts and Archives, Yale University.

Childe Harold's Pilgrimage (cantos 3–4), *Mazeppa, Parisina,* and numerous short lyrics, through to the major achievements of *Beppo* and *Don Juan* (cantos 1–4).[72] For the earlier works, the notes demonstrate a traditional reliance on context. Thus, while teaching Childe Harold, Wimsatt begins with biography ("Harold = Byron"; "Ada—biographical") and precisely locates the scenes of Harold's travels. (On one sheet, he lists various sites in Rome, such as the Apollo Belvedere, the Pantheon, St. Peter's, and the Colosseum, pictures of which he intends to bring to class.) It's somewhat touching to see a critic like Wimsatt conceding the classroom value of biography, history, and context, even becoming animated by it, while still at times struggling to make good formalist sense of Byron: at the bottom of his checklist of Roman sites, he writes a note reminding himself to "show more unity among themes."[73]

In making my way through these notes, though, it became clear to me that this emphasis on context belonged to a specific narrative arc. There is a purpose to Wimsatt's having begun with a timeline situating Byron among the other major romantics while repeatedly calling attention to his "Projection of self into eternal world." The early classes lay stress on Byron's romantic individualism, and this focus, coinciding with an emphasis on biographical context, peaks with a scrawled excerpt from Allen Tate's essays, remarking on Byron's insistent and imperious subjectivity in the face of "nature and history." Byron's impulse, in Tate's words, is "not to comprehend [nature and history] and forget himself before them, but to seek in them and impress upon them his own passions."[74] Whether they were meant to be read aloud to the class or written on the board—or neither—these scribbled words mark a turn in the trajectory of Wimsatt's "Byron," away from the romantic and individualistic and toward the more satirical and ironic sense of self in Byron's later works. (This shift in Wimsatt's teaching exactly resembles a discussion of "Byron's two manners" in one of his periodical clippings, where Byron's mature satirical style is praised over the "trite romantic way of writing—inherited, not felt—of the earlier work.")[75]

As he guides students toward the question of satire, both as a complex form that Byron masters and as an ironic mode in which he achieves distance from himself, Wimsatt seems increasingly comfortable. Byron in his teachable satiric mode embodies "that last stand of a classic mode of laughter" against what Wimsatt, in his own criticism, calls the "disorder of the age," by which he means the "sublime inflation of ideas" and the "luxury of sorry feeling" growing out of the "now notorious dissociation of sensibility."[76] His class notes indicate that at one point Wimsatt planned to bring two portraits of Byron into class—an 1823 sketch by Count D'Orsay and an 1816 drawing by G. H. Harlow—in order to help students think about the poet's strategies of satirical self-distancing. In this narrative of Byronic development, the poet comes into his own as he discards his romantic individualism. Wimsatt taught students that "[e]ven in romantic poems [Byron is] hovering often on [the] verge of satire," but that in the "better" Italian burlesque of *Beppo*, "romantic material [is] turned to grotesque."[77]

Wimsatt's investment in Byron's satirical self-distancing matches his belief that "a poetry of pure emotion is an illusion."[78] It also anticipates some of the defensive responses of Byronists, who liked to point out that the poet was actually a good match for New Critical criteria. The historicist scholar Roy Harvey Pearce, weary of such defensiveness and unwilling to cede ground to formalists, reflected in the late 1950s that "The characteristic tactic [of romanticism's defenders] is to prove, somehow, that 20th century poets, critics, and philosophers, so often nominally anti-Romantic, are actually latent

Romantics, critically sick in their very latency." Invoking the specific example of Byron, Pearce parodies the common lament of the romanticist scholar: "It is surely one of the monstrous ironies of our time, the present critical age of Irony and Ambiguity, the Period of the Poetic Paradox, that Byron, master of these, should have been so neglected by the new critics."[79] In the classroom, if not in his published criticism, Wimsatt grants Byron this mastery. The great achievement of the late satirical work, in the arc that Wimsatt draws for his students, is Byron's shedding of his romantic individualism and his arrival as a modernist poet.

This is crystallized in a sparse notation, standing free on a single note-sheet: "Byron as bridge to Eliot. / 1. Allusion as a technique / 2. Theme of ruins — / collapse of order / 3. Theme of Eden + original / Sin."[80] In presenting Byron's late work as a technical and thematic "bridge" to Eliot's *Waste Land*, Wimsatt likely has in mind as well the self-distancing procedures that Eliot would master in earlier pieces like "Prufrock" and "Gerontion." Eliot himself saw in Byron "a self that is largely a deliberate fabrication—a fabrication that is only completed in the actual writing of the lines." But he actively resisted understanding Byron as a bridge to his own work, aggressively concealing any potential identifications through a stance of pronounced disgust, both for Byron's physical appearance and for his lack of originality. Eliot, in a manner redolent of his antipathy to "puerile" Shelley, is scathing on both points: "that pudgy face suggesting a tendency to corpulence, that weakly sensual mouth, that restless triviality of expression, and worst of all that blind look of the self-conscious beauty; the bust of Byron is that of a man who was every inch the touring tragedian"; and "Of Byron one can say, as of no other poet of his eminence, that he added nothing to the language, that he discovered nothing in its sounds, and developed nothing in the meaning, of individual words."[81] For Wimsatt, however, the "bridge" metaphor offered a convenient means of consolidating Byron's value within an eminently teachable model of literary history. "I do not accept a view of literature as essentially a rebellion," he would write in the midst of the campus uprisings of the late 1960s; "I think rather of an order of expressions, and of a departure from these which is a new expression, not a destruction."[82] His belief that "tradition and history" constitute "a seamless web" also helped him to reassert the value of the modernist end of the literary-historical bridge, in a conventional trajectory moving from expressiveness to irony—from the personal lyric to the dramatic one.[83]

Wimsatt hewed closely to the New Critical view of the poem as a synthesis of dramatic parts, though he insisted that this synthesis was the consequence not of "organic" spontaneity but of conscious and deliberate verbal arrangements. In Brooks's distinctively Agrarian version of the dissociation of sensibility narrative, the cause of historical rupture (as John Guillory notes) is the rise of modern science, a fact that might be seen as contributing to Brooks's organicist conception of poetry.[84] Wimsatt, for his part, eschewed what he considered the Agrarian narrative's mystified organicism, seeing it as yet another nostalgic symptom. In his own late essay "Organic Form: Some Questions about a Metaphor" (1970), he rejected its "transcendental" unity, even if only as the (pre-dissociative) object of nostalgic longing, preferring a "homelier and humbler sort of organicism" that recognizes the poem as "a moment of spiritual activity, hypostatized, remembered, recorded, repeated." The "intimate, manifold (and hence dramatic and imaginative) 'interin-animation' of parts in a poem must surely be one of the modern critic's most carefully defended doctrines," he wrote in the same essay, using I. A. Richards's term (borrowed from Donne) for the way words and syntactic structures react together to generate meaning in a poem, rendering the poem an "all knowable" object, "all knowledge, through and through."[85]

Interinanimation between parts, a fundament of Wimsatt's anti-nostalgic science of literature, similarly defined his sense of himself as a professional. He was keenly aware of the dramatic nature of his own academic position—the fact that, as a professor, he played numerous characters. In a radio forum at Yale on "The Role of the Literary Critic," he observed that "sometimes the same critic has different jobs at different times. There are theoretical critics, practical critics, book reviewers, professors of theory, and teachers."[86] From a distance, it is understandable that these "different jobs" would not always fit neatly together. Close reading may, at times, have been a pedagogical convenience, but clearly there were aspects of the New Critical project that were more suited to published polemic than to classroom practice. Wimsatt's teaching materials convey an unmistakable sense of how he wrangled with his critical principles while attempting to forge a common ground with students.

Attempts to define the American New Criticism as either primarily theoretical or primarily pedagogical tend to miss this most practical point. "Literary theory and classroom practice are related," wrote Robert Scholes in the 1980s, "as any 'pure' or theoretical study is related to applications in the same field."[87] To go as far as to call the New Criticism "a classroom strategy [that came] to mistake itself for a critical discipline," as Hugh Kenner accused, is to get things exactly backward—as we have seen in the preceding chapter, on Cleanth Brooks's critical writing in relation to his teaching practice.[88] Kenner's claim also misses a more basic point, evident in Wimsatt's teaching of Byron, which is that for all the interinanimation between their criticism and teaching, the leading New Critics were not absolutists in the classroom.

With students, they were—as they had to be—diverse and adaptable, make-shift and improvisational, familiarly and pragmatically hybrid. Sometimes, arguments that mattered greatly to them as critics and theorists faded in significance in the working space of the seminar room, where the more pressing matter may have been (as shown in these last few chapters) to engage students with a possibly strange art form, or to guide them toward maturity, or to teach them to be critical, or ethical, or curious, or even simply to create around the reading of poems an intimate haven in an alienating institutional environment. And sometimes, the matter at hand was merely to interest students in a writer whose work challenged much of what their other classes had instilled in them.

5. The Emergence of Josephine Miles (Reading Wordsworth in Berkeley, California)

> The people born right this minute are probably going to go
> back and search the past in new ways.
> —Josephine Miles, interview, August 25, 1977

The scholar and poet Josephine Miles was many things that interest readers today: an inventive visualizer of literary information, a trailblazing data miner, an interdisciplinary adventurer, a postcritical thinker who forged a career in the midst of a critical boom.[1] Miles was what Silicon Valley types would call a "disrupter," whose computational studies of poetic language challenged professional conventions in the moment of their consolidation. Her unusual work tested the boundaries of a congealing discipline—tested even the typesetters tasked with printing her intricate handwritten numerical tables.[2] If it is tempting to think of Miles, with her prescient methods and interests, as a scholar ahead of her time, to the extent that she appears as an outlier to her era, born too soon, it is in part because the stories that get told about the rise of modern literary study tend to exclude women as well as (in a way that is systematically related) the methodological eclecticism that her work represented. Hers was an era of innovation, and she was one of its central figures, working consistently near the beating heart of her profession.

None other than William K. Wimsatt placed Miles in the middle of things. Never one to give praise lightly, Wimsatt wrote fulsomely of her significance within the field of English at mid-century, calling her work "a striking instance of a newly emergent historicocritical idiom." His review of *Eras and Modes of English Poetry* (1957) is so unusually perceptive that it is worth quoting at length:

> She is out precisely to make generalizations, to formulate viable historical
> concepts. Then in the second place, the technique has the interest and the merit
> of aiming neither simply at a contentual description (poems about melancholy,

about death, about childhood, about outdoor nature, about love, are not her theme) nor simply at a formal description (unity, coherence, emphasis, prose, metrics, metaphor, simile—these are not her theme either). Rather her method of verbal statistics, richly informed or supplemented by her own special insights, is a union of the formal and the contentual which at its best comes close to being a masterly union for generalizations about poetic history.[3]

Miles is not, Wimsatt says, an organicist—she neither close reads nor evaluates single poems conceived as living wholes. What she is, instead, is a generalizer, an amalgamator, and a practicing poet-critic, whose "method of verbal statistics" yields matter-of-fact results that are enriched by "her own special insights" as an artist.[4] Notably, Wimsatt situates Miles in an evolutionary paradigm of disciplinary change. Her "idiom," he says, is "both valid and pregnant in a way special to our own time," the metaphor denoting a power of historical gestation that is strongly grounded in its context ("present English literary scholarship and especially that scholarship in America"). In Miles, Wimsatt implies, the profession's historical-philological past visibly transitions to its "historicocritical" future. Put another way, Wimsatt sees Miles as a figure of *continuity*—a word that, together with its correlates *equilibrium, balance, steadiness, stability*, and *regularity*, constitutes Miles's own primary language of criticism.

This is a counter-nostalgic idiom, a minor register within her discipline, which downplays the distance between the literary present and the literary past by refusing the usual structuring principle of historical rupture and estrangement.[5] Miles poses this idiom assertively against the major vocabulary of her field, which includes words like *autonomy, discontinuity*, and *independence*. In doing so she creates a notion of continuity as evolution, a sense of history as a constant "equilibrium of the present," refusing the restorative Burkean notion of continuity as tradition.[6] Her muse in this, as was true for so many critics of the time, was William Wordsworth.

It's an unorthodox choice. Whether we're talking about his self-conscious break with eighteenth-century poetic modes, or the differences between his early and late styles, or the various personal turnabouts (religious, political, or otherwise) that have come to define him, Wordsworth is no easy fit with a narrative of continuity. Yet he is Miles's prime poet from start to finish.[7] Her scholarly career begins with Wordsworth (he is the subject of her dissertation and first book), and his poetry flows through her work to the very end, a stable and continuous presence. In turn, Miles reads stability and continuity into Wordsworth's generically diverse oeuvre, finding in his "classical" poetic style an "integral Wordsworth of *Prelude, Excursion*, sonnets, odes, from one end of his life to the other."[8] This consistency of style reflects a consistency of observational practice. Neither Ransom's Poet of Nostalgia nor Abrams's Poet of Homecoming, Miles's Wordsworth is a Poet of Method, who models her own critical values of patient looking and clear seeing and demonstrates "the special relation of observation to generalization" that is essential to her "descriptive" technique.[9] This is a Wordsworth who is unremittingly attentive to what Miles calls "the on-going of experience"—dedicated to the continuities of temporal change represented at the end of "Tintern Abbey," where a past-tense presence ("We stood together") is recast as a future retrospect ("Nor . . . wilt thou then forget").[10]

In this final chapter I take up Miles's counter-nostalgic (some might say counter-disciplinary) commitment to this Wordsworthian principle of continuity. It is a commitment that colors every aspect of her thinking about literary study: about the shape and wholeness of poetry, about the forms and horizons of literary periods, and about the value of interdisciplinary pursuit. As we will see, Miles eschews the notion of a poem's organic wholeness, embraces an evolutionary view of the historical flows of semantic and syntactic change, and betrays a certain indifference to the mid-century shibboleth of disciplinary autonomy. In all of these ways she presses generatively, revealingly, and also problematically against the methods and values being consolidated at the outset of higher education's liberal period, its so-called golden age.[11]

My story so far has been about the romantic investments of this period's criticism: primarily male, mostly based (sooner or later) at private universities in the North and Northeast, and devoted to the close reading of single textual objects. Miles was none of this. But to say so is not to make her the hero of a Berkeleyan progress narrative, moving optimistically westward into the technological and institutional future of knowledge production.[12] In concluding *New Critical Nostalgia* with the compulsively counter-nostalgic Miles, I turn to the paradox of a philologically trained scholar who has recently emerged as an overlooked forerunner of twenty-first-century critical trends—a figure of continuity, connecting eras, who speaks to our moment precisely because she was so much of her own. To read Miles within the historical period in which she emerged is to confront an under-reported commotion about "the future of English," a crisis once again centered on the romantic lyric.

Tabulating Poetry

Literary study, "if not precisely a science, is a species of knowledge or of learning." So wrote René Wellek and Austin Warren at the outset of *Theory of Literature* (1949)—an urgent claim at a time when science departments secured their viability (both intellectually and financially) by investing in national security.[13] It was an era, in literary study, of methodological experimentation, in which a variety of critical methods came into being under the sign of empiricism, seemingly competing to realize Ransom's oft-quoted dictum that the discipline must become "more scientific, or precise and systematic."[14] But how to account for literary art scientifically and systematically? One answer, Wellek and Warren report, was taking this shape:

> it can be done with the methods developed by the natural sciences, which need only be transferred to the study of literature. Several kinds of such transfer can be distinguished. One is the attempt to emulate the general scientific ideals of objectivity, impersonality, and certainty, an attempt which on the whole supports the collecting of neutral facts. Another is the effort to imitate the methods of natural science through the study of causal antecedents and origins; in practice, this "genetic method" justifies the tracing of any kind of relationship as long as it is possible on chronological grounds. Applied more rigidly, scientific causality is used to explain literary phenomena by the assignment of determining causes to economic, social, and political conditions. Again, there is the introduction of the quantitative methods appropriately used in some sciences, i.e., statistics, charts, and graphs. And finally there is the attempt to use biological concepts in the tracing of the evolution of literature.[15]

As you can tell from the tone, this is a report, not an endorsement. If Wellek considered "a science of literature which divorces literary study from criticism (i.e. value judgment)" to be "impossible," his list of "methods" suggests how frequently the transfer was attempted.[16] An older, "purely fact-collecting type of scholarship" (Wellek means philology) had carried heft and authority, in contrast to the perceived looseness of "appreciation" and even of ethical or aesthetic criticism.[17] Yet for all its objective rigor, philology was coming to be seen as a fusty, bygone mode in need of supersession. When the medievalist Edith Rickert championed a cutting-edge "scientific method" in a groundbreaking 1927 book heavy with visualizations, her Chicago colleague John Matthews Manly praised Rickert for meeting a "crying need . . . to turn the study of literature in a new direction," touting her book as "the sign and the cause of a new era in the study of literature."[18] The need for reading to appear "more scientific, or precise and systematic" was as pronounced as ever.

Hence the appeal of non-interpretive, numerically based techniques such as Miles's. Theodore Porter describes quantification as "a technology of distance . . . synonymous with rigor and universality"—one reason why scientific lingo became so attractive in the humanities of this period.[19] In the 1920s the word "laboratory" began to be used with increasing frequency to talk about academic reading practices, serving as a signpost for precision with a cross-disciplinary import. I. A. Richards's "laboratory approach" in *Principles of Literary Criticism* was the most famous instance of this "lit-lab" science, which Tate later scorned as "hocus-pocus" and "an elaborate cheat": "How many innocent young men—myself among them—thought, in 1924, that laboratory jargon meant laboratory demonstration!"[20] The allure of "laboratory demonstration" fed what Hugh Kenner called the New Critical "cult of the blackboard," which transformed the literature classroom into a quasi-laboratory where poetic specimens could be studied, anatomized, and diagrammed: "A typical blackboard at the end of the hour would display words encircled, with little colliding arrows; would show lines broken into phrases, with perhaps some stresses marked."[21]

A young Josephine Miles took up the challenge of laboratory demonstration in a different way, through arithmetical studies that yielded tabular content. Henry Wells called Miles's method a "laboratory technique," and when she started teaching at Berkeley in 1940, she herself told students to expect "a lab or tool course," influenced perhaps by her colleague George Rippey Stewart's 1936 textbook, *English Composition: A Laboratory Course.*[22] Miles's cultivation of empirical distance through enumerative techniques was therefore less a departure from prevailing literary methodologies (whether historicist, philological, or critical) than another way to pursue "a form of knowledge production that could fit the disciplinary model of the university"—which is also to say that this inveterate word counter and pattern seeker was not toiling eccentrically at the margins of the field but working at the profession's very heart.[23]

A formidable trilogy of arithmetical studies, heavily focused on nineteenth-century poetry, thrust Miles into professional visibility in the 1940s: *Wordsworth and the Vocabulary of Emotion* (1942), *Pathetic Fallacy in the Nineteenth Century* (1942), and *Major Adjectives in English Poetry* (1946). These led to her becoming in 1947 the first woman ever tenured by Berkeley's English Department.[24] Marjorie Levinson later named Miles as one of only five women in "the entire profession of literary studies" in the early 1970s with "the stature to serve as role models" to young female graduate students, and although that stature diminished after her death in 1985, Miles has never gone entirely missing.[25] Virtually every study of literary periodization acknowledges, at least in passing, her career-long endeavor to make statistical sense of English poetry's various eras and modes, and the exhaustive data that she amassed in nearly five decades as a computational scholar of English poetry has never ceased to find its way into the footnotes of single-author studies. Mention Miles at a conference and former students and colleagues from Berkeley step forward, eager to reminisce about spirited conversations in her Wheeler Hall office or at the Virginia Street house where, because of her debilitating arthritis, she sometimes held seminars.

It was Miles's work as a poet, known for her densely cerebral, "John Donne school" verse, that first gained her admittance to active debates about disciplinary purpose in the late 1930s. Cleanth Brooks and Robert Penn Warren published five of her poems in the *Southern Review* while she was a graduate student, an experience that she recalled as opening her up to "a new world of poetry": "The *Southern Review* was in a sense the way I felt."[26] Ransom praised her as "like Dickinson except more metaphysical and without the fundamental sentiment," and as *Kenyon Review* editor he became her "steady advisor."[27] While Miles's poetry afforded her entry to a world of scholarly conversation, it could sometimes overshadow her intellectual seriousness. Throughout a protracted correspondence with Brooks and Warren about her poems (defined, on the editors' side, by polite disregard for the young female), Miles recurrently reminded them that she was more than just a poet.[28] She tactfully commended *Understanding Poetry*—"We are having fun being half-students of yours here in California," she wrote from her first teaching job in Fresno—and eventually, she boldly took the opportunity to send them a six-page proposal for a critical project she called "Prime Words in Poetry."[29]

The proposal grew out of her dissertation, "Wordsworth and the Vocabulary of Emotion," and it involved word counts of major English poets designed to indicate lexicological shifts across historical periods. This was painstaking work, all done by hand well before the computer age.[30] Her brief lyric "Enlightenment," published in *Poetry* only the year before, is in some ways a methodological précis of the proposed work. Miles contrasts the gentle illumination of numerical data to the blinding "high powered radiance" and "archangelic doctrine" of received knowledge:

> I wish we could take a statistic with more grace, beloved
> I wish it would circle out in our minds to the very brim,
> And we could be illumined by data one by one, as by candles ...
> I wish we had one or two facts to go by,
> And a less arc-lighted kingdom to inherit.[31]

Miles's formal proposal for "Prime Words in Poetry" put great faith in data work. "Allen Tate, without venturing examples, has spoken of 'the indefinable average of poetic English,'" she wrote, but "there is no reason why the average cannot be eventually definable and exemplifiable, with enough knowledge."[32] Brooks and Warren, nonplussed by so optimistic and literal a claim to objectivity, decided not to pursue the idea for the *Southern Review*, though this began a warm correspondence on the subject.[33]

Miles's work on "Prime Words" was part of an existing trend with roots in philological study. There were plenty of literary statisticians at the time, scholars of empirical method. These included hard-core quantifiers like the Cambridge mathematician George Udny Yule, the medieval philologist Edith Rickert, and the psychologist Edward Lee Thorndike, not to mention dabblers in word counting such as Eric Partridge (who used statistical counts to establish stylistic features shared by Pope and the Romantics), William Grace (who wrote about using quantification as a teaching tool), and Oscar Firkins (who compiled and cataloged abstractions in Shelley's poetry).[34] Miles set herself apart by employing an idiom that, to use Heather Love's phrase, was "close but not deep."[35] She focused on what she called the "face values of the words on the page," self-consciously preferring this superficial approach to exploration of a text's latent depths, while nevertheless conveying her findings with the intimacy and warmth of an aesthetic critic.[36]

Miles the scholar was also the poet Josephine Miles, as many went out of their way to point out. Again and again, admirers as well as critics observed this double status, poet and critic, as explanatory of Miles's professional style. Wimsatt saw her "character" as a poet as essential to "her scholarly labors," investing them with "their peculiar kind of profit."[37] Edmond Volpe, acknowledging the worry that a computational approach "threatens to grind poetry into statistics, to replace the critic with an IBM computer," countered: "Professor Miles, however, a true lover of poetry, goes far beyond her statistics."[38] And Ransom, for a recorded conversation to accompany the third edition of *Understanding Poetry*, lamented the increasing empiricism of academic reading only to exempt Miles from the complaint: "being a poet she could count the words and tabulate the words and . . . she could come away from an hour of that and she could give you an infinite amount of the poetic quality of those verses." For Ransom, this ability to discern "poetic quality" set Miles apart from mere "linguistic scientists"—and again we see Ransom, against type, portraying evaluative criticism as the work of a personal reader:

> suppose she had not been a poet and suppose she had been a mere grammarian and not receptive to poetry? Then [her word counts] would have meant nothing. They wouldn't have really involved her; she wouldn't have been participating.[39]

Here we see the suspicion in which statistical analysis was held—such that the credit of being a practicing poet helped Miles to avoid being labeled "a mere grammarian," mechanical and philological, and to be understood instead as a participatory, responsive critic.

So this was the wider perception of Miles in her time: not merely a cold technician of literature but an imaginative poet and warm interpreter of style. Yet the glare of computational methods could still overshadow the critic's art. This was the assessment of the Columbia comparatist Henry W. Wells, who took pains to assert that Miles's "ablest" work occurs "far from her labora- tory technique"—when "her academic formalisms acquire human warmth, when her own criticism is most clearly an art." The "aesthetic method of criticism actually serves her best," Wells writes; "when her own hand is happiest, criticism turns out to be neither science nor philosophy but art."[40] Having taught in New York, Wells was probably unaware both of the pain that Miles's arthritic hands gave her and of the extraordinary work that those hands performed, not only as instruments of writing but of reading.[41] (One really must see Miles's word-counting notes, discussed below, to understand the degree to which her reading practice was also a labor-intensive writing practice, which involved writing down poems as she read them.)

Ironically, for all this idealizing of her "poetic spirit," Miles's poems were sometimes critiqued as a mere "expert's game." Less dismissive, but still in the same key, Helen Haines's review of her 1939 collection *Lines at Inter- section* commented on the poems' adherence "to what is almost a geometric design," with a scientific method, "a penetrating but delicate ultra-violet ray of insight upon the images of nature and of man imprinted on the retina of the poet's observation."[42] Miles herself refused to polarize "scientific" and "poetic," and she eschewed such labels as "computational scholar," "linguistic scientist," or "literary statistician." To her, word counts and arithmetical com- putations were mere engines of description. "The purpose," she announced at the outset of her study of poetry in the 1740s and 1840s, "is to describe in a very simple way the language most used in the poetry of two decades."[43] This attention to poetry itself—in Miles's measure, to "the language most used" in it—appealed even to intrinsic readers such as Wellek and Wimsatt. "One could almost be converted to the statistical method," wrote Wellek, extolling Miles's numerically guided historicism for being drawn from the insides of poems.[44] It was this character of Miles's statistical work that Wim- satt identified as "newly emergent"—its promise of uniting the "formal" and "contentual" with "unprecedented scrupulosity and precision of analytic observation."[45]

Seeing Poems Clearly

For Miles, statistical tabulation is a mode of seeing. It offers a means to "record the obvious," and in this it resembles scientific research that some- times (as Vivienne Koch put it in her 1952 review of *The Continuity of Poetic*

Language) "substantiates what is already known to common sense."[46] Her point, consistently, is that a received view is often at odds with empirical observation, which can be objectively tabulated to provide a sound basis for discussions of poetic style. Numbers are a guardrail to keep assumptions at bay. Thus, for all the apparent novelty of Miles's method—reviewers used words like "innovative," "original," and "unusual" to describe it —she positioned her work, if not exactly within, then at least adjacent to mainstream practices of literary study. It is worth noting that she gave a glowing review to Brooks's controversial *Well Wrought Urn*, particularly his "generous" way with single poems and the "job of description":

> Few critics are more followable in the reconstruction of the well-wrought poem, if not urn. The ten poems he describes in this book will mean the more for his having described them. . . . [W]e are so busy about interpretation and projection (and paradox); and not many see a poem clearly and describe it faithfully and easily as Mr. Brooks does.

She saw this as continuous with the "patience," "receptivity," and "straight attention to every complex structure and every simple whole" that she found demonstrated in *Understanding Poetry*.[47] Brooks matters to Miles less as a professional interpreter than as a careful, lucid teacher, able to build poems all over again using a different language: the language of description.

This is Miles's own pedagogical value as well as method. The importance of seeing poems clearly, a capacity that she claims to have learned from *Understanding Poetry*, cannot be overstated. Her earliest scholarly writings exaggerate "patience" and "straight attention" in justification of data work: a "plain readiness to observe and attend," a "mere willingness to watch the face values of the words on the page" (as if a face were the only value, and value were not a function of a system of credit and exchange).[48] To "see a poem clearly" in this way, rather than through the lens of "accepted scholarship" or nostalgic wishfulness, is Miles's desired practice, a way to meet the perceived empirical demands of the moment with what she contends is a "more continuous observation of actual poetic content than we have yet condescended to."[49]

Close reading in this way is synonymous for Miles with clearest sight and insight. Ransom's phrase "close criticism" pervades her late-1930s writings, from dissertation to grant proposals, and her early class notes reveal the succinct corrective she offered to students who misfired on an essay assignment: "Remedy: closer notes, closer reading."[50] The comparative "closer" advances Ransom's *close* into an ongoing engagement. "If we are to have more close analyses of poetic performance," she writes in "The Problem of Imagery" (1950), "we need closer understanding of the methods and materials to be analyzed."[51] Miles defended the "virtue of close criticism" against its "corresponding vice" of trying "to overleap itself and to generalize vastly."[52] Her values are physical, tactile, not abstract.

Writing to Warren in 1938, she describes poetry as "an art of words like paper-weights, loaded with connotations"—as if such connotations were a palpable substance, pressing down on words with the force of a gentle gravity.[53] A few years later, in an exchange with Brooks about Wordsworth, she expresses ambivalence about a presentism that she feels throws off this verbal weight. She begins politely: "I agree with your evaluation and do in fact feel that I've been raised, in terms of sense of values, by the books you've written and the whole Southern Review tradition." Then she drops the hammer: "I would say you lose Wordsworth by evaluating him for us today."[54] The quibble was not with Brooks's values but with a certain imperceptiveness caused by reading in terms of those values ("evaluating him for us today"). In an essay on "Critical Relativism" published that same year, 1943, she explains herself: "in the at least faintly Einsteinian world of the 1940's," some modern critics "would maintain that 18th-Century standards were just bad."[55] It was just such divergence between relative and absolute standards that drew Miles to Wordsworth's poetry in the first place; here is the opening paragraph of her 1938 dissertation:

> Wordsworth's poetry abundantly and persistently names and states emotion.
> Modern literary criticism and poetic theory tend to disbar such naming from
> poetry by definition; to warn against statement as unpoetic, the names of
> emotions particularly as unpoetic, and explicitly stated emotion as especially
> unpoetic. Wordsworth erred.

Was she yet aware of Brooks and Warren's recent attack on Shelley's passionate poetry in *Understanding Poetry*? Noting how the "discrepancy between the present theory and the actual practice" gets "easily laid" to the poet's "individual error," Miles asserts the need to "know some facts first: whether the material is indeed as persistent and abundant in this poetry as it seems, or whether one has just happened to notice it."[56] She was not disparaging New Criticism, per se, which she admired, but rather asking for a more scientific accounting of evidence. (Brooks and Warren were happy to correspond with her on this question, gave appreciative reviews to her work, and invited her to publish work alongside of theirs.)

Miles's chief interest was to establish an authoritative basis for critical discussion. Her dissertation's bibliography shows how engaged she was with the latest criticism: it is dominated by critical works of the 1930s, along with some primary materials that had recently transformed the study of Wordsworth, such as Ernest De Selincourt's editions of the 1805 *Prelude* (1926) or of the Wordsworth letters (1935–39). Brooks's *Modern Poetry and the Tradition* (1939) and Tate's essay "Tension in Poetry" (1938) were so recent that they had to be penciled into her "works cited" list when she revised it for a fellowship application the next year.[57] Miles's bibliography also includes recent scholarship by women, notable at a time when the study of English was defined by male clubbiness. On Miles's list are little-known scholars such as Edna Ashton Shearer, Elsie Smith, Annabel Newton, Marian Mead, Marjorie Barstow, Eleanor Sickels, Joan Platt, and Margaret Sherwood, in addition to more well-known ones like Edith Batho, Mary Colum, and Helen Darbishire. The inclusion is at once responsible and visibly proactive, an effort to summon a neglected recent stream of her discipline's work. This was her critical objectivity.

Miles's argument for reading-as-seeing, and for quantitative analysis as a practice of accurate observation, belongs to this animated but unsettled moment in the field, when the masculine force of erudition was giving way to values and activities associated with critical reading (attentiveness, sensitivity, inventiveness, responsiveness), though it sometimes reasserted itself under more traditional authorizing signs. Miles's dissertation on Wordsworth is her first confident foray into this world. A quantitative study of his use of direct statements of emotion, it anatomizes Wordsworth's varied techniques for naming emotion and finds that his attraction to emotion words, rather than being an innovation, grew straight out of eighteenth-century literary theory. The study is founded on word counts covering the length of Wordsworth's career (53,000 lines), along with 1,000-plus line samples of several other major and minor poets. Yet it opens unassumingly, with a set of modest, traditional "readings" that I would like to look at—not because they are particularly surprising but because they help to contextualize what Miles initially means by advocating "continuous observation of" or "straight attention" to "actual poetic content." In these pages we can see her interest in tabulation taking shape, even as the critical technique, as yet defined by careful attention to single poems, remains far from the arithmetical approach that it would lead to.

The first chapter of Miles's dissertation begins in modern criticism's most straightforward mode, by quoting Wordsworth's "Lines Written in Early Spring" in its entirety and then proceeding to a motivated description of the poem. This description is the "closer reading" that Miles sought to teach, a professional technique of attention indebted to *Understanding Poetry*:

> The poem names its feeling in every stanza. It names first the objects of observation, then the observer and the consequent emotion and thought, and that

is its regular stanzaic pattern. From the blended notes to the pleasant thoughts, from the fair works to the grieved heart, from flower to flower's enjoyment, from motion of birds to thrill of pleasure, from budding twigs to pleasure again, and finally to lament, this is the motion of the "Lines Written in Early Spring." The surface texture of the poem is made mainly of the simple names of objects and actions and qualities, and, eminently, the simple names of emotions. And this surface does not differ from the burden of the poem; its burden is, explicitly, its observation, thought, and feeling.[58]

Miles the young critic shows a talent for paraphrase that is partly the mark of her poetic sensibility, partly the signature of late-1930s professionalism. She charts the poem's oscillation between the verifiable world that Wordsworth observes and the affective world that he explores, setting up her own interest in the surface phenomenon of named emotion. "It has often been said of Wordsworth that he was a poet of both inner and outer life," she writes, but this poem is "a remarkably literal illustration of this generalization," expressing "exactly both inner and outer, sensations and soul, and one wonders at finding the whole on the surface." She notes that poems dealing in feelings do not always name those feelings, citing Tennyson's "Break, Break, Break" as an example (and again, quoting it entire): "no word" in the poem "names feeling"; its emotion exists as "aura" rather than as "statement."[59] Modern criticism advises "implying feeling" as "more effective than statement itself," but in Wordsworth, Miles says, a consistent movement from recorded sight to described feeling, from object to named emotion, constitutes a technique that the poet—if not his critics—found poetic.[60]

She next finds the same pattern in two very different kinds of poem—first "The Idiot Boy," then "Tintern Abbey"—developing a patient and uncomplicated inventory of single poems, stretching across the first eleven pages of the dissertation and culminating in a motivated summary:

> In the "Lines Written in Early Spring," there is simple motion back and forth, with the personal accents falling almost regularly on the final lines of stanzas, and the terms of joy and pleasure single and simple. In "The Idiot Boy," there is on the one hand an almost painful stress on the repetition of such single words as joy and happy, in a shadow of ballad refrain; and on the other, a more elaborate and pictorial development of feelings by physical imagery. These phases of technique are all more complex in "Tintern Abbey," with richer, both more abstract and more physical connotation, widening out from units of naming and statement into paragraph pattern upon the theme of feeling and within the field of its vocabulary.[61]

Finally, Miles gestures toward her career-defining method. This affective "vo-cabulary," registered in "three poems of widely differing scope and intent," is used "consistently once in four lines." Sometimes, she adds, Wordsworth draws from it a "plain effect"; sometimes he gets a "more slow and philo-sophical effect" from its "devices of exclamation, iteration, modification, list, metaphor"; but always, he "makes poetry out of it": "Stated emotion gives value to the thousand blended bird notes, to the boy watching the sun shine cold at night, and to the windings of his mother's search for him."[62] I am quoting from Miles's dissertation, rather than from the book that grew out of it, because its less refined approach allows us to see more clearly the pro-fessional idiom that the graduate student was aspiring toward. My summary, I should add, hardly does justice to the confidence and range of the young scholar's engagement with Wordsworth and with Wordsworth criticism, leaving one to wonder what her career might have looked like had she stuck to the genre of the intensive single-author study.

If Miles wouldn't end up devoting her career to monographs on Wordsworth, these passages help to show why. Ransom, as we've seen, turns to Wordsworth for company in the existential nostalgia of "travelling among unknown men." Miles is attracted by something quite opposite, a counter-nostalgic capacity for "straight attention" to the immediate, undistorted field of perception. Miles's Wordsworth, evident in these initial readings of her dis-sertation, is "a literalist of language," whose plain words avoid "figurative con-fusions."[63] Even emotions, she argues, Wordsworth straightforwardly names.

As Miles tells it, she initially struggled with this Wordsworth, "oppressed" by the "flat, obvious, prosaic, literal statement of feeling" that she found when she looked beyond the most taught poems. She "felt that, so exposed, it was poor stuff and poor poetry"—just "the stuff of life" in "so many words— hope, joy, fears, tears, laughter, moods, affections, passions." Modern criticism had located Wordsworth's value in a handful of brief lyrics that matched its criteria ("Rocks and stones and trees—they draw their primacy from our own great concreteness"), whereas historical scholars and appreciative readers had tended to subsume the aesthetic question in an inexact impressionism, or to judge the feeling rather than the poetry's expression of it.[64] Miles instead sought a systematic method to understand "his intentions and his ideas of poetic language." And so she set out to count "the words naming emotion and its signs" in the 53,000 lines of his *Complete Poetical Works*, enumerating around 9,000 such statements—one in every six lines, a ratio that she finds roughly consistent in every volume and through every period of his career (Figure 4).[65]

241

II. SOME POETRY FROM POPE TO WORDSWORTH

Poets	Naming per line	% Types of Context in Amplified (Half: Two Thirds)				
		General	Physical	Bestow-al	Personi-fication	Objecti-fication
Pope Essay on Man	250/1300 - 1/5	51	15	08	11	15
Armstrong Art of Health	170/ 515 - 1/3	21	47	07	14	11
Dodsley I, 200 pp.	840/5000 - 1/6	32	30	07	11	20
Johnson Vanity, London	95/ 560 - 1/6	41	27	03	19	10
Goldsmith Des.Village Traveller	130/ 870 - 1/7	49	31	--	11	09
Gray Works 1750-60 (not traced?)	200/ 750 - 1/4	18	14	16	45	07
Collins Works 1742-47	400/1400 - 1/4	21	31	07	37	04
Beattie Minstrel	300/1100 - 1/4	58	30	11	12	09
Cowper Task I,II,III	370/2450 - 1/7	32	33	21	06	08
Wordsworth Works	9000/53000- 1/6	32	30	15	09	14

Fig. 4. Josephine Miles, "Some Poetry from Pope to Wordsworth," table of "named emotion" in poetry, from "Wordsworth and the Vocabulary of Emotion," MS submitted to University of California Press, 1940. Josephine Miles Papers (BANC MSS 86/107c, carton 1, folder 60). The Bancroft Library, University of California.

Miles's prosaic Wordsworth is a far cry from the poet of the apocalyptic Imagination whom Geoffrey Hartman would introduce to the critical scene in the early 1960s, let alone from the poet of political ambivalence or linguistic indeterminacy that later generations of close readers would study.[66] He is a closer cousin to the "Victorian Wordsworth"—the poet of Nature, of feeling, of human sympathy, whose "wish," Miles says, is to be radically literal. No object, however small or mean, needs transformation or decoration to give it poetic value. It speaks for itself through the literally expressed feelings and thoughts which it awakens in its poet's breast. *Scene* plus *love* plus *prayer* is the literal vocabulary of this poetic report.[67]

Literalness, in her accounting, is akin to the simplicity of the most basic math. A good Wordsworthian poem is a "report" comprising so many verbal addends: scene + love + prayer = his "literal vocabulary." With this perception of Wordsworth's literalism, Miles makes Wordsworth her own. It also informs her reading of the Preface to *Lyrical Ballads* (1800), with its treatment of Thomas Gray's "Sonnet to Mr. Richard West." Wordsworth had printed the sonnet whole, using italics to underscore the artifices of poetic diction and personification that are the opposite of the language of genuine feeling, which he insists is that of ordinary conversation (except for rhyme and meter). Ransom, as we've seen, thinks that the fault of the sonnet is not Gray's reliance on such artifices but his existential failure to accept "natural piety": the speaker ought not have declined nature's invitation. For Miles, the problem is a vocabulary that "thrust[s] out of sight the plain humanities of nature." Wordsworth, she writes, disdains

> an abstract epithetical, rather than an active sympathetical, association of images and feelings. The scenes are "isolated" from direct human response.... It is not that Wordsworth disliked the attribution of emotion to nature; he made such attribution constantly; rather, he disliked any attribution which distorted observation, as the half-personifications of lifting fire, green garments, valleys unsmiling for sabbath well could do. The emotions of nature were shared, sympathetic, universal emotions, not devices of description and decoration which removed the objects from man's response.[68]

What Ransom calls a failure of piety, Miles calls a failure of attention. Ransom focuses on a human speaker so caught up in grief that he can't take solace in nature. Miles focuses on the field of perception, in the sonnet and in Wordsworth's critique of it: the "devices of description and decoration" that "removed the objects from man's response" yield "distorted observation." Ransom reads a troubled human speaker; Miles reads a troubled data field.

For a critic to see a poem clearly, Miles contends, the means "must necessarily be observation as detailed, enumeration as careful, separation of units as distinct, though as provisional, as possible."[69] Yet it doesn't take much to reply that Miles's method is not exactly an objective antidote or "remedy" to Gray's distortions of the data of "nature." Despite her vigorous rhetoric of neutrality, her idiosyncratic understanding of Wordsworth with its fixation on his stability is personal in ways that she does not acknowledge. What she will acknowledge is a post-Imagist taste for Wordsworthian particulars:

> today critics praise the most modern Wordsworth of the "bright blue eggs" and the "single stone" and the "reflex of a star." Indeed he was one of the first to foster such detail and suffered at the hands of his own contemporary critics for such fostering, and it seems just that what he was most blamed for he be now admired for.

But she acknowledges this taste only to join it to a longer story, one defined by Wordsworth's nurturing presence across poetry's steady stylistic evolution:

> The course of poetic history has moved steadily toward more and more im-plicative references, measures, and sentence structures, *and Wordsworth's has been part of that progress.* He prepared, as Cowper and Campbell did, for the flexible pentameters of a Shelley and a Browning, and, as Blake and Burns did, for the significant concreteness of a Keats and a Tennyson. But we lose him if we bring him down all this way in terms of what he has given us that we have used and approved.[70]

Samuel Holt Monk, for one, saw something "subjective and almost private" in the method that Miles calls objective description.[71] I think he means that her commitment to this method, and her cultivated image as a straightfor-ward observer and describer of poetry, seems overdetermined. More than any particular argument that she made about Wordsworth's poetry itself, it was this scientific procedure that defined her role in the animated professional disputes of her day.

Tabular data shaped that role. Graphic representations of poems, poets, and poetic styles embolden Miles's prose, supplementing its authority even while they deflect attention away from it. Wimsatt, who shared her visual proclivities, likened her to a travel guide whose "descriptive tour" yields a commanding prospect.[72] This was a far cry from the patient young reader of single poems who submitted "Wordsworth and the Vocabulary of Emotion" to her dissertation committee. In 1960, well into a career defined by the tabulation of poetic data, Miles would publish an entirely graphic book on the history of poetic style, subtitled *A Tabular View.* "Seen" is her keyword, not just metaphorically or cognitively, but materially. Her critical writing is visibly punctuated by italicized words, sometimes arrayed in garish catalogs meant to stand as evidence in their own right. "Wordsworth and Glitter" (1943) is exemplary. Wordsworth's use of terms such as "*false, accidental, arti-ficial, arbitrary*," Miles proposes, impl[ies] some clear assumed standard of the true, real, essential, pure, natural. What was *real* for Wordsworth? The phrase "a selection of the real language of men" is still the key to the *Lyrical Ballads* Preface, though it has as yet unlocked as many troubles as truths. The labels *excessive, extra-, over-, inflated* imply a standard of normal moderation which is established for Wordsworth by his wider theories. *Insulated, dislocated,* and *inane* imply some doctrine of natural connections. And as for *glare, gloss,* and *glitter,* pictorial as they are, they too are relative to the frame in which they shine, since excessive polish for one poetic may be necessary for another.[73]

Miles's prose is both discursive and a visual display. She shuttles between lists of Wordsworthian words and decontextualized snippets, in a strongly declarative mode that draws confidence from her numerical data. Clear seeing and countable data go hand-in-hand. In *Major Adjectives in English Poetry* (1944), Miles makes general claims based on verbal statistics and is not shy about being coercive, using "We see" no fewer than twenty-five times in just over a hundred pages—practically daring the reader to disagree.[74] Miles's second book, *Pathetic Fallacy in the Nineteenth Century* (1942), pretends to eschew critical practice altogether, summoning "the work of the poets themselves" to track the progressive decline of this particular "vocabulary of emotion." She claims (disingenuously) that her questions about its changing use are to be satisfied by "minor and detailed observation. Little debate, argument, or adding up of signposts into proof is involved."[75]

For all this insisting, Miles does worry about a naïve "trust in data as data, uninterpreted," and in practice she often elaborates her data into objective redescription.[76] The results can sound disarmingly straightforward, as in this unexceptional excerpt:

> The words appearing most often in the volumes of poetry in the bookstalls of the 1640's were these: 4 adjectives, *fair, good, great, sweet*; 10 nouns, *day, earth, eye, god, heart, heaven, love, man, soul, time*; 11 verbs, *bring, come, find, give, go, know, make, see, take, tell, think.* They took logical shape in complex declarative or exclamatory sentences about relationship, and they took melodic form to the beat of the iambic and the couplet. The poetry sounds like this "Divine Mistris" of Carew, in which are a half dozen of these words at work.[77]

Miles then presents Carew's poem itself. She is not content with mere concordancing, or to use her words, "trust in data as data." She comments on "relationship," rhetorical mode, and meter, and not least, gives a careful interpretation of the words she tabulates. In this, Wimsatt perceives "a true lover of poetry," and Ransom senses a uniquely "receptive" poet.

With this same method of calling on "simple facts," Miles elsewhere sifts out a specifically "romantic mode" of poetry:

> by about 1820 most of the leading poets' work was stanzaic in structure, while a half century before it had been mostly linear; the measures were freely trisyllabic where they had been disyllabic; by about 1820 half the major terms, the nouns, adjectives, and verbs most used by the majority, were new terms, characteristically sensory, concrete, and thus often symbolic, while oblique metaphors had taken the place of explicit similes; by about 1820 the sentence structures were more narrative than descriptive, more complex than coordinate, using more verbs and sometimes only half as many adjectives as in the century before. By about 1820, in other words, the substance and structure of poetry had physically altered in determinable degree, to carry a new attitude by a new mode of statement.[78]

This catalog of "facts" is designed to seem incontrovertible—the litany of "by about 1820" and the lists and parallel sentence structures reinforcing the strength of peroration. (Never mind that these resonant summations are debatable. With a wider base to work with and resources of technology, readers of the 2020s could dispute just about every one of these simple facts.)

Debating Miles on this is not my concern here. I am interested less in whether her claims "work" than in how she wields them, and more particularly in what compels her to approach the history of poetry as she does, through the lens of scientific inquiry and with a special fixation on continuity. "The study is based on certain hypotheses," she explains in *The Continuity of Poetic Language* (1951): "that the materials much used and much shared by poets have significance for the description of the poetry of which they are a part; and that time is a force in the establishing of the materials."[79] The *Era* yields poetry's *Mode*. How much this may be true not just of poetry but of literary criticism is an involved question, one that I turn to now.

Evolution and the Stability of Change

Miles's critical base is fundamentally a lexical archive, to be discovered, uncovered, displayed, organized, mobilized. Her very home, on Virginia Street in North Berkeley, is itself an archive: a veritable time capsule, where the books, furnishings, and fixtures bear inanimate witness to her theory of continuity in literary history. On the bookshelf there, tucked into a copy of her award-winning 1974 book *Poetry and Change*, one can find a photocopied biological classification worksheet—key to the nomenclature of species taxonomy and reminder of roiling debates about the autonomy of evolutionary paleontology that took place during Miles's first decade as a scholar.[80] Miles's adventurous investment in those debates, and in paleo-biology generally, has been overshadowed by other extra-disciplinary affiliations: friendships with the mathematician Pauline Sperry and with Betty Scott of the Berkeley "Stat Lab"; concordance work done with the help of the Cory Hall computer lab; collaboration on "factor analysis" and "stylometry" with the sociologist Hanan C. Selvin; thinking about periodization with historian Frederick Teggart's students from the Department of Social Institutions; not to mention various tense involvements with colleagues in the field of linguistics.[81] As early as 1946, however, Henry Wells, reviewing Miles's *Major Adjectives in English Poetry*, sensed the pulsing subcurrent of evolutionary paleontology: "The reader is reminded of his college classes in zoology, where bones were ascribed to certain species and fitted into their proper places." Wells waxes poetic about the marvelous views afforded by Miles's method: "On reading Miss Miles's book one feels like an enterprising fly in a zoological garden who by flitting rapidly from one species to another gains a more catholic view of nature than some less agile specialist who hangs meditating in his cubicle, speculating on one specimen only."[82]

Wells's zoological hunch speaks to the moment that he and Miles shared, one in which evolutionary questions were rampant in the academy. These questions would reach fuller flowering in Miles's next major project, her quantitative studies of poetic language in the fifth decade of each century (individual pamphlets on the 1540s, 1640s, 1740s and 1840s, and 1940s). Collected as *The Continuity of Poetic Language*, these studies argue for a principle of gentle evolutionary stability. An era's major poets, argues Miles, are not its statistical outliers or sui generis but rather expressors of major tendencies. They have been prepared for, systematically, by the "minor" poets of an earlier generation. These, says Miles, are the real innovators. Thus, Thomas Warton (d. 1790), a statistically minor writer, cultivated a germ that would blossom, through adaptations across half a century, into the "majority" style of a proto-Wordsworth:

> The specific, small, observed, new, diffusive were values for Warton. They were not in the main the values of the 1740's, his own early decade, but they were to grow, through the sensibility of Pope and Thomson, through a freer Burns and the ballads, to Wordsworth and Coleridge.[83]

Miles gives the categories "major" and "minor" a numerical basis, arguing for an evolutionary literary history characterized by gradual stylistic change. Through quantification, Miles in effect naturalizes periodization. Miles's evolutionary model of change, which she developed in part through arguments taking place in biology, extends her career-length argument for continuity. It also unsettles a consensus about field autonomy. Against the "commitment to discontinuity" and "historical contrast" that, Ted Underwood has shown, was considered as the mark of literary study's disciplinary prestige, Miles's model rejects notions of "rupture" and "contrast." "Thomas Kuhn has studied the motion of scientific revolutions, and there he says they come by little explosions," she told an interviewer, but "in arts you can see [these connections] quietly happening from just a few to more to more to more to more to the whole thing."[84] It is an argument for historical continuity that is also implicitly an argument for continuity among disciplines, evidenced by her importation of a paleo-evolutionary vocabulary.

Miles's nearest precursor in thinking about literary evolution, medieval philologist John Matthews Manly, had tried out nineteenth-century mutation theory, drawing fire from Wellek and Warren in *Theory of Literature*.[85] Miles, instead, works with a concept of evolution informed by contemporaneous work. *Eras and Modes in English Poetry* echoes both in title and subject George Gaylord Simpson's *Tempo and Mode in Evolution*, a classic of evolutionary paleontology published in 1944 in the Columbia Biological Series.[86] Miles's quantitative examination of "interrelationships of time and manner and . . . qualities and tempos of artistic change" ran parallel to debates about statistical analysis in which Simpson's work participated. In *Tempo and Mode*, Simpson sought to make sense of contradictions presented by the quantitative study of the fossil record by allowing for periods of disequilibrium in between adaptive formations:

> In phyletic evolution equilibrium of the organism-environment system is continuous, or nearly so, although the point of equilibrium may and usually does shift. In quantum evolution equilibrium is lost, and a new equilibrium is reached. There is an interval between the two equilibria, the biological analogue of a quantum, in which the system is unstable and cannot long persist without either falling back to its previous state (rarely or never accomplished in fact), becoming extinct (the usual outcome), or shifting the whole distance to the new equilibrium (quantum evolution, strictly evolution).[87]

Despite quantitatively revealed periods of instability, Simpson argued that "the data special to paleontology, principally patterns and shifts in the fossil record, could be given an evolutionary interpretation."[88] Miles adapts Simpson's argument for the "disequilibric" transitions involved in quantum evolution with her gradualist paradigm of literary change, which emphasizes the stability of the "joints" connecting one era to another. Miles proposes literary change as a form of evolution in the phyletic mode: continuous and avoidant of "the period of disequilibrium" that in quantitative studies of the fossil record "characterized the shift from one adaptive zone to another."[89]

Evolutionary paleontology would have been of interest to Miles in any case, with its attention to deviance and likeness and its imperative to understand how even the most "unlike" creatures fit into a historical pattern. "My interest has been in the similarities, rather than the differences, of poetic practice," she writes, "what in frequency and abundance most centers and joins."[90] The "joints" connecting historical eras are not sites of discontinuity and rupture but small stable parts in a continuous flow. A poem of the late 1930s, "For Futures," explores the calm she valued in transitional periods of evolutionary flux:

> When the lights come on at five o'clock on street corners
> That is Evolution by the bureau of power,
> That is a fine mechanic dealing in futures:
> For the sky is wide and warm upon that hour.
>
> But like the eyes that burned once at sea bottom,
> Widening in the gloom, prepared for light,
> The ornamental standards, the glazed globes softly
> Perceive far off how probable is night.[91]

This readiness for coming change (eyes "at sea bottom, / ... prepared for light"), she argues in *The Continuity of Poetic Language*, is typical of language's slow and steady progression from era to era: "About half the words are steady throughout, and a fourth drops away as another fourth comes in."[92] Extremes of word usage, in her model, resolve naturally, either by vanishing or evolving. Usages that are anomalous gradually grow more common and eventually become dominant.

It was a career-length claim, which adapts the "birth-death model" of speciation and extinction contemporaneously espoused by the evolutionary biologist Ernst Mayr. Miles's last book, published in the mid-1970s, repeats the 50/25/25 ratio once more: "At any one time, half the major shared terms are traditional, a quarter coming into emphasis, a quarter fading. Though some terms persist through all the centuries, often the old give place to the new with a generation or so."[93] The ever-so-slight modification of verbs in Miles's description is apt: poetry's change is a "coming into emphasis," a "fading," a "giving place to," a "dropping away." As with "Evolution by the bureau of power," the lights turn softly on while the sun still shines in order to achieve the gentlest of transitions.

I want to return to the question of periodization because it was the dominant model in academia, both critically and administratively. The Italian historiographer Benedetto Croce contended that "To *think* history is certainly *to divide it into periods*, because thought is organism, dialectic, drama, and as such has its periods, its beginning, its middle, and its end, and all the other ideal pauses that a drama implies and demands," and four decades on, Wellek viewed a contrastive periodization as "certainly one of the main instruments of historical knowledge." To periodize was to recognize "a certain scheme of norms" that had been "realized" in a given era. This was the key, Wellek argued, for an autonomous literary study—though even he betrayed ambivalence about the potentially deadening effects of defining such a scheme: if "the unity of any one period were absolute, the periods would lie next to each other like blocks of stone, without continuity of development."[94]

Early twentieth-century historiography had been strongly influenced by Darwinian ideas. Frederick Teggart, who briefly overlapped with Miles at Berkeley, wrote searchingly about the promise and the challenges of bringing scientific method, and specifically evolutionary theory, to bear on historical and social processes.[95] (In 1943, Teggart's students helped Miles to think through problems of periodization.)[96] Yet Wellek, ever dubious of imported disciplinary discourses, dismissed the influence of evolutionary theory on literary-historical thought. *Theory of Literature* suggests dispensing with the metaphor of "organism" altogether, fretting that it "leads to biological parallels not always relevant." Teggart's evolutionary conception of history "would lead merely to the abolishment of all differences between historical and natural processes, leaving the historian to subsist on borrowings from natural science."[97] The question of disciplinary autonomy was foremost for Wellek, specifically the way investing in the models of other disciplines would "crowd out strictly literary studies": "All distinctions will fall and extraneous criteria will be introduced into literature, and literature will necessarily be judged valuable only insofar as it yields results for this or that neighboring discipline."[98] This problem of "the neighboring discipline" was a crisis for the humanities in general, and for literature departments in particular.

It was with no little relief that by mid-century Wellek considered "evolution" a nearly extinct model for literary history: "Fifty and sixty years ago the concept of evolution dominated literary history; today, at least in the West, it seems to have disappeared almost completely."[99] He lists several early twentieth-century literary scholars who adopted the evolutionary model with no lasting impact, attributing their failure to reliance on an out-of-date (nineteenth-century) concept from an out-of-place discipline (biology) to explain modern works of art. Miles and F. W. Bateson are mentioned in passing as "the only exceptions I know" to "the general rejection of the concept of literary evolution."[100] But it seems that rejection was a process rather than a certain fact, and it is significant that this remains a question today, not only in the abstract, but for administrators looking to reduce faculty lines by collapsing or erasing historical periods or by privileging an ideal of "consilience" serviceable in the process of dismantling programs.

Periodization was the major model of mid-century professional literary study, a "scheme of norms" that charted historical study. It extracts stability from flux, offering "a way," as Timothy Reiss writes, "to break up what is seen as the motion of human life, experience, and events through history into discrete moments that are comprehensible because each *in itself* is not subject to major historical change. Periods become their own agents."[101] Miles's approach, however, locates stability in the long flux itself. The periodizing nostalgia that identifies the discrete spirit of an age while defining aftercomers as exiles from its zeitgeist gives way, in her counter-nostalgic work, to a paradigm in which "the motion" from one age to the next is its own form of comprehensibility.[102] Replacing Wellek's "scheme of norms" with a period's verbal materials in order to establish its dominant "mode," Miles asserts the agency of time, which she says constrains writers in their choice of materials and thus determines the historical trajectory of literature.

Taking issue with Miles's model in 1950, Rosemond Tuve sarcastically cites "the horridly intractable cold fact that the poet, not the Time nor the Reader, wrote the poem—first."[103] But in *Eras and Modes in English Poetry*, Miles would reaffirm her evolutionary paradigm, now focusing on syntax rather than vocabulary and on whole centuries rather than single decades. She calls this a "descriptive principle of period sequence," using proportions of adjectives, nouns, and verbs to identify each era's syntactical norm or "mode."[104] She names these modes *clausal* (active, predicative, verb-driven: Chaucer, Burns, Browning, Hardy), *phrasal* (substantive, lofty, descriptive, noun- and adjective-heavy: Milton, Keats, Tennyson), and *balanced* (classical, intermediate, "an attempt at stasis" in response to one of the two extremes: Spenser, Pope, Wordsworth, Arnold, Eliot). In her purview, the sweep of literary history shows a regular alternation between modes—a resolutely moderate pattern defined by periodical reversions to balance:

> Classifying the poetry written from 1500 to 1900 in accordance with this distinction, we discover a sequence which runs as follows: clausal, clausal, balanced; clausal, clausal, balanced; phrasal, phrasal, balanced; clausal, clausal, balanced. In other words, there are four groups, one in each century, each begun by an extreme and terminated by a balance. No periods of extreme come immediately together, because each is followed by moderation in a balanced form.[105]

Here again, Miles's critical consensus-building is evident. Formerly "we see," it's now an objective "we discover," with the lay of the land there for all to behold.

Though the narrative is given a bit modestly, the stakes are high: "an apparent period of moderation in the latter part of each [century] seems to mediate the preceding and ensuing extremes." The gravitational pull of equilibrium here is immense. While critics could—and did—quibble over which poets got classed with which syntactical modes (is Shelley really a "balanced" poet? does Tennyson have more in common with the "phrasal" Blake than with the "clausal" Browning?), Miles's broad thesis is the stability of literature, with "gradual modifications and renewals" moving inexorably forward "in a single direction."[106] Usage could occasionally *look* back to the past, but it would never *go* back. "The poetry of an era does not in any whole sense return to the poetry of another. The line of development is largely one-directional."[107] (Not the least of continuities is Miles's own critical narrative: the sentence just quoted was published in 1951, the next in 1957.) The "forward motion of usages never allows a mode exactly to recur, but progressively alters materials even while it is recalling structures."[108] As she argues in *The Primary Language of Poetry in the 1940's* (1951), the metaphysical revival (of which she was part) represents not a nostalgic restoration of a previous era's verse but the flowering of a distinctively modern mode, inclusive of but not determined by elements of the past. In this literary version of Dollo's law of irreversibility, by which "a whole organism never reverts completely to a prior phylogenetic stage," Miles's paradigm of continuity distinguishes her from the source- and influence-hunters of early-century comparative literature.[109] There was no "danger of a return to a kind of 19th century philological academicism" (Vivienne Koch's concern regarding Miles's computational studies) any more than of a forward leap into literary macroanalysis (Miles doesn't take on more than she can read, nor even more than she can write; she copies out every line in her "database" by hand). Her method was, in its own time, rather more modest than its massive investment of labor would suggest, self-consciously belonging to her own discipline's gradual evolution.[110]

Miles's professional emergence in the decade of the Modern Synthesis is strangely apt. If, as she contends, "time provides a bond for poets," it does so for scholars too.[111] The debates about evolution, quantitative study of specimens, and disciplinarity, taking place in many different fields, are the historical situation in which she worked. And the exhaustive word-counting notes preserved in Berkeley's Bancroft Library, to which I now turn, convey this sense of limitation in the most material form possible.[112] The work of five decades, undertaken mainly on Miles's enclosed Virginia Street patio, they represent the most literal form of description—the writing down of poems—and provide a striking evidence base for her theory of continuity.

Wordsworth, "instructively realigned"

In 1965, Miles was asked to review a handful of new concordances for *Victorian Studies*.[113] Coming late in a career dedicated to the principle of continuity—and in the midst of a decade defined by (among other things) discontinuity—Miles's review stands out as a meditation on the "disjointed" beauties of an old-fashioned and nearly obsolete form. "A concordance reader is pleased to read such segments as the following," she writes, proceeding to quote what she calls an "aesthetically delightful" selection from Thomas Walsh's *Concordance to the Poems of Wallace Stevens*:

DEJECTED. Dejected his manner to the turbulence. (C29–12
DELAYS. Could ever make them fat, these are delays (Sombre 69–15 P
DELICATE. A minor meeting, facile, deli- cate. (C 35–5
    And not a delicate ether star-impaled (Havana 144–1
    Except for delicate clinkings not ex- plained. (Descrip 340–16
DELICATELY. So delicately blushed, so humbly eyed (C 44–13
DELIGHT. From madness or delight, with- out regard (Monocle 17–12

In a reflexive exercise, Miles ruminates on the aesthetic impact of these "oddly disjointed yet instructively realigned verses." She reads the concordance excerpt, with its "repetitive stress pattern" and "mysterious associations," as a kind of verse form, descending from the anaphora of the syllable "DE" and reorganized according to a "strict alphabetizing of each word" in the work. This agent-less sorting process yields illuminations: "*Dejected, delays, delight*—what do they share but the artifice of the alphabet? Well, also the meaningful *de-* prefix, and a similar stress pattern, both made more vivid by the rigor of their arrangement, even before considering their mysterious associations with manner and madness." Miles imagines "the concordance reader" as a reader-for-pleasure—a reader who, more than merely consulting an informational resource, enjoys its aesthetic effects, such as "a finely implicative breaking up and reconstructing of poetic relations," which produces "marvelous information" as well as a "simple enjoyment from page to page."[114]

What is the relation of Miles's concordance-poetry to the graphs, tables, and other visualizations filling her books and papers? This is the work to which she and her hard-tasked typesetters dedicated so much time, and I'd say that these, too, are at once aesthetic objects and wellsprings of "marvelous information." They possess a beauty of their own, which exceeds their heuristic value or their status as graphic redescriptions of poetry. The aesthetic impact of these published visualizations is poignantly felt when their originals are encountered face-to-face in the Bancroft Library, an abundance of cartons stuffed with sheets of paper, most of them crisscrossed with Miles's tiny, disciplined cursive—the fossil record of her voluminous reading.[115] In part this poignance is a function of the archival space itself, which casts a nostalgic halo over the artifacts held and kept safe there. To see the graphic record of Miles's work, including makeshift tables and on-the-fly calculations that never made it into print, is to understand how enormously creative this visual and handwritten aspect of her scholarly undertaking was. Hardly a comedown from her prose or verse stylings, Miles's handmade visualizations of literary data are like her chiseled poems: designed for complexity and clarity.

In turning to these preserved word counts, I enter into traces of a reading practice, approaching them the way Miles approached passages from a concordance: as if they were a new poetry. Pasanek remarks that "whatever else Miles is doing [through her word counting], she is reading—reading many, many poems in an extremely laborious manner."[116] And whenever Miles is reading, she is also writing—literally writing a poem down (de-scribing it), word by word and line by line, in new designs intended to make "marvelous information" visible. Such "breaking up and restructuring" of poems metaphorically conflates scholarly work with her own painful experiences as a child, when Miles was subjected to "casts and operations and various drastic methods" aimed at easing her acute rheumatoid arthritis. One of these therapies involved breaking the bones throughout her body and resetting them—disjointment with a vengeance.[117] Her disjointing and realigning of poems represents a kind of corporeal refutation to disembodied modes of (Kantian, Arnoldian, and New Critical) disinterest; it is a serious reinvestment in the idea of poetry as a living whole.

This work extends her preference for continuity over its privileged antonym, autonomy. Although this is often overstated—Brooks, for one, conceded organic unity as an ideal often contested by poetic ruptures—autonomy did have prestige, and no little value. Mary Poovey argues that "a model of the autonomous text as an organic whole enabled critics to achieve a degree of methodological rigor that resembled the procedural objectivism of science," with the result that "almost all of the literary criticism published in the U. S. since the 1940s is organized, either explicitly or implicitly, by the trope of the organic whole."[118] Miles, however, has a different notion of poetic wholeness. Wimsatt's calm observation (cited at the outset of this chapter) that Miles eschews "the recent American enterprise of organistic analysis" undersells the point. "I never believed that the work of art was all that autonomous," she said late in life; "I always wanted to keep relating it to other things a little bit—strands of context."[119] This is not the contextualism we're familiar with; Miles's "context" is nothing less than the modifications of syntax across a thousand lines of a single poet's work, or the flows of linguistic change between poet and poet, era and era.

Miles's word-counting notes capture these flows both numerically and visually. Methodically compiled across five decades, they represent a formidable body of critical labor, enshrining her reading of hundreds of poets—from canonical English figures (Chaucer, Shakespeare, Spenser, Donne, Milton, Pope, Wordsworth, Tennyson) to less regarded ones (John Chalkhill, Thomas Campbell, Anna Seward), and from classical authors and medieval balladeers to her contemporaries (including some word counts of her own verse). The small sheets that hold these notes allow us to glimpse an early working expression of modern literary study, from a time when various practices of distance and detachment were being contested.[120] Systematically grouped into bunches of about twenty to thirty octavo-sized loose-leaf sheets, each covered front to back with tiny handwriting, the word counts show poem after poem sorted into columns of adjectives, nouns, and verbs, with slight variations dependent on the specific project. Generally the columns furthest to the left and right (adjectives and verbs) are sporadically filled, while that in the center (nouns) is so tightly crammed as to be nearly unreadable. The final few pages in each bundle are given over to scribbled summation—totals, proportions, equations, tables, and cryptic observations about the meaning of it all.

Before turning to a couple of examples, I need to emphasize again that, for Miles, such word counts served a practical purpose. They were a heuristic device, a tool for systematically sorting the verbal "data" of poetry so that it could be readily extracted and interpreted. Miles never published these counts, and it may not have occurred to her that they would be read outside of this instrumental function (much as it didn't occur to concordance makers that a reader such as Miles would experience *their* work aesthetically). In opening these transcriptions up to an essentially visual reading, I simply mean to show how Miles's conception of poetry as a data field changes the nature of the poetry she studies. To some readers, these transformations of poetic material will recall "*l'art concret*, in particular concrete poetry and its elements of montage, linguistic awareness, and the use of language as acoustic and visual material"; others will find them exceedingly un- or anti-poetic, antagonistic to "the care for thick verbal structure, and for the agencies of construction, that distinguishes literary aesthetics from informational communication."[121]

These extremes of response recall the varieties of disciplinary reading being contested in Miles's day—and still in ours. Like the italicized word lists that feature in her prose, these organized notations of individual poems, giving Miles's counting method a tangible shape, draw attention to the deformative effects of other, mixed reading-and-writing practices: editing, translating, paraphrasing, "deep" close reading, scanning, descriptive appreciation, and digitally assisted visualization, to name just a few.[122]

Neither pictures nor even exactly graphs, these arresting artifacts vividly record an approach to reading that has little use for the paradigms of autonomy and unity. Instead of affirming a lyric's intricate complexity, these materials show Miles's procedure unraveling the lyric, extricating and disordering its verbal units into an artifact that resists (if it doesn't entirely dispense with) reading as we think of it.[123] A brief but representative example of this method involves a late lyric by Wordsworth, "Evening Voluntary XI." The poem in its entirety reads:

> The Crescent-moon, the Star of Love,
> Glories of evening, as ye there are seen
> With but a span of sky between—
> Speak one of you, my doubts remove,
> Which is the attendant Page and which the Queen?[124]

Here is a poem after Miles's own heart—five lines that delicately interrogate the structure of seeing, exploring what it means to describe a constellation and then to name its parts. Miles never "reads" this poem in any of her books, though, content to subsume it as a data point within her poetic spreadsheets. Her system (undertaken in this case by an unnamed research assistant) arrays discrete words in three columns, sorted according to parts of speech but otherwise in the order they appear in the poem—adjectives on the far left, nouns in the middle, verbs on the far right. Words that don't fit these categories are either attached as part of a larger phrase or eliminated. The resulting form is completely different from Wordsworth's original (Figure 5):

	Crescent-moon	Star	
	Love		
	Glories	evening	are seen
	span	sky	
	doubts		speak
			remove
attendant	Page	Queen	is

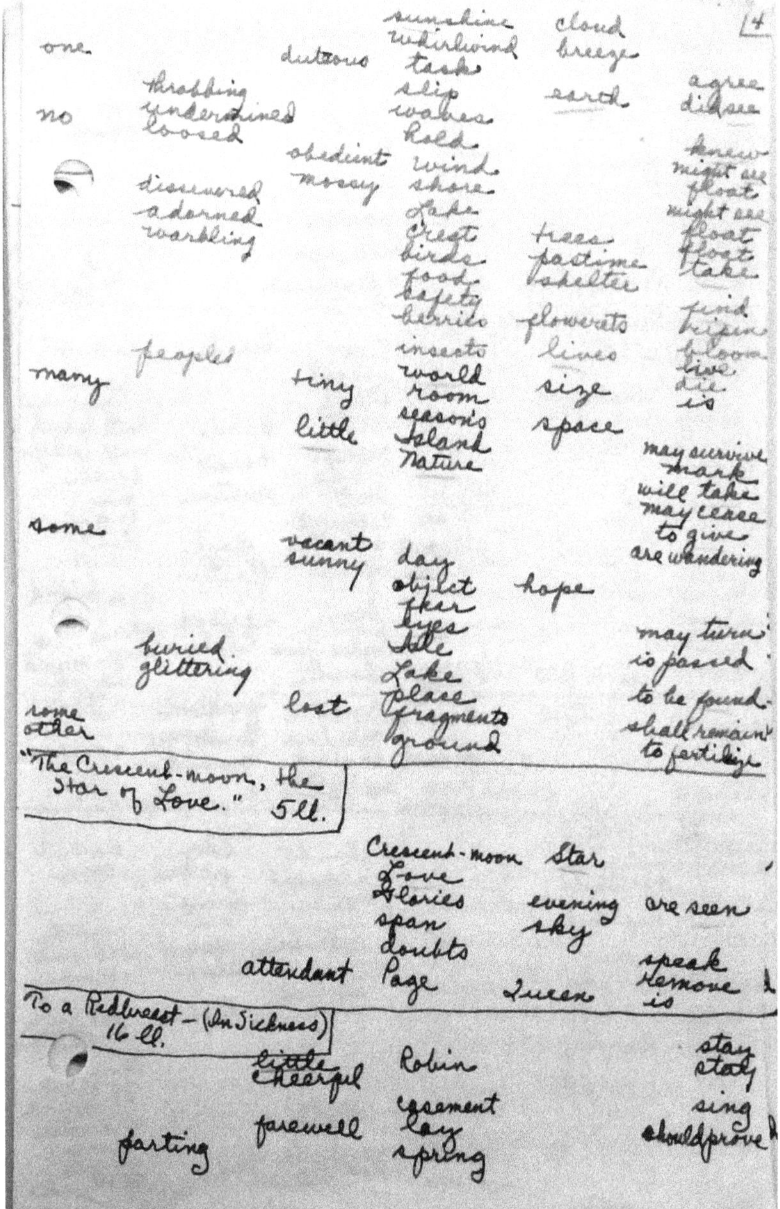

Fig. 5. Word-counting notes for Wordsworth's "The Crescent-moon, the Star of Love," Josephine Miles Papers (BANC MSS 86/107c, carton 6, folder 106). The Bancroft Library, University of California.

Because Wordsworth's poem is so brief, we can see Miles's process at a glance. Most conspicuous is the way white space is inflated on the page. On this whitened ground float words rendered into fundamental building blocks; other words are just eliminated. Wordsworth's line "The Crescent-moon, the Star of Love," is a pair of appositives, each occupying half of the opening tetrameter line. In the Milesian reorganization, *Crescent-moon* and *Star* are adjacent objects perched atop the verbal structure. We see word units, not a poetic line. Instead of reading left to right or line by line, a reader's eye might be drawn, after the initial pairing *moon/star*, toward the noun cluster on the left (*Love, Glories, span, doubts*); or might turn after *span* toward *sky*, drawn by the alliteration, or by the way the concept ("span [of] sky") is incarnated in the blank that separates the words.

The treatment of "Evening Voluntary XI" is a snapshot of the procedure's challenge to the presumed unity of the text-object. Miles seeks, by selectively disjointing the poem into its component parts, to reveal its "encoded discourse" (as Alan Liu might have it).[125] In the process, she radically defamiliarizes the act of reading, representing it as a string of consequential decisions. This is the "stochastic" mode that Lisa Samuels and Jerome McGann point to as the hallmark of "reading backward," a seemingly random yet "highly regulated" reordering of the lyric that effectively defamiliarizes it. By inhibiting the linear reading of a poem and disturbing the impulse to understand the poem as "communicative discourse," Miles's word graphs exemplify what Samuels and McGann call "deformance"; they are at once disruptive of "the poem itself" (i.e., de-forming that neat unity) and indicative of the multifarious ways in which form is constituted.[126]

Yet Miles's word-counting technique has a curiously reparatory effect when it comes to the longer, meditative "Lines composed a few miles above Tintern Abbey." Critics of the 1930s and '40s tended to regard "Tintern Abbey" unfavorably, as doctrinally "unsound" (according to Norman Foerster) or as grammatically and logically "muddled" (William Empson's judgment)—though in her dissertation, Miles treated it as an exercise in evolutionary vocabulary, characterized by "its loving variation": a "play of change over the simple words like joy, fear, grief; a shift from term to synonym, from pictorial to rational image, from description to comparison, from item to list."[127] Miles's graphic rendering of the poem's verbal surface similarly recasts it, projecting a steady progress from discontinuity to stability. Coherence and stability here refer not to the organic body of a poem as disclosed through a careful examination of paradoxes and ambiguities, nor to the unified body of a poem's religious ideas, but to its patterned distribution of grammar. The classic lyric of nostalgic revisiting, which uses memory to open up a new line of development, "Tintern Abbey" is perplexed in this rendering, its multiple temporalities flattened into a graphic display of forward motion.

Miles's notes on "Tintern Abbey" occupy eight sides (four sheets) of paper, with the first recto covering nearly all of the poem's 22-line invocation (Figure 6). The word order of the opening lines is nearly untouched by Miles's method; though the line breaks change, it retains a logical syntax that demonstrates Wordsworth's mastery of "the sentence sound" (to use Frost's term). The ruminative horizontality of Wordsworth's pentameter line, meanwhile, gives way—not surprisingly, given the organizational principle at work—to a more measured and deliberate look:

```
Five          years        have passed
five
              summers
              w. the length
of five
    long                 winters!   + again I hear
rolling       these waters
      [sweet]  mt.-springs
with a (soft)
        inland  murmur            Do I behold
These steep
    + lofty   cliffs
on a wild
    secluded  scene             impress
              thoughts
of more deep  seclusion          + connect
              the landsc.
              w. the quiet
              of the sky¹²⁸
```

In some ways this is unremarkable. It might be said that the new groupings created by the columns draw attention to aspects of Wordsworth's technique—the lulling sibilance and internal rhyming of his adjectives (*five, five, five, long, rolling, sweet, soft, inland, steep, lofty, wild, secluded, deep*), for instance, or the generally insubstantial or fluid quality of his nouns (*years, summers, length, winters, waters, mt.-springs, murmur, thoughts, quiet, sky*, the major exception being *cliffs*). The new proximity of *mt.-springs* to *summers* and *winters* might even encourage us to consider the absence of a "fall" from this pastoral beginning.

Although Miles frequently preserves the structure of the original poem,

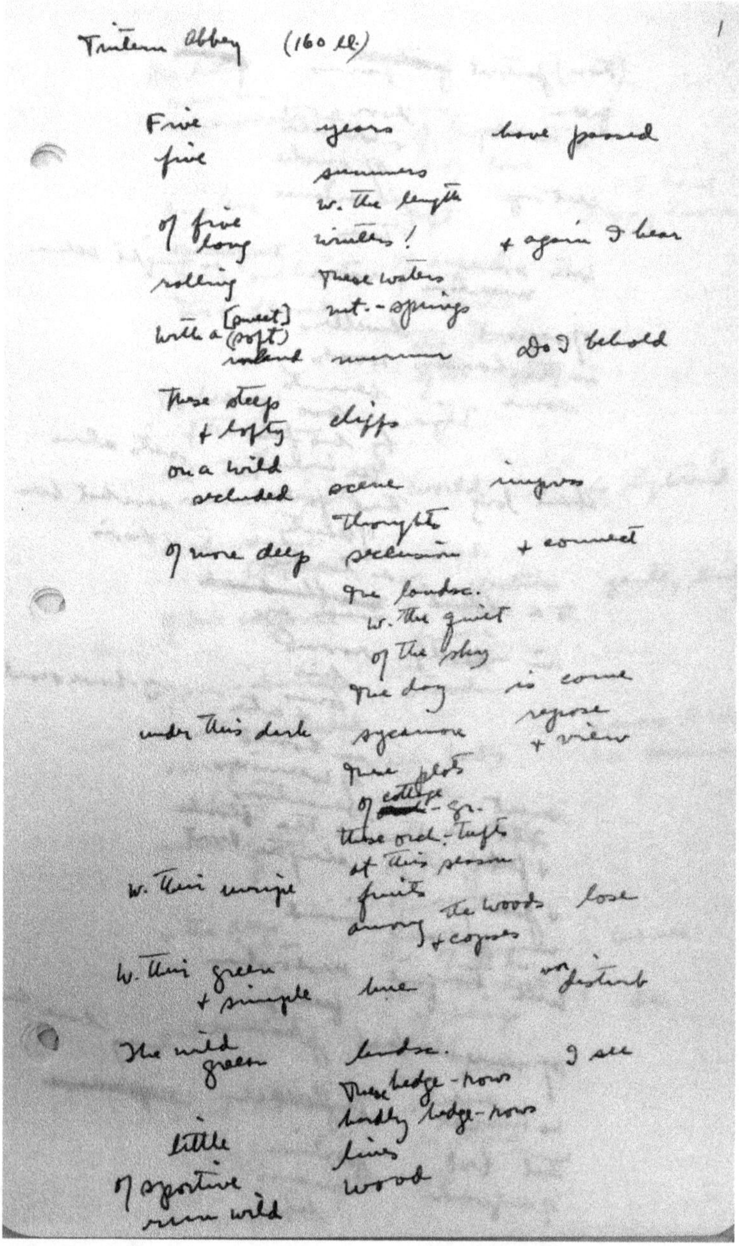

Fig. 6. Josephine Miles, word-counting notes for Wordsworth's "Lines composed a few miles above Tintern Abbey" (beginning), Josephine Miles Papers (BANC MSS 86/107c, carton 6, folder 106). The Bancroft Library, University of California.

there is something unstable about her notation as well. In treating other poems, she sometimes employs mathematical symbols to indicate the repetition of words, but here, where one might expect *five²* or *five³*, her notation keeps in place Wordsworth's incantatory syntax. There are a couple of glitches: she charts *rolling* as an attributive adjective ("waters, rolling from their mountain-springs"), and twice bundles the subjective noun "I" into verb phrases ("and again I hear"; "Do I behold")—minor grammatical events, to be sure, though they predict the instability of what follows. Particularly arresting, in Miles's system, is the way the qualifying manner of the poem's invocation comes through:

<pre>
                                  I see

                     These hedge-rows
                     hardly hedge-rows
        little   lines
     of sportive   wood
        run wild
</pre>

Throughout her scansion, Miles binds demonstrative adjectives to the noun phrase (*these* hedge-rows), and here, once again, she keeps the subjective pronoun with the verb and shifts the participial verb phrase "[has] run wild" to the adjective column. (*Hardly* is technically an adverb, modifying the absent "are.") Such choices remind us that, in this poem of reflection, verbs ("sent up in silence"; "supplied by thought"; "made quiet") tend toward the descriptive while subjectivity is aligned with vision. There is also a formal revelation: just where objective perception breaks down (*these→hardly*), descriptive terms inject some subjectivism into the syntax (*little, sportive, wild*), a fact that is illustrated by the leftward tilt of the graphic rendering.

But for all the verbal completeness of these early passages in Miles's transcription, the poem soon frays. About midway through, it becomes sparser in appearance, a change that reflects the lyric's growing uncertainty. Wordsworth's syntax looks progressively more fickle, less "naturally" connective, with empty verbiage filling the poem at crucial moments where the speaker needs to make his case. This aspect of the poem's syntax is evident enough in Wordsworth's original (indeed all this is in keeping with Miles's admission that the goal of her method is "to record the obvious"):

<pre>
                Though absent long,
        These forms of beauty have not been to me
        As is a landscape to a blind man's eye:
</pre>

But oft, in lonely rooms, and mid the din
Of towns and cities, I have owed to them
In hours of weariness, sensations sweet,
Felt in the blood, and felt along the heart,
And passing even into my purer mind
With tranquil restoration . . .

But it is aggressively registered in Miles's transcription, where verbs drop out almost entirely after *have not been* and *as is*, ceding to a cluster of nouns:

Absent long	these forms	have not been	
	of beauty	as is	
	a landsc.		
to a blind	~~to a blind man's~~		
	man's eye		
in lonely	rooms		
	din		
	towns	I have owed	
	+ cities		
	in hours		
	of weariness		
sweet	sensations		
felt	in the blood		
+ felt	along the heart		
+ passing			
my purer	mind		
with. tranquil	restoration		

The centering of weight in the noun column, soon followed by a tilt to the left-hand/adjective side, is visibly marked by indeterminacy, as Miles struggles to decide (in an ironic ekphrasis) whether "blind man" is a compound noun. Similar unbalancings occur at other moments of transition or strong assertion, such as a sudden verb-heaviness on page two verso ("I dare / to hope / I was / I came / I founded") and again on page three recto ("faint I / nor mourn / nor murmur / have followed / I wd. believe / I have learned / to look").

Part of the formal drama of Wordsworth's lyric is its recalibration of diffuse energies in the concluding apostrophe. The verbal knots or densities that mark much of the central section of Miles's deformance accordingly disappear as the speaker's benediction for his sister summons a renewed harmony among parts of speech:

                              shall e'er prevail
cheerful   faith   or disturb
~~all~~   all   which we behold
full   of blessings   is
                 the moon   let
                      walk   shine
in thy solitary ~~solitary~~   ~~walk~~
The misty   mt. winds   + let
                                    be free
    in after   years   to blow
These wild   ecstasies   shall be
    into a sober pleasure   Matured
                 thy mind   shall be
for all   a mansion
    lovely   forms
                 thy memory   be
                 as a dwelling-place
For all
    Sweet   sounds
                 + harmonies

The intimacy of this address heralds a return of the smooth, Wordsworthian
sentence sound, demonstrated in the balance among the columns of Miles's
notation. Though this balance is temporarily imperiled, one last time, by a
doubtful turn in the discourse ("If solitude, or fear, or pain, or grief . . ."), this
setback amplifies the poem's ultimate sense of recovery:

                    If solitude
                       or fear
                       or pain   should be
                       or grief
                    thy portion
   what healing   thoughts
      of tender   joy   wilt thou
                                        remember
                 my exhortations
                                     If I shd. Be
                    thy voice   I can no more
   thy wild   eyes   hear
                    nor catch

```
                    these gleams
     of past              existence      wilt thou
                                            forget
                      on the banks
     of this delightful   stream        we stood
                      a worshipper
     unwearied           of nature       came
                      in that service   rather say
     with warmer        love
[page break]
     with far deeper  zeal

                                          nor wilt thou
         of holier     love                 then forget
       after many      wanderings
           many        years
                       of absence
       these steep     woods
         + lofty       cliffs
       + this green
          pastoral     landsc.            were to me
       more dear       for thy sake
```

Miles's notation foregrounds the lack of verbs through much of the poem, conveying Wordsworth's emphasis on things and on feelings, rather than on bodily actions. The body in "Tintern Abbey" is more feeling machine than corporal agent—hence the visible grouping of physical verbs around the reminiscence of sensuous boyhood (*came, bounded, led, sought*), and the reliance on cognitive and perceptual verbs here at the end (*remember, hear, forget, say*). Coinciding with a new balance between adjectival, nominal, and verbal elements, this resurgence of a cognitive and perceptual vocabulary signals the poem's wishful recuperative argument—now given an expressive structure—in which losses in the domain of sensuous pleasure are compensated by gains in the domain of imaginative vision.

Miles's method instantiates this structural coherence, realigning "Tintern Abbey" and graphically revealing its verbal patterning as an echo of its central story of stability and continuity. It's a story she's clearly invested in, one that dispenses with the poem's subtle (or unsubtle) signs of doubt. Thus, while Miles calculates Wordsworth's adjective–noun–verb ratio throughout *Lyrical Ballads* as a "classical" 9-16-9, "Tintern Abbey" comes in at an adjective- and noun-heavy (and verb-light) 10-17-7—more akin to the "phrasal" or "sublime" mode of a Milton or Keats. In the poem's closing movement, however, balance returns. Far from a muddle, when transformed into its arrayed parts of speech it visually conveys this ultimate recovery of equipoise, echoing its central argument for continuity: "for such loss, I would believe, / Abundant recompense."

That of course is a famously insecure argument, its uncertainty marked by the mournful intrusion of those three wavering words, "I would believe." An avowedly "superficial" account of poetry's "surfaces" is ill-equipped to detect this characteristic hesitance of Wordsworthian lyric.[129] "Tintern Abbey" in particular resists flowing forward in time; it "halts," Susan Wolfson observes, "in (uncertain) difficult ways: syntactic tortures and self-interruptions, qualifications of *if* and *perhaps*, restraints of *may* and *might*, assertions pouncing on hesitations, affirmations by denial."[130] A "radically literal" style this is not. To be fair, the graphic artifacts found among Miles's word-counting notes are neither substitutes for her method nor criticism in their own right. They are real-time records of a specific kind of reading, and not in themselves readings of poems (as we conceive of this term).

They do, though, bear a relation of contiguity to Miles's technique of semantic analysis, and as such they shed light on that technique's constraints when it comes to a poetry that is more mournful than it admits. The nostalgia marked by the Wordsworthian title verb "revisiting" may be within the ken of such analysis, but there is also "a kind of nostalgia that is . . . integral to the very reading of verse," as Ruth Abbott writes, a "backward-looking attention to the rhythmic past of the poem we are in the middle of reading" as well as an "expectation or even longing for that rhythmic past to return as reading continues."[131] This sense of the poem's existence in time is yet another version of the nostalgic impulse that disciplinary criticism works so hard to repress or deny, its frustrated longing to recover reading's reference—whether historical, linguistic, or otherwise—from the bare traces that language leaves behind. Something gets lost in the laborious effort to deny such losses. The "on-going of experience," as conceptual model for Miles's (steady, diligent, continuous) surveying of thousands upon thousands of lines of poetry, may offer much in clear knowledge, but it invariably loses the nuances discoverable only by halting—such as the soft tones of doubt that, falling between the lines or beneath the surfaces of poems, prove so difficult to count.

Coda

"The method is not statistical; it is merely provisionally descriptive."[132] This tentative note, entering Miles's prose around 1950, conveys a growing sense of her method's inadequacy to some poems. The pejorative phrase "merely descriptive," of course, is only too common in scholarly writing, reflecting description's lack of intellectual prestige, yet because Miles cares for individual words, we ought to note the other half of her doubled adverb: *provisionally*, meaning "temporarily" or "provided only for the moment."[133] The implication is that a numerical description should serve only until a better description becomes possible, and so on, as if all description were bound to give way to further description while always coming up short against the text itself—that old longing, once again, at the core of literary study.

Just as the word "description" contains "writing" in its root, the word "provisional" contains "sight," and its rhetorical diminishment here hints at Miles's declining faith in "merely" seeing as a basis for description. The change in tone may have had something to do with recent reviews of her work on poetry of the 1640s. Prominent scholars like Tuve, Monk, and the linguist James Sledd were less concerned with Miles's counting technique in itself ("there is no reason why criticism should not use any method it can lay its hand upon," conceded Tuve) than with her specific use of it: if "statistical methods are chosen, we must of course apply them with the rigor their nature demands."[134] They questioned Miles's rigor on several fronts, including her choice of representative texts (1640s republications of poems written many decades earlier, *The Dunciad* as the specimen of 1740s-era Pope, Eliot's *Four Quartets* for the 1940s) and her reliance on the line as the basic unit for measuring verbal frequencies (which played loose with the fact that some lines are longer or bear more structural weight than others).[135] The "method somehow seems not quite adequate to the analysis of poetry," chided Monk, and Tuve also pointed to the discrepancy between method and analysis, citing Miles's prose commentaries as "extra-to the method."[136] Ironically, whereas formalist critics tended to give Miles a pass for her method because they found her a sensitive reader, historicists saw the dichotomy between her tables and her prose as a source of embarrassment, exposing a quaint "poet's criticism" beneath the (insufficiently rigorous) data.[137]

This retreat to a qualified mode of description occurs fairly rapidly at the end of her pamphlet on *The Primary Language of Poetry in the 1740's and 1840's*, her follow-up to the study of the 1640s which Tuve, Monk, and some others had so harshly assessed. The final paragraph begins with a confident catalog of what statistical study makes "possible to observe":

> It is possible to observe, as we have here, that all the traits of language, its sound, its sentence structure, and its vocabulary, alter together, over a period of time like a century, to compose a new major pattern with a certain stability and con-

tinuity. It is possible to observe how specifically the alterations are commented on and encouraged by the critics of the time; how conscious is the process.[138]

The confidence gained from an ostensibly clear line of sight, though, brings Miles to an impasse: "But first we must know much more." Rhetorically humbled, she ends the book in a recessive register: "This present study has found certain minimum facts," she writes, which "for all their ramifications in this text, are not adequate to suggest definitions; but they should be adequate to provide a small part of definition when poetry is read in the light of its whole world."[139]

Just a year later, Miles would positively revalue her accounting of the surface. Conceding that "what is newly counted might well have been guessed" (what Wells more harshly called her "distressingly familiar conclusions"), she says, "But this is just my interest, in a sense to record the obvious. . . . I do not quote poems to reveal new entities, but rather to repeat, over and over, the main lines of agreements in the various forms they take."[140] This privileging of tautology and repetition—another inheritance from Wordsworth, key to the *Lyrical Ballads* "experiment"—feeds her larger thesis about historical continuity: "the obvious, to-be-guessed continuities need still to be seen in the shades of their combination," because being "so basic to every poem" they become "difficult to observe."[141] This difficulty, she argues, is a modern Wordsworthian concern:

> The power of the Wordsworthian mode for our day is the mind's excursive power, the change and commotion in the world of spirit. In its harmonious regularity and cumulative stress it demands meditation; in its accords, sympathy; in its balanced literalness, a steady observation. *All these are difficult for us.* An age of symbol, passion, and irony is not much good at a common view or a general concern or even a strong abstract statement in a determined meter. But we can learn. And Wordsworth's can be the poetry not only from which, but toward which, we proceed.[142]

Miles considers Wordsworth as Brooks had, in terms of "today." Whereas she had accused Brooks of "los[ing] Wordsworth" by evaluating him in terms of present tastes, here she invests with some urgency in Wordsworth's pedagogical power "for us." She points specifically to the connective character of Wordsworth's poetry, its understated sense of continuity across "the long dull stretches of verse" that a poet "of more than fifty thousand lines is apt to write."[143] This thoroughgoing dedication to continuities "difficult to observe"—steady progress and slow change, present blossomings and new emergences—doubles as Miles's rejection of autonomy. ("It breaks up the idea of autonomy, and it goes to the idea of continuity": this was her comment on Jonathan Culler's *Structuralist Poetics*.)[144]

In a minor register, Miles's career-long thesis reflects some of the challenging aspects of her lived experience—a relation that she herself never invoked, and which I have only hinted at. Miles did not identify in terms of her disability (though others identified her), and she declined to participate in the activist struggle for disability rights (though the Independent Living Movement started in Berkeley).[145] Still, it must be acknowledged that autonomy was a profoundly troubled notion for her. Throughout her adult life, arthritic flareups would stiffen her body, making it impossible to walk and challenging even to operate a wheelchair. She lived with her mother for most of her life and often had to be carried by students in and out of the classrooms where she taught.[146] Her early poems press on questions of personal independence and aesthetic autonomy, conflating mental and bodily exertions such that risking an idea can feel like stepping gingerly onto a twig in the underbrush (as in her poem "Scholarly Procedure").[147] Another poem describes a literature class as the site of a collective "straining of effort" among colleagues, intellectual pursuit doubling as a fantasy of physical nimbleness that leaves participants "breathless with promise of our own conclusion." But the round seminar table is more than an image of escape; it is "a circle we are bound for," which is to say that it is just the sort of paradoxical world that Miles herself inhabited.[148] "All our roads go nowhere," she begins "On Inhabiting an Orange," another early lyric that artfully limns the tension between aspiration and constraint:

> All our footsteps, set to make
>   Metric advance,
>   Lapse into arcs in deference
>   To circumstance.[149]

There is, as we have already seen, a guardedness or distance in Miles's poetry and scholarly prose, expressed here as "deference / To circumstance," and elsewhere as submission to history's "forward-carrying force."[150]

This makes her a peculiar object of our recent critical nostalgia. Much of this book has explored the various forms of attachment that define modern reading practices and our ways of thinking about the past. But in Miles we encounter a multifaceted sense of *detachment*: a distance from the will to unity, from the care for autonomy, from conventional ways of thinking about English. Her word-counting method, her critique of organicism, and her argument for continuity all seem to invite biographical study, and yet she never quite authorizes such an approach. She remains elusive and difficult to locate in her work. Three-quarters of a century later, these distances complicate efforts to recover Miles for our new histories of literary study, evoking a lost mode of resistance to her era's disciplinary orthodoxies and signaling a need—one that she herself foresaw—for new ways to search the past of criticism.

Epilogue:
The Fields of Learning

In 1951 William K. Wimsatt, then chair of the MLA's division on Poetics and Literary Theory, wrote to Josephine Miles asking if she could fly to Detroit to help him with that year's meeting. He pointed to the generous travel funding he believed was provided by West Coast universities: "I understand that you people at California get financial backing for such trips—as, alas, we do not."[1] It's a somewhat unremarkable piece of professional correspondence, setting aside the fact (likely unbeknownst to Wimsatt) that funding would not have been Miles's main obstacle to travel. But it also sheds light on its moment. Wimsatt perceived the large public research university as an institution on the rise, and he found a symbol for that emergence, for the sense of an old dispensation giving way to a new one, in "California": an idealized horizon where ocean and highway together signify endless possibilities of movement, the epitome of what Celeste Langan calls "the ideology of freedom as automobility."[2] Surely a young professor *there*, of all places, could go wherever she wished.

The anecdote is slight enough in itself, yet it touches on a pair of themes that have coursed through this book's chapters. Wimsatt's mention of Miles's home base points to a growing slippage between regional and professional forms of belonging in the mid-century academy—what Christopher Jencks and David Riesman have termed "the academic revolution" of the 1950s and '60s.[3] Wimsatt's reference to the research funding provided by the University of California, meanwhile, calls attention to the emergence of the signature postwar American institution, soon to be theorized by Clark Kerr as the "multiversity," which was altering the landscape of higher education even as it incorporated and simulated certain pastoral features of the traditional private colleges.[4]

John Crowe Ransom and Josephine Miles, subjects of this book's first and last chapters, dwell on these themes from opposite perspectives and with very different feelings. For Ransom, writing about Louisiana State University in the early 1930s, the transformation of an old Baton Rouge plantation into a state-run and nationally oriented university is ironic, suffusing the outwardly pastoral collegiate setting with the violence of history and incongruities of progress. For Miles, working at California's flagship institution in the volatile 1960s, pastoral is invoked not in reference to a façade of leafy quads and ivied stones but in praise of a forward-moving knowledge infrastructure: the disciplines, those professional fields of learning tilled by scholars, which together yield the contemporary university's intellectual harvest. For both Ransom and Miles, romantic organicism looms large. Ransom's caustic representation of the modern state university, artificially "planted" atop a slave plantation, is practically a parody of the Coleridgean vision of "multeity in unity," that organic ideal in which things are "for the most part in their right places."[5] Miles's "multeity," however, defines a distinctly counter-nostalgic conception, in which the university's many parts are held together not organically but administratively, a stable mechanism that carries its own warming promise of a secure institutional home.

The juxtaposition between these divergent institutional pastorals, one written in the Deep South of the 1930s and one written on the West Coast in the 1960s, pits a backward-looking agrarianism against a cautious enthusiasm about modern institutions. But this is no simple progress narrative: Ransom's nostalgic mode is tinged with his characteristic irony, while Miles's enthusiasm about the multiversity papers over some of that institution's darker elements. Together, they point forward to a new age of the university that was in some sense catalyzed by the ostensibly insular engagements with romantic lyric that this book has explored—an irony that I reflect on in my closing pages.

"progress is often destruction"

In "The Aesthetic of Regionalism" (1934), John Crowe Ransom dwells with a complicated nostalgia on the modern American university, in a representation charged with Agrarianism's racial politics.[6] From the very start, the essay reads as dramatic monologue, written in the persona of an intellectual outsider who refers to himself in the third person as, by turns, a "philosophical regionalist," a "traveling regionalist," a "distant eclectic," and an "expert traveler." Whether riding the rails through rural New Mexico on the way to an academic conference, or driving through the Mississippi Delta en route to give a lecture, this speaker—an ironized version of Ransom himself—espouses the precious regionalism of a privileged white class, whose members dabble in local cultures like wine connoisseurs sampling vintages of different areas, some "more charming than others."[7] Folding its view of the other into a narcissistic projection of his own desires, this is regionalism *as an aesthetic*, and a specifically Kantian one at that, where the objects are framed and appreciated from an enabling vehicular distance.

The regionalism of Louisiana—as if there were only one—provides the centerpiece of the essay's closing pages, as Ransom heads toward Baton Rouge to give a talk at the new state university campus. Louisiana is introduced as if it were an Appellation of Origin, the "most distinct [regionalism] among the Deep South varieties," "charming" both in natural features ("its live-oaks hung with moss, its sub-tropical flora, its waters, its soft air") and cultural ones ("the finish of its old French features, and its domestic architecture, which is not surpassed in the world").[8] Ransom makes no secret of the fact that he experiences the place as an outsider. He is a "visiting regionalist in Baton Rouge," and moreover an academic—though he consigns this fact to the distance of a footnote, telling the reader that the essay as a whole was "presented as a speech to The Graduate Club of Louisiana State University at Baton Rouge."[9] The significance of his academic status permeates the essay, clarifying its dramatic persona as a specifically professorial role, characterized by scholarly detachment.

A trio of interrelated developments in Baton Rouge's built landscape organize the essay's conclusion: the gaudy state capitol; next to it, the abandoned U.S. Army barracks (also the former site of the state university); and two miles south, the new university campus. Ransom's account of these three sites is an exercise in Agrarian valuation.[10] The description of the capitol dominates, though it really exists in the end to set off a rumination on the two other sites. In Ransom's account, the capitol is defined by its extravagance and eclecticism: "The State of Louisiana took its bag and went shopping in the biggest market; it came back with New York artists, French and Italian marbles, African mahogany, Vesuvian lava for the paving."[11] T. S. Eliot had dubiously praised the South as "less industrialised and less invaded by foreign races," yet in this depiction of the capitol skyscraper, industrialism and cosmopolitanism find their material expression.[12] Ransom writes that the capitol "could almost as easily stand in Topeka or Harrisburg or Sacramento as in Baton Rouge."[13] The repressed doppelgänger, as so often in Agrarian xenophobic representation, is the region's formerly enslaved population, brought in from abroad.

Xenophobia takes many forms in Agrarian writing: fear of incursion by mechanical industry and capitalist profiteers; fear of the city as an economic center that would draw white farmers away from the land; fear of racial and cultural others who might usurp upon white rural culture. Here it crystallizes in the set-piece description of the capitol, a hodgepodge of materials from other places. Posed against this "shameless eclecticism," though, is the idyllic new university campus, whose "builders," Ransom writes, "conceived a harmonious plan for the campus in a modified Spanish" which "suits the regional landscape, and is not altogether foreign to the regional history." Compared to the "bold" and "sumptuous" state capitol building, introduced in the very next sentence, Louisiana State's "harmonious" campus plan is the very image of regional propriety, defined by Robert Penn Warren as an effort to realize an "appropriate relation to the past."[14]

As Ransom's tortured litotes suggests, however, this "example of regional architecture perfectly adapted to its environment" is more complicated than it initially appears.[15] In that phrase, "not altogether foreign," we hear the unreliable voice of the traveling regionalist, whose casual nominalization ("a modified Spanish") reflects his connoisseur-like approach. The material realities of higher education are kept at arm's length. The university's physical move from downtown's historically rich army barracks to an old plantation plot two miles away had been prompted, we are told, by a need for "more room and larger buildings": at four thousand students and growing, the much larger "plant of the new University" required more "economical" buildings than the barracks could provide.[16] Its transplantation was in keeping with what Ransom elsewhere calls the modern state's "forward-looking and hundred per-cent Americanism," but here that "Americanism" is obscured in the contrast with the ostentatiously non-regional capitol.[17]

Compare this outsider's account of Baton Rouge architecture to an insider's account of Vanderbilt University, written by Ransom's friend and fellow Agrarian Donald Davidson. Whereas Ransom treats the co-mixture between institutional necessity and regional environment as a matter of uneasy compromise, Davidson gives a romantic view of Vanderbilt. Unlike its large public counterpart in Chapel Hill, a hub for New South advocates (like Howard Odum) which Davidson disdained as an essentially Northern and pluralist institution, Vanderbilt is rendered as organic to the South. Davidson first figures higher education as a formal garden, containing growths that are imported from around the world:

> The academic enclosure was intended—as all universities are—to be a center of diffusion of knowledge brought in from points far distant in time and space—from here, there, and yonder—from anywhere but the local terrain—to be handed out again, neatly processed, for the benefit of the local inhabitants.

In the formal garden that is Vanderbilt, however, "the local terrain" asserts itself, leading to "something native and spontaneous—an infusion from the surrounding country into our academic enclosure":

The South did not sit down quietly and wait to be benefited by Vanderbilt University. It dropped seeds within the enclosure. Unbidden, they grew, while Chancellor Kirkland and the Board of Trust were busy with other matters. And presently the University, considerably to its surprise, suddenly found itself diffusing something it had never officially provided for: the fruit of a literary tradition risen out of native stock, unregistered, unscheduled, certainly unaccredited, but all the same hardy, insistently proliferous, and sometimes as prickly as black locust.[18]

In presenting literary study at Vanderbilt as an "unbidden," "hardy," and "proliferous" growth, Davidson acts out a rural, nativist fantasy of the elite national university. His Vanderbilt is both institutional and pastoral, though its pastoral aspects overcome its institutional necessities. Knowledge that is "never officially provided for," that is "unregistered, unscheduled, certainly unaccredited," grows organically like "fruit" from "native stock," while administrators and bureaucratic managers keep "busy with other matters." Mark McGurl describes the challenge of authenticity for large regional institutions in the 1930s: how to "go national and also, as we say, keep it real?"[19] Davidson's is the pastoral of the university at its most extreme, designed to preserve Vanderbilt's national stature while staking some of that stature on its authentic regionalism. In Ransom's dramatized critique, by contrast, a word like "plant" cedes all of its organic connotations to the language of industry: "the much larger *plant* of the new university." It also calls attention to the historically scarred land upon which this "larger plant" was planted: the Gartness Plantation.

The word "campus," summoning the semi-rural ideal of American higher education, is etymologically rooted in the Latin for "field"; by the turn of the twentieth century, more than three-quarters of American colleges and universities were using "campus" to describe their grounds.[20] In Ransom's account, though, where the "campus" is described as a technical "plant" located on a former "plantation," the pastoral connotation is a grotesque perversion of rural innocence. The irony is deepened by the complex backstory of the particular campus he describes. As he certainly knew (or at least learned during his visit to Baton Rouge), the renowned Olmsted firm had originally been tapped to design the grounds of Louisiana State. This was already problematic for the aesthetic of regionalism, given that the Olmsted name was indistinguishable from the semi-rural character of American public space. Grand walking parks in numerous American cities owed their landscape aesthetics to Frederick Law Olmsted and his sons, and the college design boom of the early twentieth century made the "Olmsted Look" a ubiquitous feature of American academia. Standing on the Louisiana State quadrangle, one could almost as easily be standing in Rochester or Stanford as in Baton Rouge.[21]

Olmsted envisioned college as a parklike setting, rooted in the natural terrain and adaptable to other terrains, and his family firm designed no fewer than 250 U.S. universities between the late 1800s and the 1950s. The Olmsteds' adaptable regional aesthetic leads Schryer to the trenchant observation that Ransom identifies "the local region" with "the history of the research university in the United States," an identification that anticipates both his move to Kenyon and the professionalist claims of "Criticism, Inc." Yet to observe with Schryer that "The architecture of Louisiana State University is no more indigenous to Baton Rouge than the architecture of the state capitol" is also to discern Ransom's central irony, for regionalism itself, in "The Aesthetic of Regionalism," is a condition of vitiation.[22] The moment a regionalism is detected, it is already of a second order. As Ransom says elsewhere in the essay: "we scarcely know for certain of any regional culture anywhere that can be called, in strictness, 'indigenous.' A regional culture ordinarily represents an importation, or series of importations, that has been lived with and adapted for so long that finally it fits, and looks 'native.' "[23] The aesthetic compromise of the university's builders with the local environment reflects this essential inauthenticity of Ransom's regionalist aesthetic, which sits at a distance from the indigenous (it only "*looks* 'native'") and represents an adaptation over time (it only "*finally* . . . fits").[24]

As it turns out, the principal style of the Baton Rouge campus that Ransom visited in 1933 was not a "modified Spanish" at all. In a classic Louisiana story, the state legislature in 1922 refused to pay the Olmsted firm for its six years of work on the campus design. A German-born architect named Theodore Link, brought in to complete the design, scrapped much of the Olmsteds' landscape-based plan and redesigned three-fourths of the university's main buildings in an Italian Renaissance style based on the Venetian architect Andrea Palladio. After just a year, Link passed away, and the university hired yet another firm, the New Orleans–based Wogan and Bernard, to finish. The "modified Spanish" that Ransom's philosophical regionalist so much admires, which likely refers to the "vaguely Spanish Mission–style buildings" that appear in the Olmsteds' original design plans, is, as it happens, nothing more than an archival relic.[25] To look only slightly beneath the surface of Ransom's prose is to confront the comic mistakenness of his academic traveler.

At the essay's end, Ransom inserts a third term into the unstable dyad of campus and capitol: the city's old army barracks. Built around 1820 on what are now the capitol grounds, the barracks became part of the State University complex in 1886; Ransom alludes to them in his first mention of "the new buildings of the State University":

> The old buildings still stand, or at least the "Barracks" do, in the heart of the city; the others had to go, since the city needed their room, and the University, with four thousand students, needed still more room and larger buildings. The old buildings are simple, genuine, and moving; precisely the sort of thing that would make a European town famous among the tourists. When the much larger plant of the new University was constructed it seems probable that buildings on the order of the Barracks but on the new scale would not have been economical, nor successful. . . .[26]

The barracks convey a sense of dislocation without ever having been moved themselves. They are out of place because the place itself has changed. Built on the site of former French, British, and Spanish forts, they were an important army base during the Mexican-American War and then passed hands from the Union to the Confederacy and back to the Union in the early 1860s. They evoke the area's complex history, but only residually. They "still stand," but in a context to which they bear no reference, metonymic for what has vanished: the "old buildings" that "had to go" because the growing city and then the growing university needed the space. As opposed to the "new buildings" of a university whose increasing enrollments demanded "still more room," these "old buildings" are "simple, genuine, and moving." Ransom adds with a wink that they are "precisely the sort of thing that would make a European town famous among the tourists"—famous, that is, among traveling regionalists like himself, who take the inaccurate measure of an environment they do not fully grasp.[27]

The barracks, however, return at essay's end as the symbol of a deeper historical loss. The "harmonious plan" and "modified Spanish" of the new university might seem to offer the main contrast with Huey Long's audacious Capitol skyscraper, but this other "strange juxtaposition" reveals how much the new campus and the new Capitol building actually have in common. The regionalist has little use for the big new institution, and in the essay's closing sentence, he shunts aside the university altogether to recover an original contrast between the modest, low-lying barracks and the "magnificent indiscretion" soaring over them. For the nostalgic traveler, what resonates is "the ironic perpetuation of the old Barracks"—not the barracks themselves, but the fact of their improbable survival, in a place that no longer has any use for them. Originally built to house itinerant people, their residual power is their condition of obsolescence. Like poetry in its "distal" relation to lyric's "prose core," discussed in Chapter 1, the barracks are at once the essence of the place, holding within themselves the region's prosy history, and simultaneously out of place, foreign to the logic of the modern and practical state. To employ the terms of Ransom's poetics, they are "an order of existence which [is] crumbling." Their unlikely survival bespeaks the Agrarian regionalist's "understanding that what is called progress is often destruction"—the elegiac closing words of "The Aesthetic of Regionalism."[28]

"The motion is forward"

Ransom's regionalism gravitates toward the "simple, genuine, and moving" forms of the pre-modern university. Josephine Miles's regionalism, by contrast, is institutionalist and deliberately non-nostalgic. "The special qualities of this region are not qualities of nostalgia and regret," she writes of her home state of California: "The motion is forward—toward horizons, toward speculation."[29] Automobility may have been California's ideology of freedom, but for Miles the West Coast with its large investments in research and public education brought about a different kind of freedom—call it a methodological freedom, or a freedom from the stifling autonomy of a single discipline, which confirmed new forms of connection and community. Though her seclusion out West was enforced by circumstances that made travel hard, distance was also connection in this new world of academic exchange, and the topographical expanse separating her from the early epicenters of literary close reading augmented the intellectual mobility encouraged by her institutional environment. Statistical knowledge was a vehicle for forward motion, a means of critiquing and cutting loose from fixed positions. It promised "a view from nowhere" that, particularly as a woman with a disability, Miles seemed to be denied. And it put her in the conversation (the view from nowhere was still, after all, a view).[30]

Counter to the typical associations of California, Miles did not fantasize about crossing the sea, did not tap into that reverse-nostalgia which looks dreamingly toward the horizon's abstract future. Instead, California represented for her a secure boundary. Of her poem "After This, Sea," she said that "it is about how it feels to be living at the edge of a continent as we do here."[31] The poem itself begins by invoking this coastal limit:

This is as far as the land goes, after this it is sea.
This is where my father stopped, being no sailor;
Being no Beowulf nor orient-spice hungry,
Here he let horizons come quietly to rest.[32]

As in "On Inhabiting an Orange," which describes an ascent that gently presses up against the atmospheric limit, Miles's California is defined by its location "at the edge of the continent." The storied Californian horizon contains the sense of an ending, bounded by an untraversable force that re-directs to habitable land and a known past: "here we are at bay, / Facing back on the known street and roof, all flight / Spent."[33]

The repeated rebound effect depicted here, turning back from the ocean and toward "the known street," is essentially Milesian.[34] As an undergrad-uate she'd been discouraged by a professor who said that "nobody could write a poem who couldn't take to the road": "I was in a sense doomed," she recalled, "by not riding the freights."[35] But Miles moved in other ways. When Cleanth Brooks and Robert Penn Warren published her poems in the *Southern Review* along with an admiring review by Morton Zabel (editor of *Poetry Magazine*), she experienced it as a salutary relocation, from her own California to a new and invigorating "poetic world": "In Los Angeles it is hard to know one's place in any poetic world, and in the one Mr. Zabel puts me in there's more oxygen than I'd expect to have capacity for."[36] Straying from "the work itself" by ranging across different modes of knowledge, too, she found transporting and reassuring: Miles once described her restlessness in the face of "whole poems" so vivid that she turned to extra-textual "facts" for relief from them.[37] When she thought about her Berkeley graduate stu-dents, she similarly described the intellectual energy of scholarly conversation as growing out of a frustrated encounter with limitation:

> I act as adviser to graduate students; after they have their papers settled, they ask me where is the nearest beach. I tell them this is not southern California and they are disappointed; they have their swimming suits on under their jeans. They are all ready to plunge. But from this disappointment they will recover in time for their first classes. This is the momentum, the energy, brought to the promised land; whatever promises are broken, the energy builds on the original imagination.[38]

Repelled from the hoped-for "plunge," students return to "the promised land" of the seminar table, where movement is intellectualized, its energies combustible: "Bent with the need / The words take speed / And we lean and follow where they lead."[39]

As we saw in Chapter 5, Miles centers her critique of organicism in a difficult-to-observe continuity—the Wordsworthian "on-going of experi-ence." For Ransom, Wordsworth's "My Heart Leaps Up" acts as a salve to his chronic psychic alienation and homelessness; the "natural piety" that he reads into the poet's "days bound each to each" softens the jarring discontinuities of modern life. For Miles, less inclined to consider a discrete *each* and *each*, it is the general principle of evolution, of continuity with what is already established, that serves for piety. This is, she argues, how a profession works:

> The fact that the major terms and structures of poets in any one time are so alike suggests a profession of poetry, within a profession of literature, an ongoing art in which individuals share to various degrees, forming, shaping, and guiding to their own individual purposes, but never far from center, as if the art were a culture of its own, moving in expression of the culture.[40]

The character of poetry at "any one time" evolves with the culture and reflects the regulated workings of "a profession of literature." This intrinsic constraint ("never far from center") paradoxically doubles as a reassuring freedom, as Miles shores herself against extremes of instability by piously locating herself in her own profession's "forward-carrying" stream.[41]

This stream was no gently gliding and recursive romantic river but a tributary of a much larger body: the multiversity, an institution composed of many different communities (not just one) and held together through an administrative apparatus (and not through common backgrounds, knowledges, and values). In this multidimensional and massively productive "city of intellect," less high-minded in conception than Cardinal Newman's liberal "Idea," a management model of individual and complementary colleges, schools, and divisions would yield marketable knowledge.[42] The realization of Kerr's 1960 Master Plan was to stoke controversy in the years following, when the university's intimacy with state authority combined with what some perceived as a reduction of community members to academic production units. But in its dual promise of egalitarianism and excellence, his mechanistic ideal wove a powerful spell. A "university must serve a knowledge explosion and a population explosion simultaneously," Kerr wrote, and as Miles admiringly concurred, what a place like Berkeley "does best, and what few universities in the country or the world do better," is allow those "who possess insight and curiosity enough to learn at the very frontiers of knowledge" to achieve their "birthright" of an "education at every point adapted to those most eager to explore the unknowns."[43]

Miles's optimism runs counter to the prevailing narrative of critical university studies, which tells us that the pastoral image of the university faded as an emergent "hermeneutics of suspicion" coincided with the institutional suspicion articulated by thinkers like Althusser and Foucault.[44] This suspicion had crucially been shaped by Kerr's account of the American multiversity as a pluralistic arm of the state, coterminous with intellectual power, economic might, and military force: "The university and segments of industry are becoming more and more alike," he wrote in *The Uses of the University*; "The two worlds are merging, physically and psychologically."[45] Miles was not unaware of these dangers, and her fidelity to the concept of the multiversity was hardly absolute. After the 1960s she could deride Berkeley as essentially "a functioning financial body . . . interested in facts and forces."[46] In a later lyric called "Retrospective," she considers her complicity with the university's military entanglements:

> Once I didn't think that much about making the bomb.
> In the halls I turned
> Away from the machinists who made it,
> I said sorry
> To Japanese friends, especially one from Hiroshima
> . . .
> Look what I have been doing,
> I have been making the bomb, creating,
> Letting be created, the following real people:
> John Mitchell, General Westmoreland,
> Sheriff Madigan, John Mitchell,
> The list keeps sticking so it doesn't get to the bit names.[47]

The listed names testify to the compromises that Kerr's multiversity entailed. Sheriff Madigan authorized police violence against Berkeley campus protesters, General Westmoreland commanded U.S. forces in Vietnam, and the repeated "John Mitchell" (a kind of circuitry error: the "list keeps sticking") suggests both the famously tarnished Attorney General and the less well-known namesake of the "Mitchell Fountain" at the base of Berkeley's Campanile: the campus armorer who maintained the University Cadets' practice weapons from 1895 to 1904. This other John Mitchell was awarded a Congressional Medal for his service in the Indian Wars, and he represents the university's longer history of military involvement—dating all the way back to the 1862 Morrill Act, which established military instruction on campus.[48] "How to keep from making / John Mitchell, General Westmoreland," Miles concludes the poem, indicating the ethical challenges of teaching at the intersection between School and State.

These challenges notwithstanding, Miles continued in the late 1960s to understand her home university more or less optimistically, as a timely emergence on the academic horizon—a force for continuity that joined past with present and discipline with discipline. Cultivating a sense of community out of this institutional idea, Miles shifts her critique of organicism into a wider scale. Against Abraham Flexner's conception of the university as "a highly vitalized organism," she accepts Kerr's opposing notion of the university as a competitive mechanism, "a pluralistic organization with many component parts," capable of serving "individual faculty entrepreneurs" who are not bound to their local disciplinary homes.[49] The notion of the "field" as a community of scholars unified around a shared intellectual interest becomes for her a metaphor for pastoral departure "toward horizons, toward speculation." In her poem "Fields of Learning," quoted in this book's epigraph, the literary topos of "starting out" brings the speaker away from her familiar patrimonial fields and into an enlivening medley of knowledges, scientific and technical as well as humanistic, which collectively define a progress toward futurity: "they figure us, they figure / Our next turning."

"Fields of Learning" is the title piece of a slim volume that Miles published in 1968 to mark her university's centennial (Figure 7). Dedicated "In debt to Berkeley," the poems depict disciplinary field and pastoral field alike as idyllic and sustaining, aligning academic life with Virgilian pastoral.[50] The whole marks a celebration of academia's interdependent fields of learning—those joining and centering sites of exchange (and change) with which Miles so strongly identified. She wrote many of the poems in *Fields of Learning* based on freshman textbooks for her students' other courses, books that she and her faculty colleagues regularly read so that they could mentor more effectively, and which she found "illuminated with vitality."[51] Several poems share a title with an academic subject: "Biology," "Physics," "Economics," "Law," "Botany," "History," "Political Science." One poem, "Office," depicts the warm sense of community among students and faculty that percolates around the semi-institutional and semi-intimate institution of office hours.[52] In this poem's sequence of student voices, we hear from the "homesick" student from Hong Kong whose mother writes poems, from the overachiever "hot on the trail of Dryden's brother-in-law," from the activist who wants her Viet Nam petition signed, from the passerby who stops to admire the view from Miles's window—and finally from the professor herself, asserting a patient and teacherly "Let's take some time to talk about sequences."[53] The volume's final poem, "Paths," revisits the pastoral topos:

Going out into the fields of learning,
We shake the dew from the grasses.
All is new.
The paths we make through the wet grasses shine
As if with light.

Fig. 7. Josephine Miles, Draft cover for *Fields of Learning: Poems for the Centenary Year at Berkeley*, 1968. Josephine Miles Papers (BANC MSS 86/107c, carton 1, folder 17). The Bancroft Library, University of California.

There is a beautiful lyricism here, picking up on the conversion of physical movement that we have seen in Miles's other poems. Grassy "paths" crossing metaphorical "fields" transform the abstract routes students travel through a major into something wondrous and innocent: "They go where we take them, where they go."[54] Miles gave *Fields of Learning* "to all the administrators," as well as to friends, students, colleagues, and chairs; not a single administrator replied, she wryly recalled, but she received "fascinating letters from teachers of physics and teachers of biology."[55] Together its poems constitute an institutional pastoral, written at a time of visible crisis and structural transition, which brings together a multidisciplinary community of students and teachers while expressing Miles's basic faith in the multiversity's novel and non-organistic model.

Miles's Berkeley is still today a focal point of a complicated nostalgia, signifying at once a lost golden age of activism and the contrary belief that a "fiercely forward-looking" radicalism bears no truck with bygone critiques of progress.[56] Mario Savio and the student-power movement of the 1960s decried Kerr's institutional model as "a public utility serving the purely technical needs of society," and Paul Goodman complained that there was "no growing up" in these "little models of the Organized System itself."[57] In "the minds of alienated students," writes Roger Geiger, "the ills of the multiversity stemmed above all from its bondage to other dehumanizing institutions of American society"; thus undergraduates protested specialized disciplinary expertise as irrelevant to their academic experience, just another sign of the university's enthrallment by the State. They also won the right to evaluate their teachers, enroll in independent studies, and take classes on a pass-fail basis.[58]

These developments had all been supported by the enfranchisement of the student reader, emanating from close-reading practices that, in effect if not in intent, quietly broke down certain structures of intellectual authority. Even as the postwar university grew into a behemoth defined above all by its great size, the literature classroom afforded a space in which a different set of power relations could be modeled and experienced. A 1968 Select Committee Report on education at Berkeley singled out the English Department for its teaching and especially for its "fine tradition" of involving senior faculty in lower-division instruction. (It also showed that the bulk of arrested student protesters had majored in humanities disciplines.) The "Muscatine Report," as it was known—an intriguing pendant to Miles's *Fields of Learning*, published that same year—concluded that "big universities must somehow try to be as personal and as student-involved as are many smaller colleges and universities."[59]

Looking more closely at the curriculum at Miles's Berkeley in that decade, one finds a sign of the times in the fortunes of academic romanticism. Secured as a professional subfield with the 1961 establishment of *Studies in Romanticism*, romantic studies blossomed in a campus climate where egalitarianism and emotion mattered, and where adolescence held a newly won authority. A marginal and merely occasional object of study in 1960, when about one romantic per year was taught as a "major author," it grew into an integral part of the English curriculum by the end of the decade: Keats and Blake were both taught twice as single-author seminars in the academic year 1968–69, and the following year, 1969–70, saw the romanticism survey course expanded into a two-semester sequence.[60] The field was plowed and ready for M. H. Abrams's *Natural Supernaturalism* in 1971, a fulcrum for definition and resistance that all but determined the growth of romantic studies in the coming decades.

Changing with the times, too, was Brooks and Warren's revolutionary, discipline-defining textbook. In the late 1960s, publishers' reports for a new edition of *Understanding Poetry* found it inadequate to "the new mood in colleges and universities"; in one reviewer's words, "The book has a little too much the sense of I know, you don't, so I'll tell you."[61] Another reviewer recommended a more direct appeal to the tastes of students: "I am not suggesting that the editors include John Lennon in *Understanding Poetry*, but . . . this is something I feel necessary to make the material more relevant to the tastes, interests, and backgrounds of our students."[62] Brooks and Warren proved adroit and responsive, adding more women and poets of color to their selections—Warren, apparently more eager than Brooks, scribbled "yes" in the margins alongside one report's recommendation for a new section on "Protest and Propaganda Poetry, Black Poets, Plath, Sexton."[63] Students' new status as consumers in a competitive commercial environment was to be respected.

This points to one of the central ironies of the American New Criticism: originating (and eventually repudiated) as a nostalgic intellectual movement set against the intrusion of "foreign matter" into the pure field of "the poem itself," and flourishing as a "corporate" arrangement espousing the idea of the discipline as the "business" of scholars, its student-oriented classroom pedagogy ultimately helped nudge the university toward a new era of student agency and student resistance. It is not too far a leap from Ransom's ideal of the seminar as a "public discussion" among mature participants, or from Brooks's classroom where students felt comfortable expressing their boredom with a poem—or from countless other classes taught on the premise that students were tired of being "lectured *at*"—to the massive reimagining of intellectual authority represented by student-initiated courses, student evaluations of faculty teaching, student-directed curricular renovations, and the like.[64] And not only in the United States, for what began as a North American story with inputs from Europe became, after World War II, part of a global story about democratization and imperial reach. Of the many European scholars who moved to American universities during and after the war, some, like René Wellek, Erich Auerbach, and Geoffrey Hartman, helped to transform close reading into what came to be known, simply, as "Theory." Others, like the Italian comparatist Remo Ceserani, returned home to lecture and publish on the New Critics. (His 1960 essay on Ransom's poetics, published in the Italian periodical *Studi Romani*, remains one of the most clear-eyed accounts of the American New Criticism that has been written.)[65]

The self-proclaimed "conservative revolution" of *Understanding Poetry*, catalyzed by a series of hyper-cathected engagements with romantic poetry, thus moved strangely into alignment with the romantic revolutions of the postwar era. American close reading became part of a worldwide story about the democratization of knowledge. Yet its self-consciously "corporate" aspects also prefaced a darker story—a kind of institutional anti-pastoral—encompassing (among other things) violence toward student activists, the populist suspicion of expertise, the financialization and entrepreneurialization of knowledge, and the alienation of labor within the late-capitalist university.[66] Our New Critical nostalgia may fantasize dubiously about mid-century "English" as an institutional Eden from which we have been expelled. But as we consider the feelings of profound loss that imbue our supposedly anti-nostalgic mission as professional intellectuals, the widespread sense that there is "something missing" from the ways we read, engage our students, and interact with the varied communities to which we belong, it is worth remembering that nostalgia can express attachments to the past that go beyond mere dream-chasing or "heart's-desire" thinking—that its longings might even be integral to the disciplinary imagination, intimating a critical resistance to the unjust features of the present, and asserting the ultimately reasonable belief that academic life can be made better.[67]

Acknowledgments

I owe thanks to many people for their support during the decade or so that I've worked on this project, beginning with my friends, colleagues, and students at Louisiana State University. I can't imagine this book without Elsie Michie, who read each of its chapters more than once, often on short notice, and always with acumen and care. Dan Novak, Pallavi Rastogi, and Sharon Weltman scoured every word of my initial drafts, helping to give them shape and pushing me to see what they might become. Chris Barrett and Benjy Kahan repeatedly engaged my work with perspicacity and enthusiasm. Many other colleagues listened, shared insights, and encouraged me; my thanks to Nolde Alexius, Michael Bibler, Lauren Coats, Jennifer Davis, Lara Glenum, Rick Godden, Fahima Ife, Madoka Kishi, Joseph Kronick, Michelle Massé, Rick Moreland, Keith Sandiford, Sue Weinstein, and Michelle Zerba. I am grateful to June Pulliam for her help with the index, to Alexandra Chiasson, Makayla Jenkins, and Eta Nurulhady for their research assistance, and to Rachel Augustine, Jodi Scott Elliot, Christie Lauder, Jiwon Min, Eta Nurulhady, and Austin Svedjan for the camaraderie of our weekly writing sessions, which kept me going throughout the worst of the pandemic.

The opening pages of *New Critical Nostalgia* remark on the recent surge of melancholy over a supposedly dying profession, but the profession as I've experienced it in writing this book is anything but moribund—or maybe I've just lucked out in finding so many colleagues, within my field and beyond, willing to read and converse. For dialogue that has sustained me, I thank Elaine Auyoung, Samuel Baker, Jeremy Braddock, Marshall Brown, Jay Dickson, Cassandra Falke, Anne-Lise François, Sonia Hofkosh, Yohei Igarashi, Paul Kelleher, Charles Mahoney, Peter Manning, Brian McGrath, Tom McLean, Omar Miranda, Olivia Loksing Moy, Jonathan Mulrooney, Anahid Nersessian, Stephen Orgel, Ivan Ortiz, Hollis Robbins, Emily Rohrbach, Bea Sanford, Emily Sun, Mark Taylor, and Deanne Williams. Parts of this book were shared with audiences at the University of Connecticut, Princeton University, Sonoma State University, and UCLA, and I am grateful to Jonathan Grossman, Cailey Hall, Yohei Igarashi, Hollis Robbins, and Kelly Swartz for those opportunities and the feedback that they generated. Meetings of the North American Society for the Study of Romanticism and the International Conference on Romanticism have been indispensable sources of collegiality and encouragement, and I would like to acknowledge the boards of these organizations and the hosts of their annual conferences. My thanks as well to Brian Bates, Noah Comet, Anne-Lise François, Celeste Langan, Alexander Walton, and Orrin N. C. Wang, who edited journal issues in which portions of this book appeared and gave valuable advice in the process.

Kevis Goodman read the entire manuscript with extraordinary sensitivity, shared with me as penetrating an appraisal as I could have hoped for, and talked me through aspects of the argument that I was revising; I am profoundly grateful to her. Heartfelt thanks, too, to my writing partner Sarah Allison, who saw all of these chapters in varying states of illegibility and consistently offered insight, reassurance, and meaningful critique; to Chad Wellmon, whose thorough reading of the manuscript generated a series of questions that guided me through its revision; to Alex Woloch, for countless generative conversations and for responding illuminatingly to drafts at two critical moments; to Brad Pasanek, who read my work, shared his archival research with me, and even showed me around Josephine Miles's Virginia Street house; and to Ken Gross and Bill Galperin, for detailed commentary on drafts of individual chapters. Throughout the writing of this book, I've often found myself transported back to the intense and formative classrooms of Adrienne Donald and Starry Schor, who first pushed me to read through the surface of criticism's language.

I owe a special debt to Susan Wolfson. Already a source of much kindness over the years, Susan on two separate occasions—and with almost inconceivable attentiveness—made her way through messy manuscripts and provided rigorous, informed, and illuminating commentaries that doubled as roadmaps for revision. Her intelligence made these chapters much better than they otherwise would have been; I can't thank her enough.

My work on this project benefited from a transformative year spent at the University of Rochester Humanities Center in 2018–2019. I'm grateful to Joan Rubin, the Center's founding director, for creating such a welcoming and generative environment; and to my fellow Fellows, who taught me an enormous amount about my subject: Chris Haufe, Lihong Liu, Kathryn Mariner, William Miller, and Anna Rosensweig. I feel great appreciation, as well, for the audiences who attended the Center's seminars and provided insightful feedback, especially Ken Gross, Bette London, James Longenbach, and Joanna Scott.

I would like to thank my dedicated department chairs between 2012 and

2022, Rick Moreland, Elsie Michie (again), and Joseph Kronick, who helped me secure institutional support for this book. This support included an English Department Regent's Research Grant, a pair of College of Humanities and Social Science travel grants, a Provost's Fund for Innovation in Research Faculty Travel Grant, a Manship Summer Grant, and a year-long ATLAS Grant sponsored by the State of Louisiana, and for those awards I am grateful to the English Department, the College of Humanities and Social Science, the Provost's office, and the Louisiana Board of Regents. I also wish to acknowledge Robin Collor, who coordinated those grant funds, and the indefatigable Ann Whitmer, who as Assistant Dean and Grants Coordinator has helped me every step of the way.

Many librarians have gone out of their way to help me locate relevant faculty papers. My thanks to the staffs of the University of California's Bancroft Library, Cornell University's Kroch Library, Dillard University's Library Archives and Special Collections, LSU's Department of Special Collections in Hill Memorial Library, Southern University's Archives and Manuscripts Department, Vanderbilt University's Special Collections and University Archives, Xavier University of Louisiana's University Archives and Special Collections, and Yale University's Beinecke Rare Book and Manuscript Library and Department of Manuscripts and Archives in Sterling Library. Thanks as well to Laura Theobald for her industrious assistance at several of these libraries, and to Benjamin Meiners for transcribing materials in the Washington University in St. Louis Special Collections.

I am indebted to the entire editorial team at Fordham University Press, including Tom Lay, Kem Crimmins, Eric Newman, and Courtney Lee Adams, and to Sara Guyer and Brian McGrath, the Lit Z series editors, for helping to make *New Critical Nostalgia* a reality. I'm immensely thankful to Angel Albarrán and Anna Cabrera for allowing one of their photographs to grace the book's cover.

A version of Chapter 3 was published as "Reading Keats Together: Cleanth Brooks and the Collegiate Public," *Keats and Popular Culture*, ed. Brian Bates, *Romantic Circles Praxis* (September 2020): https://romantic-circles.org/praxis/popkeats/praxis.2020.popkeats.rovee.html. An early iteration of Chapter 4 appeared as "Not Donne, but Byron: American Criticism and the Mid-Century Classroom," *The Byron Journal* 45 (2017): 75–90. Several sentences in Chapters 3 and 5 are extracted, respectively, from "Trashing Keats," *ELH* 75 (2008): 993–1022, and "Counting Wordsworth by the Bay: The Distance of Josephine Miles," *European Romantic Review* 28 (2017): 405–412. I thank these journals for their permission to include these materials here.

Giovanna Ceserani has unwaveringly supported my work on this book, in ways both too small to name and too large to fathom. My gratitude to her knows no bounds.

New Critical Nostalgia really began back in the 1990s, during a series of weekly tutorials in which Lucy Newlyn impressed upon me—then a naïve admirer of Wordsworth—the importance of thinking critically about the history of romantic studies. I had no idea, at the time, that I'd later return to this subject in earnest. I was, however, conscious of feeling inspired, and of beginning to think that literary study might be a profession I'd like to enter. I am singularly appreciative to Lucy for her encouraging and exacting mentorship.

My mother was an English minor who held onto her copy of *Understanding Poetry* and loved talking about it. My stepfather went to school on the G. I. Bill and believed fervently in public higher education. I certainly owe some of my interest in this book's subject to them, and I'm sorry that they're no longer around to read it. The same goes for the wise and bighearted Remo Ceserani, who told me so much, so colorfully, about the academic world that he encountered as a wide-eyed visiting scholar in New Haven and Berkeley in the 1950s and 1960s. Just a few months after Remo's unexpected passing in 2016, I was touched to come across a special folder bearing his name among Ransom's correspondence at Vanderbilt. It would have been gratifying, and a lot more fun, to have finished this book in his good company.

Notes

Introduction: Our Elegiac Professionalism

1. The "vague sense of loss" that I allude to here is not to be confused with the strong feelings produced by the rampant insecurity of academic life, particularly with respect to the uncertain future of literary study and the humanities in general. Some of that discourse has found a focus in responses to John Guillory's *Professing Criticism: Essays on the Organization of Literary Study* (Chicago and London: U of Chicago P, 2023). I use the collective pronoun in my chapter title and throughout this book not to claim a uniform universal identity for the discipline or to incarnate a false sense of community, but simply to denote a general formation with a shared professional membership—"the discipline"—in which I assume most readers to be co-participants. However, following Eve Sedgwick, I also employ the universalizing claim to explore complex problems associated with it, including the extent to which it even holds true. On Sedgwick's universalizing claims, see Ramzi Fawaz, who writes that "for Sedgwick the universal is primarily a space for hypothesizing, for making conjectures about what is going on around us, what is tending to happen, despite our many differences"; "An Open Mesh of Possibilities: The Necessity of Eve Sedgwick in Dark Times," in *Reading Sedgwick*, ed. Lauren Berlant (Durham, NC: Duke UP, 2019), 13.

2. Ellen Rooney, "Form and Contentment," *MLQ: Modern Language Quarterly* 61 (2000): 24; Roland Greene, "The Heroic Age of Spenser Studies: Roche After Fifty Years," *Arcade: Literature, the Humanities, and the World* (May 7, 2014): http://arcade .stanford.edu/blogs/heroic-age-spenser-studies-roche-after-fifty-years. The dates of this "heroic" or "golden age" can slide around a bit: J. B. Lethbridge moves it backward to the 1960s and 1970s ("Preface," *Edmund Spenser: New and Renewed Directions* [Teaneck, NJ: Fairleigh Dickinson UP, 2006], 17), William Logan deems the period from the 1920s to the 1950s "a golden age of modern literary criticism" ("Forward into the Past: Reading the New Critics," *Virginia Quarterly Review* 84 [2008]: 253), while W. J. T. Mitchell names the 1980s as criticism's "golden age" ("The Golden Age of Criticism: Seven Theses and a Commentary," *London Review of Books* 9, no. 12 [25 June 1987]: 16). Whenever this idyllic disciplinary past is said to have been, however—and it is never any later than the 1980s—most would probably agree that its roots are in the postwar boom of the American university.

3. Marjorie Levinson, "What Is New Formalism?," *PMLA* 122 (2007): 560; Joseph North, *Literary Criticism: A Concise Political History* (New Haven: Yale UP, 2017), 147. For the long-lost philological "unity of knowledge," see James Turner, *Philology: The Forgotten Origins of the Modern Humanities* (Princeton: Princeton UP, 2014), 1–123. Gregory Nagy observes "the nostalgia of philology for the Muses of inspired performance," which Seth Lerer cites in describing "nostalgia" as a feature "that lies at the heart of the

rhetoric of philology"; Gregory Nagy, "Homeric Questions," *Transactions of the American Philological Association* 122 (1992): 19; Seth Lerer, *Error and the Academic Self: The Scholarly Imagination, Medieval to Modern* (New York: Columbia UP, 2002), 10.

4. For the "method wars," see Rita Felski, "Introduction," *New Literary History* 45 (2014): v. Examples of recent methodological returns include Adelene Buckland and Beth Palmer (eds.), *A Return to the Common Reader: Print Culture and the Novel, 1850–1900* (Burlington, VT: Ashgate, 2011); Rachel Sagner Buurma and Laura Heffernan, *The Teaching Archive: A New History for Literary Study* (Chicago: U of Chicago P, 2020); Jonathan Loesberg, *A Return to Aesthetics: Autonomy, Indifference, and Postmodernism* (Stanford: Stanford UP, 2005); and Edward W. Said, "The Return to Philology," *Humanism and Democratic Criticism* (New York: Columbia UP, 2004), 57–84.

5. David Lowenthal, "Nostalgia Tells It Like It Wasn't," in *The Imagined Past: History and Nostalgia*, eds. Martin Chase and Christopher Shaw (Manchester: Manchester UP, 1989), 18–32. I am grateful to Kevis Goodman for conversation on the complexity of nostalgia (which I discuss at greater length below), and also for her book's rigorously historicized discussion of nostalgia's relation to notions of displacement and mobility, both across geographical space and within the body and mind: Kevis Goodman, *Pathologies of Motion: Historical Thinking in Medicine, Aesthetics, and Poetics* (New Haven and London: Yale UP, 2022).

6. Edward Said, "Opponents, Audiences, Constituencies and Community," *Critical Inquiry* 9 (1982): 22, 24. It's important to emphasize Said's repudiation of academic "*noninterference*," which underscores the fact that the object of his mourning is "the role of letters" and not the New Criticism itself. For the politics of criticism in Said, as well as for the mistaken identifications involved in an Arnoldian nostalgia for New Critical "noninterference," see Russ Castronovo, "What Are the Politics of Critique? The Function of Criticism at a Different Time," in *Critique and Postcritique*, eds. Elizabeth Anker and Rita Felski (Durham, NC: Duke UP, 2017), esp. 235–41.

7. Geoffrey Galt Harpham, *The Humanities and the Dream of America* (Chicago: U of Chicago P, 2011), 189.

8. *General Education in a Free Society: Report of the Harvard Committee* (Cambridge: Harvard UP, 1945), 108. For the Redbook as a "wartime document" that "links the humanities with national identity and security," see Harpham, *The Humanities and the Dream of America*, 153–61.

9. Mary Poovey, "The Twenty-First-Century University and the Market: What Price Economic Viability?," *differences: A Journal of Feminist Cultural Studies* 12 (2001): 8.

10. This 1948 piece is a good caution against idealizations of the postwar humanities: "Today . . . we are re-examining the position of literature in our schools and colleges, and we find that the physical sciences and the practical, applied arts and sciences are flourishing, while the so-called 'humanities,' including literature, are being pushed aside"; Marvin T. Herrick, "Can the Study of Literature Be Revived?," *College English* 10.3 (1948): 146–47.

11. William M. Chace, "The Decline of the English Department," *The American Scholar* 78 (Autumn 2009): 33.

12. Jacob Burckhardt, "Fall of the Humanists in the Sixteenth Century," *The Civilization of the Renaissance in Italy*, trans. S. G. C. Middlemore (New York: Macmillan, 1914), 272–73.

13. Several clusters on the subject have appeared in recent years: see, e.g., "Close Reading," *ADE Bulletin* 149 (2009): 8–25; "The Way We Read Now," eds. Stephen Best and Sharon Marcus, *Representations* 108 (2009); "Learning to Read," eds. Evelyne Ender and Deidre Shauna Lynch, *PMLA* 130 (2015): 539–45, 666–749; and "Description Across Disciplines," eds. Sharon Marcus et al., *Representations* 135 (2016). See also Rita Felski, *The Limits of Critique* (Chicago: U of Chicago P, 2015); Eve Kosofsky Sedgwick, "Paranoid Reading and Reparative Reading, or, You're So Paranoid, You Probably Think This Introduction Is About You," in *Novel Gazing: Queer Readings in Fiction*, ed. Eve Kosofsky Sedgwick (Durham, NC: Duke UP, 1997); Franco Moretti, *Distant Reading* (London: Verso, 2013); Heather Love, "Close but Not Deep: Literary Ethics and the Descriptive Turn," *New Literary History* 41 (2010): 371–91; and Elaine Freedgood and Cannon Schmitt, "Denotatively, Technically, Literally," *Representations* 125 (2014): 1–14.

14. Elaine Auyoung, "What We Mean by Reading," *New Literary History* 51 (2020): 93.

15. Poovey, "The Twenty-First-Century University and the Market," 3.

16. N. Katherine Hayles, "How We Read: Close, Hyper, Machine," *ADE Bulletin* 149 (2010): 63.

17. John Guillory calls close reading "a modern academic practice with an inaugural moment, a period of development, and now perhaps a phase of decline"; "Close Reading: Prologue and Epilogue," *ADE Bulletin* 149 (2010): 8. Isolating that "inaugural moment" has proven irresistible; for Guillory, the fountainhead is I.A. Richards/Cambridge/1929. See also (among many others) Marijeta Bozovic, "Whose Forms? Missing Russians in Caroline Levine's *Forms*," *PMLA* 132 (2017): 1181–86; Rachel Sagner Buurma and Laura Heffernan, "The Canon in the Classroom: T. S. Eliot's Modern English Literature Tutorial and *The Sacred Wood*," *PMLA* 33 (2018): 264–81; Joshua Gang, "Behaviorism and the Beginnings of Close Reading," *ELH* 78 (2011): 1–25; Benjamin Morgan, "Critical Empathy: Vernon Lee's Aesthetics and the Origins of Close Reading," *Victorian Studies* 55 (2012): 31–56; and North, *Literary Criticism*, 26–36.

18. Frank Jordan, ed., *The English Romantic Poets: Review of Research and Criticism*, 3rd ed. (New York: Modern Language Association, 1972), 62.

19. David Wagenknecht et al., "How It Was," *Studies in Romanticism* 21 (1982): 565.

20. T. E. Hulme, "Romanticism and Classicism," in *Speculations: Essays on Humanism and the Philosophy of Art,* ed. Herbert Read (New York: Harcourt, Brace and Company, 1924), 118, 126.

21. James Chandler, *England in 1819: The Politics of Literary Culture and the Case of Romantic Historicism* (Chicago: U of Chicago P, 1998), 137. Chandler remarks on this historical pattern in the process of lamenting romanticism's "lost . . . pride of place" in the later twentieth century (136–37). See also Jonathan Arac, *Critical Genealogies: Historical Situations for Postmodern Literary Studies* (New York: Columbia UP, 1987), 11–113; and Marjorie Levinson, who writes that "Romanticism has often served as the profession's laboratory for research and development of new topics, methods, and critical aims"; *Thinking Through Poetry: Field Reports on Romantic Lyric* (Oxford: Oxford UP, 2018), 1.

22. T. S. Eliot, "The Music of Poetry" (1942), in *On Poetry and Poets* (London: Faber, 1957), 28; T. S. Eliot, *The Use of Poetry and the Use of Criticism* (Cambridge: Harvard UP, 1933), 26.

23. Cleanth Brooks, *Community, Religion, and Literature: Essays* (Columbia: U of Missouri P, 1995), 148–49. Brooks's biographer writes that while at Vanderbilt, "Percy

Shelley ... was Cleanth's idea of a poet"; Mark Royden Winchell, *Cleanth Brooks and the Rise of Modern Criticism* (Charlottesville: U of Virginia P, 1996), 34.

24. Austin Warren, *The Letters of Austin Warren*, ed. George Panichas (Macon, GA: Mercer UP, 2011), 161.

25. T. S. Eliot, "Shelley and Keats," in *The Use of Poetry and the Use of Criticism* (Cambridge: Harvard UP, 1933), 80. For further discussion of Frederick Pottle's and Eliot's reminiscences of Shelley, see Chapter 2. Conversion could go the other way as well: Robert Penn Warren would later credit Brooks with turning him on to Wordsworth, writing "that it was Cleanth's theorizing that finally converted me to Wordsworth— from whose work I had long been alienated by some stupid courses in the subject"; "Brooks and Warren," *National Endowment for the Humanities* (newsletter) 6, no. 2 (1985): 2. Brooks claimed that it was through being forced to teach the romantics starting in the late 1950s at Yale that he became willing to admit the merits of a romantic poetics that he had long been cavalier about. "Few poems by Wordsworth will, I believe, more richly repay close reading than this particular poem," his lecture notes indicate that he told students of "The Old Cumberland Beggar"—one of many moments in his teaching materials where Brooks evinces an obvious fondness for the poetry he is commonly thought to have rejected; Cleanth Brooks, "Lectures for the Romantic Seminar" ("'The Old Cumberland Beggar,' 'Resolution and Independence,' 'Michael,' and 'The Ruined Cottage'"), Cleanth Brooks Papers (YCAL MSS 30, box 112, folder 1), 4, Beinecke Rare Book and Manuscript Library, Yale University.

26. Frederick Pottle, typescript of lecture for English 150, delivered c. 1935. Frederick Pottle Papers (MS 1605, box 17), Yale University Manuscripts and Archives, Yale University. See Chapter 2 for discussion of this phenomenon in Pottle and Eliot.

27. T. S. Eliot, "A Romantic Aristocrat," in *The Sacred Wood: Essays on Poetry and Criticism* (New York: Alfred Knopf, 1921), 27; John Crowe Ransom, "Criticism, Inc.," *Selected Essays of John Crowe Ransom*, eds. Thomas Daniel Young and John Hindle (Baton Rouge: Louisiana State UP, 1984), 96–97. Jean Starobinski explains modern nostalgia as posing problems of maturation and "integration into the adult world": "We no longer speak of disease but of reaction; we no longer underline the desire to return but, on the contrary, the failure of adaptation. ... We emphasize ... the lack of adaptation to the new society which the individual must live in. The theory of nostalgia put the accent on the original environment (on the *Heim*); the theory of inadaptation accentuates the paramount necessity of reintegration into an existing *milieu*"; Jean Starobinski, "The Idea of Nostalgia," trans. William S. Kemp, *Diogenes* 14 (1966): 101, 103. College students experiencing their "first significant breaking away from home" were believed peculiarly susceptible to "the nostalgia-reaction," leading to a bevy of medical studies on nostalgic undergraduates in the 1930s and '40s; see Willis H. McCann, "Nostalgia: A Review of the Literature," *Psychological Bulletin* 38 (1941): 171, and Ernst Kretchmer, *A Text-Book of Medical Psychology* (London: Oxford UP, 1934), 187. On the burgeoning interest in "mental hygiene" and "the problematique of nostalgic college and university students" in the 1930s and 1940s, see Nauman Naqvi, "The Nostalgic Subject: A Genealogy of the 'Critique of Nostalgia,'" *CIRSDIG* (Centro Interuniversitario per le Ricerche sulla Sociologia del Diritto e delle Istituzioni Giuridiche), Working Paper 23 (2007): 42–43. Predictably, as we see in Chapter 2, it was Shelley who was generally affiliated with the pathology; see Graham Hough's assessment in *The Romantic Poets* (London: Hutchinson

House, 1953), 122: "Nearly all the contacts of this vivid and subtle mind with the outer world show a certain failure of adaptation."

28. John Crowe Ransom, "Preface," *The World's Body*, viii.

29. Hulme, "Romanticism and Classicism," 127.

30. Gerald Graff, *Professing Literature: An Institutional History* (Chicago and London: U of Chicago P, 1987), 146.

31. John Taylor, "Bloom's Day: Hanging Out with the Reigning Genius of Lit Crit," *New York* (November 5, 1990): 56.

32. Richard H. Fogle, *The Imagery of Keats and Shelley: A Comparative Study* (Chapel Hill: U of North Carolina P, 1949), 242; Fogle, "Romantic Bards and Metaphysical Reviewers," *ELH* 12 (1945): 221.

33. Frederick Pottle, "The Case of Shelley," *PMLA* 67 (1952): 601.

34. By "field" I mean "romantic studies," though it might be argued that "crisis" is the discipline's prevailing mode as well; James F. English observes: "English has been issuing warnings and alarms regarding the grim realities of its current condition" ever "since its first emergence as part of the higher educational curriculum"; *The Global Future of English Studies* (London: Wiley-Blackwell, 2012), 5.

35. Orrin N. C. Wang, *Romantic Sobriety: Sensation, Revolution, Commodification, History* (Baltimore: Johns Hopkins UP, 2011), 36.

36. This was Susan Wolfson and William Galperin's argument, made at the round-table "'Romanticism' in Crisis," for a rubric they named "The Romantic Century"; "The Romantic Century," *Romantic Circles* (1996): http://www.romantic-circles.org /reference/misc/confarchive/crisis/crisisa.html.

37. For the economic backdrop of the late-century crisis, see Christopher New-field's bracing chapter on "English's Market Retreat" in *Unmaking the Public University: The Forty-Year Assault on the Middle Class* (Cambridge: Harvard UP, 2008), 142–58; and Poovey, "The Twenty-First-Century University and the Market," 3–6. For the broad curricular context, see Clifford Adelman, *The Empirical Curriculum: Changes in Post-secondary Course-Taking, 1972–2000* (Washington: US Department of Education, 1995).

38. Aidan Day, *Romanticism: The New Critical Idiom*, 2nd ed. (New York: Routledge, 2012), 84; Wagenknecht et al., "How It Was," 562; Chandler, *England in 1819*, 489.

39. M. H. Abrams, "Structure and Style in the Greater Romantic Lyric," in *From Sensibility to Romanticism: Essays Presented to Frederick A. Pottle*, eds. Frederick W. Hilles and Harold Bloom (New York: Oxford UP, 1965), 527–60.

40. Wagenknecht et al., "How It Was," 558, 567, 563.

41. Eric Lindstrom, "Teaching Romanticism, Poetics, and Lyric Theory," *Teaching Romanticism and Literary Theory*, ed. Brian McGrath, *Romantic Circles Praxis* (December 2016): https://romantic-circles.org/pedagogies/commons/teaching_romanticism /pedagogies.commons.2016.teaching_romanticism.lindstrom.html, para. 13.

42. Wang, *Romantic Sobriety*, 287.

43. For this correlation, and for an innovative trace-history of the discipline's past (what she calls a "history from within"), see Levinson, *Thinking Through Poetry*, 1.

44. Mary Poovey, "The Model System of Contemporary Literary Criticism," *Critical Inquiry* 27 (2001): 435.

45. Cleanth Brooks, "Irony and 'Ironic' Poetry," *College English* 9 (1948): 237.

46. Jacques Barzun, *Romanticism and the Modern Ego* (Boston: Little, Brown, and Co.,

1943), 187–88; "America and the Intellectual," *Time* (June 11, 1956): 70; Jon Klancher describes the correlation between postwar pluralistic democracy, British romantic culture, and romantic studies in a seminal essay on the subject: "Romantic Criticism and the Meanings of the French Revolution," *Studies in Romanticism* 28 (1989): 481.

47. Klancher, "Romantic Criticism and the Meanings of the French Revolution," 489.

48. Klancher, "Romantic Criticism and the Meanings of the French Revolution," 464. For the intimate relation between the "helplessly elegiac" romantic lyric and "the very form of our literary criticism," see Levinson, "The New Historicism: Back to the Future," *Thinking Through Poetry*, 61.

49. Reinhart Koselleck, "Crisis," trans. Michaela W. Richter, *Journal of the History of Ideas* 67 (2006): 358, 371. Richter translates the entry for "Krise" in Koselleck's eight-volume historical lexicon of political terms, the *Geschichtliche Grundbegriffe* (1972–97).

50. Koselleck, "Crisis," 359.

51. René Wellek, "The Crisis of Comparative Literature," in *Concepts of Criticism*, ed. Stephen G. Nichols Jr. (New Haven: Yale UP, 1963), 282; Paul de Man, "The Crisis of Contemporary Criticism," *Arion: A Journal of Humanities and the Classics* 6 (1967): 44. De Man's essay reappeared as "Criticism and Crisis," the first chapter of *Blindness and Insight* (Minneapolis: U of Minnesota P, 1971), 3–19. For de Man, the "crisis of criticism" is the self-scrutiny and self-separation involved in the act of criticism; he even synonymizes the words: "genuine crisis or criticism" (44). For other views of the relation between "criticism" and "crisis," see Tobin Siebers, *The Ethics of Criticism* (Ithaca: Cornell UP, 1988), 14–15; William E. Cain, *The Crisis in Criticism* (Baltimore: Johns Hopkins UP, 1984); and W. J. T. Mitchell, "911: Criticism and Crisis," *Critical Inquiry* 28 (2002): 567–72.

52. Jonathan Kramnick and Anahid Nersessian, "Form and Explanation," *Critical Inquiry* 43 (2017): 668.

53. See Ellen Rooney, *Seductive Reasoning: Pluralism as the Problematic of Contemporary Literary Theory* (Ithaca: Cornell UP, 1989), especially her discussion of E. D. Hirsch and disciplinarity on 66–84. On the culture of academic argument, crucial to a liberal-democratic tradition and characteristic of the theoretical turn that grew out of this period, see Amanda Anderson, *The Way We Argue Now: A Study in the Cultures of Theory* (Princeton: Princeton UP, 2009). See also Heather Love's anticipatory nostalgia for the notion: "the point now is to hold on to the spaces in which we can disagree with each other, whether generously or churlishly. . . . It is possible that some day we will stop fighting with each other. But that might happen only when there is nothing left to fight for"; "Response," *PMLA* 135 (2020): 1019–20.

54. Robert Bernasconi, *How to Read Sartre* (New York: Norton, 2007); Stella Sandford, *How to Read Beauvoir* (New York: Norton, 2007). For examples of the genre, see Mortimer Adler, *How to Read a Book: The Art of Getting a Liberal Education* (New York: Simon and Schuster, 1940); I. A. Richards, *How to Read a Page* (New York: Norton, 1942); Bertrand Russell, *How to Read and Understand History* (Girard, KS: Haldeman-Julius, 1943); Llewellyn Jones, *How to Read Books* (New York: Norton, 1930); and J. B. Kerfoot, *How to Read* (Boston: Houghton Mifflin, 1916).

55. Terry Eagleton, *How to Read a Poem* (Oxford: Blackwell, 2011), 1.

56. R. W. Short, "The Dilemma Presented by Historical Scholarship," *College English* 5 (1944): 214.

57. Short, "The Dilemma Presented by Historical Scholarship," 214.

58. Laurence R. Veysey, *The Emergence of the American University* (Chicago: U of Chicago P, 1965), 34–67.

59. H. A. White, "Clear Thinking for Army Trainees," *College English* 5 (1944): 444.

60. William Riley Parker, "English in Wartime: A Suggestion and an Illustration," *College English* 4 (January 1943): 236.

61. G. H. Estabrooks, "Campus Revolution," *Saturday Evening Post* 206 (18 September 1943): 14–15.

62. For the link between American nationalism and the humanities after the war, see Harpham, *The Humanities and the Dream of America*, 13–15, 145–63.

63. William DeVane, "The English Major," *College English* 3 (1941): 48.

64. Herrick, "Can the Study of Literature Be Revived?," 146–47, 149.

65. Jane Gallop, "The Historicization of Literary Studies and the Fate of Close Reading," *Profession* (2007): 183.

66. Elizabeth Nitchie, *The Criticism of Literature* (New York: Macmillan, 1928).

67. Edith Rickert, *New Methods for the Study of Literature* (Chicago: U of Chicago P, 1927); Edwin Greenlaw, *The Province of Literary History* (Baltimore: Johns Hopkins UP, 1931), ix–x; Elisabeth Wintersteen Schneider, *Aesthetic Motive* (New York: Macmillan, 1939). Greenlaw, a Spenserian at Chapel Hill before moving to Johns Hopkins in the mid-1920s, was responding to the New Humanist Norman Foerster's accusation that historically minded scholars were "deserters" of literature; *The American Scholar: A Study in Litterae Inhumaniores* (Chapel Hill: U of North Carolina P, 1929), 23–24. Rickert, an expert in English philology who was immensely productive as an editor particularly (but not exclusively) of medieval writing, famously collaborated with her Chicago colleague John Matthews Manly for four decades, producing what is known as "the Manly-Rickert text" of *The Canterbury Tales* (1940); she has recently begun to receive her due as a pioneering figure not only in Chaucer studies but in the quantitative analysis and visualization of literary history. Schneider, professor at Temple and later UC Santa Barbara (and onetime president of the College English Association), is like Nitchie and Rickert an undeservedly obscured figure in twentieth-century literary studies—and also, like Nitchie, a romanticist, with books on Hazlitt and on Coleridge to go along with several others in the field of poetics.

68. Rita Felski, *Uses of Literature* (Oxford: Blackwell, 2008), 2. I am grateful to Alex Woloch for conversation on this point.

69. John Crowe Ransom, "Reconstructed but Unregenerate," *I'll Take My Stand: The South and the Agrarian Tradition. By Twelve Southerners* (1930; Baton Rouge: Louisiana State UP, 2006), 6.

70. On Ransom's summoning "the forced migrations of the slave trade" and "others who were forced to leave home," see Jennifer K. Ladino, *Reclaiming Nostalgia: Longing for Nature in American Literature* (Charlottesville: U of Virginia P, 2013), 53.

71. Ransom, "Criticism, Inc.," 93–94.

72. Thomas Daniel Young, *Gentleman in a Dustcoat: A Biography of John Crowe Ransom* (Baton Rouge: Louisiana State UP, 1976), 299–301.

73. See Paul Bové, "Agriculture and Academe: America's Southern Question," *boundary2* 14 (1986): 169–96; Graff, *Professing Literature*, 147–59; Marc Jancovich, *The Cultural Politics of the New Criticism* (Cambridge: Cambridge UP, 1993); Alexander

MacLeod, "'Disagreeable Intellectual Distance': Theory and Politics in the Old Regionalism of the New Critics," in *Rereading the New Criticism*, eds. Miranda B. Hickman and John D. McIntyre (Columbus: Ohio State UP, 2012), 184–94; and Stephen Schryer, *Fantasies of the New Class: Ideologies of Professionalism in Post–World War II American Fiction* (New York: Columbia UP, 2011), 29–54.

74. Linda Hutcheon, "Irony, Nostalgia, and the Postmodern," *Methods for the Study of Literature as Cultural Memory*, eds. Raymond Vervliet and Annemarie Estor (Atlanta: Rodopi, 2000), 195.

75. Susan J. Wolfson, *Formal Charges: The Shaping of Poetry in British Romanticism* (Stanford: Stanford UP, 1997), 1.

76. North, *Literary Criticism*, 154, 125, 148.

77. North, *Literary Criticism*, 147.

78. Alastair Bonnett, *Left in the Past: Radicalism and the Politics of Nostalgia* (New York: Continuum, 2010), 7.

79. Michael Löwy and Robert Sayre, "Figures of Romantic Anti-Capitalism," *New German Critique* 32 (1984): 56.

80. Johannes Hofer, "Medical Dissertation on Nostalgia" [*Dissertatio Medica de Nostalgia, oder Heimwehe*], trans. Carolyn Kiser Anspach, *Bulletin of the History of Medicine* 2 (1934): 376–91. On clinical nostalgia, see Starobinski, "The Idea of Nostalgia," 81–103; Peter Fritzsche, "How Nostalgia Narrates Modernity," in *The Work of Memory: New Directions in the Study of German Society and Culture*, eds. Alon Confino and Peter Fritzsche (Urbana: U of Illinois P, 2002), 62–85; Andreea Decui Ritivoi, *Yesterday's Self: Nostalgia and the Immigrant Identity* (New York: Rowman and Littlefield, 2002), 13–42; Naqvi, "The Nostalgic Subject," 4–51; Goodman, *Pathologies of Motion*, 74–112; Michael S. Roth, "Dying of the Past: Medical Studies on Nostalgia in Nineteenth-Century France," *Memory, Trauma, and History* (New York: Columbia UP, 2012), 23–38; and Thomas Dodman, *What Nostalgia Was: War, Empire, and the Time of a Deadly Emotion* (Chicago: U of Chicago P, 2018).

81. Erasmus Darwin, *Zoonomia; or, The Laws of Organic Life* (1794–96), vol. 2 (Philadelphia: Edward Earle, 1818), 314–15. On nostalgia in the late eighteenth and early nineteenth century, see Starobinski, "The Idea of Nostalgia," 92–100; Goodman, *Pathologies of Motion*, 86–109, 113–44; and Dodman, *What Nostalgia Was*, 93–123.

82. For nostalgia's significance in modern criminology, see Naqvi, "The Nostalgic Subject," 29–38; Elisabeth Bronfen, *The Knotted Subject: Hysteria and Its Discontents* (Princeton: Princeton UP, 1998), 243–89; and Ritivoi, *Yesterday's Self*, 13–20.

83. David J. Flicker and Paul Weiss, "Nostalgia and Its Military Implications," *War Medicine* 4 (1943): 383, 386. See also C. L. Wittson, H. I. Harris, and W. A. Hunt, "Cryptic Nostalgia," *War Medicine* 3 (1943): 57–59; and C. L. Wittson, H. I. Harris, and W. A. Hunt, "Detection of the Neuropsychiatrically Unfit," *United States Naval Bulletin* 40 (1942): 342–46. All are discussed by Naqvi in his eye-opening genealogy of the diagnosis in "The Nostalgic Subject," 24–29.

84. Naqvi, "The Nostalgic Subject," 9; Fritzsche, "How Nostalgia Narrates Modernity," 62.

85. Nicholas Dames, "Nostalgia and Its Disciplines," *Memory Studies* 3 (2010): 270.

86. Long before "campus" became synonymous with "pastoral," Hofer presented his

seminal dissertation on nostalgia in an encomium that conveyed the fragile collegiality between an authoritative mentor and his anxious disciple: "present[ed] for examination, to his friend of learning, the president, in the very ancient university of Rauracum, a man most enterprising and distinguished. . . . I hope only that the kindness of the Reader will bear in mind that a young man has written this and has been the first to treat a new material"; Hofer, "Medical Dissertation on Nostalgia," 379–80.

87. Nicholas Dames, *Amnesiac Selves: Nostalgia, Forgetting, and British Fiction, 1810–1870* (Oxford: Oxford UP, 2001), 6.

88. Svetlana Boym, *The Future of Nostalgia* (New York: Basic Books, 2001), 50.

89. Fritzsche, "How Nostalgia Narrates Modernity," 66, 65.

90. On the "compulsive, repetitive, nostalgic desire for the archive, an irrepressible desire to return to the origin, a homesickness," see Jacques Derrida, *Archive Fever: A Freudian Impression*, trans. Eric Prenowitz (Chicago and London: U of Chicago P, 1996), 91. See also Jonathan Boulter, *Melancholy and the Archive: Trauma, History, and Memory in the Contemporary Novel* (London and New York: Continuum, 2011); and Arlette Farge, *The Allure of the Archives* (1989), trans. Thomas Scott-Railton (New Haven: Yale UP, 2013).

91. Lisa Jardine, *Temptation in the Archives: Essays in Golden Age Dutch Culture* (London: UCL P, 2015), viii.

92. Lorraine Daston, "The Time of the Archive," *Science in the Archives: Pasts, Presents, Futures*, ed. Lorraine Daston (Chicago: U of Chicago P, 2017), 330.

93. Daston, "The Time of the Archive," 329.

94. This is a self-reinforcing cycle, since the underfunding (for example) of archives at historically Black institutions ensures that the profession's Black history is neglected and undervalued. For important work on this problem with respect to disciplinary history, see Michael Bibby, "The Disinterested and Fine: New Negro Renaissance Poetry and the Racial Formation of Modernist Studies," *Modernism/Modernity* 20 (2013): 485–501; Buurma and Heffernan's chapter on J. Saunders Redding in *The Teaching Archive*, 107–32; and Andy Hines, *Outside Literary Studies: Black Criticism and the University* (Chicago: U of Chicago P, 2022).

95. On the way "schematic narratives" such as this "underwrite" disciplinary identity while papering over "the reality of intellectual untidiness," see Stefan Collini, *The Nostalgic Imagination: History in English Criticism* (Oxford: Oxford UP, 2019), 10–11.

Chapter 1: Ransom's Melancholy (Reading Wordsworth in Gambier, Ohio)

1. John Crowe Ransom Papers (box 3, folders 4–6), Vanderbilt University Special Collections, Vanderbilt University.

2. William Wordsworth, "I travell'd among unknown Men," *Wordsworth's Poetry and Prose: A Norton Critical Edition*, ed. Nicholas Halmi (New York: W. W. Norton, 2013), 392–93. The last of the Lucy poems to be written, in 1801, this was the only one of them not to appear in *Lyrical Ballads*. Though intended for the 1802 edition, it was not published until *Poems, in Two Volumes* (1807). See Richard Matlack, "Wordsworth's Lucy Poems in Psychobiographical Context," *PMLA* 93 (1978): 47, 60–61; Pamela Woof, "The 'Lucy' Poems: Poetry of Mourning," *The Wordsworth Circle* 30 (1999):

28–36; and Jared Curtis, "A Note on the Lost Manuscripts of William Wordsworth's 'Louisa' and 'I travell'd among unknown Men,'" *The Yale University Library Gazette* 53 (1979): 196–201.

3. John Crowe Ransom, "The Third Moment," qtd. in Thomas Daniel Young, "The Evolution of Ransom's Critical Theory: Image and Idea," in *The New Criticism and After*, ed. Thomas Daniel Young (Charlottesville: UP of Virginia, 1976), 27–28; Ransom, *The New Criticism* (Norfolk, CT: New Directions, 1941), 280.

4. Stephen Schryer, *Fantasies of the New Class: Ideologies of Professionalism in Post-World War II American Fiction* (New York: Columbia UP, 2011), 41.

5. Hugh Kenner, "The Pedagogue as Critic," in *The New Criticism and After*, ed. Thomas Daniel Young (Charlottesville: UP of Virginia, 1976), 36.

6. Gerald Graff, *Professing Literature: An Institutional History* (Chicago and London: U of Chicago P, 1987), 155.

7. John Fekete, *The Critical Twilight: Explorations in the Ideology of Anglo-American Literary Theory from Eliot to McLuhan* (New York: Routledge, 1977), 44; Paul Bové, "Agriculture and Academe: America's Southern Question," *boundary2* 14 (1986): 115; Langdon Hammer, *Hart Crane and Allen Tate: Janus-Faced Modernism* (Princeton: Princeton UP, 2017), 26. Some other influential accounts of Ransom's turn from Agrarianism to the profession that have helped shape my own include Graff, *Professing Literature*, 147–59; Marc Jancovich, *The Cultural Politics of the New Criticism* (Cambridge: Cambridge UP, 1993); Alexander MacLeod, "'Disagreeable Intellectual Distance': Theory and Politics in the Old Regionalism of the New Critics," in *Rereading the New Criticism*, eds. Miranda B. Hickman and John D. McIntyre (Columbus: Ohio State UP, 2012), 184–94; and Schryer, *Fantasies of the New Class*, 29–54.

8. Louis D. Rubin, Jr., "A Critic Almost Anonymous: John Crowe Ransom Goes North," in Young, ed., *The New Criticism and After*, 6–7.

9. After Brooks's move to Yale in 1947, Vanderbilt's alumni magazine ran a feature titled "Why the Academic Hegira to the North?," *The [Vanderbilt] Alumnus* (April–May 1947): 6.

10. Thomas Daniel Young, "New Critics," in *The New Encyclopedia of Southern Culture*, vol. 9: "Literature," ed. M. Thomas Inge (Chapel Hill: U of North Carolina P, 2014), 104. This narrative has gained widespread purchase: see Terry Eagleton's description of "the long trek from Nashville, Tennessee, home of the Fugitives, to the East Coast Ivy League universities" as the analog to the New Critics' rising influence (the "rebel merg[ing] into the image of his master"); *Literary Theory: An Introduction* (1983), Anniversary Edition (Oxford: Blackwell, 2008), 43.

11. Qtd. in Thomas Daniel Young, *Gentleman in a Dustcoat: A Biography of John Crowe Ransom* (Baton Rouge: Louisiana State UP, 1976), 288.

12. Wallace Stevens, telegram, Ransom Papers (box 5, folder 16).

13. Attention to the emigration of white intellectuals obscured other, more substantive migrations, such as the violently enforced transport of an enslaved population from Africa to the American South, and the subsequent migration, contemporary with Ransom's Agrarian phase, of some six million Black people out of the South and to the North and West of the United States. Richard Wright tellingly recalled exhorting himself in terms diametrically opposed to Ransom's: "The first conclusion I arrived at [as a

young person] was this: Get out of the South as soon as is humanly possible." Wright's well-known phrase about leaving the South has been popularized in the title of Isabel Wilkerson's *The Warmth of Other Suns: The Epic Story of America's Great Migration* (New York: Random House, 2011). His comment about "getting out" was made during his NAACP Spingarn Medal Acceptance Speech in 1941; qtd. in Jeff Karem, *The Romance of Authenticity: The Cultural Politics of Regional and Ethnic Literatures* (Charlottesville: UP of Virginia, 2004), 173.

14. Samuel Holt Monk and Lawrence Lee, telegrams, Ransom Papers (box 5, folder 16).

15. John Crowe Ransom, *Selected Letters*, eds. Thomas Daniel Young and George Core (Baton Rouge: Louisiana State UP, 1984), 217.

16. Ransom, qtd. in Young, *Gentleman in a Dustcoat*, 287.

17. Donald Davidson, qtd. in Mark G. Malvasi, *The Unregenerate South: The Agrarian Thought of John Crowe Ransom, Allen Tate, and Donald Davidson* (Baton Rouge: Louisiana State UP, 1997), 76.

18. On Davidson, see Paul V. Murphy, *The Rebuke of History: The Southern Agrarians and American Conservative Thought* (Chapel Hill: U of North Carolina P, 2001), 92–113. For a nuanced and even-handed assessment of Davidson's response to Ransom's situation, read as a kind of diagnosis of "why the New Critics left their old regionalism behind," see MacLeod, "'Disagreeable Intellectual Distance,'" 190–91.

19. Regionalist writings of the time lend a sense of inevitability to Ransom's move. While Tate claimed that "The Southern writer should if possible be a Southerner in the South," he added that in the absence of a regional "machinery of publication," Southern writers of his generation were fated to go north; Allen Tate, "The Profession of Letters in the South," *Virginia Quarterly Review* 11 (1935): 174. The South itself, in Agrarians' eyes, was already permeated by the North: the competing regionalism of New South progressives like Howard Odum's Chapel Hill group self-consciously embraced—or in the eyes of the Vanderbilt Agrarians, capitulated to—the North's scientific habits of thought. Ransom himself critically observed this assimilative tendency, writing in 1934 that "Southern regionalism has to fight for its life," and observing that even "University Reviews" such as the *Sewanee Review* and the *Virginia Quarterly Review* had become "perfectly eclectic"—a synonym, in the Agrarian lexicon, for pejoratives such as "progressive" and "cosmopolitan"; John Crowe Ransom, "Regionalism in the South," *The New Mexico Quarterly* 4 (1934): 110.

20. John Crowe Ransom, *Land! The Case for an Agrarian Economy* (1932), ed. Jason Peters, intro. Jay T. Collier (South Bend: U of Notre Dame P, 2017), 12; "Teacher, Ex-Pupil at Kenyon Talk Only Poetry," *Columbus Citizen-Journal* (May 1, 1968): 1; John Crowe Ransom to Donald Davidson, June 10, 1939, Ransom Papers (box 11, folder 10).

21. "Fifty Seniors Don Cap and Gown," *Kenyon Collegian* (June 13, 1938): 1. About half of the students who matriculated in 1934 graduated, with the main reasons given for attrition being financial and vocational. See "College Opens Doors to 114 Select Frosh," *Kenyon Collegian* (September 16, 1937): 1; "Eighty of Large Frosh Class Pledged by Fraternities," *Kenyon Collegian* (October 4, 1934): 1. Since the 1920s Ransom had been teaching four courses at a time, including freshman and upper-division Composition courses that enrolled up to a hundred students per term, and Modern Literature

courses with thirty students each. To Robert Graves, Ransom described "growing a
bit stale" in his "present unrelieved monotony," and with one child in college and another on the way, he also was facing significant financial obligations; qtd. in Young,
Gentleman in a Dustcoat, 127. To make ends meet he sought teaching wherever he could
during the summers, while neglecting his own writing. As he wrote Davidson in the
April following his move, he still faced a summer full of teaching gigs ("two and a half
weeks at Kentucky; a week at Murray; a week at University of Chattanooga; and six
weeks at Texas") but was finally "recovering solvency": "I don't know how I could
have managed if I had stayed on at Vanderbilt"; Ransom to Davidson, April 29, 1938,
Donald Davidson Papers (box 11, folder 10), Vanderbilt University Special Collections,
Vanderbilt University.

22. Mark McGurl, *The Program Era: Postwar Fiction and the Rise of Creative Writing*
(Cambridge: Harvard UP, 2009), 149; "Why?," *Chattanooga Times* (February 22, 1947),
Cleanth Brooks Papers (box 90, folder 1922), Beinecke Rare Book and Manuscript
Library, Yale University. An unattributed poem found among Brooks's papers attests
the crisis. Titled "Mr. Cleanth Brooks Enters Into Yale," it is in the voice of an LSU
student (though the title suggests that it might have been written in mockery by a
Yale student) lamenting the intrusion upon regional identity by private "business" and
consoling himself by numbly throwing peanut shells at the university's caged Bengal
tiger mascot: "Southern Culture is a State of Mind and increasingly only that . . . / And
this / Is none of my damned business. Let us go / And throw shelled peanuts at Mike";
[Anonymous], "Mr. Cleanth Brooks Enters Into Yale," Brooks Papers (box 90, folder
1922).

23. Cleanth Brooks's letter is reprinted in "An Alumnus Raises a Question: Why the
Academic Hegira to the North?," *The [Vanderbilt] Alumnus* (April–May 1947): 6; Brooks
Papers (box 90, folder 1922).

24. This elision of the American New Criticism's sociocultural roots began to be
noticed as early as the 1960s; see John Dixon Hunt, "The American 'New Criticism,'"
Critical Survey 2 (1966): 201: "To most people nowadays [New Criticism] means only
'close reading,' but such a pedagogical residue is scarcely faithful to the original impulses and doctrines of the movement."

25. Henry Holt and Company, Advertisement for *Understanding Poetry*, *The Saturday
Review* (August 3, 1946), in Brooks Papers (series 2, box 50, folder 903).

26. See Norman E. Nelson and Clarence D. Thorpe, "Criticism in the Twentieth
Century: A Bird's Eye View," *College English* 8 (1947): 395–405; Frederick A. Pottle,
"The New Critics and the Historical Method," *The Yale Review* 43 (1953): 14–23;
Clarence L. Kulisheck, "The New Criticism and the New College Text," *Journal of
Higher Education* 25 (1954): 173–78; Richard James Calhoun, "The New Criticism Ten
Years After," *South Atlantic Bulletin* 26 (1960): 1–6. An exception that proves the rule
is Robert Gorham Davis's contribution to *The American Scholar* in 1950, in which he
aligns the Southern New Critics with "a general intellectual assault on the assumptions of democratic liberalism"; Robert Gorham Davis, "The New Criticism and the
Democratic Tradition," *The American Scholar* 19 (1949–50): 11. Davis's claim elicited a
firestorm of response that dragged out across nearly two years, showing just how flam-
mable the political and historical subtext could be; among many that took offense at

what they perceived as a "charge of fascism," see Yvor Winters, "The Reader Replies," *The American Scholar* 19 (1950): 380.

27. Stanley Hyman, *The Armed Vision* (New York: Alfred A. Knopf, 1947), 75–76.

28. Hyman, *The Armed Vision*, 217, 318, 76.

29. Bové, coining a shorthand, defines the "PS" as an anti-critical antiquarian whose unhistoricized scholarship betrays a "desire for a return to mythicized origins among what must be seen, by any standard, as a leading conservative and still unyieldingly anti-Marxist element within not only the academic critical profession, but the Reaganized culture as a whole"; "Agriculture and Academe," 172. For an astute assessment of Bové's argument—and in general for an essential history of "the South" as object of literary and cultural study—see Michael Kreyling, *Inventing Southern Literature* (Jackson: UP of Mississippi, 1998).

30. For the "stalk of cotton" as Agrarian emblem of organicism, see Andrew Nelson Lytle, "The Hind Tit," *I'll Take My Stand: The South and the Agrarian Tradition. By Twelve Southerners* (1930; Baton Rouge: Louisiana State UP, 2006), 210.

31. Graff, *Professing Literature*, 146.

32. See Schryer, *Fantasies of the New Class*, 41–54; and MacLeod, "'Disagreeable Intellectual Distance,'" 184–94. I owe much to Schryer's and MacLeod's intensely detailed accounts, which have transformed earlier understandings of Ransom's turn from Agrarianism to professionalism through their attention to questions of disciplinary specialization and cultural geography.

33. Alistair Bonnett, *Left in the Past: Radicalism and the Politics of Nostalgia* (New York: Bloomsbury, 2010), 170.

34. John Crowe Ransom, "Criticism, Inc.," *Selected Essays of John Crowe Ransom*, eds. Thomas Daniel Young and John Hindle (Baton Rouge: Louisiana State UP, 1984), 93–94.

35. Only a year before, in "What Does the South Want?," Ransom had differentiated between "Eastern business interests" he considered "predatory," and local industries capable of fostering "regional autonomy": "there is practically nobody, even in the economically backward South, who proposes to destroy corporate business"; John Crowe Ransom, "What Does the South Want?," *Virginia Quarterly Review* 12 (1936): 187. This subtle gradation between the industrial and professional also applies to field boundaries, as Ransom's benign attitude toward "incorporation" brings *regional* autonomy into dialogue with *disciplinary* and *aesthetic* autonomy.

36. For the "salesmanship" of the theatrical lecturer, see Ransom, "Criticism, Inc.," 100.

37. Ransom, "Criticism, Inc.," 95.

38. Ransom, "Criticism, Inc.," 95.

39. Ransom, "Criticism, Inc.," 95.

40. Ransom, "Criticism, Inc.," 99–100.

41. Ransom, "Criticism, Inc.," 104.

42. Ransom, "Criticism, Inc.," 97, 101. For "dryasdust philology," see Jerome J. McGann, *A New Republic of Letters: Memory and Scholarship in the Age of Digital Reproduction* (Cambridge: Harvard UP, 2014), 49.

43. Ransom, "Criticism, Inc.," 96–97.

44. Ransom, "Criticism, Inc.," 96–97.

45. Ransom, "Criticism, Inc.," 105.

46. I. A. Richards, *Practical Criticism: A Study of Literary Judgment* (London: Kegan Paul, Trench, Trubner, 1929), 12.

47. Ransom, "Criticism, Inc.," 106.

48. Ransom, "Criticism, Inc.," 105.

49. Viktor Shklovsky, "Art, as Device" (1917), *Theory of Prose*, trans. Benjamin Sher (Normal, IL: Dalkey Archive P, 1998), 5; Theodor F. Adorno, *Minima Moralia: Reflections from Damaged Life* (1951), trans. E. F. N. Jephcott (London: New Left Books, 1974), 222; John Crowe Ransom, "The Tense of Poetry" (1935), *The World's Body*, 237.

50. Brooks, *The Well Wrought Urn: Studies in the Structure of Poetry* (New York: Harcourt Brace, 1947), x.

51. John Crowe Ransom, "Poetry: A Note in Ontology," in *Selected Essays*, 52.

52. John Crowe Ransom, "Criticism as Pure Speculation," in *Selected Essays*, 138.

53. Ransom, "Criticism as Pure Speculation," 138.

54. Ransom, "Criticism, Inc.," 106; Ransom, *The New Criticism*, 280.

55. Catherine Gallagher, "Formalism and Time," *Modern Language Quarterly* 61 (2000): 238.

56. Ransom, "Criticism, Inc.," 105.

57. Ransom, "Criticism, Inc.," 105.

58. W. K. Wimsatt, Jr. and M. C. Beardsley, "The Affective Fallacy," *Sewanee Review* 57 (1949): 49.

59. John Crowe Ransom, "The Bases of Criticism," *Sewanee Review* 52 (1944): 569.

60. Ransom, "Criticism, Inc.," 105 (emphasis added).

61. Ransom, "The Bases of Criticism," 567; "Distal," in W. A. Newman Dorland, *The American Illustrated Medical Dictionary* (Philadelphia: W. B. Saunders, 1917), 312.

62. Ransom, "The Bases of Criticism," 567.

63. Ransom, "The Bases of Criticism," 567.

64. Ransom, "Criticism, Inc.," 105.

65. Frederic Jameson, "Nostalgia for the Present" (1989), in *Close Reading: The Reader*, eds. Frank Lentricchia and Andrew DuBois (Durham, NC: Duke UP, 2003), 231.

66. Ransom, "Humanism at Chicago," *Kenyon Review* 14 (1952): 658. For poetry's mediation of this "here and now," see Kevis Goodman, who describes (in ways that illuminate Ransom's uneasy response to a disciplinary situation that he helped create), "the *unpleasurable* feeling" of "recording and recognizing 'history-on-the-move,' or . . . of treating or recreating the historical process as a present participle"; *Georgic Modernity and British Romanticism: Georgic and the Mediation of History* (Cambridge: Cambridge UP, 2004), 3.

67. Ransom, "William Wordsworth: Notes Toward an Understanding of Poetry," *Kenyon Review* 12 (1950): 499.

68. See Christopher Jencks and David Riesman, *The Academic Revolution* (Garden City, NY: Doubleday, 1968).

69. Ransom, "Criticism, Inc.," 102.

70. *The Department of English at Indiana University Bloomington 1868–1970* (Bloomington: Indiana University Board of Trustees, 1971), 134.

71. Ransom, "William Wordsworth," 507.

72. Ransom, "A Poem Nearly Anonymous" (1933), *The World's Body* (New York: Charles Scribner's Sons, 1938), 3; Ransom, *The New Criticism*, 115–19.

73. Ransom, "William Wordsworth," 249.

74. M. H. Abrams, "Introduction: Two Roads to Wordsworth," *Wordsworth: A Collection of Critical Views* (Englewood Cliffs, NJ: Prentice-Hall, 1972), 2.

75. M. H. Abrams, *Natural Supernaturalism: Tradition and Revolution in Romantic Literature* (New York: Norton, 1971), 288.

76. In this, Ransom anticipates (and perhaps influences) Geoffrey Hartman, who in the 1960s would align Wordsworthian maturity with an *agita* or "anxiety" not typically associated with the rural poet of nature. Hartman's body of work frequently bears traces of his admiration for Ransom. He is the rare critic who detects the "tongue in cheek" quality of "Criticism, Inc." ("Paul de Man's Proverbs of Hell," *London Review of Books* 6, no. 5 [March 15, 1984]: 8). In his memoir, Hartman recalls attending the Indiana School of Letters right around the time Ransom was writing his essay on Wordsworth, and later in that decade, when Hartman received an offer of an associate professorship at Kenyon, he suspected it "was at the urging of John Crowe Ransom, who had read *The Unmediated Vision*"; *A Scholar's Tale: Intellectual Journey of a Displaced Child of Europe* (New York: Fordham UP, 2007), 31, 189.

77. Brooks, *The Well Wrought Urn*, 3–9; Cleanth Brooks, *Modern Poetry and the Tradition* (Chapel Hill: U of North Carolina P, 1939), 3–6.

78. William Wordsworth, *Letters of William and Dorothy Wordsworth*, eds. Ernest de Selincourt and Chester L. Shaver, 2nd ed. (Oxford: Oxford UP, 1967), 1: 586.

79. Brooks, *The Well Wrought Urn*, 7, 208.

80. Ransom, "William Wordsworth," 503, 504.

81. Ransom, "William Wordsworth," 499.

82. Ransom, "William Wordsworth," 504.

83. Ransom, "William Wordsworth," 503.

84. Even his idiosyncratic definition of "Meters," the least visualizable of the four terms, attributes to phonetics a visual impact by incorporating a scalar metaphor: "they mean to enlarge the poetic concretion by enforcing those phonetic values which belong to the medium and are independent of the semantic referent"; Ransom, "William Wordsworth," 505.

85. Ransom, "William Wordsworth," 505.

86. Ransom, "William Wordsworth," 505.

87. Ransom, "William Wordsworth," 506.

88. I. A. Richards, *Practical Criticism*, 204.

89. I. A. Richards, *Basic in Teaching: East and West* (London: Kegan Paul, Trench, Trubner & Co., 1935), 56; Richards, *Practical Criticism*, 195. On Richards and Basic English in historical relation to techniques of close reading, see Yohei Igarashi, "Statistical Analysis at the Birth of Close Reading," *New Literary History* 46 (2015): 485–504.

90. I. A. Richards, *Basic English and Its Uses* (New York: Norton, 1943), 107–9.

91. Ransom, "William Wordsworth," 506.

92. Richards, *Practical Criticism*, 227.

93. John Crowe Ransom, "The South: Old or New?," *Sewanee Review* 36 (1928): 146.

94. John Crowe Ransom, "The Concrete Universal II," in *Selected Essays*, 286.

95. Ransom, "William Wordsworth," 500.

96. Ransom, "William Wordsworth," 501–502.

97. Ransom, "William Wordsworth," 503.

98. Ransom, "William Wordsworth," 503.

99. Ransom, "William Wordsworth," 503.

100. Ransom, "William Wordsworth," 502.

101. Ransom, "William Wordsworth," 503.

102. Ransom, "William Wordsworth," 504.

103. Ransom, "William Wordsworth," 504.

104. Ransom, "William Wordsworth," 507.

105. Jonathan Culler has commented on the indeterminacy of the phrase "close reading" by remarking that its opposite "is not distant reading but something like sloppy reading, or casual reading"; "The Closeness of Close Reading," *ADE Bulletin* 149 (2010): 20.

106. Ransom, "William Wordsworth," 511.

107. Ransom, "William Wordsworth," 512, 508.

108. Ransom, "William Wordsworth," 509.

109. For redundancy and tautology in relation to accounts of nostalgia in eighteenth-century medical literature and romantic conceptualizations of reading, see Kevis Goodman, *Pathologies of Motion: Historical Thinking in Medicine, Aesthetics, and Poetics* (New Haven and London: Yale UP, 2022), esp. 174–89; I quote from her account of Wordsworthian tautology on 181.

110. Ransom, "William Wordsworth," 515–16.

111. Ransom, "William Wordsworth," 516.

112. See Peter Manning, "Wordsworth's Intimations Ode and Its Epigraphs," *Journal of English and Germanic Philology* 82 (1982): 526–40. The epigraph in 1807's *Poems, in Two Volumes*, "Paulò majora canamus" ("Let us sing somewhat more loftily"), was from Virgil's *Eclogue* 4.1.

113. John Crowe Ransom, "Modern with a Southern Accent," *Virginia Quarterly Review* 11 (1935): 191–92.

114. In addition to this ostensible "Southern quality," Wordsworth had also been a constant fixture in the nineteenth-century Southern imagination, not only for his anti-industrialist regionalism but for his recuperative poetics of natural harmony. Henry Timrod, so-called poet laureate of the Confederacy, raved "that nobody could devote a month or many months to that grand old bard, without being made wiser and better"; qtd. in Edd Winfield Parks, *Ante-Bellum Southern Literary Critics* (Athens: U of Georgia P, 1962), 213–14. The *Columbia [SC] Phoenix* of June 15, 1865 (1:64) featured a front-page article titled "Wordsworth on Taste and Culture," in which the poet's "sincere love of nature" offered an antidote to the traumatic postwar transition, displayed in several articles on the same page that detailed numerous military orders calling in various ways on Southerners, "after these years of blood and suffering," to "acquiesce in the result of battle," the need to grow crops, cultivate nature, and so on. Wordsworth's name thus stands prominently atop a page whose content centers on restoring nature's harmony; he is the muse of postwar balance.

115. M. H. Abrams, "*The Prelude* and *The Recluse*: Wordsworth's Long Journey Home," in *Wordsworth: A Collection of Critical Essays* (New York: Prentice-Hall, 1972), 161.

116. Ransom to Davidson, April 11, 1951, Davidson Papers, (box 11, folder 10).

117. "Teacher, Ex-Pupil at Kenyon Talk Only Poetry," 1.

118. John Crowe Ransom, "Art and the Human Economy," *Kenyon Review* 7 (1945): 685.

119. Kenyon College itself was relatively calm for 1968, with a conservative political science department and a reputation for analytical conversations about politics rather than for direct activism. Terry Robbins, one of the three Weathermen killed in a 1970 New York townhouse explosion, entered Kenyon in 1964 and started a chapter of SDS there, but he dropped out because of his difficulty in gathering support on such a conservative campus.

120. Ransom, "Art and the Human Economy," 687.

121. I take a cue from Marjorie Levinson, who cautioned Wordsworth's Reagan-era readers that "the prolific contraries of Romantic poetry and criticism . . . are not our family of conflicts, which is to say, they are not prolific for us"; Marjorie Levinson, *Wordsworth's Great Period Poems* (Cambridge: Cambridge UP, 1986), 57.

Chapter 2: Shelley's Immaturity

1. Cleanth Brooks, *Modern Poetry and the Tradition* (Chapel Hill: U of North Carolina P, 1939), 237; John Crowe Ransom, *Selected Letters* (Baton Rouge: Louisiana State UP, 1985), 73; Ransom, "Survey of Literature," *Poems and Essays* (New York: Alfred Knopf, 1955), 63 (lines 17–18); Allen Tate and John Peale Bishop, *The Republic of Letters in America: Correspondence*, ed. Thomas Daniel Young and John J. Hindle (Lexington: UP of Kentucky, 1981), 141, 142–43. Forty years later, Paul Foot revived the motif of "Shelley's balls" with a different emphasis, telling the story of the annual "Eights Week" attacks on the poet's naked Victorian-era statue at University College, Oxford—an act of vandalism that Foot reads as a metaphor for Shelley's "castration" by editors ensconced mainly "at British places of learning": "'We've got Shelley's balls!' was the plummy cry of triumph which would echo through the quadrangles," while college officials "shrugged their shoulders and sought out a mason, who replaced the missing parts"; Paul Foot, *Red Shelley* (London: Sidgwick & Jackson, 1980), 9–10.

2. Carlos Baker, *Shelley's Major Poetry: The Fabric of a Vision* (Princeton: Princeton UP, 1948), 11.

3. On these contending versions of "Shelley," see Timothy Webb, *Shelley: A Voice Not Understood* (Manchester: Manchester UP, 1977), 1–32.

4. Percy Bysshe Shelley, *The Letters of Percy Bysshe Shelley*, ed. F. L. Jones (Oxford: Clarendon P, 1964), 2:310. Twentieth-century readers could have discerned in this myth of Shelley's arrested development a prevalent formulation of homosexuality as an "aberration" associated with stunted growth—what Freud called "a certain arrest of sexual development"; "Letter to an American Mother" (1935), in Ronald Bayer, *Homosexuality and American Psychiatry: The Politics of Diagnosis* (Princeton: Princeton UP, 1981), 27. Heather Love summarizes the Freudian framework: "homosexuality is often seen as a result of a failure of maturation or a failure to overcome primary cathexes, and it

has been associated with narcissism and infantilism as well as with incomplete or failed gendering"; *Feeling Backward: Loss and the Politics of Queer History* (Cambridge: Harvard UP, 2007), 21–22. For the Freudian trope of "arrest" see also Henry Abelove, "Freud, Male Homosexuality, and the Americans," in *The Lesbian and Gay Studies Reader*, eds. Henry Abelove, Michéle Aina Barale, and David M. Halperin (New York: Routledge, 1993), 381. Freud's portrayal of homosexuality as a form of arrested development echoed nineteenth-century sexologists such as Karl Heinrich Ulrichs, Richard Freiherr von Krafft-Ebing, and Havelock Ellis. Richard C. Sha argues that Shelley hints at an evolutionary model of sexuality in his "Discourse on the Manners of the Antient Greeks" (the preface to his 1818 translation of Plato's *Symposium*); "The Use and Abuse of Alterity: David Halperin and Percy Shelley on Ancient Greek Sexuality," *Historicizing Romantic Sexuality*, ed. Richard C. Sha, *Romantic Circles Praxis* (January 2006): http://www.rc.umd.edu/praxis/sexuality/sha/sha.html, para. 39.

5. On the abuse of Keats along gendered lines, with implications for the sexualized reception of Shelley, see Susan J. Wolfson, "Feminizing Keats," in *Critical Essays on John Keats*, ed. Hermione de Almeida (Boston: G. K. Hall & Co., 1990), 317–53.

6. See Susan J. Wolfson, "'Slow Time,' 'a Brooklet, Scarce Espied': Close Reading, Cleanth Brooks, John Keats," in *The Work of Reading: Literary Criticism in the 21st Century*, eds. Anirudh Sridhar, Mir Ali Hosseini, and Derek Attridge (New York: Palgrave Macmillan, 2021), 199–206.

7. Brooks, *Modern Poetry and the Tradition*, 50; Cleanth Brooks, *The Well Wrought Urn: Studies in the Structure of Poetry* (New York: Harcourt Brace, 1947), 255; Brooks, *Modern Poetry and the Tradition*, 237. Plenty of critics, of course, describe compelling versions of irony in Shelley. See, for example, Harold Bloom, *The Visionary Company*, 2nd ed. (Ithaca: Cornell UP, 1971), 282–362; Stuart Curran, *Poetic Form and British Romanticism* (New York and Oxford: Oxford UP, 1986), 80–82; and Andrew Franta, "Audience, Irony, and Shelley," in *British Romanticism: Criticism and Debates*, ed. Mark Canuel (London: Routledge, 2015), 170–79.

8. Brooks, "Irony and 'Ironic' Poetry," *College English* 9 (1948): 234. Arguing that Brooks "is perhaps too quick to credit Shelley's sincerity" in "Ode to the West Wind," Andrew Franta observes that "Shelley's speaker does, after all, respond to his failure to internalize nature by impaling himself on it"; Franta, "Audience, Irony, and Shelley," 173.

9. Frederick Pottle, "The Case of Shelley," *PMLA* 67 (1952): 599. Shelleyans liked to say that the New Critics were reading the wrong poems, cherry-picking "weaker" private lyrics that Shelley never intended for the public eye; see, for example, G. M. Matthews, who recasts Shelley as "modest," "reticent," and "private": "A total of seven or eight 'personal' lyrics in twelve volumes of verse, only half of these in the last eleven volumes—a modest ration, one might think, for a monotonously self-regarding narcissist whose genius was essentially lyrical. . . . This is all. It now seems necessary to ask: how is it that so reticent a poet has gained a reputation for emotional exhibitionism? . . . To treat these intimate verses ('you may read them to Jane, but to no one else,—and yet on second thoughts I had rather you would not') as if they were manifestoes is rather like breaking into a man's bathroom in order to censure his habit of indecent exposure"; "Shelley's Lyrics," in D. W. Jefferson, ed., *The Morality of Art: Essays Presented to G. Wilson Knight* (London: Routledge and Kegan Paul, 1969), reprinted in *Shelley's*

Poetry and Prose, eds. Donald H. Reiman and Sharon B. Powers (New York: Norton, 1977), 682.

10. *English Romantic Poets*, eds. James Stephens, Edwin L. Beck, and Royall H. Snow (Cincinnati: American Book Company, 1933), xxxiv.

11. Deidre Shauna Lynch, *Loving Literature: A Cultural History* (Cambridge: Harvard UP, 2014), 65.

12. Abbott C. Martin, "Dark Inscrutable Workmanship: Poetry for Grown People," *The Sewanee Review* 50 (1942): 398.

13. A word about vocabulary: the militaristic terminology used to describe the response to Shelley—"attack," "assault," "offensive," and so forth—is significantly the New Critics' own. They seem really to have seen themselves as engaged in what we nowadays would call a culture war, their vocabulary reflecting a self-conscious sense of embattlement. See, for example, the correspondence between Tate and Brooks, in which the word *attack* features repeatedly—all page numbers cited in *Cleanth Brooks and Allen Tate: Collected Letters, 1933–1976*, ed. Alphonse Vinh (Columbia: U of Missouri P, 1976): "Your *attack* bodes well for our symposium" (Brooks to Tate, 65); "I haven't seen the Horace Gregory *attack*. . . . As a matter of fact, the slurring reference to Gregory in my books was probably sufficient . . . to account for his *attack*" (Brooks to Tate, 68); "Chauncey Brewster Tinker was at the lecture. He said to someone, 'Why doesn't somebody throw a stool at him?' Maybe we can throw some stools (pun) at him or his like in our *attack*" (Tate to Brooks, 68–69); "The M.L.A. had need of thee when Mr. Bush read his *attack*. . . . Those *attacked* were you, Empson, John, and I. John got the roughest treatment . . ." (Tate to Brooks, 146); "I wonder if you have sent the MS. . . . I think that it is worthwhile to make the *attack* soon" (Brooks to Tate, 23); "Do we need to *attack* the leftists? It seems to me they are as liquidated as the Confederate Army" (Tate to Brooks, 69); "I get extreme private admiration and public *attack*" (Brooks to Tate, 24); "Last Saturday the New England CEA met here at Yale with a program featuring an *attack* and a defense of critical methods" (Brooks to Tate, 168); "your essay . . . centers the fight right at the crucial point—I'm convinced more and more that positivism is the real enemy and that the only sound strategy is to *attack* there" (Brooks to Tate, 76). This last letter includes Brooks's explanation of his rhetorical self-arming: "It's my considered opinion, Allen, that in academic matters one ought never to use the rapier when the meat-axe will do. That's not to claim that I wield it with nonchalance or special grace. But no other weapon will work on the academic politician" (76).

14. Mary Wollstonecraft Shelley, "Note to Queen Mab" (1839), in *The Complete Poetical Works of Percy Bysshe Shelley* (1839), ed. H. Buxton Forman, 2nd ed. (London: Reeves and Turner, 1886), 1: xl. On the challenges the editor Mary Shelley had to navigate in rehabilitating Shelley, see Susan J. Wolfson, "Editorial Privilege: Mary Shelley and Percy Shelley's Audiences," in *The Other Mary Shelley*, eds. Audrey Fisch, Anne K. Mellor, and Esther H. Schor (New York: Oxford UP, 1993), 39–72.

15. Everard Meynell dates the essay on Shelley to 1889 (it was published posthumously in 1909) in *The Life of Francis Thompson* (New York: Charles Scribner, 1913), 98.

16. Edward Trelawney, *Recollections of the Last Days of Shelley and Byron* (Boston: Ticknor and Fields, 1858), 13.

17. Charles Kingsley, "Thoughts on Shelley and Byron" (1853), rpt. in *Literary and General Lectures and Essays* (London: Macmillan, 1890), 53. The difference between viewing Shelley as a "beardless boy" and viewing him as a "monster" was usually developmental: advocates for Shelley saw him as *pre*-pubescent—boyish, asexual, and innocent—while detractors deemed him as having crossed over into adolescent limbo, a period in life "when the individual has developed full sexual capacity but has not yet assumed a full adult role in society." See Patricia Meyer Spacks, *The Adolescent Idea: Myths of Youth and the Adult Imagination* (New York: Basic Books, 1981), 7. For the contrast between the "animal" Shelley and the "ethereal" Shelley in his nineteenth-century reception, see Timothy Morton, "Receptions," in *Cambridge Companion to Shelley*, ed. Timothy Morton (Cambridge: Cambridge UP, 2006), 36.

18. John Stuart Mill, "The Two Kinds of Poetry" (1833), rpt. in *Early Essays by John Stuart Mill* (London: George Bell, 1897), 228–29.

19. Mill, "The Two Kinds of Poetry," 228. On Mill's treatment of "adolescent" Shelley, particularly as this gets related to style in Shelley's reception, see Jane Stabler, "Shelley Criticism from Romanticism to Modernism," in *The Oxford Handbook to Percy Bysshe Shelley*, ed. Michael O'Neill (Oxford: Oxford UP, 2013), esp. 661–66.

20. F. R. Leavis, "Shelley," *Revaluation: Tradition and Development in English Poetry* (New York: George W. Stewart, 1947), 167; C. S. Lewis, "Shelley, Dryden, and Mr. Eliot," *Selected Literary Essays*, ed. Walter Hooper (Cambridge: Cambridge UP, 1969), 204. On Shelley's reputation for speed and the affective perspective that readers must assume to render such a judgment, see William Keach's chapter "Shelley's Speed" in *Shelley's Style* (New York: Routledge, 1984), esp. 154–56 for a survey of statements such as those by Leavis, Bloom, and Lewis.

21. Leavis, "Shelley," 206.

22. See, for example, remarks by George Santayana ("Shelley seems hardly to have been brought up"), Irving Babbitt ("He was the perfect example of the nympholept"), and Aldous Huxley ("Ugh! Think of his treatment of women—shocking, really shocking. . . . He wasn't born a man; he was only a kind of fairy slug with the sexual appetites of a schoolboy"). George Santayana, "Shelley: Or the Poetic Value of Revolutionary Principles," *Winds of Doctrine* (New York: Charles Scribner's Sons, 1913), 158; Irving Babbitt, *Rousseau and Romanticism* (Boston and New York: Houghton Mifflin Company, 1919), 263, 161; Aldous Huxley, *Point Counter Point* (London: Chatto and Windus, 1928), 119.

23. Paul Elmer More, "Shelley," *Shelburne Essays*, seventh series (Boston and New York: Houghton Mifflin, 1910), 6–7; Pottle, "The Case of Shelley," 598. Running parallel to such judgments—and contemporary with Brooks's and Warren's time in graduate school—there was also a 1925 psychological account by the proto-queer theorist Edward Carpenter, who sympathetically worked out Shelley's "repressed (and hence unconscious) homosexual impulses of comrade-love." The "tender sadness and vague self-pitying emotion" of Shelley's poetry, Carpenter argued, reflect "a homosexual component in his make-up" which is "typical of a certain stage of adolescence"; "Shelley remained to some degree fixed at this phase." Edward Carpenter, *The Psychology of the Poet Shelley* (London: Taylor and Francis, 1925), 87, 60–61. See also Robert Metcalf Smith, *The Shelley Legend* (New York: Charles Scribner, 1945), a lurid and error-filled attack on Shelley's morals that drew on Carpenter's book. *The Psychology*

of the Poet Shelley turned out to be an elaborate fiction in its own right, based on the account of a "Dr. George Barnefield," who happened to be Carpenter himself.

24. The political Shelley, as Paul Foot tells us, had already been "sheltered from young people" by a "process of censorship and omission"—no danger of infecting young people with socialism—but the lyrical Shelley, despite the handwringing cited above, remained pedagogically central, taught even in New Humanist classrooms. See Foot, *Red Shelley*, 11; and Austin Warren's report on Irving Babbitt's teaching in *The Letters of Austin Warren*, ed. George Panichas (Macon, GA: Mercer UP, 2011), 161.

25. Esther Raushenbush, *Literature for Individual Education* (New York: Columbia UP, 1942), v.

26. Elizabeth Geen, "Some Thoughts on Higher Education for Women," *Pi Lambda Theta Journal* 29 (1951): 164, 175.

27. Thomas Clark Pollock, "English for Maturity," *College English* 10 (1949): 246, 247–48.

28. Pollock, "English for Maturity," 250.

29. John Crowe Ransom, Miscellaneous Fragments (undated), John Crowe Ransom Papers (box 4, folder 12), Vanderbilt University Special Collections, Vanderbilt University.

30. René Wellek, *English Criticism, 1900–1950* (1986), *A History of Modern Criticism*, 6 vols. (New Haven: Yale UP, 1955–86), 5: 190–91.

31. Brooks, *The Well Wrought Urn*, 81; Tate, *The Republic of Letters in America*, 78; W. K. Wimsatt, Jr., "The Concrete Universal," *The Verbal Icon: Studies in the Meaning of Poetry* (Lexington: UP of Kentucky, 1954), 82.

32. John Crowe Ransom, "Preface," *The World's Body* (New York: Charles Scribner's, 1938), viii.

33. One of the "master narratives" of nineteenth-century thought, according to Andrew Elfenbein, was "the development away from a youthful, immature Byronic phrase [*sic*] to a sober, adult 'Victorian' phase." The New Critics tweaked this narrative by substituting Shelley for Byron. While Byron dwindled into a matter of relative indifference to them, Shelley came to embody an immature, adolescent sensibility that had to be (first) disciplined and (finally) overcome. See Andrew Elfenbein, *Byron and the Victorians* (Cambridge: Cambridge UP, 1995), 88–89.

34. [Cleanth Brooks and Robert Penn Warren], "Sophomore Poetry Manual," Cleanth Brooks Papers (YCAL MSS 30, box 31, page 69), Beinecke Rare Book & Manuscript Library, Yale University. On precursors to *Understanding Poetry* such as the "Sophomore Poetry Manual" and *An Approach to Literature*, as well as the teaching methods consolidated by such classroom texts, see Tara Lockhart's excellent "Teaching with Style: Brooks and Warren's Literary Pedagogy," in *Rereading the New Criticism*, eds. Miranda B. Hickman and John D. McIntyre (Columbus: The Ohio State UP, 2012), 195–217.

35. T.S. Eliot, *The Use of Poetry and the Use of Criticism* (Cambridge: Harvard UP, 1933), 80. For Shelley's charged significance to Eliot, see Peter Lowe, *Christian Romanticism: T. S. Eliot's Response to Percy Shelley* (Amherst, NY: Cambria P, 2006); and George Franklin, "Instances of Meeting: Shelley and Eliot: A Study in Affinity," *ELH* 61 (1994): 955–90.

36. Eliot, *The Use of Poetry*, 80–83.

37. Eliot, *On Poetry and Poets* (London: Faber, 1957), 28.

38. Robert Browning, *Pauline* (1833), *Robert Browning: The Major Works*, ed. Adam Roberts (Oxford: Oxford UP, 1997), 1–28. For another statement of the distinctiveness of the youthful encounter with Shelley's poetry, as compared with the philosophical or academic reading, see Edmund Gosse, "Shelley in 1892," *Questions at Issue* (London: William Heinemann, 1893), 210–11: "We must throw ourselves back to what we were at twenty, and recollect how dazzling, how fresh, how full of colour, and melody, and odour, this poetry seemed to us. . . . We took him for what he seemed, 'a pard-like spirit, beautiful and swift,' and we thought to criticise him as little as we thought to judge the murmur of the forest or the reflections of the moonlight on the lake. He was exquisite, emancipated, young like ourselves, and yet as wise as a divinity. We followed him unquestioning, walking in step with his panthers, as the Bacchantes followed Dionysus out of India, intoxicated with enthusiasm." On Shelley's institutional status in the British university curriculum of the late nineteenth century, see Anthony Kearney, "Reading Shelley: A Problem for Late Victorian English Studies," *Victorian Poetry* 36 (1998): 59–73; and Mark Kipperman, "Absorbing a Revolution: Shelley Becomes a Romantic, 1889–1903," *Nineteenth-Century Literature* 47 (1992): 187–211.

39. T. S. Eliot, "Reflections on Contemporary Poetry," *The Egoist* (July 1919): 39–40. See the sensitive discussion in Franklin, "Instances of Meeting," 956–58.

40. Eliot, "Reflections on Contemporary Poetry," 40. Many thanks to Kenneth Gross for helpful conversation about this passage.

41. T. S. Eliot, *The Sacred Wood: Essays on Poetry and Criticism* (New York: Alfred Knopf, 1921), 27. The phrase "uncertain disease" is Kevis Goodman's, drawn from the eighteenth-century Scottish physician William Cullen, for whom it captured "the provoking difficulty that nostalgia (*Heimweh, maladie du pay*) posed to the classification practices of eighteenth-century disease taxonomies." I don't wish to press too directly an equivalence between "Shelley" and this "uncertain disease," though Goodman's searching account of eighteenth-century nostalgia as a "disease of unhappily or unwillingly dislocated persons" aligns somewhat with Eliot's and others' perception that subjective disorientation, the displacement of the self from the self, could be an outcome of reading Shelley. In light of Goodman's alternative phrase "an uncertain unease" (a lesser pathology?), I note this fascinating report from Peter Manning about Brooks's teaching of Shelley: "I inherited from Cleanth Brooks in the only class on the Romantics I ever took a certain *unease* about Shelley. 'I won't speak about Shelley' he said, leaving it to the students to sustain the discussion for several days; 'My views about Shelley are in print, and I don't wish to spoil pleasure for anybody else'"; Kevis Goodman, *Pathologies of Motion: Historical Thinking in Medicine, Aesthetics, and Poetics* (New Haven and London: Yale UP, 2022), 31, 112, 118; Peter Manning, email to author, August 4, 2022.

42. Cleanth Brooks, *Community, Religion, and Literature: Essays* (Columbia: U of Missouri P, 1995), 148–49. "My training and personal impulses prepared me for only the romantics," he added; "In my own senior year, I at last began to grow up."

43. Pottle's audiences at Yale were exclusively male, but in "The Case of Shelley" he generalizes the phenomenon to include female students as well: "From the first appearance of Shelley's poems down at least to the year 1917 (and I can hardly have been the

last to experience it) his poems had a unique power to intoxicate and to enthrall sensitive young men and women, to operate upon them with the force of a sudden conversion"; "The Case of Shelley," 594. The world's most eminent Boswellian and author of the important rehabilitative essay on Shelley, Pottle is nowadays best remembered through his relationships with others: dissertation supervisor to Harold Bloom (whose *Shelley's Mythmaking* cites Pottle's "The Case of Shelley" no fewer than fifteen times), honoree of the Festschrift *From Sensibility to Romanticism* (a veritable who's-who of postwar criticism), and Brooks's most patient and formidable adversary (targeted in *The Well Wrought Urn*, he engaged in collegial dispute with Brooks throughout the next decade). Pottle's recurrently supporting role in the history of the discipline is probably due to his humility and general disinclination for polemic—he seems to have been as kindly regarded as anyone in the field of English—but it does little justice to his significance as a textual critic and literary theorist. The present book, I'm afraid, places him in a similarly supporting role. It is also a crucial role, however, for Pottle is a reliable commentator whose even-handed assessments can clarify elements of our received disciplinary narrative.

44. Frederick Pottle, manuscript of lecture for English 150, delivered c. 1935. Frederick Pottle Papers (MS 1605, box 17, folder 47), Yale University Manuscripts and Archives, Yale University. Quotations from Pottle's lectures in the coming pages are all from this manuscript.

45. Goodman, *Pathologies of Motion*, 32.

46. Frederick Pottle, *The Idiom of Poetry* (1941), 2nd ed. (Ithaca: Cornell UP, 1946), 151–52.

47. Spacks, *The Adolescent Idea*, 5.

48. Pottle seems to have replaced this number whenever he repeated the lecture in subsequent years; in the manuscript, "of thirty-six" is crossed through with a pencil, and "little short of fifty" scribbled in above.

49. Pottle, *The Idiom of Poetry*, 83.

50. Robert Browning knew this: "I shall go mad if I recall that time!"; *Pauline*, 12 (line 429).

51. Pottle, manuscript of lecture for English 150, Pottle Papers (box 17, folder 47).

52. Louise Dudley, *The Study of Literature* (New York: Houghton Mifflin, 1928), v; Howard Foster Lowry and Willard Thorp, *Oxford Anthology of English Poetry* (New York: Oxford UP, 1935), v.

53. Eliot, "Reflections on Contemporary Poetry," 40.

54. Cleanth Brooks, Jr. and Robert Penn Warren, *Understanding Poetry: An Anthology for College Students* (New York: Henry Holt, 1938), xiii.

55. Paul E. Reynolds, "Textbook Seminal and Sound," *CEA Critic* 13.8 (November, 1951): 7; Clarence L. Kulisheck, review of *Poems for Study*, *CEA Critic* 16.3 (March, 1954): 5.

56. Kulisheck, review of *Poems for Study*, 5.

57. Garrick Davis, "The Well-Wrought Textbook," *Humanities* 32 (2011): 24.

58. Handwritten note on Sara Teasdale's "I Shall Not Care," typescript of "Instructor's Manual" for *Understanding Poetry* (4th ed.), Brooks Papers (YCAL MSS 30, box 50).

59. Gertrude Slaughter, "Percy Bysshe Shelley, 1822–1922," *The North American Review* 216 (1922): 67; Foot, *Red Shelley*, 257.

60. Brooks and Warren, *Understanding Poetry*, v.

61. M. H. Abrams, Oral History interview with Jonathan Culler and Neil Hertz, February 18, 2008, M. H. Abrams Papers (14–12–4080, CD-437), Kroch Library, Division of Rare and Manuscript Collections, Cornell University.

62. Brooks and Warren, *Understanding Poetry*, 416, 363, 219.

63. Robert Scholes, *Textual Power: Literary Theory and the Teaching of English* (New Haven: Yale UP, 1985), 62.

64. The analysis of "The Indian Serenade" appears in Brooks and Warren, *Understanding Poetry*, 320–23; except where noted, all quotations of this analysis refer to these pages.

65. Hugh Kenner, *The Art of Poetry* (New York: Holt, Rinehart and Winston, 1959), 35–36.

66. H.R. Swardson, "The Heritage of the New Criticism," *College English* 41 (1979): 416–17.

67. Richard H. Fogle, *The Imagery of Keats and Shelley: A Comparative Study* (Chapel Hill: U of North Carolina P, 1949), 274; Pottle, "The Case of Shelley," 605.

68. Percy Shelley, "The Indian Serenade," in *Understanding Poetry*, 319–20.

69. Shelley, *Shelley's Poetry and Prose*, 369–70. For "dramatic lyric," see Robert Langbaum, *The Poetry of Experience: The Dramatic Monologue in Modern Literary Tradition* (1957; Chicago and London: U of Chicago P, 1985); Ralph Rader, "The Dramatic Monologue and Related Lyric Forms," *Critical Inquiry* 3 (1976): 131–51; and Carol D. Christ, *Victorian and Modern Poetics* (Chicago: U of Chicago P, 1986), 15–52.

70. See Burton R. Pollin, *Music for Shelley's Poetry: An Annotated Bibliography of Musical Settings of Shelley's Poetry* (New York: Da Capo P, 1974). Pollin lists 165 settings of "To —" ("Music, when soft voices die"), and 150 of "The Indian Serenade."

71. Chauncey B. Tinker, "Shelley's Indian Serenade," *Yale Library Gazette* 25 (1950): 71–72.

72. Fogle, *Imagery of Keats and Shelley*, 85.

73. Jane Marcus, "Britannia Rules the Waves," in *Decolonizing Tradition: New Views of Twentieth-Century "British" Literary Canons*, ed. Karen Lawrence (Urbana: U of Illinois P, 1992), 137.

74. Allen Tate characteristically writes of death in Donne as a kind of manly, virtuous consummation, arguing that "the moment of death is like the secret communion of lovers." Here is another stick for a New Critic to beat Shelley with: Shelley's lover can't even die like a man, departing in not-so-secret "communion" with himself; Tate, "The Point of Dying: Donne's Virtuous Men," *Sewanee Review* 61 (1953): 76.

75. The textual history provided here is based mainly on the account by Donald Reiman and Michael O'Neill, editors of *Percy Bysshe Shelley*, vol. 8: *Fair-Copy Manuscripts of Shelley's Poems in European and American Libraries* (New York and London: Garland Publishing, 1997), xvi–xvii, 329–40.

76. Trelawney, *Recollections*, 150.

77. Robert Browning to Leigh Hunt, 6 October 1857, *The Correspondence of Leigh Hunt, edited by His Eldest Son* (London: Smith, Elder and Co., 1862), 2: 266.

78. Qtd. in B. C. Forbes, *How to Get the Most Out of Business* (1927; rpt. New York: Cosimo, 2006), 191.

79. Reiman and O'Neill, *Percy Bysshe Shelley*, 339. *La Clemenza di Tito* was a popular opera in Tuscany, where the Shelleys lived mostly between summer 1819 and spring 1822. Staged in London in July 1817, it was also reviewed by Leigh Hunt in *The Examiner*. Emanuele Senici writes of the duet, "Ah Perdona," that it "was undoubtedly the most famous piece of the opera in Britain" during the first half of the nineteenth century; "'Adapted to the Modern Stage': *La Clemenza di Tito* in London," *Cambridge Opera Journal* 7 (1995): 9.

80. Some scholars have speculated that Shelley imagined the lines being sung to Mozart's score, but there is little evidence for such a claim—and the fact that both pieces are in Mary's hand would in any case render manuscript evidence tenuous. See Buxton Forman, "Shelley, Metastasio, and Mozart: 'The Indian Serenade,'" *The Athenaeum* no. 4175 (7 November 1907): 550–51; and Theodore Fenner, *Leigh Hunt and Opera Criticism: The "Examiner" Years, 1808–1821* (Lawrence: UP of Kansas, 1972), 221.

81. See Seth Lerer, *Error and the Academic Self: The Scholarly Imagination, Medieval to Modern* (New York: Columbia UP, 2002), 253: "The old philology . . . always lurks in the background not just of the New Criticism but of high theory."

82. The chapter on "How Poems Come About" involves literary, intellectual, and historical materials, authorial intention, and the creative process. Reproducing a manuscript of A. E. Housman's "The Immortal Part" and including it as an insert, Brooks and Warren pursue an intensive reading of the poem in order to speculate on Housman's creative process. The manuscript exists not to complicate the notion of the unitary "poem itself" but, on the contrary, to reinforce it by hypostatizing the progress from "original idea to . . . finished poem"; "Now we are primarily interested in the nature of the poem and its quality: we are critics and appreciators of poetry. . . . The poem is what we want in the end and . . . a knowledge of the materials that went into the poem or of the process by which it came to be, cannot change the nature of the poem itself"; Brooks and Warren, *Understanding Poetry*, 2nd ed. (1950), 617–18, 591.

83. James Turner, *Philology: The Forgotten Origins of the Modern Humanities* (Princeton: Princeton UP, 2014), 298. Roman Jakobson is reputed to have said, "Philology is the art of reading slowly"; Calvert Watkins, "What Is Philology?' in *On Philology*, ed. Jan M. Ziolkowski (University Park and London: Pennsylvania State UP, 1990), 25.

84. "A Conservative Revolution," Promotional material, Brooks Papers (YCAL MSS 30, box 46).

85. David Daiches, *The Novel and the Modern World* (Chicago: U of Chicago P, 1939), 213, 217–18.

86. Allen Tate, "The Function of Criticism" (1941), *Reason in Madness: Critical Essays* (Salem, NH: Ayer Co., 1988), 17.

87. Jerome J. McGann, *The Beauty of Inflections: Literary Investigations in Historical Method and Theory* (Oxford: Clarendon P, 1988), 114; Brooks and Warren, *Understanding Poetry* (2nd ed.), xxi. On "the dialectic *with* historicism" that tends to get elided in critiques of New Criticism, see Susan J. Wolfson, *Formal Charges: The Shaping of Poetry in British Romanticism* (Stanford: Stanford UP, 1997), 8–9.

88. See Turner, *Philology*, 265–75, to which this account is indebted.

89. Frances Ferguson, "Philology, Literature, Style," *ELH* 80 (2013): 325; Frances Ferguson, "Now It's Personal: D. A. Miller and Too-Close Reading," *Critical Inquiry* 41 (2015): 532.

90. Ferguson, "Philology," 325.

91. For the work of editing that Brooks and Warren's correspondence describe, see James A. Grimshaw, "Cleanth Brooks and Robert Penn Warren: Notes on Their Literary Correspondence," *Mississippi Quarterly* 48 (1994–95): 93–104.

92. Brooks and Warren, *Understanding Poetry* (2nd ed.), xxi.

93. John Crowe Ransom, "William Wordsworth: Notes Toward an Understanding of Poetry," *Kenyon Review* 12 (1950): 507. On lyric understatement as an alternative to lyric poetry's (especially romanticism's) association with excess, hyperbole, and overstatement, see Brian McGrath, *Look Round for Poetry: Untimely Romanticisms* (New York: Fordham UP, 2022), 23–40.

94. This was the description given in Sotheby's 1962 catalog, when the manuscript said to have been discovered on Shelley's body was sold at auction; Reiman and O'Neill, *Percy Bysshe Shelley*, 331.

95. Leavis, "Shelley," 207.

96. Brooks and Warren, *Understanding Poetry*, 296–319.

97. Brooks and Warren, *Understanding Poetry*, 323–33.

98. Brooks and Warren, *Understanding Poetry*, 319.

99. Immanuel Kant, "An Answer to the Question: What Is Enlightenment?," trans. James Schmidt, in *What Is Enlightenment? Eighteenth-Century Answers and Twentieth-Century Questions* (Berkeley: U of California P, 1996), 58; Cleanth Brooks, Jr. and Robert Penn Warren, "General Introduction," *An Approach to Literature*, eds. Brooks, John Thibaut Purser, and Warren (Baton Rouge: Louisiana State UP, 1936), 6.

100. For an excellent treatment of Pottle and his major rehabilitative essay, see Chapter 9, "The Case of Shelley," in James Chandler, *England in 1819: The Politics of Literary Culture and the Case of Romantic Historicism* (Chicago: U of Chicago P, 1998), esp. 489–98.

101. Pottle, "The Case of Shelley," 605.

102. Pottle, "The Case of Shelley," 605–6.

103. Pottle, manuscript of lecture for "English Poets of the 19C," delivered 1956. Pottle Papers (MS 1605, box 14, folder 13–19).

104. Fogle, *The Imagery of Keats and Shelley*, 274.

105. Eliot, *The Use of Poetry*, 80. On the insinuation of biography into the twentieth-century critical reading of Shelley, see Webb, *A Voice Not Understood*, 25–37 (including mention of "The Indian Serenade" on 35–37). On the gendered assumptions about "sensitivity" and politics that often inform such complaints, see Catherine Maxwell, *The Female Sublime from Milton to Swinburne: Bearing Blindness* (Manchester: Manchester UP, 2009), 94–104. Anthony Kearney argues that it was Edward Dowden's 1886 biography that made it "no longer possible to study [Shelley] without dragging unpalatable biographical facts into the critical assessments. The poetry was tarnished by the biography"; "Reading Shelley," 61.

106. Brooks and Warren, *Understanding Poetry*, 232.

107. Thomas Jefferson Hogg, *Shelley at Oxford* (London: Methuen, 1904), 12; Thomas Love Peacock, *Memoirs of Percy Bysshe Shelley*, ed. H.F.B. Brett-Smith (London: Henry

Frowde, 1909), 16; Trelawney, *Recollections*, 122; *The Collected Letters of Thomas and Jane Welsh Carlyle*, ed. C. de L. Ryals et al., vol. 27 (Durham and London: Duke UP, 1999), 65; Leavis, "Shelley," 211; René Wellek, "The Concept of 'Romanticism' in Literary History," *Comparative Literature* 1 (1949): 191.

108. Lewis Charles Tatham, Jr., *Shelley and His Twentieth-Century Detractors* (Dissertation, University of Florida, 1965), 22.

109. M. Eunice Mousel, "Falsetto in Shelley," *Studies in Philology* 33 (1936): 588, 609.

110. Brooks and Warren, *Understanding Poetry*, 295.

111. Handwritten note for "To Ianthe," typescript of "Instructor's Manual" for *Understanding Poetry* (2nd ed.), Brooks Papers (YCAL MSS 30, box 50).

112. The deletion of this sentence is one of only two revisions they made to the entire essay. The other revision was to the very next sentence, where they removed "amusement or disgust" (as responses of a reader to the poem) with the slightly more understated "glib and easy exaggeration" (as descriptions of the poem itself).

113. Allen Tate, "Understanding Modern Poetry," *The English Journal* 29 (1940): 268.

114. Graham Hough, *The Romantic Poets* (London: Hutchinson House, 1953), 122.

115. Kulisheck, review of *Poems for Study*, 5.

116. Clarence L. Kulisheck, "Time for a New Indoor Sport," *College English* 13 (1952): 313.

117. Compelling exceptions include Judith Chernaik, *The Lyrics of Shelley* (Cleveland: P of Case Western Reserve U, 1972), 150–54; Matthews, "Shelley's Lyrics," 688–89; Maxwell, *The Female Sublime from Milton to Swinburne*, 97–100; Jessica Quillen, *Shelley and the Musico-Aesthetics of Romanticism* (New York: Routledge, 2016), 140–42; and Paul A. Vatalaro, *Shelley's Music: Fantasy, Authority, and the Object Voice* (Surrey: Ashgate, 2009), 137–38.

118. A. M. D. Hughes, *The Nascent Mind of Shelley* (Oxford: Clarendon P, 1942); Kenneth Neill Cameron, *The Young Shelley: Genesis of a Radical* (New York: Macmillan, 1950). More recently, William Keach has made a strong case for the classroom teaching of the adolescent Shelley: "We miss a tremendous opportunity if we don't begin with Shelley when he was exactly our students' age, eighteen to twenty-one, experimenting with writing and with sex as many of them do, trying to negotiate new social and financial relations with his family—and throwing himself into a life of serious political activism that most students these days find impossible even to imagine, much less to realize"; "Young Shelley," in *Early Shelley: Vulgarisms, Politics and Fractals*, ed. Neil Fraistat, *Romantic Circles Praxis* (August 1997): https://romantic-circles.org/praxis/early shelley/keach/keach.html, para. 2.

119. Cameron, *The Young Shelley*, 15, 106–7, 37, xi; Foot, *Red Shelley*, 10. Foot echoes Frederick Engels, *The Condition of the Working Class in England in 1844*, trans. Florence Kelley Wischnewetzky (London: Swan Sonnenschein, 1892), 240: "Shelley, the genius, the prophet, . . . find[s] most of [his] readers in the proletariat; the bourgeoisie owns only castrated editions, family editions, cut down in accordance with the hypocritical morality of today."

120. Orrin N. C. Wang, *Fantastic Modernity: Dialectical Readings in Romanticism and Theory* (Baltimore: Johns Hopkins UP, 1996), 190.

121. Harold Bloom, *Shelley's Mythmaking* (Ithaca: Cornell UP, 1959). Bloom's biggest complaint about the New Critics was that, not knowing how to read Shelley, they

simply didn't: "Critics as eminent as Eliot, Leavis, Tate, Brooks, and Ransom, among others, have assured us that the bulk of it is not good poetry, without evidencing that they know it well enough to judge dispassionately"; 110.

122. Pottle, "The Case of Shelley," 608.

Chapter 3: Brooks and the Collegiate Public, Reading Keats Together

1. The phrase "Keats's well-wrought urn" appears, for instance, in George Bornstein, *Representing Modernist Texts: Editing as Interpretation* (Ann Arbor: U of Michigan P, 1991), 265; Nimal Dass, *Rebuilding Babel: The Translations of W.H. Auden* (Amsterdam and Atlanta: Rodopi, 1993), 36; David Fairer, *Organising Poetry: The Coleridge Circle, 1790–1798* (Oxford and New York: Oxford UP, 2009), 32; Richard Haw, *Art of the Brooklyn Bridge: A Visual History* (New York: Routledge, 2008), 187; Richard Keller Simon, *Truth Culture: Popular Culture and the Great Tradition* (Berkeley: U of California P, 1999), 123; and Aron Vinegar and Michael J. Golec, *Relearning from Las Vegas* (Minneapolis: U of Minnesota P, 2009), 85.

2. Ernest Bernbaum, "Keats, Shelley, Byron, and Hunt: A Critical Sketch of Important Books and Articles Concerning Them Published in 1940–1950," *Keats-Shelley Journal* 1 (1952): 73; J. R. MacGillivray, *Keats: A Bibliography and Reference Guide with an Essay on Keats' Reputation* (Toronto: U of Toronto P, 1949), lxxxi.

3. Frederick Pottle, class notes for "English Poets of the Nineteenth Century," 1956, Frederick Pottle Papers (MS 1605, box 14, folder 13), Yale University Manuscripts and Archives, Yale University.

4. Cleanth Brooks, "The Artistry of Keats: A Modern Tribute," *The Major English Romantic Poets: A Symposium in Reappraisal*, eds. C. D. Thorpe, C. Baker, and B. Weaver (Carbondale: Southern Illinois UP, 1957), 246. Worth noting is that this reparative essay comes two decades after Brooks's rough treatment of "Ode on a Nightingale" in the first edition of *Understanding Poetry*, where Keats's ode is carted out (like Shelley's "Indian Serenade") as an example of a weak, defective poem; Cleanth Brooks, Jr. and Robert Penn Warren, *Understanding Poetry* (New York: Henry Holt, 1938), 408–13. On Brooks's early pedagogical framings of Keats, see Susan J. Wolfson, "'Slow Time,' 'a Brooklet, Scarce Espied': Close Reading, Cleanth Brooks, John Keats," in *The Work of Reading: Literary Criticism in the 21st Century*, eds. Anirudh Sridhar, Mir Ali Hosseini, and Derek Attridge (New York: Palgrave Macmillan, 2021), 199–206.

5. John Keats, *Letters of John Keats 1814–1821*, ed. H. E. Rollins, 2 vol. (Cambridge UP, 1958), 1: 394.

6. Keats, *Letters*, 2: 144.

7. Keats, *Letters*, 2: 163. On Keats's complex relation to gender, in his own writing and in criticism of his work, see Alan Bewell, "Keats's 'Realm of Flora,'" *Studies in Romanticism* 31 (1992): 71–98; Margaret Homans, "Keats Reading Women, Women Reading Keats," *Studies in Romanticism* 29 (1990): 341–70; Greg Kucich, "Gender Crossings: Keats and Tighe," *Keats-Shelley Journal* 44 (1995): 29–39; Anne K. Mellor, "Keats and the Complexities of Gender," in *The Cambridge Companion to Keats*, ed. Susan Wolfson (Cambridge and New York: Cambridge UP, 2001), 214–29; Marlon B. Ross, "Beyond the Fragmented Word: Keats at the Limits of Patrilineal Language," in *Out of Bounds: Male Writers and Gender(ed) Criticism*, ed. Laura Claridge and Elizabeth Langland (Amherst:

U of Massachusetts P, 1990), 110–31; Susan J. Wolfson, "Feminizing Keats," in *Critical Essays on John Keats*, ed. Hermione de Almeida (Boston: G. K. Hall & Co., 1990), 317–53.

8. Keats, *Letters*, 2: 146.

9. For an influential recasting of Keats's precious aestheticism contemporaneous with the New Criticism's own recasting, see Douglas Bush, *Mythology and the Romantic Tradition in English Poetry* (Cambridge: Harvard UP, 1937), 418–28. On the Harvard School's philosophically "mature" Keats, see Christopher Rovee, "Trashing Keats," *ELH* 75 (2008): 1002–3, 1013–14.

10. Cleanth Brooks, *The Well Wrought Urn: Studies in the Structure of Poetry* (New York: Harcourt Brace, 1947), 156. On eroticism in the ode, see Barbara Johnson, *The Feminist Difference: Literature, Psychoanalysis, Race, and Gender* (Cambridge: Harvard UP, 1998), 129–35; Peter Manning, "Reading and Ravishing: The 'Ode on a Grecian Urn,'" in *Approaches to Teaching Keats's Poetry*, eds. Walter H. Evert and Jack W. Rhodes (New York: Modern Language Association, 1991), 131–36; Deborah Pope, "The Dark Side of the Urn: A Re-Evaluation of the Speaker of 'Ode on a Grecian Urn,'" *Essays in Literature* 10 (1983): 45–53; and Froma I. Zeitlin, "Keats in His Tradition: On Ravishing Urns," in *Rape and Representation*, eds. Lynn A. Higgins and Brenda R. Silver (New York: Columbia UP, 1991), 278–303. As Pope notes, the specter of sexual violence in the poem has long been recognized as a feature of the poem by canonical Keats criticism, though with quite variable emphases; "The Dark Side of the Urn," 46.

11. Shelley, for all his gatekeeping, at least kept trying. See Stephen Behrendt, *Shelley and His Audiences* (Lincoln: U of Nebraska P, 1989); and Susan J. Wolfson, "Editorial Privilege: Mary Shelley and Percy Shelley's Audiences," in *The Other Mary Shelley*, eds. Audrey Fisch, Anne K. Mellor, and Esther H. Schor (New York: Oxford UP, 1993), 39–72.

12. Douglas Mao, "The New Critics and the Text-Object," *ELH* 63 (1996): 246.

13. John Crowe Ransom, "Shakespeare at Sonnets," *The World's Body* (New York: Charles Scribner's, 1938), 280; Allen Tate, *Essays of Four Decades* (Chicago: Swallow P, 1968), 527; Brooks, *The Well Wrought Urn*, 233.

14. John Guillory, *Cultural Capital: The Problem of Literary Canon Formation* (Baltimore: Johns Hopkins UP, 1993), 165, 173–74. On the significance of the urn in Guillory's argument, see Mao, "The New Critics and the Text-Object," 236–37.

15. Brooks, *Understanding Poetry*, 21.

16. Cleanth Brooks, "Literature as Paideia," typescript of lecture [n.d.], Cleanth Brooks Papers (YCAL MSS 30, box 74, folder 1465), Beinecke Rare Book and Manuscript Library, Yale University.

17. Cleanth Brooks, *The Hidden God: Studies in Hemingway, Faulkner, Yeats, Eliot, and Warren* (New Haven: Yale UP, 1963), 3.

18. Gerald Graff writes that "putting the emphasis on the literary text itself . . . seemed a tactic ideally suited to a new, mass student body that could not be depended on to bring to the university any common cultural background"; *Professing Literature: An Institutional History* (Chicago and London: U of Chicago P, 1987), 173. Guillory notes that Graff makes no claim for the democratizing intentions of New Critical pedagogy, yet the basic association is nonetheless commonly made. For an example of the optimistic rhetoric, see Norman Norwood Holland: "The 'New Criticism' opened the great tradition of English literature to people of any or no cultural inheritance. . . . In an

upwardly mobile society, students whose parents had never graduated from high school could be *littérateurs*"; *The Critical I* (New York: Columbia UP, 1992), 68. More nuanced, Douglas Mao enriches our understanding of this counter-hierarchical tendency by arguing that the New Criticism's emphasis on the text-object in itself, rather than on the scholarly origins and contexts that enable its study, served a paradoxically leveling function: "the primary aim of the New Critics in this area was . . . to bring 'difficult' poetry to the widest possible audience by showing that one can engage complexity without devoting one's lifetime to the mastery of historical and biographical contexts"; "The New Critics and the Text-Object," 248.

19. Franco Moretti, "The Slaughterhouse of Literature," *MLQ* 61 (2000): 209n3.

20. Cleanth Brooks, *Modern Poetry and the Tradition* (Chapel Hill: U of North Carolina P, 1939), 237.

21. Guillory, *Cultural Capital*, 170–71.

22. Richard R. Werry, "A Public for Poetry," *College English* (1948): 8, 13.

23. John Crowe Ransom, "Theory of Poetic Form," *Texas Quarterly* 9 (1966): 190.

24. Hugh Kenner, "Pedagogue as Critic," 38. Kenner did his Ph.D. with Brooks in the 1950s. I use the term "protegé" advisedly: responding late in his life to this same essay's critique of certain aspects of the New Critical enterprise, Brooks takes offense in a way that is unusual for him, in a nearly five-page digression that hints at something deeper than critical disagreement: Brooks, *Community, Religion, and Literature*, 83–87.

25. Mark Ciabattari, *Social History of the United States: The 1940s* (Santa Barbara: ABC-CLIO, 2009), xix, 176.

26. Daniel A. Clark, "The Two Joes Meet—Joe College, Joe Veteran: The G.I. Bill, College Education, and Postwar American Culture," *History of Education Quarterly* (Summer 1998): 174.

27. Meghan Wilson, "The Forgotten GI: The Servicemen's Readjustment Act and Black Colleges, 1944–54," in *Historically Black Colleges and Universities: Triumphs, Troubles, and Taboos*, eds. Marybeth Gasman and Christopher L. Tudico (New York: Palgrave Macmillan, 2008), 94–97. HBCU administrators supposed that they got about 40% of what "they estimated they would require"; James A. Atkins, "Negro Educational Institutions and the Veterans' Educational Facilities," *Journal of Negro Education* 17 (1948): 152. This underfunding had the effect of artificially suppressing the (still massive) surge in new enrollments, writes Hilary Herbold, since more than twenty thousand Black men were denied admission for the academic year 1946–1947 due to a lack of resources and physical space; Hilary Herbold, "Never a Level Playing Field: Blacks and the GI Bill," *The Journal of Blacks in Higher Education* 6 (1995): 104–8.

28. Joseph A. Baker, "Which Generation?," *The CEA Critic* 19.9 (December 1957): 2–3; Karl Shapiro et al., "The Careful Young Men: Tomorrow's Leaders Analyzed by Today's Teachers," *The Nation* 184.10 (March 9, 1957): 208.

29. Darrel Abel, "Intellectual Criticism," *The American Scholar* 12 (1943): 415.

30. Baker, "Which Generation?," 2–3.

31. Brooks, *Modern Poetry and the Tradition*, 67–68.

32. Keith W. Olson, "The G.I. Bill and Higher Education: Success and Surprise," *American Quarterly* 25 (1973): 596, 602.

33. Olson, "The G.I. Bill and Higher Education," 596.

34. Wilson, "The Forgotten GI," 96.

35. Mark McGurl, *The Program Era: Postwar Fiction and the Rise of Creative Writing* (Cambridge: Harvard UP, 2009), 66. See also Kathleen J. Frydl, *The G.I. Bill* (Cambridge UP, 2009), 222–62.

36. Olson, "The G.I. Bill and Higher Education," 606; Frydl, *The G.I. Bill*, 314.

37. McGurl, *The Program Era*, 61. Christopher Findeisen counters that McGurl "misinterprets mass education as a form of egalitarianism," describing mass education as one of neoliberal America's most successful ideological tools: "During the past sixty years or so, the higher-educational system has been one of America's most effective technologies for sustaining the ideology of equal opportunities, and it has done this by orchestrating the myth of systemic inclusion"; "Injuries of Class: Mass Education and the American Campus Novel," *PMLA* 130 (2015): 296, 294. Meanwhile, for African Americans the dream of systemic inclusion was barely even mythical. Despite an "overall increase in education levels in the black community," going to college was for most less about "meritocratic class mobility" than about gaining a wider range of occupational skills and securing a modicum of financial security; Kathleen J. Fitzgerald, *Recognizing Race and Ethnicity: Power, Privilege, and Inequality* (Boulder, CO: Westview P, 2014), 283–84. See also Beth Bailey, "Losing the War," *Reviews in American History* 39 (2011): 196–204; Herbold, "Never a Level Playing Field," 104–8; and Sarah E. Turner and John Bound, "Closing the Gap or Widening the Divide: The Effects of the G.I. Bill and World War II on the Educational Outcomes of Black Americans," *Journal of Economic History* 63 (2003): 145–77. Approaching these dynamics from a slightly later historical vantage, Roderick A. Ferguson describes mass education's ideology of upward social mobility, predicated on "the incorporation . . . of difference," as belonging to the State's "practices of exclusion and regulation" of minorities; *The Reorder of Things: The University and Its Pedagogies of Minority Difference* (Minneapolis: U of Minnesota P, 2012), 12.

38. Joan Shelley Rubin, *The Making of Middlebrow Culture* (Chapel Hill: U of North Carolina P, 1992), 306.

39. "Twenty-Seven Great Books of the World," *The New York Times Book Review* (July 6, 1941): 6; qtd. in Rubin, *The Making of Middlebrow Culture*, 232.

40. Huntington Cairns, Allen Tate, and Mark Van Doren, *Invitation to Learning* (New York: Random House, 1941), 188, 233.

41. Clark Kerr, "The Schools of Business Administration," in *New Dimensions of Learning in a Free Society* (Pittsburgh: U of Pittsburgh P, 1958), 66. Kerr was speaking at the inauguration of Edward Litchfield as the University of Pittsburgh's new chancellor. He updated many of the ideas in the speech for his landmark book, *The Uses of the University* (Berkeley: U of California P, 1963). On Kerr's Pittsburgh speech, and especially his discussion of the university as the "crossroads of society," see Ethan Schrum, "To 'Administer the Present': Clark Kerr and the Purpose of the Postwar American Research University," *Social Science History* 36 (2012): 499–523. See also in the same issue, which is an assemblage of essays commemorating the fiftieth anniversary of *The Uses of the University*, Paul H. Mattingly, "Clark Kerr: The Unapologetic Pragmatist," 481–97; and Christopher P. Loss, "From Pluralism to Diversity: Reassessing the Political Uses of *The Uses of the University*," 525–49.

42. Kerr, "The Schools of Business Administration," 31; Olson, "The G.I. Bill and Higher Education," 607; Frydl, *The G.I. Bill*, 316–18.

43. Frederick Pottle, typescript of lecture, "Current Developments on the Teaching of English Literature at Yale," 1966, Pottle Papers (MS 1605, box 21, folder 78).

44. Bruce A. Kimball, *Orators and Philosophers: A History of the Idea of Liberal Education* (New York: College Entrance Examination Board, 1995), 119. For a succinct introduction to the "liberal-free" and "oratorical" (or "*artes liberales*") ideals, see Geoffrey Galt Harpham, *The Humanities and the Dream of America* (Chicago: U of Chicago P, 2011), 11–18.

45. Kimball, *Orators and Philosophers*, 238; Harpham, *The Humanities and the Dream of America*, 12–13.

46. John Crowe Ransom, "The Teaching of Poetry," *Kenyon Review* 1 (1938): 82–83.

47. Donald Davidson, "A Mirror for Artists," *I'll Take My Stand: The South and the Agrarian Tradition. By Twelve Southerners* (1930; Baton Rouge: Louisiana State UP, 1977), 34.

48. Ransom, "Criticism, Inc.," *Selected Essays of John Crowe Ransom*, eds. Thomas Daniel Young and John Hindle (Baton Rouge: Louisiana State UP, 1984), 102–3.

49. Ransom, "Criticism, Inc.," 99.

50. Ransom, "Criticism, Inc.," 100.

51. Bonnie G. Smith, *The Gender of History: Men, Women, and Historical Practice* (Cambridge: Harvard UP, 2000), 105–16. See also Lorraine Daston, "The Academies and the Unity of Knowledge: Disciplining the Disciplines," *differences* 10 (1998): 67–86; Wolfgang J. Mommsen, "Historical Study in West Germany," *Historical Study in the West*, intro. Boyd C. Shafer (New York: Appleton-Century-Crofts, 1968), 81–99; and James Turner, *Philology: The Forgotten Origins of the Modern Humanities* (Princeton: Princeton UP, 2014), 299–310.

52. Ephraim Everton, qtd. in Smith, *The Gender of History*, 105–7.

53. Smith, *The Gender of History*, 113.

54. Cleanth Brooks and Robert Penn Warren, "The Liberal Arts and the Art of Reading," typescript of lecture [1938?], Brooks Papers (YCAL MSS 30, box 72, folder 1408), 3.

55. Cleanth Brooks and Robert Penn Warren, Instructor's Manual to *Understanding Poetry*, typescript, 1972, Brooks Papers (YCAL MSS 30, box 50), n.p.

56. Tony Stoneburner, "The Seminars of the Sixties," *Teacher & Critic: Essays by and About Austin Warren*, eds. Myron Simon and Harvey Gross (Los Angeles: Plantin P, 1976), 152.

57. See Irvin A. Derbigny, *General Education in the Negro College* (Stanford: Stanford UP, 1947), 91, 153–57; Earl J. McGrath, *The Predominantly Negro Colleges and Universities in Transition* (New York: Teachers College, 1965), 96–97; Buell G. Gallagher, *American Caste and the Negro College* (New York: Columbia UP, 1938), 354–55, 364–67. Intriguingly, the "Brooks and Warren Revolution" arrived at different HBCUs at different times, complicating any straightforward narrative about the interrelation between disciplinary trends and teaching practices. For instance, at Xavier University (New Orleans), the postwar "Introduction to Literature" course was a survey of "the world's literary masterpieces," which until 1953 stressed "our cultural inheritance" from these master-

pieces; it was not until 1957 that the goal of the class became the "Interpretation, appreciation, and criticism" of literary works—a new Brooksian emphasis, albeit one that lasted only five years, since in 1962 the objective changed again to a "tracing" of the "historical development of English literature." "English 201: Introduction to Literature," *Xavier University Bulletin*, vols. XXVI–XXXVIII (1949–1964). Across town at Dillard University, meanwhile, the advertised postwar practice was "rapid readings," the opposite of the "closeness" taught by *Understanding Poetry*; "English 315, 316: English Poetry of the Nineteenth Century," *The Dillard Bulletin* (1951–1953).

58. Jack Stillinger, "Fifty-nine Ways of Reading 'Ode on a Grecian Urn,'" *Ode on a Grecian Urn: Hypercanonicity and Pedagogy*, ed. James O'Rourke, *Romantic Circles Praxis* (October 2003): https://romantic-circles.org/praxis/grecianurn/contributorsessays /grecianurnstillinger.html, para. 3, 6.

59. Qtd. in Thomas Daniel Young, *Gentleman in a Dustcoat: A Biography of John Crowe Ransom* (Baton Rouge: Louisiana State UP, 1976), 417.

60. Robert Withington, "The Critic and the Student," *College English* 11 (1950): 282.

61. Austin Warren, "In Search of a Vocation," in *Teacher & Critic*, 25.

62. Myron Simon, "The Spirit of Community," in *Teacher & Critic*, 118, 125–26.

63. Austin Warren, "True and False Shepherds," in *Teacher & Critic*, 51.

64. Warren, "In Search of a Vocation," 25; Warren, "True and False Shepherds," 51. Originally composed in 1947, Warren submitted the article to *PMLA* under the title "Good Teaching."

65. "A Shoutin' Oratorio, Including a Brief, Perhaps Superfluous Coda, in Commemoration of a Brand New Addition to the Yale Faculty; the English Department, To Be Exact," *The Yale Record* (September 22, 1947), 15. Brooks Papers (YCAL MSS 30, box 90, folder 1923).

66. Randall Stewart, "New Critic and Old Scholar," *College English* 15 (1953): 106.

67. "Many of them approached a Shakespeare sonnet or Keats's 'Ode to a Nightingale' or Pope's 'Rape of the Lock' much as they would approach an ad in a Sears-Roebuck catalogue or an editorial in their local newspaper"; Cleanth Brooks, "Forty Years of *Understanding Poetry*," in *Confronting Crisis: Teachers in America*, eds. Ernestine P. Sewell and Billi M. Rogers (Arlington: U of Texas at Arlington P, 1979), 168.

68. Susan J. Wolfson, *Formal Charges: The Shaping of Poetry in British Romanticism* (Stanford: Stanford UP, 1997), 239.

69. Rachel Sagner Buurma and Laura Heffernan, *The Teaching Archive: A New History for Literary Study* (Chicago: U of Chicago P, 2020), 143.

70. See the alert reading in Buurma and Heffernan, *The Teaching Archive*, 142–43.

71. Cleanth Brooks, "Contemporary Poetic Theory and Practice [English 71]," Brooks Papers (YCAL MSS 30, box 81, folder 1657), 28.

72. Brooks, "Contemporary Poetic Theory and Practice [English 71]," 5–6.

73. Jewel Spears Brooker, "In Conclusion: Literature and Culture in the Last Essays of Cleanth Brooks," *South Atlantic Review* 60 (1995): 131.

74. On Brooks's *The Well Wrought Urn* as a "landmark of public pedagogy," see Susan J. Wolfson, "Tennyson's Tears, Brooks's Motivations," in *The Question of the Aesthetic*, ed. George Levine (Oxford: Oxford UP, 2022), 221–42.

75. Brooks, *The Well Wrought Urn*, 152.

76. Brooks, *The Well Wrought Urn*, 152.

77. Allen Tate, "A Reading of Keats (II)," *The American Scholar* 15 (1946): 195–96; Earl R. Wasserman, *The Finer Tone: Keats' Major Works* (Baltimore: Johns Hopkins UP, 1953), 3.

78. Brooks, *The Well Wrought Urn*, 154, 152.

79. Brooks, *The Well Wrought Urn*, 153.

80. Brooks, *The Well Wrought Urn*, 154.

81. Brooks, *The Well Wrought Urn*, 153.

82. Brooks, *The Well Wrought Urn*, 154.

83. Brooks, *The Well Wrought Urn*, 165, 151.

84. Brooks, *The Well Wrought Urn*, 155.

85. Helen Vendler, "'Tintern Abbey': Two Assaults," *Bucknell Review* 36 (1992): 181.

86. Brooks, *The Well Wrought Urn*, 154–55, 152, 157.

87. Brooks, *The Well Wrought Urn*, 155.

88. Brooks, *The Well Wrought Urn*, 163.

89. Brooks, *The Well Wrought Urn*, 163.

90. Brooks, *The Well Wrought Urn*, 160–61.

91. William Empson, "Thy Darling in an Urn," *Sewanee Review* 55 (1947): 697.

92. W. B. Yeats, *A Vision* (London: Palgrave Macmillan, 1962), 3. On Yeats's haunting by Keats's imagination (as in this allusion's neglect of the little town's status as merely "a retrojected surmise"), see Susan J. Wolfson, *Romantic Shades and Shadows* (Baltimore: Johns Hopkins UP, 2018), 178–79.

93. Cleanth Brooks, "Southern Literature: The Wellsprings of Its Vitality," *Georgia Review* 16 (1962): 250.

94. Brooks, *The Well Wrought Urn*, 162.

95. William Empson, *The Structure of Complex Words* (London: Chatto and Windus, 1951), 369.

96. Brooks, *The Well Wrought Urn*, 161 (emphasis added).

97. Brooks, *The Well Wrought Urn*, 161.

98. Brooks, *The Well Wrought Urn*, 162 (emphasis added).

99. Brooks, *The Well Wrought Urn*, 162.

100. See Susan J. Wolfson, *The Questioning Presence: Wordsworth, Keats, and the Interrogative Mode in Romantic Poetry* (Ithaca: Cornell UP, 1986), 301–5, 317–28.

101. Frederic Jameson, "From Criticism to History," *New Literary History* 12 (1981): 374.

102. Theodor W. Adorno, *Aesthetic Theory*, ed. and trans. Robert Hullot-Kentor (Minneapolis: U of Minnesota P, 1997), 121.

103. Theodor W. Adorno, "Valéry Proust Museum," *Prisms*, trans. Samuel and Shierry Weber (Cambridge: MIT P, 1981), 181.

104. Sianne Ngai, "The Cuteness of the Avant Garde," *Critical Inquiry* 31 (2005): 843.

105. "Brooks Warns of Jeopardy to Education," *New Haven Evening Register* (March 7, 1949), Brooks Papers (YCAL MSS 30, box 90, folder 1923).

106. James Gollin, "Cleanth Brooks Remembered," *The American Scholar* 64 (1995): 257.

107. Brooks, *The Well Wrought Urn*, 166.

Chapter 4: The Case of Byron

1. Cleanth Brooks, Jr. and Robert Penn Warren, *Understanding Poetry: An Anthology for College Students* (New York: Henry Holt, 1938), 187–88, 266–68, 288–89.

2. William K. Wimsatt, Jr. and Cleanth Brooks, *Literary Criticism: A Short History* (New York: Knopf, 1957); René Wellek and Austin Warren, *Theory of Literature* (New York: Harcourt Brace, 1949); W. K. Wimsatt, Jr. and M. C. Beardsley, "The Affective Fallacy," *Sewanee Review* 57 (1949): 44, 55.

3. Cleanth Brooks, *Community, Religion, and Literature: Essays* (Columbia: U of Missouri P, 1995), 88–89.

4. A pair of 1937 essays represents the closest thing to an exception. But T. S. Eliot, author of "Byron," in *On Poetry and Poets* (London: Faber and Faber, 1969), 193–206, generally dissociated himself from the New Criticism, and was aloof from the disciplinary concerns that gave it impetus; and René Wellek's "Mácha and Byron," in *The Slavonic and East European Review* 15 (1937): 400–412, belongs to Wellek's London period (before the war led him to move to Iowa, where he became familiar with the American New Critics) and focuses on the Czech romantic, in any case, arguing against the common assumption that he was a Byronist.

5. Catherine Gallagher, "The History of Literary Criticism," *Daedalus* 126 (1997): 135.

6. W. H. Auden, "The Life of a That-There Poet," *The Dyer's Hand and Other Essays* (New York: Random House, 1962), 405.

7. Peter J. Manning, "Childe Harold in the Marketplace: From Romaunt to Handbook," *MLQ* 2 (1991): 185. See also Northrop Frye: "With Byron the Personality Is, So to Speak, Built In to the Poetry"; Northrop Frye, "Nature and Homer" (1958), *Fables of Identity: Studies in Poetic Mythology* (New York: Harcourt Brace Jovanovich, 1963), 44.

8. Tom Mole, *Byron's Romantic Celebrity: Industrial Culture and the Hermeneutic of Intimacy* (Basingstoke and New York: Palgrave Macmillan, 2007), 23.

9. Class notes for "The Age of Wordsworth," February 13, 1967, Cleanth Brooks Papers (YCAL MSS 30, series 7, box 112), Beinecke Rare Book and Manuscript Library, Yale University.

10. This was a word even in Byron's own lifetime: the translation of the poetry and the personality into a signature style. See, among other exemplary accounts, those by Andrew Elfenbein, *Byron and the Victorians* (Cambridge: Cambridge UP, 1995), 47–89; Clara Tuite, *Lord Byron and Scandalous Celebrity* (Cambridge: Cambridge UP, 2015); and Susan J. Wolfson, *Romantic Interactions: Social Being and the Turns of Literary Action* (Baltimore: Johns Hopkins UP, 2010), 211–89.

11. Matthew Arnold, "Byron" (1881), in *The Complete Prose Works of Matthew Arnold*, ed. R. H. Super, vol. 9 (Ann Arbor: U of Michigan P, 1973), 225; Austin Warren, "Kenneth Burke: His Mind and Art," *Sewanee Review* 41 (1933): 356. Warren is paraphrasing Kenneth Burke, *Counter-Statement* (Berkeley: U of California P, 1931), 58: "Mute Byrons (potential Byrons) were waiting in more or less avowed discomfiture for the formulation of Byronism, and when it came they were enchanted. Again and again through Byron's pages they came upon the minutiae of their Byronism . . . and continued enchanted."

12. See, e.g., Susan J. Wolfson's assessment of "Byron's casual style" as conveying claims "about poetic diction, about the ration of aesthetic labor and discursive grace

that a poetic object ought to exhibit, and about the bearing of these matters on lines of commerce between a poet and his readers"; *Formal Charges: The Shaping of Poetry in British Romanticism* (Stanford: Stanford UP, 1997), 134.

13. Pottle, class notes for "English Poets of the Nineteenth Century" (MS 1605, box 14, folder 13).

14. For the phrase's double-meaning, see Mary Francis Gyles, "Nero Fiddled While Rome Burned," *The Classical Journal* 42 (1947): 211–17.

15. Cleanth Brooks, *The Well Wrought Urn: Studies in the Structure of Poetry* (New York: Harcourt Brace, 1947), 217, 235.

16. René Wellek, "Philosophy and Postwar American Criticism," in *Concepts of Criticism*, ed. Stephen G. Nichols Jr. (New Haven: Yale UP, 1963), 329.

17. Brooks, *The Well Wrought Urn*, 235.

18. Class notes for "The Age of Wordsworth," February 13, 1967, Brooks Papers (series 7, box 112).

19. Term examination for "The Age of Wordsworth," May 25, 1960, Brooks Papers (series 7, box 112).

20. Rachel Sagner Buurma and Laura Heffernan, *The Teaching Archive: A New History for Literary Study* (Chicago: U of Chicago P, 2021), 14.

21. Caroline Franklin, *Byron* (London and New York: Routledge, 2007), 96–100; Jane Stabler (ed. and intro.), *Byron* (London: Longman, 1998), 3–7. For more granular summaries one has to go to the nearer vantage of the 1950s: Bernbaum, "Keats, Shelley, Byron, and Hunt," 73–85; Leslie A. Marchand, "Recent Byron Scholarship," *English Miscellany* 3 (1952): 125–40; and Theodore Raysor, *The English Romantic Poets: A Review of Research* (New York: Modern Language Association, 1956), 165–83. For a survey of this wave of historicist writing on Byron, see "Lord Byron," in Percy Bysshe Shelley et al., *Shelley and His Circle, 1773–1822*, vol. 3, ed. Kenneth Neill Cameron (Cambridge: Harvard UP, 1961–70), 321.

22. Austin Warren, *Becoming What One Is* (Ann Arbor: U of Michigan P, 1995), xv; Austin Warren, *Teacher & Critic: Essays by and About Austin Warren*, eds. Myron Simon and Harvey Gross (Los Angeles: Plantin P, 1976), 86; René Wellek, *Discriminations* (New Haven: Yale UP, 1970), 40; Yvor Winters, "Problems for the Modern Critic of Literature," *Hudson Review* 9 (1956): 328; John Crowe Ransom, "Criticism, Inc.," *Selected Essays of John Crowe Ransom*, eds. Thomas Daniel Young and John Hindle (Baton Rouge: Louisiana State UP, 1984), 98.

23. Johns Hopkins, long a stronghold for the Lovejovian history of ideas, was the epicenter of this pluralist shift starting in the late 1940s. Literature scholars like Marjorie Hope Nicolson, Raymond Dexter Havens, and Lois Whitney all were influenced by A. O. Lovejoy, the philosopher who convened the cross-disciplinary History of Ideas Club beginning in 1923. But Leo Spitzer's arrival from Europe as chair of Romance Philology in the 1940s introduced *explication du texte* and gave Lovejoy an intellectual adversary, provoking an increased dialectic among approaches. This culminated, as Ronald Paulson writes, in the "watershed" year of 1949, marking the start of a "fruitful wedding of the history of ideas with the explication of the poem itself"; Paulson, "English Literary History at the Johns Hopkins University," *New Literary History* 1 (1970): 562. That year the romanticist Earl Wasserman was hired, and the recently ar-

rived Renaissance scholar D. C. Allen published two books, one in a history-of-ideas vein and one more formalist in orientation. By the end of the 1960s, "the Hopkins atmosphere" would be characterized by "pluralism and a commitment to interdisciplinary exploration" (Paulson, "English Literary History," 559), with the still-strong history of ideas camp balanced by hybrid scholars like Wasserman and Allen, phenomenologists like Georges Poulet, Jean Starobinski, and J. Hillis Miller, the poet-critic Pedro Salinas, the anthropological philosopher René Girard, and the artistic-literary historian Paulson. Paulson, "English Literary History," 559–64. See also Anthony Grafton, "The History of Ideas: Precept and Practice, 1950–2000 and Beyond," *Journal of the History of Ideas* 67 (2006): 1–32; and Richard Macksey, "'Particles of Nether-Do': A Controversy of Critics, 1876–1976," *Modern Language Notes* 91 (1976): i–vi.

24. Robert B. Heilman, *A Life in Letters*, eds. Edward Alexander, Richard Dunn, and Paul Jaussen (U of Washington P, 2009), 84.

25. *The Literary Correspondence of Donald Davidson and Allen Tate*, eds. John Tyree Fain and Thomas Daniel Young (U of Georgia P, 1974), 151.

26. T. G. Steffan, *Modern Philology: A Journal Devoted to Research in Medieval and Modern Literature* 44 (1947): 141. At its inception in 1903, the journal had been titled simply *Modern Philology*—which was actually not simple at all, considering philology's traditional focus on ancient, biblical, and medieval texts. Starting in August 1944, it appeared with the new subtitle featuring the word "research," to define the specific kind of work represented in the journal's pages. The stated inclusion of "Modern Literature" among the fields traditionally associated with philological work was also reflective of a wider shift. The moderns had been implicit in the journal's mission from the start (the very first issue, though weighted heavily toward medieval and ancient traditions, included essays on Goethe and Shakespeare), but in the 1940s, with modern poetry increasingly the subject of critical study and classroom discussion, *Modern Philology*'s new subtitle emphasized that it, too, could accommodate yet newer texts. In the early 2000s, the journal updated its subtitle once more, finally confirming what had long been true in practice by placing criticism and historical study on an equal footing: *Modern Philology: Critical and Historical Studies in Literature, Medieval through Contemporary*. See Richard Strier, "Editorial Statement," *Modern Philology* 103 (2005): 1–3.

27. Allen Tate, "Poetry and the Absolute," *Sewanee Review* 35 (1927): 44.

28. Bertrand Russell, "Byronic Unhappiness," *The Conquest of Happiness* (London and New York: Routledge, 2012), 115.

29. Bertrand Russell, *A History of Western Philosophy* (New York: Simon and Schuster, 1972), 747. The chapter on Byron was an expansion of Russell's 1940 article "Byron and the Modern World," *Journal of the History of Ideas* 1 (1940): 24–36. A colloquy between Arthur O. Lovejoy and Leo Spitzer, which takes Russell's thesis to the concept of "romanticism," is also relevant here. In "The Meaning of Romanticism for the Historian of Ideas" (*Journal of the History of Ideas* 2 [1941]: 257–78), Lovejoy had tied the "romantic" ideas of "organicism, dynamism, and diversificationism" to the rise of Hitlerism, arguing that their "fusion" had been "a factor in the production of the state of mind upon which the totalitarian ideologies depend for their appeal" (272). Spitzer, in "Geistesgeschichte vs. History of Ideas as Applied to Hitlerism" (*Journal of the History of Ideas* 5 [1944]: 191–203), countered that Lovejoy's "conclusion that present events

can be blamed on the great Romantic thinkers" ignored "the vast differences between the two [historical] climates" (200). He argued that those ideas represent "the bodily or vital feelings of a healthy organism," which must be distinguished "from the unhealthy, hectic fanaticism of the Hitlerites" (202, 194). See also Lovejoy's "Reply to Professor Spitzer" in the same issue (204–19). On this exchange, see Grafton, "The History of Ideas: Precept and Practice," 7–8.

30. Kenneth Burke, "Careers Without Careerism," *Kenyon Review* 7 (1945): 165.

31. David Erdman, "Lord Byron and the Genteel Reformers," *PMLA* 56 (1941): 1065; André Maurois, *Byron* (New York: D. Appleton, 1930), 206.

32. Erdman, "Lord Byron and the Genteel Reformers," 1075.

33. Erdman, "Lord Byron and the Genteel Reformers," 1093–94.

34. Erdman, "Lord Byron as Rinaldo," *PMLA* 57 (1942): 229–30.

35. Leslie Marchand, "Lord Byron and Count Alborghetti," *PMLA* 64 (1949): 976, 987, 1000, 990.

36. M. H. Abrams, *Natural Supernaturalism: Tradition and Revolution in Romantic Literature* (New York: Norton, 1971), 13.

37. Anne Kostelanetz Mellor, *English Romantic Irony* (Cambridge: Harvard UP, 1980); Jerome J. McGann, *The Romantic Ideology* (Chicago: U of Chicago P, 1983), 22.

38. René Wellek, "The Concept of 'Romanticism' in Literary History," *Comparative Literature* 1 (1949): 147.

39. Jerome J. McGann, "Rethinking Romanticism," *ELH* 59 (1992): 736, 737.

40. Jeffrey J. Williams, "A Life in Criticism: An Interview with M. H. Abrams," *Minnesota Review* 69 (2007): 73; M. H. Abrams, *The Mirror and the Lamp: Romantic Theory and the Critical Tradition* (Oxford and New York: Clarendon P, 1953), 167–77, 184–225; Abrams, "Organic Aesthetics," undated fragment discarded from final MS of *The Mirror and the Lamp*, M. H. Abrams Papers (14–12–4080, box 6, folder 47), Kroch Library, Division of Rare and Manuscript Collections, Cornell University.

41. Williams, "A Life in Criticism," 72–73.

42. Jonathan Arac points out that the full title, *The Mirror and the Lamp: Romantic Theory and the Critical Tradition*, expresses in both its halves the appeal of paradox, with the final term gently evoking New Critical root-texts like Cleanth Brooks's *Modern Poetry and the Tradition* and T. S. Eliot's "Tradition and the Individual Talent"; Jonathan Arac, *Critical Genealogies: Historical Situations for Postmodern Literary Studies* (New York: Columbia UP, 1987), 77. Herbert Lindenberger, reviewing *Natural Supernaturalism* in the early 1970s, suggests a more personality-based explanation for this apparent methodological in-betweenness: "When Mr. Abrams describes his procedure as one that will 'bring out important elements of both *continuity* and *change*,' or when he subtitles his book '*Tradition* and *Revolution* in Romantic Literature,' we recognize one who rejects the innovative, exciting, 'untenable' thesis in favor of compromising, synthesizing, clarifying"; Herbert Lindenberger, review of *Natural Supernaturalism*, *English Language Notes* 10 (1972): 153. I would add that these couplings can just as easily be read in terms of Abrams's historical thesis, as is reflected by the fact that his book began as a history-of-ideas dissertation with the very same title. Abrams's editor even wished to drop "The Mirror and the Lamp" altogether, leaving the "Romantic Theory and Critical Tradition" as the full title (he thought this snappier). Abrams half-conceded, asking to keep

a single "the." Only the "splenetic" last-second urging of his old Harvard tutor, Arthur Colby Sprague, prevented it from appearing as *Romantic Theory and the Critical Tradition*, a title that Sprague feared was "pedantic, and so dull he'd already forgotten it." Persuaded by Sprague, Abrams pleaded with the editor to change the title back. (It is fair to wonder whether a book titled *Romantic Theory and the Critical Tradition* would have placed twenty-fifth on the Modern Library's list of the Top 100 non-fiction books of the twentieth century.) M. H. Abrams to Lee Grove, 12[?] Nov. 1952, Abrams Papers (14–12–4080, box 11, folder 2).

43. Various teaching materials, Abrams Papers (14–12–4080, box 2, folders 1, 20, 36, 41, 42, 58; box 5, folder 16).

44. Class notes for English S-150c, "Poetry of the Romantic Period," Abrams Papers (14–12–4080, box 2, folder 1; box 5, folder 36).

45. Abrams, *The Mirror and the Lamp*, 49, 139.

46. Diploma from the War Manpower Commission, 3 Aug. 1944, Abrams Papers (14–12–4080, box 17, folder 7).

47. The famous phrase is from C. P. Snow, *The Two Cultures and the Scientific Revolution* (Cambridge: Cambridge UP, 1959). Abrams joins a minor tradition of literary scholars who led double lives during wartime (including his longtime colleague at Cornell, Stephen Parrish, who worked as a code breaker for the Office of Naval Intelligence during World War II and, again, in Korea). The philologists and medievalists John Matthews Manly (president of MLA in the 1910s) and Edith Rickert (an early statistical analyst) both enlisted in the cryptographic unit of military intelligence during the first World War. That unit was staffed by a number of humanists primarily from Yale and Chicago, including Chauncey Tinker. See Henry Veggian, "From Philology to Formalism: Edith Rickert, John Matthews Manly, and the Literary/Reformist Beginnings of U.S. Cryptology," *Reader* 54 (Spring 2006): 67–90. A few decades later, the CIA had a through-line to students of Agrarian New Critics; see Frances Stonor Saunders, *The Cultural Cold War: The CIA and the World of Arts and Letters* (New York: The New P, 1999), 197–211.

48. Harvard Psycho-Acoustic Laboratory reports, Abrams Papers (14–12–4080, box 17, folder 1, and box 16, folders 34–38).

49. Williams, "A Life in Criticism," 82.

50. M. H. Abrams, "The Transformation of English Studies, 1930–1995," *Daedalus* 126 (1997): 115.

51. M. H. Abrams, "The Fourth Dimension of the Poem," in *The Fourth Dimension of a Poem and Other Essays* (New York: Norton, 2012), 1–29. Jonathan Culler jokingly mentioned the "secret lab" as a source for the "fourth dimension" during a weekend celebration of Abrams's career, saying that it might just have taken fifty years for the idea to blossom; "M. H. Abrams at 100: A Weekend Celebration," *English at Cornell: A Newsletter from the Department of English* 16 (Winter 2013): 2.

52. Abrams to R. D. Havens, 15 Feb. 1945, Abrams Papers (14–12–4080, box 17, folder 6).

53. Robert Gorham Davis, "The New Criticism and the Democratic Tradition," *The American Scholar* 19 (1949–50): 9–19; Thomas Bender, "Politics, Intellect, and the American University, 1945–1995," *Daedalus* 126 (1997): 10.

54. For "tact" as the essential quality of the critic, see M. H. Abrams, "How to Do Things with Texts," *Doing Things with Texts: Essays in Criticism and Critical Theory*, ed. Michael Fischer (New York and London: W. W. Norton, 1989), 294.

55. Abrams, "The Transformation of English Studies," 115.

56. See J. Hillis Miller, "On Edge: The Crossways of Contemporary Criticism," *Bulletin of the American Academy of Arts and Sciences* 32 (1979): 13–32; and M. H. Abrams, "Construing and Deconstructing," *Doing Things with Texts: Essays in Criticism and Critical Theory*, ed. Michael Fischer (New York: Norton, 1989), 314–32. On Abrams's "oddly formalist" reaction to Miller, see Marc Redfield, *Theory at Yale: The Strange Case of Deconstruction in America* (New York: Fordham UP, 2015), 69–74. The debatable characterization of Miller as "destroyer" and "magician" is by Vincent Leitch, "The Lateral Dance: The Deconstructive Criticism of J. Hillis Miller," *Critical Inquiry* 6 (1980): 603.

57. Abrams, "The Transformation of English Studies," 115, 119, 118, 122.

58. M. H. Abrams, "A Reply," in *High Romantic Argument: Essays for M. H. Abrams*, ed. Lawrence Lipking (Ithaca: Cornell UP, 1981), 174 (emphasis added).

59. John Crowe Ransom, "Reconstructed but Unregenerate," *I'll Take My Stand: The South and the Agrarian Tradition. By Twelve Southerners* (1930; Baton Rouge: Louisiana State UP, 2006), 1 (emphasis added).

60. M. H. Abrams, "Unconscious Expectation in the Reading of Poetry," *ELH* 9 (1942): 243, 244.

61. Williams, "A Life in Criticism," 73.

62. Hugh Kenner, "The Pedagogue as Critic," in *The New Criticism and After*, ed. Thomas Daniel Young (Charlottesville: UP of Virginia, 1976), 37.

63. W. K. Wimsatt, Jr. and M. C. Beardsley, "The Intentional Fallacy," *Sewanee Review* 54 (1946): 468–88; Wimsatt and Beardsley, "The Affective Fallacy," 31–55; René Wellek, "The Literary Theory of William K. Wimsatt," *Yale Review* 66 (1976): 178.

64. Wimsatt and Beardsley, "The Affective Fallacy," 31.

65. W. K. Wimsatt, "Battering the Object: The Ontological Approach," in *Contemporary Criticism*, eds. Malcolm Bradbury and David Palmer (London: Edward Arnold, 1970), 74.

66. Wimsatt and Beardsley, "The Intentional Fallacy," 477; Wimsatt and Brooks, *Literary Criticism*, 253.

67. Wimsatt and Brooks, *Literary Criticism*, 284.

68. Wimsatt and Brooks, *Literary Criticism*, 284. For "dissociation of sensibility" as a "disorder of the age"—referring to poetry written after the seventeenth century—see W. K. Wimsatt, Jr., "The Augustan Mode in English Poetry," *ELH* 20 (1953): 14.

69. "Sociologist Predicts End of Romantic Love," news item (cut from *New York Times*, 18 May 1967), William Kurtz Wimsatt, Jr. Papers (MS 769, series 1, box 1, folder 17), Yale University Manuscripts and Archives, Yale University.

70. Wimsatt Papers (series 1, box 7, folder 99).

71. W. K. Wimsatt, "Horses of Wrath: Recent Critical Lessons," *Hateful Contraries: Studies in Literature and Criticism* (Lexington: UP of Kentucky, 1966), 35.

72. This wide range is indicated in the notes themselves and is also given in a "List of Suggested Assignments in Byron" from 1942; Wimsatt Papers (series 1, box 7, folder 98).

73. Wimsatt Papers (series 1, box 7, folder 99).

74. Wimsatt Papers (series 1, box 7, folder 99).

75. Wimsatt Papers (series 1, box 7, folder 98). The article, "Poet of Two Styles," is cut from the front page of the *Times Literary Supplement* for 15 July 1949.

76. Wimsatt, "The Augustan Mode," 14.

77. Wimsatt Papers (series 1, box 7, folder 100).

78. Wimsatt and Beardsley, "The Affective Fallacy," 37.

79. Roy Harvey Pearce, "Romantics, Critics, Historicists," *The Hudson Review* 10 (1957): 448.

80. Wimsatt Papers (series 1, box 7, folder 100).

81. Eliot, "Byron," 203, 197, 203.

82. W. K. Wimsatt, "Imitation as Freedom—1717–1798," *New Literary History* 1 (1970): 216. Wellek remarks that "Actually Wimsatt had an absorbing interest in biography and literary history," the key point being that these could help as *description* but not in *evaluation*: "Wimsatt insists on the distinction between genetic and descriptive accounts of literature"; Wellek, "The Literary Theory of William K. Wimsatt," 190.

83. Wellek, "The Literary Theory of William K. Wimsatt," 186. "Expressiveness" is to be distinguished from "expression," which Wimsatt calls "the master concept" of aesthetics, "not really separable from anything that is either represented or formed in any kind of art." Unlike romantic expressiveness, expression in its "wide sense" refers broadly and formally to "articulation, abstraction, symbolization, significance 'incarnate' in a form." W. K. Wimsatt, "Sparshott on Aesthetics: A Guided Tour," *The Review of Metaphysics* 20 (1966): 85, 82.

84. John Guillory, *Cultural Capital: The Problem of Literary Canon Formation* (Baltimore: Johns Hopkins UP, 1993), 158. See Mark Jancovich's related claim, that the Southern New Critics responded to a world in which "the rationalizing tendencies of industrial capitalism and bourgeois thought created a distinction between thought and feeling"; Marc Jancovich, *The Cultural Politics of the New Criticism* (Cambridge: Cambridge UP, 1993), 29.

85. W. K. Wimsatt, "Organic Form: Some Questions about a Metaphor," in *Romanticism: Vistas, Instances, Continuities*, eds. David Thorburn and Geoffrey Hartman (Ithaca: Cornell UP, 1973), 37, 22, 34, 29. See Frances Ferguson, "Organic Form and Its Consequences," *Land, Nation and Culture, 1740–1840: Thinking the Republic of Taste*, eds. Peter de Bolla, Nigel Leask, and David Simpson (New York: Palgrave Macmillan, 2005), esp. 225–29.

86. Transcript of "Yale Reports" broadcast (March 31, 1963), Wimsatt Papers (series 3, box 42, folder 19).

87. Robert Scholes, *Textual Power: Literary Theory and the Teaching of English* (New Haven: Yale UP, 1985), 18.

88. Kenner, "The Pedagogue as Critic," 37.

Chapter 5. The Emergence of Josephine Miles (Reading Wordsworth in Berkeley, California)

1. The recent surge of work on Miles—I am thinking especially of Brad Pasanek's meditation on the scale of academic labor in her "extreme reading" practice, and Rachel Sagner Buurma's and Laura Heffernan's revealing dive into her teaching ar-

chive—is testament to this interest, and both Pasanek's and Buurma and Heffernan's writing has served as a timely antidote to a restorative nostalgia that projects desires for consensus onto an idealized view of the mid-century. See Brad Pasanek, "Extreme Reading: Josephine Miles and the Scale of the Pre-Digital Digital Humanities," *ELH* (2019): 355–86; and Rachel Sagner Buurma and Laura Heffernan, *The Teaching Archive: A New History for Literary Study* (Chicago: U of Chicago P, 2021), 154–82.

As a woman in a largely male profession, and as a professional who contended and worked through a severe physical disability, Miles has come to represent for many critics (especially in the gender-troubled field of digital humanities) a lost lineage ripe for recovery. For her place in digital history, see Pasanek, "Extreme Reading," 355–57; Buurma and Heffernan, *The Teaching Archive*, 158; Rachel Sagner Buurma and Laura Heffernan, "Search and Replace: Josephine Miles and the Origins of Distant Reading," *Modernism/Modernity Print Plus* 3.1 (2018): https://modernismmodernity.org/forums /posts/search-and-replace; Rosanne G. Potter, "Statistical Analysis of Literature: A Retrospective on 'Computers and the Humanities,' 1966–1990," *Computers and the Humanities* 25 (1991): 402; Mario Wimmer, "Josephine Miles (1911–1985): Doing Digital Humanism with and without Machines," *History of Humanities* 4 (2019): 329–34; and Trisha N. Campbell, "Josephine Miles: A Digital Reprocessing," *Provocations* 1 (2015): http://ccdigitalpress.org/reconstructingthearchive/campbell.html. Histories of the digital humanities often cite Father Roberto Busa, who in 1949 undertook work supported by IBM, as "the well-known beginning" of "humanities computing"; Susan Hockey, "The History of Humanities Computing," in *A Companion to Digital Humanities*, eds. Susan Schreibman et al. (New York: Blackwell, 2008), 4. Miles, however, did large-scale statistical analyses by hand beginning in the late 1930s, and in the 1950s she collaborated with scientists at Berkeley's Cory Lab on computer concordances; see Josephine Miles, *Poetry, Teaching, and Scholarship: Oral History Transcript and Related Material, 1977–1980*, interview by Ruth Teiser and Catherine Harroun for Regional Oral History Office (Berkeley: The Bancroft Library, 1980), 124–26. For a particularly thoughtful effort to complicate the origin-story of digital humanities, see Steven E. Jones, *Roberto Busa, S.J., and the Emergence of Humanities Computing: The Priest and the Punched Cards* (New York, 2016). On Miles and disability, Susan M. Schweik's work is exemplary; see "The Voice of 'Reason,'" *Public Culture* 13 (2001): 485–505, and "Josephine Miles's Crip(t) Words: Gender, Disability, 'Doll,'" *Journal of Literary Disability* 1 (2007): 49–60. See also Zofia Burr, *Of Women, Poetry, and Power: Strategies of Address in Dickinson, Miles, Brooks, Lorde, and Angelou* (Urbana: U of Illinois P, 2002), 67–112; Carolyn Smith, "Old-Age Freedom in Josephine Miles's Late Poems, 1974–79," in *Aging and Gender in Literature*, eds. Anne M. Wyatt-Brown and Janice Rossen (Charlottesville: UP of Virginia, 1993); and Eve Kosofsky Sedgwick, who anticipated the intersectional turn in scholarship in "The Vibrant Politics of Josephine Miles," *Epoch* 31 (1982): 62–76.

2. In one instance, recalled in an interview, Miles had to pay an unnamed "heroic woman at our press who was a major typist" to work out the complex visuals for her folio *Renaissance, Eighteenth-Century, and Modern Language in English Poetry: A Tabular View* (Berkeley: U of California P, 1960); Miles, *Poetry, Teaching, and Scholarship*, 123. Although the term "disrupter" has become a somewhat dubious term of praise for Silicon Valley entrepreneurs, Miles—a lover of words—might have appreciated its etymology

(from the Latin *dis-rumpere*, meaning "to break apart") and history of medical usage (used in the fifteenth century to refer to the "laceration of tissue").

3. W. K. Wimsatt, Jr., review of *Eras and Modes in English Poetry*, *The Journal of English and Germanic Philology* 57 (1958): 326.

4. Wimsatt, review of *Eras and Modes in English Poetry*, 327.

5. We might discern in Miles's preferred vocabulary of literary-historical continuity a forerunner of Jonathan Goldberg and Madhavi Menon's "unhistoricism," which questions the privileging of alterity and difference in the dominant thinking of history; "Queering History," *PMLA* 120 (2005): 1608–17. For other alternatives that variously echo Miles's idea of continuity, see Rita Felski, "Context Stinks!," *New Literary History* 42 (2011): 573–91.

6. Josephine Miles, *Poetry and Change: Donne, Milton, Wordsworth, and the Equilibrium of the Present* (Berkeley: U of California P, 1974).

7. In calling Wordsworth Miles's "prime poet," I mean that he came first in her career and subsequently provided consistent intellectual grounding for her. But he was, to be clear, far from being her *favorite* poet: "I've written a lot on Wordsworth" and "I like him now; I don't love him. The poet that I like the best, W. B. Yeats, I've written very little on"; *Poetry, Teaching, and Scholarship*, 183.

8. Josephine Miles, *Eras and Modes in English Poetry* (Berkeley: U of California P, 1957), 125. Continuity had been a feature of the family-sponsored Victorian Wordsworth: "It is true, 'the child was father of the man,' and there is a continuous stream of identity flowing from the earliest to his latest poems"; Christopher Wordsworth, *Memoirs of William Wordsworth*, 2 vols. (London: Moxon, 1851), 1: 4–5.

9. Miles, *Eras and Modes*, 137.

10. Josephine Miles uses "the on-going of experience" in the Preface added to her 1965 reissue of *Wordsworth and the Vocabulary of Emotion* (Berkeley: U of California P, 1965), xi.

11. On Miles's critique of New Critical organicism within a history of disability as a cultural construct, see Christopher Rovee, "Counting Wordsworth by the Bay: The Distance of Josephine Miles," *European Romantic Review* 28 (2017): 405–12.

12. The irony, which I touch on in my Epilogue, is that Miles's home city of Berkeley was named for the idealist philosopher Bishop George Berkeley, whose 1752 "Verses on the Prospect of Planting Arts and Learning in America" prophesies a "Westward . . . course of empire," in which Europe's "decay" gives way to "another golden age" in "distant lands"; *The Works of George Berkeley*, vol. 4 (*Miscellaneous Works, 1707–1750*), ed. Alexander Campbell Fraser (Oxford: Clarendon Press, 1901), 365–66. Many thanks to Kevis Goodman for pointing this out.

13. Wellek and Warren, *Theory of Literature*, 4.

14. John Crowe Ransom, "Criticism, Inc.," *Selected Essays of John Crowe Ransom*, eds. Thomas Daniel Young and John Hindle (Baton Rouge: Louisiana State UP, 1984), 93.

15. René Wellek and Austin Warren, *Theory of Literature* (New York: Harcourt Brace, 1949), 4.

16. René Wellek, "The Concept of Evolution in Literary History," *Concepts of Criticism*, ed. Stephen G. Nichols, Jr. (New Haven: Yale UP, 1963), 52.

17. René Wellek to Josephine Miles, February 28, 1943, Josephine Miles Papers (BANC MSS 86/107, box 9, folder 11), Bancroft Library, University of California.

18. Edith Rickert, *New Methods for the Study of Literature*, intro. John Matthews Manly (Chicago: U of Chicago P, 1927), v, ix. On Rickert, see Buurma and Heffernan, *The Teaching Archive*, 88–102.

19. Quantification, Porter adds, was uniquely fitted to interdisciplinary work, being "well suited to communication that goes beyond the boundaries of locality and community"—beyond, that is, the constraints of a particular field. Theodore M. Porter, *Trust in Numbers: The Pursuit of Objectivity in Science and Public Life* (Princeton UP, 1995), ix.

20. Allen Tate, "The Present Function of Criticism" (1940), *Limits of Poetry: Selected Essays: 1928–1948* (New York: Swallow P, 1948), 9. For Richards and "laboratory" pedagogy, see Buurma and Heffernan, *The Teaching Archive*, 66–88.

21. Hugh Kenner, "The Pedagogue as Critic," in *The New Criticism and After*, ed. Thomas Daniel Young (Charlottesville: UP of Virginia, 1976), 43–44.

22. Miles, Class notes for English 1A, 1940, Miles Papers (carton 8, folder 47); George R. Stewart, Jr., *English Composition: A Laboratory Course*, vol. 1 (New York: Henry Holt, 1936). Stewart's book still sits on Miles's bookshelf in her former North Berkeley house. It is included in a meticulous inventory of Miles's books that was produced and shared with me by Brad Pasanek. On Miles's "workshop-style pedagogy," see Buurma and Heffernan, *The Teaching Archive*, 154–57.

23. David R. Shumway, *Creating American Civilization: A Genealogy of American Literature as an Academic Discipline* (Minneapolis: U of Minnesota P, 1994), 232.

24. Josephine Miles, *Wordsworth and the Vocabulary of Emotion* (Berkeley: U of California P, 1942); Josephine Miles, *Pathetic Fallacy in the Nineteenth Century* (Berkeley: U of California P, 1942); and Josephine Miles, *Major Adjectives in English Poetry* (Berkeley: U of California P, 1944).

25. Marjorie Levinson, "Revisionist Reading: An Account of the Practice," *Studies in the Literary Imagination* 30 (1997): 129. Levinson suggests as "a generous estimate" that there may have been ten such women in the profession, but only five "come to mind": Miles, Barbara Lewalski, Marjorie Hope Nicolson, Rosemund Tuve, and Ruth Wallerstein.

26. Miles, *Poetry, Teaching, and Scholarship*, 66; Josephine Miles [interview], "The Poetry Scene at Berkeley, 1918–Ca. 1956," 14, typescript of interview with Eloyde Tovey, May 19, 1981, Miles Papers (carton 8, folder 6).

27. John Crowe Ransom to Miles, March 23, 1944, Miles Papers (box 5, folder 5); Miles [interview], "The Poetry Scene at Berkeley, 1918–Ca. 1956," 13.

28. During the protracted exchange about her poems, Brooks and Warren changed their mind about some of them, requested substitutions for other poems that they liked less, then failed to return and eventually lost the physical manuscripts of yet others ("most humiliating," conceded Brooks). Robert Penn Warren to Miles (September 21, 1937; January 14, 1938; January 10, 1939; April 12, 1939; and May 11, 1939), and Brooks to Miles (November 8, 1939, and November 27, 1939 [quoted]), *Southern Review* Records (YCAL MSS 694, series 1, box 4), Beinecke Rare Book and Manuscript Library, Yale University.

29. Miles to Robert Penn Warren (July 8, 1938, February 12, 1939, and March 27, 1939), *Southern Review* Records (series 1, box 4).

30. See Pasanek for the daunting "pre-digital scale of word-by-word reading"; "Extreme Reading," 356. As Buurma and Heffernan describe, in the 1950s Miles "led a team to create the first computational literary concordance," picking up the task of a concordance to Dryden from a recently deceased colleague; *The Teaching Archive*, 11. On the female labor that made Father Roberto Busa's concordance work possible, see Melissa Terras and Julianne Nyhan, "Father Busa's Female Punch Card Operatives," in *Debates in Digital Humanities*, eds. Matthew K. Gold and Lauren F. Klein (Minneapolis: U of Minnesota P, 2016), 60–65.

31. Josephine Miles, "Enlightenment," *Poetry* 53 (1939): 238.

32. Josephine Miles, "Prime Words in Poetry," typescript, Miles Papers (carton 3, folder 77).

33. Warren to Miles, April 12, 1939, *Southern Review* Records (series 1, box 4).

34. George Udny Yule, *The Statistical Study of Literary Vocabulary* (Cambridge UP, 1944); Rickert, *New Methods for the Study of Literature*; Edward Lee Thorndike, *The Teacher's Word Book* (New York: Teachers College, Columbia University, 1921); Eric Partridge, *Eighteenth-Century English Romantic Poetry* (Paris: É. Champion, 1924), 72; William J. Grace, "Teaching Poetic Appreciation Using Quantitative Analysis," *College English* 1 (1939): 222–27; Oscar W. Firkins, *Power and Elusiveness in Shelley* (Minneapolis: U of Minnesota P, 1937). See Yohei Igarashi, "Statistical Analysis at the Birth of Close Reading," *New Literary History* 46 (2015), 485–504, for an excellent account of word counting and literary analysis in the age of philology (which, he demonstrates, was also the age of Richards).

35. Heather Love, "Close but Not Deep: Literary Ethics and the Descriptive Turn," *New Literary History* 41 (2010): 371–91.

36. Josephine Miles, "Devotation and Criticism," [5], Miles Papers (carton 3, folder 34).

37. Wimsatt, review of *Eras and Modes in English Poetry*, 321–22.

38. Edmond L. Volpe, review of *Eras and Modes in English Poetry*, *Books Abroad* 32 (1958): 190.

39. Transcription of conversation between Cleanth Brooks, Warren, and Ransom, Cleanth Brooks Papers (YCAL MSS 30, series 2, box 50, folder 895), Beinecke Rare Book and Manuscript Library, Yale University.

40. Henry W. Wells, review of *The Primary Language of Poetry in the 1940's*, *American Literature* 24 (1952): 265–66.

41. There is no way to know. Wells refers to Miles's "courage" at the start of the review, and in a review of her previous book, he exaggeratedly described her criticism as "nimble," "agile," metaphorizing her scholarly technique (in terms that suggest over-compensation) as "acrobatic," like "walking a tight-rope," with "the circus glamour of being spectacular." But this is as likely to express the physicality pervasively ascribed to scholarly exertions at the time. See Henry W. Wells, review of *Major Adjectives in English Poetry: From Wyatt to Auden*, *American Literature* 18 (1946): 266–67.

42. Helen E. Haines, "Lutanists of Winter," newspaper unidentified, Miles Papers (carton 8, folder 16). This review likely appeared in the *Pasadena Star-News*, as Haines wrote weekly reviews for them from 1914 to 1959; see Mary Robinson Sive, "Helen E. Haines, 1872–1961: An Annotated Bibliography," *The Journal of Library History* (1966–1972) 5 (1970): 158.

43. Josephine Miles, *The Continuity of Poetic Language: The Primary Language of Poetry, 1540's–1940's* (Berkeley: U of California P, 1951), 161. Miles's individual studies of the 1540s, 1640s, 1740s and 1840s, and 1940s were first published as pamphlets, then assembled to form the book *The Continuity of Poetic Language*; I refer throughout to the book.

44. René Wellek to Josephine Miles, January 3, 1944. In an earlier letter, sent after having reviewed Miles's Wordsworth book, Wellek praised her method: "I wish there were more people in American scholarship who are interested in such literary questions. . . . On the whole, I feel, that there must come a change away from the purely fact-collecting type of scholarship to studies concentrating on the actual work of art and its devices"; Wellek to Miles, February 28, 1943, Miles Papers (BANC MSS 86/107, box 9, folder 11), Bancroft Library, University of California.

45. Wimsatt, review of *Eras and Modes in English Poetry*, 326–27.

46. Miles, *Continuity*, 534; Vivienne Koch, review of *The Continuity of Poetic Language*, *Poetry* 79 (1952): 366.

47. Josephine Miles, review of *The Well Wrought Urn*, *Journal of Aesthetics and Art Criticism* (1947): 185–86.

48. Miles, "Devotation and Criticism," [3].

49. Josephine Miles, "More Semantics of Poetry," *Kenyon Review* 2 (1940): 502.

50. Josephine Miles, "Postscript, July 27, 1942," typescript, Miles Papers (carton 3, folder 74); Josephine Miles, "Weights and Measures in Poetry," typescript, c. 1940, Miles Papers (carton 3, folder 98); *Poetry, Teaching, and Scholarship*, 85; Josephine Miles, Class notes for English 1B, University of California at Berkeley, 1940, Miles Papers (carton 8, folder 48).

51. Josephine Miles, "The Problem of Imagery," *Sewanee Review* 58 (1950): 526.

52. Miles, "Weights and Measures in Poetry," Miles Papers (carton 3, folder 98).

53. Miles to Warren, July 8, 1938, *Southern Review* Records (series 1, box 4).

54. Miles to Brooks, November 7, 1943, Miles Papers (box 1, folder 45).

55. Josephine Miles, "Critical Relativism," *Kenyon Review* 5 (1943): 138.

56. Josephine Louise Miles, typescript of "Wordsworth and the Vocabulary of Emotion" (dissertation), Miles Papers (carton 1, folder 59), 1.

57. Miles, typescript of "Wordsworth and the Vocabulary of Emotion" (dissertation), 253, 260.

58. Miles, typescript of "Wordsworth and the Vocabulary of Emotion" (dissertation), 2.

59. Miles, typescript of "Wordsworth and the Vocabulary of Emotion" (dissertation), 3.

60. Miles, *Wordsworth and the Vocabulary of Emotion*, 15.

61. Miles, typescript of "Wordsworth and the Vocabulary of Emotion" (dissertation), 11.

62. Miles, typescript of "Wordsworth and the Vocabulary of Emotion" (dissertation), 12.

63. Miles, *Continuity*, 360.

64. Miles, *Eras and Modes*, 128.

65. Miles, *Wordsworth and the Vocabulary of Emotion*, 4, 22.

66. See Geoffrey H. Hartman, "A Poet's Progress: Wordsworth and the *Via Naturaliter Negativa*," *Modern Philology* 59 (1962): 214–24.

67. Miles, *Continuity*, 358.

68. Miles, *Continuity*, 361–62.

69. Miles, *Vocabulary of Poetry*, 2.

70. Miles, *Eras and Modes*, 135–36 (emphasis added).

71. Samuel Holt Monk, review of *The Primary Language of Poetry in the 1640's, 1740's and 1840's, and 1940's, Journal of English and Germanic Philology* 51 (1952): 426.

72. Wimsatt, review of *Eras and Modes in English Poetry*, 325–26.

73. Josephine Miles, "Wordsworth and Glitter," *Studies in Philology* 40 (1943): 557.

74. Josephine Miles, *Major Adjectives*, 420–21. Note the strikingly similar tone in the later work of Franco Moretti, which also draws authority from reference to visualizable evidence; see, e.g., the various essays assembled in Moretti's *Distant Reading* (New York: Verso, 2013).

75. Miles, *Pathetic Fallacy*, 4.

76. Miles, "The Freshman at Composition," *College Composition and Communication* 2 (1951): 9.

77. Miles, *Continuity*, 4–5.

78. Miles, *Eras and Modes*, 121–22.

79. Miles, *Continuity*, 161.

80. I am indebted to Brad Pasanek for kindly guiding me through Miles's house and sharing with me his detailed inventory of the house's contents, which includes a notation about this worksheet.

81. For Miles's relationships with women in other disciplines, especially Math, see *The Women's Faculty Club of the University of California, Berkeley, 1919–1982*, interviews conducted by Suzanne B. Riess, Regional Oral History Office, The Bancroft Library Berkeley, California, 1981–82. For Scott, see Amanda L. Golbeck, *Equivalence: Elizabeth L. Scott at Berkeley* (Boca Raton, FL: CRC P, 2017). For Miles's IBM-assisted concordance work and the lab at Cory Hall, see Buurma and Heffernan, "Search and Replace: The Origins of Distant Reading"; and Miles, *Poetry, Teaching, and Scholarship*, 124–26. For her work on stylometry, see Josephine Miles and Hanan C. Selvin, "A Factor Analysis of the Vocabulary of Poetry in the Seventeenth Century," in *The Computer and Literary Style: Introductory Essays and Studies*, ed. Jacob Leed (Kent: Kent State UP, 1966), 116–27; and Pasanek, "Extreme Reading," 372–73. For Miles's tense involvement with linguistics within the field of English and with Berkeley's Department of Linguistics, see Miles, *Poetry, Teaching, and Scholarship*, 111–14.

82. Wells, review of *Major Adjectives in English Poetry: From Wyatt to Auden*, 267.

83. Miles, *Continuity*, 355.

84. Ted Underwood, *Why Literary Periods Mattered: Historical Contrast and the Prestige of English Studies* (Stanford: Stanford UP, 2015), 161; Miles, *Poetry, Teaching, and Scholarship*, 242.

85. See John Matthews Manly, "Literary Forms and the New Theory of the Origin of Species," *Modern Philology* 4 (1907): 577–95; and Wellek, "The Concept of Evolution," 42–45. For a good overview of the species concept in relation to literary form, see Jonathan Kramnick and Anahid Nersessian, "Form and Explanation," *Critical Inquiry* 43 (2017): 663–67.

86. A peculiar feature of *Eras and Modes*—where the presence of evolutionary paleontology is perhaps most strongly felt—is the near total absence of footnotes. This is

a departure from Miles's previous publications, where footnotes lay bare the statistical, historical, and scientific "strands of context" that inform her scholarship. It is as though she has so thoroughly internalized her contexts by the time of *Eras and Modes* (or is so thoroughly spoken by them) that citation has become superfluous.

87. Simpson, *Tempo and Mode*, 207.

88. Christopher Haufe, "Wonderful Death," manuscript in preparation (2018), 5.

89. Haufe, "Wonderful Death," 8; "Equilibrium" was to become yet another of Miles's keywords. It is included in the title of her final collection, *Poetry and Change: The Equilibrium of the Present*, which reverberates with a new (and uncannily apt) formulation from the field of evolutionary biology: "punctuated equilibrium," explained in a now classic essay by Niles Eldredge and Stephen Jay Gould in 1972 as an evolutionary process consisting of long periods of changelessness punctuated by sudden bursts of rapid change. See Niles Eldredge and S. J. Gould, "Punctuated Equilibria: An Alternative to Phyletic Gradualism," in *Models in Paleobiology*, ed. Thomas J. M. Schopf (San Francisco: Freeman, Cooper & Co., 1972), 82–115.

90. Miles, *Continuity*, 384.

91. Josephine Miles, "For Futures," *Lines at Intersection* (New York: Macmillan, 1939), 45.

92. Miles, *Continuity*, 498.

93. Miles, *Poetry and Change*, 59.

94. Benedetto Croce, *History: Its Theory and Practice*, trans. Douglas Ainslie (New York: Harcourt Brace, 1921), 112; Wellek and Warren, *Theory of Literature*, 268, 278 (the preface attributes its "Literary History" chapter to Wellek). Marshall Brown alertly notes that the placement of "periodization" at the end of *Theory of Literature* "marks it as both the crown of Wellek's ambitions and the biggest thorn in his side"; "Periods and Resistances," *MLQ: Modern Language Quarterly* 62 (2001): 311. On early practices of comparative literature, including Wellek's critique of source study and the search for influences over a systematic tracing of literary-historical periods, see Underwood, *Why Literary Periods Mattered*, 115–26.

95. Among several works, see Frederick J. Teggart, *Prolegomena to History: The Relationship of History to Literature, Philosophy, and Science* (Berkeley: U of California P, 1916), 87–125; and Frederick J. Teggart, *Theory and Process of History* (Berkeley: U of California P, 1941). A copy of the latter is preserved on Miles's bookshelves, thoroughly marked-up with her pencil.

96. "Right now we're working here on the single problem of 'period,' mostly with the aid of Teggart's students in social institutions, and we are all at a loss and confused. (We seem at the moment to have a sort of nucleus and wave theory by the tail)!"; Miles to Brooks, November 7, 1943, Miles Papers (box 1, folder 45).

97. Wellek and Warren, *Theory of Literature*, 17, 267.

98. René Wellek, "Literary History," in *Literary Scholarship: Its Aims and Methods*, ed. Norman Foerster (Chapel Hill: U of North Carolina P, 1941), 109.

99. Wellek, "The Concept of Evolution," 37. On "the long-drawn-out disintegration" of Victorian and Edwardian culture's evolutionary framework as "a founding moment for the modern form of disciplines like philosophy, literary criticism, and anthropology," see Stefan Collini, "Company Histories: CamU PLC and SocAnth Ltd.,"

English Pasts: Essays in History and Culture (New York and Oxford: Oxford UP, 1999), 282.

100. Wellek, "The Concept of Evolution," 37.

101. Timothy J. Reiss, "Perioddity: Considerations on the Geography of Histories," *MLQ* 62 (2001): 433.

102. For a different formulation and use of "counter-nostalgia," see Jennifer K. Ladino, *Reclaiming Nostalgia: Longing for Nature in American Literature* (Charlottesville and London: U of Virginia P, 2012), 15: "Nostalgia becomes 'counter-' when it is strategically deployed to challenge a progressivist ethos. Counter-nostalgia is nostalgia with a critical edge."

103. Rosemond Tuve, review of *The Primary Language of Poetry in the 1640's*, *Modern Language Notes* 65 (1950): 62.

104. Miles, *Eras and Modes*, 2.

105. Miles, *Eras and Modes*, 3.

106. Miles, *Eras and Modes*, viii.

107. Miles, *Continuity*, 503.

108. Miles, *Eras and Modes*, 6.

109. Stephen Jay Gould, "Evolutionary Paleontology and the Science of Form," *Earth-Science Reviews* 6 (1970): 201. Gould also points out, in terms suited to Miles's crossover theorizing, that Dollo is relevant not merely to the evolution of biological life but to history, both as an example of history and as a form or template for historical change: "Dollo's law is not an adjunct of evolutionary theory. It is a statement, framed in terms of animals and their evolution, of the nature of history; or, put another way, it is an affirmation of the historical nature of evolutionary events"; 208. On the comparatist evolutionary tradition, indicted by Wellek, see Underwood, *Why Literary Periods Mattered*, 117–19.

110. Koch, review of *The Continuity of Poetic Language*, 366–67. On the disproportion between Miles's "efforts" and "results," see Pasanek, "Extreme Reading," 366.

111. Miles, *Continuity*, 153.

112. On "limit" as a keyword in Miles's work, see Pasanek, "Extreme Reading," 359. See also Miles's own multivalent reflection (which Pasanek quotes): "in an existential world making choices is everything. It's when choices are limited that it's easy to make intelligent decisions and my choices were always very limited"; Miles, *Poetry, Teaching, and Scholarship*, 291.

113. Josephine Miles, review of *Concordance to the Poems of Matthew Arnold* et al., *Victorian Studies* 8 (1965): 290–92.

114. Miles, review of *Concordance to the Poems of Matthew Arnold* et al., 290.

115. The word counts are predominantly in Miles's distinctive handwriting, but since she employed graduate student assistants, there are some counts in recognizably different hands. She describes her employment of student assistants in *Poetry, Teaching, and Scholarship*, 128.

116. Pasanek, "Extreme Reading," 375.

117. Miles, *Poetry, Teaching, and Scholarship*, 4.

118. Mary Poovey, "The Model System of Contemporary Literary Criticism," *Critical Inquiry* 27 (2001): 432, 435. On Poovey's argument, see Frances Ferguson, "Or-

ganic Form and Its Consequences," *Land, Nation and Culture, 1740–1840: Thinking the Republic of Taste*, eds. Peter de Bolla, Nigel Leask, and David Simpson (New York: Palgrave Macmillan, 2005), 223–40.

119. Miles, *Poetry, Teaching, and Scholarship*, 90.

120. See Amanda Anderson, *Forms of Distance* (Princeton: Princeton UP, 2006). For the history of scientific objectivity, see Lorraine Daston and Peter Galison, *Objectivity* (New York: Zone Books, 2007).

121. Wimmer, "Josephine Miles," 333; Susan J. Wolfson, *Romantic Shades and Shadows* (Baltimore: Johns Hopkins UP, 2018), 37.

122. See Lisa Samuels and Jerome McGann, "Deformance and Interpretation," *New Literary History* 30 (1999): 46.

123. Rachel Feder's account of "archival reading" has been helpful to me in thinking about how to approach Miles's word-count notes. Thinking through the ways "archival forms of knowledge resist or at least challenge traditional modes of reading," Feder describes "archival reading" as "a particular type of textual criticism focused . . . on the experience of encountering an archival text" that eludes "conventional genre categories"; "The Experimental Dorothy Wordsworth," *Studies in Romanticism* 53 (2014): 543, 541.

124. There are four different bundles for Wordsworth's poetry among Miles's notes; this poem appears in a bundle containing counts of *The Complete Poetical Works of William Wordsworth*, Miles Papers (carton 6, folder 106). Miles's edition for this bundle was *The Complete Poetical Works of William Wordsworth*, ed. John Morley (London: Macmillan, 1930).

125. Alan Liu, "Transcendental Data: Toward a Cultural History and Aesthetics of the New Encoded Discourse," *Critical Inquiry* 31 (2004): 49–84, esp. 52–59.

126. Samuels and McGann, "Deformance and Interpretation," 36, 28; Theodor Adorno, "On Lyric Poetry and Society," *Notes to Literature*, trans. Shierry Weber Nicholsen (New York, 1991), 1: 43–44. Spun from a playful statement by Emily Dickinson ("Did you ever read one of her Poems backward, because the plunge from the front overturned you?"), Samuels and McGann's concept of deformance combines resonances of "performance" and "deformity." By systematically disordering a poem's verbal units, it promises to strip its film of familiarity, to "release or expose [its] possibilities of meaning" by "short-circuit[ing] the sign of prose transparency and reinstall[ing] the text—any text, prose or verse—as a performative event, a made thing." On "deformance" and its intimacy with computational analysis, see Stephen Ramsay, *Reading Machines: Toward an Algorithmic Criticism* (Urbana: U of Illinois P, 2011), 32–38.

127. Norman Foerster, "The Esthetic Judgment and the Ethical Judgment," in *The Intent of the Critic*, ed. Donald A. Stauffer (Princeton: Princeton UP, 1941), 76; William Empson, *Seven Types of Ambiguity*, 2nd edn. (London: Chatto and Windus, 1949), 154; Miles, typescript of "Wordsworth and the Vocabulary of Emotion" (dissertation), 10. For Empson's complicated disapproval of Wordsworth's poem, see Nicholas Halmi, "Two Types of Wordsworthian Ambiguity," in *Romantic Ambiguity: Abodes of the Modern*, ed. Sebastian Domsch (Trier: Wissenschaften Verlag Trier, 2017), esp. 37–40. See also Leavis's comments on Wordsworth's "innocently insidious trick" in the poem, by which "a scrupulous nicety of statement" obscures "the argument from which he will emerge, as it were inevitably, with a far from inevitable conclusion"; F. R. Leavis, *Reval-*

uation: Tradition and Development in English Poetry (New York: George W. Stewart, 1947), 162. For a complex assessment, see Wimsatt's comments on "Tintern Abbey" and the "curious split" or "parceling of the landscape" that results from the romantic "dramatization of the spiritual through the use of the faint, the shifting, the least tangible and most mysterious parts of nature"; W. K. Wimsatt, Jr., "The Structure of Romantic Nature Imagery," *The Verbal Icon* (Lexington: UP of Kentucky, 1954), 110–11. For a mid-century recuperation of "Tintern Abbey" along New Critical lines as "a unified and significant whole," see James Benziger, "Tintern Abbey Revisited," *PMLA* 65 (1950): 154–62.

128. According to her notesheets, Miles's text of *Lyrical Ballads* is the 1798 edition reproduced in *The English Replicas* facsimile series (Bradford and London: Payson and Clarke, 1927). Miles's word-count of "Tintern Abbey" is in the bundle for *Lyrical Ballads, with a Few Other Poems*, Miles Papers (carton 6, folder 106).

129. Miles, *Continuity*, 2.

130. Susan J. Wolfson, "Poem upon the Wye," in *The Oxford Handbook of William Wordsworth*, eds. Richard Gravil and Daniel Robinson (Oxford: Oxford UP, 2015), 192.

131. Ruth Abbott, "Nostalgia, Coming Home, and the End of the Poem: On Reading William Wordsworth's *Ode: Intimations of Immortality from Recollections of Early Childhood*," *Memory Studies* 3 (2010): 211.

132. Miles, *Continuity*, 166.

133. On the recurrence of "merely descriptive" in disciplinary writing, see Sharon Marcus, Heather Love, and Stephen Best, "Building a Better Description," *Representations* 135 (2016): 1–2.

134. Tuve, review of *The Primary Language of Poetry in the 1640's*, 61.

135. Monk, review of *The Primary Language of Poetry*, 427; James Sledd, review of *The Primary Language of Poetry in the 1640's*, *Modern Philology* 47 (1949): 141–42. See also Tuve, with exasperation, in her review of *The Primary Language of Poetry in the 1640's*, 61: "If 'the time' is so important, with common expression 'drawn in for nourishment like the air we breathe,' what of the fact that three of these poets were dead before the decade began? that one, Donne, had not breathed (the air of this place at any rate) for *nine* years?"

136. Monk, review of *The Primary Language of Poetry*, 427–28; Tuve, review of *The Primary Language of Poetry in the 1640's*, 61.

137. On Tuve's thorough debunking, see Pasanek, who also comments incisively on the rhetoric of disability that Tuve invoked; Pasanek, "Extreme Reading," 370.

138. Miles, *Continuity*, 371–72.

139. Miles, *Continuity*, 372.

140. Wells, review of *The Primary Language of Poetry in the 1940's*, 265; Miles, *Continuity*, 534.

141. Miles, *Continuity*, 534–35. On Wordsworthian tautology as "homesickness by other means," a "mode of bibliopathology" that might suggest connections with Miles's practice, see Kevis Goodman, *Pathologies of Motion: Historical Thinking in Medicine, Aesthetics, and Poetics* (New Haven: Yale UP, 2022), 174–89.

142. Miles, *Eras and Modes*, 144 (emphasis added).

143. Miles, *Eras and Modes*, 128.

144. Miles, *Poetry, Teaching, and Scholarship*, 138.

145. Miles stated in a late interview that "independence today, especially in relation to disablement, means physical independence or personal independence. It's very
curious, but really, neither of those crossed my mind very much"; Miles, *Poetry, Teaching, and Scholarship*, 74. Susan Schweik, who shows "the 'strangeness' of disability" to
be ubiquitous across Miles's writing, discusses the challenges of invoking "an activist,
social model of disability as a tool for reading Miles," and generously explores Miles's
avoidance of such identifications, speculating that the "delegitimated" status of disability and its accompanying "ideology of rehabilitation" would have been powerful
incentives to fashion herself "as both agreeable and capable"; "The Voice of 'Reason,'"
488–90, 493.

146. Miles, *Poetry, Teaching, and Scholarship*, 228. See Schweik, "The Voice of 'Reason,'" 485–505; and Thom Gunn, "In Memoriam: Josephine Miles," *California Monthly*
95.6 (June–July 1985): 29.

147. Josephine Miles, "Scholarly Procedure," *Poetry* 53 (1939): 237. For "movement"
in Miles's poetry, see Burr, *Of Women, Poetry, and Power*, 88–90.

148. Josephine Miles, "Custom of Exercise: Seminar," *Poetry* 53 (1939): 236.

149. Josephine Miles, "On Inhabiting an Orange," *Collected Poems: 1930–1983*
(Urbana: U of Illinois P, 1983), 6–7.

150. Miles, *Continuity*, 503.

Epilogue: The Fields of Learning

1. William K. Wimsatt, Jr. to Josephine Miles, August 15, 1951, Josephine Miles
Papers (box 9, folder 18), Bancroft Library, University of California.

2. Celeste Langan, "Mobile Disability," *Public Culture* 13 (2001): 663.

3. In Jencks and Riesman's account, colleges and universities became less associated
with the intimacies of traditional regional culture (parochial, prejudicial, religious, par-
ticularist) and more with the impersonalism of a liberal institutional culture (complex,
objective, urbane, universalist), while faculty increasingly thought of themselves as "independent professionals" beholden to their discipline more than to their institution or
locale; Christopher Jencks and David Riesman, *The Academic Revolution* (Garden City,
NY: Doubleday, 1968), 14.

4. Clark Kerr, *The Uses of the University* (Berkeley: U of California P, 1963), 15.

5. Samuel Taylor Coleridge, "On the Principles of Genial Criticism," *Shorter Works
and Fragments*, eds. H. J. and J. R. de J. Jackson (Princeton: Princeton UP, 1995), 1: 372;
John Crowe Ransom, "Reconstructed but Unregenerate," *I'll Take My Stand: The South
and the Agrarian Tradition. By Twelve Southerners* (1930; Baton Rouge: Louisiana State UP,
2006), 14. For the organic ideal of "multeity in unity" in its relation to New Criticism,
see Cleanth Brooks, "The Organic Theory of Literature," in *Literature and Belief: English
Institute Essays, 1957*, ed. M. H. Abrams (New York: Columbia UP, 1958), 63; Jonathan
Arac, *Critical Genealogies*, 81–95; and Michael Clark, "The Genealogy of Coherence
and the Rhetoric of History in American New Criticism," in *Criticism, History, and
Intertextuality*, eds. Richard Fleming and Michael Payne (Lewisburg, PA: Bucknell UP,
1988), 17–60.

6. Ransom's academic professionalism is usually identified with "Criticism, Inc.," though Stephen Schryer has persuasively demonstrated its nascent presence in this earlier essay in *Fantasies of the New Class: Ideologies of Professionalism in Post–World War II American Fiction* (New York: Columbia UP, 2011), 44–47.

7. John Crowe Ransom, "The Aesthetic of Regionalism," *Selected Essays of John Crowe Ransom*, eds. Thomas Daniel Young and John Hindle (Baton Rouge: Louisiana State UP, 1984), 45–46, 56–57. Ransom's "philosophical regionalist" professes himself struck by the violent effects of "the machine economy" on Black people who work the land for next to nothing, yet he no sooner acknowledges the racial injustice before his eyes, flouting the "well-bred instinct [that] argues *against noticing*" (in Toni Morrison's phrase), than he intellectualizes it away, reducing Black life to a symbol for the South's regional variety. Centering the white philosophical regionalist's freedom to travel and to offer commentary on non-white lives that pass in and out of his gaze, Ransom demonstrates the exploitative character of an *aesthetic* of regionalism. Toni Morrison, *Playing in the Dark: Whiteness and the Literary Imagination* (Cambridge: Harvard UP, 1992), 10.

8. Ransom, "The Aesthetic of Regionalism," 54, 56–57.

9. Ransom, "The Aesthetic of Regionalism," 57.

10. Absent from the built landscape in Ransom's essay is a palpably repressed fourth term: the campus of Southern University and A&M College, the historically Black land-grant institution located (from 1914) a few miles to the north, in Scotlandville, then the largest majority-Black community in Louisiana.

11. Ransom, "The Aesthetic of Regionalism," 57.

12. T. S. Eliot, *After Strange Gods: A Primer of Modern Heresy* (London: Faber and Faber, 1934), 17.

13. Ransom, "The Aesthetic of Regionalism," 58.

14. Ransom, "The Aesthetic of Regionalism," 57; Robert Penn Warren, "Literature as Symptom," in *Who Owns America?*, eds. Herbert Agar and Allen Tate (Boston: Houghton Mifflin, 1936), 272–73.

15. Schryer, *Fantasies of the New Class*, 46.

16. Ransom, "The Aesthetic of Regionalism," 57.

17. John Crowe Ransom, "The South: Old or New?," *Sewanee Review* 36 (1928): 139.

18. Donald Davidson, "Preface," *Pursuit: Anthology of Stories and Poems* (1951), qtd. in "The Southern Writer and the Modern University," *Georgia Review* 12 (1958): 25–26.

19. Mark McGurl, *The Program Era: Postwar Fiction and the Rise of Creative Writing* (Cambridge: Harvard UP, 2009), 149–50.

20. "Campus," coined most likely in allusion to Campus Martius in ancient Rome, was originally used as a synonym for college grounds at Princeton in the 1770s, when (instead of "yard" or "green") it referred to the grassy space in front of Nassau Hall. See Paul Venable Turner, *Campus: An American Planning Tradition* (Cambridge: MIT P, 1984), 47.

21. On the Olmsted firm and its work for American universities, see Francis R. Kowsky, "College and School Campuses," in *The Master List of Design Projects of the Olmsted Firm*, eds. Lucy Lawliss et al. (Washington: National Association of Olmsted Parks, 2008), 117–32; Jonathan Coulson et al., *University Planning and Architecture: The Search for Perfection* (New York: Routledge, 2015), 19–21, 141–47; Sheldon Rothblatt, *The*

Modern University and Its Discontents: The Fate of Newman's Legacies in Britain and America (Cambridge: Cambridge UP, 2006), 70–78; and Turner, *Campus: An American Planning Tradition*, 41–45.

22. Schryer, *Fantasies of the New Class*, 46–47.

23. Ransom, "The Aesthetic of Regionalism," 53.

24. At its worst extreme, this ideal of a "transplanted regionalism" nurtured the Agrarian belief in the South as a haven for European whites, the closest thing to a miniature European civilization that one could find outside of Europe: "The Fathers of the Republic . . . were European regionalists, and they set about to apply to their new regions as much of their European regionalism as was applicable"; Ransom, "The Aesthetic of Regionalism," 52.

25. J. Michael Desmond, *The Architecture of LSU* (Baton Rouge: Louisiana State UP, 2013). Desmond's is the definitive account of the campus's design.

26. Ransom, "The Aesthetic of Regionalism," 57.

27. Ransom, "The Aesthetic of Regionalism," 57.

28. Ransom, "The Aesthetic of Regionalism," 58. Ransom sounds a less elegiac note in his last essay for the *Kenyon Review* in 1959: "in the last resort education is a democratic process, in which the courses are subject to the election of the applicants, and a course even when it has been elected can never rise above the intellectual passion of its pupils, or their comparative indifference. So, with the new generation of students, Milton declines in the curriculum; even Shakespeare has lost heavily; Homer and Virgil are practically gone. The literary interest of the students today is ninety per cent in the literature of their own age; more often than not it is found in books which do not find entry into the curriculum. . . . It may be that we in the elite tradition of Phi Beta Kappa have held too hard and too long by our traditional literature, and have become culturally a little effete and devitalized." John Crowe Ransom, "The Idea of a Literary Anthropologist," *Kenyon Review* 21 (1959): 139–40.

29. Miles, "Comment" (n.d.), Miles Papers (carton 3, folder 32).

30. Nagel, *The View from Nowhere*, 70: "The question is how limited beings like ourselves can alter their conception of the world so that it is no longer just the view from where they are but in a sense a view from nowhere, which includes and comprehends the fact that the world contains beings which possess it, explains why the world appears to them as it does prior to the formation of that conception, and explains how they can arrive at the conception itself."

31. Miles, "Comment" (n.d.), Miles Papers (carton 3, folder 32); "Have you been writing verse during all these years, Miss Miles?," interview, 1939, Miles Papers (carton 3, folder 45).

32. Josephine Miles, *Collected Poems: 1930–1983* (Urbana: U of Illinois P, 1983), 5–6.

33. Miles, *Collected Poems: 1930–1983*, 6.

34. Josephine Miles, *The Continuity of Poetic Language* (Berkeley: U of California P, 1951), 358.

35. Josephine Miles, *Poetry, Teaching, and Scholarship: Oral History Transcript and Related Material, 1977–1980*, interview by Ruth Teiser and Catherine Harroun for Regional Oral History Office (Berkeley: The Bancroft Library, 1980), 37.

36. Josephine Miles to Cleanth Brooks, December 26, 1939, *Southern Review* Records (YCAL MSS 694, series 1, box 4), Beinecke Rare Book and Manuscript Library, Yale University.

37. Miles, "Teaching English Lyric Poetry," [n.d.], Miles Papers (carton 3, folder 93).

38. Miles, "Comment," [n.d.], Miles Papers (carton 3, folder 32).

39. Josephine Miles, "Custom of Exercise: Seminar," *Poetry* 53 (1939): 236.

40. Josephine Miles, *Poetry and Change: Donne, Milton, Wordsworth, and the Equilibrium of the Present* (Berkeley: U of California P, 1974), 217.

41. Miles, *Continuity*, 503.

42. Clark Kerr, "The Schools of Business Administration," in *New Dimensions of Learning in a Free Society* (Pittsburgh: U of Pittsburgh P, 1958), 66; Jonathan R. Cole, *The Great American University* (New York: Public Affairs, 2009), 134, 140.

43. Kerr, *Uses of the University*, 28; Miles, "Academic Plan 1974–1979," [n.d.], Miles Papers (carton 3, folder 27), 1–2.

44. Paul Ricouer, *Freud and Philosophy: An Essay on Interpretation* (New Haven: Yale UP, 1970). On this line of institutional critique, as well as for a spirited argument about "the need to safeguard a stable institutional home" against "various forms of existential threat," see Mark McGurl, "Ordinary Doom: Literary Studies in the Waste Land of the Present," *New Literary History* 41 (2010): 337, 340–41.

45. Kerr, *Uses of the University*, 31–32.

46. Miles, *Poetry, Teaching, Scholarship*, 243.

47. Miles, *Collected Poems: 1930–1983*, 190–91.

48. Harvey Helfand, *University of California, Berkeley: An Architectural Tour* (New York: Princeton Architectural P, 2002), 52.

49. Abraham Flexner, *Universities: American, English, German* (1930), intro. Clark Kerr (New Brunswick, NJ: Transaction Books, 1994), 231; Clark Kerr, "Introduction," in Flexner, *Universities*, xxi; Kerr, *The Uses of the University*, 15.

50. Josephine Miles, *Fields of Learning* (Berkeley, CA: Oyez, 1968).

51. Miles, *Poetry, Teaching, Scholarship*, 158.

52. Though the poem is titled "Office," in manuscript it was titled "Office Hour"; Miles Papers (carton 1, folder 16). In an interview, Miles reminisced about the warmth of community that pervaded her department at the end of the day, when many professors held their office hours: "at six o clock at night, all English Department doors were open, and at every desk you saw a professor leaning over a desk with a student's paper before him and the student listening and asking questions about the paper. That's the picture that I have of the English Department of Wheeler Hall teaching"; Miles, *Poetry, Teaching, Scholarship*, 141.

53. Miles, *Fields of Learning*, 19–20.

54. Miles, *Fields of Learning*, 25.

55. Miles, *Poetry, Teaching, Scholarship*, 159.

56. Alastair Bonnett, *Left in the Past: Radicalism and the Politics of Nostalgia* (New York: Continuum, 2010), 1. On nostalgia as a type of "false memory" fundamentally at odds with "the critique of progress," see Christopher Lasch, *The True and Only Heaven: Progress and Its Critics* (New York: Norton, 1991), 113, 14.

57. Free Speech Movement, "We want a university," in *The Berkeley Student Revolt: Facts and Interpretations*, eds. Seymour Martin Lipset and Sheldon S. Wolin (Garden City, NY: Anchor Books, 1965), 213; Paul Goodman, *The Community of Scholars* (New York: Random House, 1962), 8.

58. Roger L. Geiger, *Research and Relevant Knowledge: American Research Universities Since World War II*, 2nd ed. (New Brunswick, NJ: Transaction Publishers, 2008), 236.

59. Charles Muscatine et al., *Education at Berkeley: Report of the Select Committee on Education* (Berkeley and Los Angeles: U of California P, 1968), 40, 24–25, [jacket cover].

60. *General Catalogue, 1968–69* (University of California, Berkeley), 297–98; *General Catalogue, 1969–70* (University of California, Berkeley), 311.

61. Anonymous readers' reports on *Understanding Poetry*, 3rd ed. (n.d.; c. 1967), Robert Penn Warren papers (YCAL MSS 51, Series 1, box 202, folder 3571).

62. James McKillop, reader's report on *Understanding Poetry*, 3rd ed. (December, 1967), Robert Penn Warren papers, YCAL MSS 51, Series 1, box 202, folder 3571.

63. Anonymous readers' reports on *Understanding Poetry*, 3rd edition (n.d.; c. 1967), Robert Penn Warren papers (YCAL MSS 51, Series 1, box 202, folder 3571).

64. "A Conservative Revolution," Promotional material, Cleanth Brooks Papers, Beinecke Rare Book & Manuscript Library, YCAL MSS 30, box 46.

65. Remo Ceserani, "Sulle Teorie Poetiche Di John Crowe Ransom," *Studi Americani* 8 (1960): 307–37.

66. Among many versions of this less optimistic story (one needn't look far these days to find them), Roderick A. Ferguson's accounts in *The Reorder of Things: The University and Its Pedagogies of Minority Difference* (Minneapolis: U of Minnesota P, 2012), and *We Demand: The University and Social Protests* (Oakland: U of California P, 2017), most powerfully unsettle the usual narratives told about student agency and student-led movements. Ferguson hints at a radically different way of understanding New Critical pedagogy: that for all its positive impact on student agency, it was also a prelude to the effort at containing "the social ruptures that student and social movements produced in the 1950s, '60s, and '70s"; *We Demand*, 68.

67. For the critique of "heart's-desire poetry" which "denies the real world by idealizing it," see John Crowe Ransom, "Preface," *The World's Body* (New York: Charles Scribner's Sons, 1938), viii.

Index

Christopher Rovee is Robert Penn Warren Professor of English at Louisiana State University. He is author of *Imagining the Gallery: The Social Body of British Romanticism*.

Printed in the USA
CPSIA information can be obtained
at www.ICGtesting.com
JSHW020843191223
53974JS00006B/232